Models of Understanding Text

Publications of the University of Georgia Institute of Behavioral Research:

Britton/Pellegrini • Narrative Thought and Narrative Language

Schwanenflugel • The Psychology of Word Meanings

Martin/Tesser • The Construction of Social Judgments

Britton/Graesser • Models of Understanding Text

Models of Understanding Text

Edited by

Bruce K. Britton
University of Georgia

Arthur C. Graesser
University of Memphis

Routledge
Taylor & Francis Group
LONDON AND NEW YORK

First published 1996 by Lawrence Erlbaum Associates, Inc.

Published 2022 by Routledge
4 Park Square, Milton Park, Abingdon, Oxon OX14 4RN
605 Third Avenue, New York, NY 10017

Routledge is an imprint of the Taylor & Francis Group, an informa business

Publisher's Note

The publisher has gone to great lengths to ensure the quality of this reprint but points out that some imperfections in the original copies may be apparent.

Library of Congress Cataloging-in-Publication Data

Models of understanding text / edited by Bruce K. Britton, Arthur C. Graesser.
p. cm.
Includes bibliographical references and index.
1. Comprehension. 2. Reading comprehension. 3. Psycholinguistics. I. Britton, Bruce K. II. Graesser, Arthur C.
BF325.M63 1996
401'.41—cd20 95-5085
CIP

ISBN 13: 978-0-805-81848-2 (hbk)
ISBN 13: 978-0-805-81849-9 (pbk)

For Product Safety Concerns and Information please contact our EU representative: GPSR@taylorandfrancis.com
Taylor & Francis Verlag GmbH, Kaufingerstraße 24, 80331 München, Germany.

CONTENTS

Preface vii

1 New Models of Deep Comprehension 1
Arthur C. Graesser, Shane S. Swamer, William B. Baggett, and Marie A. Sell

2 A Predication Semantics Model of Text Comprehension and Recall 33
Althea Turner, Bruce K. Britton, Paul Andraessen, and Deborah McCutchen

3 Extending Capacity-Constrained Construction Integration: Toward "Smarter" and Flexible Models of Text Comprehension 73
Susan R. Goldman, Sashank Varma, and Nathalie Coté

4 Effects of Prior Knowledge on Text Comprehension: A Simple Modeling Approach 115
Suzanne Mannes and Marie St. George

5 A Model of Narrative Comprehension and Recall **141**
Charles R. Fletcher, Paul van den Broek, and Erik J. Arthur

6 A "Landscape" View of Reading: Fluctuating Patterns of Activation and the Construction of a Stable Memory Representation **165**
Paul van den Broek, Kirsten Risden, Charles R. Fletcher, and Richard Thurlow

7 The Role of Inferential Processing in Reading Ability **189**
Debra L. Long, Mark R. Seely, Brian J. Oppy, and Jonathan M. Golding

8 Metaphor as a Constraint on Text Understanding **215**
Raymond W. Gibbs, Jr.

9 Toward a Model of Literary Comprehension **241**
Rolf A. Zwaan

10 Understanding and Resolving Arguments: The Dynamics of Negotiation **257**
Nancy L. Stein, Ronan S. Bernas, David J. Calicchia, and Anne Wright

11 The Structure-Building Framework: What It Is, What It Might Also Be, and Why **289**
Morton Ann Gernsbacher

12 The Mental Models Theory of Language Comprehension **313**
Alan Garnham and Jane Oakhill

13 Five Metaphors for Text Understanding **341**
Arthur C. Graesser and Bruce K. Britton

Author Index **353**

Subject Index **361**

PREFACE

The field of text and discourse processing has matured dramatically during the last 20 years, spawning approximately 20 new journals and 10 new societies. As researchers have dissected the different levels of text analysis (i.e., surface structure, semantics, pragmatics, rhetorical organization, world knowledge, the referential situation model), they have accumulated an impressive body of empirical findings. They have achieved a more explicit and detailed understanding of the representations at each level, as well as the cognitive processes that are involved in the construction of these representations. The intricacies of some of these levels (e.g., pragmatics, world knowledge, and the situation model) were quite mysterious 20 years ago, and, thus, most researchers avoided these levels. Fortunately, however, enough researchers have cultivated interests at each level for a balanced perspective on comprehension mechanisms to evolve.

One sign of progress in a field is the emergence of sophisticated theoretical models that are supported by empirical data. A sophisticated model has an explicit declaration of its assumptions about representations and cognitive processes. Ideally, these assumptions are articulated with analytical and quantitative precision. A sophisticated model furnishes clear-cut predictions that can be falsified when submitted to empirical tests. The contributors to this volume have developed models of text comprehension. They have also tested the validity of these models by collecting data from comprehenders either during comprehension or after comprehension is completed.

This volume is the product of a conference on Models of Understanding Text. The conference convened in March 1991 under the auspices of the Cognitive Studies Group of the Institute for Behavioral Research at the University of Georgia. The 3-day conference featured extended presentations by Bruce Britton, Morton Gernsbacher, Art Graesser, and Walter Kintsch. Each of these participants nominated several researchers whose contributions would provide a comprehensive and state-of-the-art volume. The result represents a full range of active modeling efforts in the field of text and discourse processing. The contributions of the editors have been placed first, followed by the others in alphabetical order.

Acknowledgments are due to the funding agencies and institutions that supported the conference and the work of the two editors. The conference was cosponsored by the Institute for Behavioral Research (with special thanks to its Director, Abraham Tesser), the Department of Psychology, and the Artificial Intelligence Research Group at the University of Georgia. The research of the first editor was supported by the Learning Abilities Measurement Program (LAMP) of Armstrong Laboratories (funded by the Air Force Office of Scientific Research, with special thanks to Patrick Kyllonen and John Tangney), the Office of Naval Research (with thanks to Susan Chipman), the National Reading Research Center (funded by the Office of Educational Research and Improvement of the Department of Education), and the cosponsors of the conference. The research of the second editor was supported by the Office of Naval Research (with thanks, once again, to Susan Chipman), the Institute for Intelligent Systems, and the Center for Applied Psychological Research at the University of Memphis, an established center of excellence in the state of Tennessee.

Bruce K. Britton
Arthur C. Graesser

CHAPTER

1

NEW MODELS OF DEEP COMPREHENSION

Arthur C. Graesser
Shane S. Swamer
William B. Baggett
Marie A. Sell
University of Memphis

This chapter presents new models of comprehension that we have been developing in recent years. These models focus on deeper levels of comprehension (which involve pragmatics, inferences, and world knowledge) rather than shallow levels of comprehension (such as lexical processing, syntactic parsing, and the interpretation of explicit text). Early research in the psychology of language and discourse processing emphasized the shallow levels of comprehension. It was easier to measure and manipulate factors directly associated with the surface text than to struggle with barely visible mechanisms at the deep levels. There were many theories about the surface levels, enough theories to occupy everyone's time for several decades. However, researchers came to recognize the pressing need to explore the deep levels. They discovered that the deep levels often have a greater impact on reading time, memory, decision making, and judgment than do the shallow levels. They also identified interesting ways in which deep levels interacted with shallow levels of processing. The *zeitgeist* has shifted from the shallow to the deep levels of comprehension.

The research reported in this chapter investigates three rather diverse components of deep comprehension: dialogue patterns, generation of knowledge-based inferences, and question asking. Each of these components has interested researchers in discourse processing and natural language comprehension, but adequate psychological theories have not yet evolved. This chapter attempts to fill the void by sketching new models that explain the systematicity within each of these three components. It is beyond the scope of this chapter to cover all of the literature on dialogue patterns, inference generation, and question asking.

Instead, this chapter is designed to sketch new models, report selected empirical support for each model, and identify promising directions for expanding the models.

DIALOGUE PATTERNS: PREDICTING THE NEXT SPEECH ACT CATEGORY

The content of many conversations seems very predictable. For example, consider the following initial exchange of a telephone conversation:

> Art (after the telephone rings): Hello.
>
> Shane: Is this Art?
>
> Art: Yeah. Oh, Shane! How's it going?
>
> Shane: Oh, pretty good.
>
> Art: So what can I do for you?
>
> Shane: I have a question about this one analysis. . . .

There are clear expectations about which speech acts are appropriate at each turn. The conversation would be incoherent if the same speech acts were randomly ordered. When person A asks a question, person B is expected to formulate a reply to the question. A promise from person A normally elicits gratitude from person B. A greeting elicits a counter-greeting or acknowledgment. Conversation patterns are very regular (if not completely scripted) during greetings, introductions, business transactions, restaurant conversations, and most other speech exchanges. This systematicity is not confined to speech. There are vestiges of these regularities in the rhetorical structures embodied in narrative text and even in expository text.

Researchers in discourse processing, sociology, and sociolinguistics have analyzed prominent dialogue patterns (Clark & Schaefer, 1989; D'Andrade & Wish, 1985; Goffman, 1974; Graesser, 1992; Mehan, 1979; Schegloff & Sacks, 1973; Turner & Cullingford, 1989). Some of the systematicity resides at a categorical level that is independent of the world knowledge, beliefs, and goals of the speech participants; that is, there are appropriate and inappropriate orderings of speech act categories. Schegloff and Sacks (1973) analyzed the adjacency pairs of conversational turns to answer the following question: Given that one speaker utters a speech act in category C during turn *n*, what is the appropriate speech act category for the other speaker at the next, adjacent turn ($n + 1$)? The most common adjacency pair is the [Question → Reply-to-question] sequence. The adjacency pair analysis considers only one speech act as prior context when generating predictions for the subsequent speech act. However, researchers have identified larger sequences of dialogue patterns. Mehan (1979) identified a triplet that occurs frequently in classroom environments, which is illustrated in the following sequence:

Teacher question: What is the capital of Florida?

Student answer: Athens.

Teacher evaluation of answer: No, that's not right.

Counter-clarification questions produce a quadruple sequence:

Question A: Where did you go yesterday?

Question B: Yesterday morning?

Answer B: Yeah, in the morning.

Answer A: To Jack's, for breakfast.

There are longer sequences of dialogue patterns, but the longer sequences have rarely been investigated.

The knowledge accumulated in the study of dialogue patterns has been fragmented and largely untested. No one has developed a model that ties together the assorted observations. No one has quantified the extent to which these patterns account for the speech acts in naturalistic conversation. There is no model that is sufficiently broad in scope that it could be applied to any conversation or text. In view of these shortcomings, we developed two models that attempt to capture the systematicity in speech act sequences. The two models have radically different computational architectures: a connectionist architecture and a symbolic architecture.

The two models are based on the assumption that the stream of conversation (or text) can be segmented into a linear sequence of speech act categories. There have been extensive debates over what speech act categories are needed for a satisfactory analysis of human conversation (Austin, 1962; Bach & Harnish, 1979; D'Andrade & Wish, 1985; Searle, 1969). We adopted a slightly modified version of D'Andrade and Wish's (1985) set of speech act categories. Their categories were both theoretically motivated and empirically adequate in the sense that trained judges agreed on the assignment of categories. The eight categories of speech acts are:

1. *Question* (Q): Interrogative expression that is not an indirect request (e.g., "What is your name?").
2. *Reply to question* (RQ): Speech act that answers a previous question (e.g., "My name is Marie.").
3. *Directive* (D): A request in an imperative form for the listener to do something (e.g., "Shut the door.").
4. *Indirect directive* (ID): A request in a nonimperative form for the listener to do something (e.g., "Could you shut the door?, I would appreciate it if you'd shut the door.").
5. *Assertion* (A): A report about some state of affairs that could be true or false, but does not directly answer a previous question (e.g., "I went to Minneapolis last week., Minnesota is cold in March.").

6. *Evaluation* (E): An expression of sentiment or judgment about some entity, fact, event, or state of affairs (e.g., "That's ridiculous!, That's right.").
7. *Verbal response* (R): A spoken acknowledgment of the previous speech act by the other person (e.g., "Uh-huh.").
8. *Nonverbal response* (N): A nonverbal acknowledgment of the previous speech act by the other person (e.g., a head nod).

Because there are two speakers in a dialogue, each speech act in a conversation can fall into one of 16 categories (2 speakers × 8 basic speech acts = 16). A Juncture (J) category was also included to signify lengthy pauses in a conversation and excerpts that are uninterpretable to judges. In summary, the stream of dyadic conversation was segmented into a sequence of speech acts and each speech act was assigned to 1 of 17 speech act categories.

Sell et al. (1991) used this 17-category speech act scheme in their analysis of 90 conversation involving pairs of children. Dyads of second-graders and sixth-graders were videotaped for 10 minutes in three different contexts: playing 20 questions, solving a puzzle, and free play. The dyads were further segregated according to how well they knew each other: mutual friends (A and B liked each other), unilateral friends (A liked B, but B neither liked nor disliked A), and acquaintances (A and B did not like or dislike each other). All of the children in the dyads were from the same classroom and so they were never strangers. Sell et al. (1991) reported that the 17-category speech act scheme could be successfully applied to the 16,657 speech acts in this corpus (hereafter, called the "Sell corpus"). The 17 categories were sufficient in that all of the speech acts in the Sell corpus fit into one of the 17 categories. The categories were sufficiently reliable because trained judges agreed on which category to ascribe to the speech acts; the Cohen's kappas were .82, .76, and .74 for the question, puzzle, and free-play task, respectively.

The goal of our models was to capture the systematicity in the sequential ordering of the speech act categories. That is, to what extent can the category of speech act $n + 1$ be successfully predicted, given the sequence of speech acts 1 through n? A *hit rate* is the likelihood that a theoretically predicted category actually occurs in the data, as specified in Formula 1.

$$\text{hit rate} = p(\text{category } C \text{ occurred at } n + 1 \text{ category } C \text{ is predicted by the model at } n + 1) \tag{1}$$

A hit rate is not a satisfactory index of the success of a model, however, because it is not adjusted for the likelihood that the speech act could occur by chance. For example, if a particular speech act category occurred in the corpus 90% of the time, there would be a high hit rate, assuming that the model predicted that category most of the time. A satisfactory index of the success of the model would need to control for the baserate likelihood that the predicted speech act occurred in the empirical distribution of speech act categories (called the a posteriori distribution). For example, the baserate likelihoods of the speech act categories in the Sell corpus were .21, .14, .04, .02, .40, .03, .07, .03, and .07 for categories Q, RQ, D, ID, A, E, R, N, and J, respectively. We computed a *goodness-of-prediction (GOP) index* that corrected for the baserate likelihood that a speech act category would occur by chance, as specified in Formula 2.

$$\text{GOP index} = [\text{hit rate}(\text{category } C) - \text{baserate}(\text{category } C)] / [1.0 - \text{baserate}(\text{category } C)] \quad (2)$$

The model allows for more than one speech act category at observation $n + 1$. In this case, Formulas 1 and 2 are still correct except that the values are based on a set of categories rather than a single category.

Recurrent Connectionist Network

Researchers in the connectionist camp of cognitive architectures developed a recurrent network that is suitable for capturing the systematicity in the temporal ordering of events (Cleeremans & McClelland, 1991; Elman, 1990). The recurrent connectionist network preserves in the network an encoding of all previous input, and uses this information to induce the structure underlying temporal sequences.

There are four layers of nodes in the recurrent network, as shown in Fig. 1.1. The *input layer* specifies the category of speech act n. There are 17 nodes in the input layer, one for each speech act category. The appropriate node is activated when speech act n is received. For example, if Person 1 asked a question, then the Q1 node would be activated in the input layer of the network. The *output layer* contains the predictions for speech act $n + 1$. There are 17 output nodes, one for each speech act category. An output node has an activation value that reflects the degree to which the network predicts that output node. For example, if the input were Q1 we would expect RQ2 to receive a high activation value in the output layer, thereby capturing the regularity that people are expected to answer questions that others ask. The *hidden layer* captures higher order constituents that are activated by speech act n. Hidden layers are frequently implemented in connectionist architectures to capture internal cognitive mechanisms (Rumelhart & McClelland, 1986). The hidden layer is needed when direct input–output mappings fail to capture systematicity in the data. There are 10 nodes in the hidden layer of our network. The *context layer* allows the network to induce temporal sequences. The context layer stores the activations from the hidden layer of the previous step in the speech act sequence (as designated by the fixed weights of 1 in Fig. 1.1). The activations of the hidden layer at step n depend on: (a) the input at n and (b) the activation of the context layer at n (which was the hidden layer at $n - 1$). Therefore, the hidden layer is receiving information about present and past inputs. The resulting activation pattern of the 10 nodes of the hidden layer at step n is subsequently copied into the context layer at step $n + 1$. The context layer must have the same number of nodes as the hidden layer (10 nodes in our model).

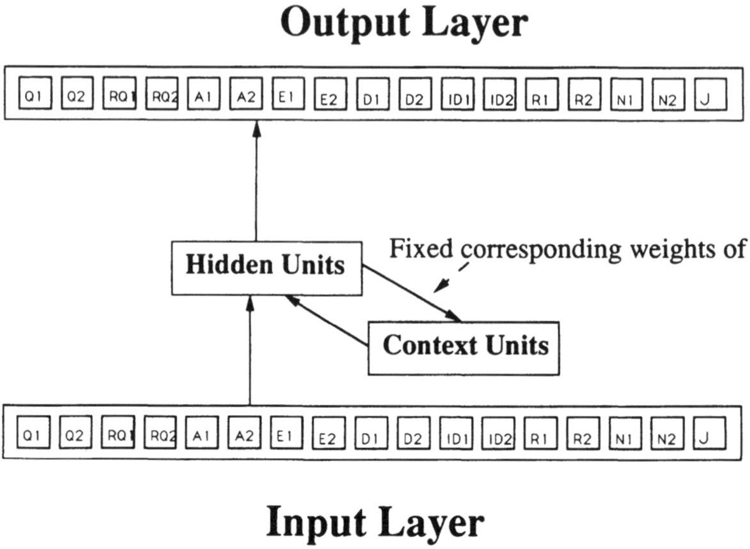

FIG. 1.1. Recurrent connectionist network for speech act prediction.

There are a total of 440 connections that are allowed to vary in the weight space of this model. There are 170 connections between the input layer and the hidden layer (i.e., 17 input nodes and 10 hidden layer nodes). Similarly, there are 170 connections from the hidden layer to the output layer. The other 100 nodes link the 10-node context layer to the 10-node hidden layer. There are also connections from the hidden layer to the context layer that are fixed at 1. In preliminary simulations, we varied the number of nodes in the hidden layer and the context layer (from 6 to 14 nodes). However, the success of the model did not depend on the number of nodes in these layers.

The recurrent connectionist network was used to simulate predictions for the 16,657 speech acts in the Sell corpus (see Swamer et al., 1993). The network was trained on 12 passes through the corpus (i.e., the performance of the network had clearly settled and reached an asymptote). We performed eight different simulations, with each run having a different set of random initial weights in the weight space. Performance measures were averaged over these eight simulations.

The performance of the recurrent network was evaluated by computing two different GOP indices (see Formula 2). A *maximal activation* GOP index considered only one output node as the predicted speech act category for step $n + 1$. The predicted category was the one that received the highest activation value in the output layer. The maximal activation GOP index was found to be .29. The hit rate in this analysis was .38 and the baserate was .12. Therefore, the likelihood of correctly predicting the next speech act category was .29, over and above adjustments for baserates. An *above-threshold* GOP index enabled the network to accommodate multiple speech act categories at each step; all output nodes that met or exceeded a threshold activation level were acceptable predictions for step $n + 1$. Preliminary tests revealed that a threshold of .18 provided an optimal fit to the data. On average, 1.9 speech acts were above threshold at any given step in the conversation. The above-threshold GOP index was found to be .38. The hit rate was .57 and the baserate was .30. These results support the claim that there is systematicity in the sequencing of speech act categories in dyadic conversation. Although no one would be surprised about this systematicity, the model established a foundation for quantifying the systematicity and for simulating speech act sequences.

We performed follow-up analyses to answer additional questions about the dialogue patterns. We found that the recurrent network had a significantly better fit to the data than a back propagation network that considered only speech act n when predicting $n + 1$. This back propagation network was identical to the recurrent network in Fig. 1.1 except that it included no context layer of nodes. The fact that the recurrent network improved the GOP index supports the claim that there is greater systematicity than predicted by Schegloff and Sacks' (1973) analysis of adjacency pairs. How much context is used in predicting the next speech act category? We found that only three speech acts of context significantly affected performance. When we plotted GOP scores as a function of the number of speech acts of context that were entered into the connectionist network, we found no significant difference between three speech acts of context and four or more speech acts of context. Thus, quadruple sequences were the highest order dialogue patterns in the Sell corpus. It is interesting to note that this upperbound is compatible with previous theoretical observations in the literature (i.e., counter-questions involved quadruple sequences) and with limitations of working memory.

Follow-up analyses revealed that the type of task in which the children were engaged had a robust impact on GOP indices. The maximal activation GOP indices were .38, .07, and .18 in the question, puzzle, and free play task, respectively. This suggests that the children engaged in parallel monologues in the puzzle task, whereas the 20-questions game placed substantial constraints on the dialogues. In contrast, the age of the children and the type of social relationship (i.e., mutual friends, unilateral friends, versus acquaintances) had no impact on the GOP indices.

Recursive Transition Network

The same speech act data also were simulated by a model that adopted a symbolic computational architecture. The symbolic model consisted of a recursive transition network, or RTN (Jacobs, 1983; Stevens & Rumelhart, 1975). The advantage of a symbolic architecture is that the investigator can trace and articulate the dialogue patterns that explain systematicity in the data. In contrast, it is difficult to identify patterns in a weight space from a connectionist model and relate such patterns with theory.

Figure 1.2 shows a recursive transition network that we constructed to fit the Sell corpus from both data and theory. As regards data, a number of patterns emerged inductively when we inspected the 17 × 17 transition matrix between speech act n and speech act $n + 1$. This matrix computes the likelihood that a particular category C_i occurred at step $n + 1$, given that category C_j occurred at step n. As regards theory, some patterns were anticipated on the basis of common sense and theoretical developments in the literature. Following Clark and Schaefer (1989), for example, the RTN in Fig. 1.2 segregates a Contribution from an Acknowledgment of the contribution by the other party. There are four modules that emanate from the Contribute node (Interrogate, Inform, Direct, and Evaluate) and that capture four of the basic goals of communication. Counter-clarification questions (i.e., k-Interrogate) are embedded in the second step of the Interrogate, Direct, and Evaluation modules. The Challenge module is a reaction of person A in situations in which person B tries to evaluate something or person B tries to get A to do something (i.e., the Direct and Evaluate modules, respectively).

The RTN in Fig. 1.2 includes seven modules. Each module has two or three state nodes and a set of arcs that emanate from each state node. The arc specifies the set of legal speech act categories and the set of recursively embedded modules that are legal at that point. The speech act categories are the same eight categories that were defined earlier: Q, RQ, D, ID, A, E, V, and N. There are seven recursively embedded modules: Contribute, Acknowledge, Interrogate, Direct, Evaluate, Inform, and Challenge. It should be noted that $_i$ and $_k$ are indices that identify which of the two individuals is speaking. In some cases, the same individual produces a sequence of speech acts. In other cases, the turn transfers to the other person.

The RTN generates a set of legal speech acts at each step of the conversation. A speech act at $n + 1$ is legal if there is at least one path in the family of alternative paths that emanate from speech act n. A hit occurs when speech act $n + 1$ matches one of the legal alternatives. Hit rates and GOP indices can be computed in the same way as for the recurrent connectionist network (see Formulas 1 and 2). There is an all-or-none prediction of each speech act at step $n + 1$ in this model, whereas there are continuous activation values in the output layer of the connectionist model. A maximal activation GOP index cannot be computed in the RTN whenever there is more than one legal alternative at a step (which is normally the case). Therefore, we were left only with the above-threshold GOP index to evaluate the performance of the RTN model.

We used the RTN in Fig. 1.2 to simulate the speech acts in the Sell corpus. The GOP index was .39, whereas the hit rate was .83 and the baserate was .72. This GOP index compares favorably with the .38 GOP index in our test of the recurrent connectionist model. However, it is important to point out that the mean number of speech acts legal at each step was quite high (10.6) in the RTN model compared to the number of above-threshold alternatives in the recurrent

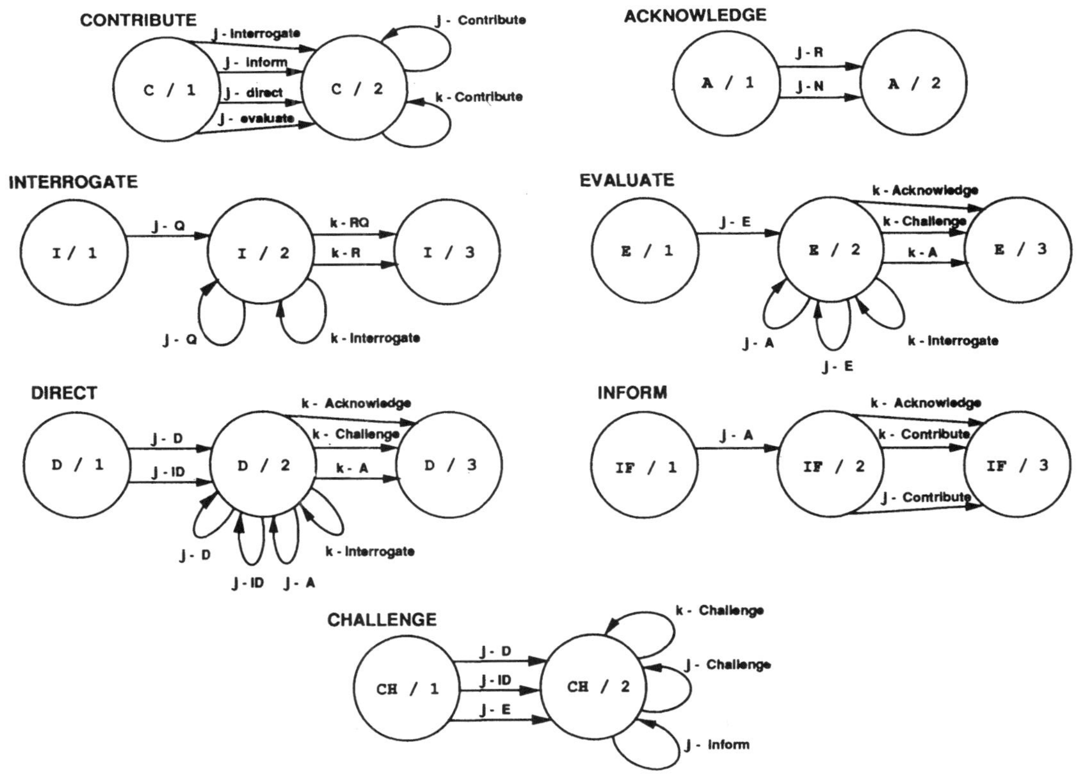

FIG. 1.2. Recursive transition network for speech act prediction.

model (1.9). In a more direct comparison between the models, we adjusted the threshold of the connectionist model so that it had approximately 10.6 above-threshold speech acts per step. The GOP index was .53 in that simulation of the recurrent network. Therefore, it appears that the RTN captures approximately 74% (.39 / .53) of the systematicity that was detected in the recurrent connectionist network.

We currently are tuning the RTN in an effort to improve its predictive power. One improvement consists of adding or deleting links in an effort to improve the GOP scores. Because there are seven modules, there are a finite number of alternative RTN's to test. For example, there are 30 alternative arcs emanating from each node because there are two speakers, eight speech act categories, and seven higher-order modules. Each of the seven modules has only one node in which there is uncertainty about the alternative arcs, which results in 210 possible RTNs to test. A second improvement we are considering is to assign weights to each arc, reflecting the frequency in which the arc is traversed. The weights would reduce the number of legal alternatives that exceed some threshold at a particular step. The extent to which these modifications improve the RTN model awaits future research.

Expanding the Models

Both the connectionist model and the symbolic RTN model need to be tested further on additional samples of speech acts. The Sell corpus was collected from children between the ages of 7 and 12. Adult conversations might produce more complex RTNs that take more than three speech acts of context into consideration. We currently are testing the two models on a corpus of speech acts from tutoring sessions involving college students. It is possible to focus on particular conditions, such as the speech act sequences that occur when "why" questions are answered. The generality of these models can be evaluated only after they are tested in a variety of speech samples.

Another important task for future research is to include additional levels of knowledge in the models and determine whether the GOP indices improve. For example, we currently are analyzing the *pragmatic mode* of the interaction to determine whether this level of knowledge improves the ability of each model to predict speech acts. Examples of pragmatic modes are argument, collaborations, assistance, play, and greeting. Presumably, the dialogue patterns would differ substantially among these pragmatic modes. The recurrent connectionist model could be expanded by adding a set of nodes in the input layer that specifies the pragmatic mode. As a consequence, the number of nodes in the hidden layer and context layer might also need to be increased. The RTN model could be expanded by placing conditions on the traversal of each arc at a particular state (e.g., traverse arc A at state S only if the speech participants are in the play mode). *Augmented recursive transition networks* (ARTNs) are created when conditions are placed on arc traversals. Levels of knowledge beyond the pragmatic mode could also be added. Even the type of domain knowledge (e.g., procedural, taxonomic, causal, logical) or the particular topic (e.g., geography, mathematics, art) could be specified. Each level of knowledge could increase the value of the GOP index. We could then determine which levels or combinations of levels were primarily responsible for predicting speech act categories.

These models could be expanded to multiple-agent architectures in which agents interact in parallel (Minsky, 1975; Brooks, 1991). Each speaker would function as an agent with its own connectionist model or RTN. For each agent, there would be some specification as to when the agent initiates a turn, interrupts another agent, or provides backchannel feedback (i.e., verbal and nonverbal acknowledgments). The agents would interact in parallel.

GENERATING KNOWLEDGE-BASED INFERENCES DURING STORY COMPREHENSION

Readers generate a variety of knowledge-based inferences when they comprehend stories. They can generate inferences about the spatial setting and layout, properties of objects, traits of story characters, the knowledge and beliefs of characters, the goals and plans that motivate the characters' actions, the manner of executing actions, the causes of events, future episodes in the plot, the attitudes and motives of the writer, the appropriate emotional reactions of the reader, and so on. There has been extensive research and debate over which of these classes of inferences are made during comprehension (i.e., online) and which are made only when prompted by a task after comprehension is completed (i.e., offline) (Graesser & Bower, 1990; Graesser & Kreuz, 1993; Kintsch, 1993; Magliano & Graesser, 1991; McKoon & Ratcliff, 1992; Singer, 1988; Whitney, 1987). The issue addressed in this section, therefore, is which knowledge-based inferences are generated online during story comprehension?

There are important reasons for concentrating on stories. Narrative text has a closer correspondence to everyday experience than does expository text (Bruner, 1986; Mandler, 1984; Nelson, 1986; Schank, 1990). Both stories and everyday experiences involve people performing actions in pursuit of goals, the occurrence of obstacles to goals, and emotional reactions to obstacles. The background knowledge and concepts in stories also are familiar to adult readers. In contrast, the purpose of writing expository text is to inform the reader about new concepts, generic truths, and technical material. Consequently, many knowledge-based inferences are generated during the comprehension of narrative text, whereas expository text invokes comparatively few inferences (Britton, van Dusen, Glynn, & Hemphill, 1990; Graesser, 1981).

Knowledge-based inferences are those inferences that are constructed whenever knowledge structures from long-term memory are activated and incorporated into the meaning representation of the text. The meaning representation consists of the *textbase* and the *referential situation model* (van Dijk & Kintsch, 1983; Garnham & Oakley, this volume; Glenberg, Meyer, & Lindem, 1987; Johnson-Laird, 1983; Kintsch, 1988; Morrow, Greenspan, & Bower, 1987). The textbase contains explicit text propositions and a small number of inferences that provide local semantic coherence between propositions. The referential situation model (or mental model) is a lifelike mental representation of the people, setting, actions, goals, and events that are either explicitly mentioned or inferentially suggested by the text. The background knowledge structures include both *generic* packages of world knowledge, such as scripts, stereotypes, frames, or schemata and *specific* memory representations of a prior experience, text, or excerpt from the text being comprehended. It normally takes more time to access and reconstruct information from a specific knowledge structure than from a generic knowledge structure because specific knowledge structures are not overlearned and automatized. A knowledge-based inference is copied directly or inherited from a knowledge structure during comprehension. Alternatively, a novel knowledge-based inference is constructed after several iterative cycles of searching memory and accumulating knowledge from multiple information sources (Just & Carpenter, 1992).

Knowledge-based inferences do not include transient activations of information in a knowledge structure (generic or specific) that are never incorporated into the meaning representation of the text. Knowledge-based inferences also do not include logic-based inferences derived from systems of domain-independent formal reasoning, such as propositional calculus, predicate calculus, or theorem proving (Rips, 1990), or quantitative and statistical inferences derived from formulas and quantitative procedures (Kahneman, Slovic, & Tversky, 1982). Inferences that are products of logical, statistical, and quantitative reasoning are normally difficult to derive and thus, they would not be generated online within the time constraints of normal reading (250–400 words per min).

Table 1.1 presents some examples of knowledge-based inferences in the context of the story "The Czar and His Daughters." The inferences are those possible when the reader comprehends the explicit action *A dragon kidnapped the daughters*. Six categories of knowledge-based inferences are illustrated in Table 1.1:

1. *Superordinate goal*: A goal that motivates an agent's intentional action.
2. *Subordinate goal/action*: A goal, plan, or action that specifies how an agent's intentional action is achieved.
3. *Causal antecedent*: An inference on a causal chain, or bridge, between the explicit action, event, or state being comprehended and the prior passage context.
4. *Causal consequence*: An inference on a forecasted causal chain emanating from the explicit clause being processed. These include physical events and new plans of agents, but not emotions.

TABLE 1.1
Example Story and Possible Inferences

The Czar and His Daughters

Once there was a Czar who had three lovely daughters. One day the three daughters went walking in the woods. They were enjoying themselves so much that they forgot the time and stayed too long. A dragon kidnapped the three daughters. As they were being dragged off they cried for help. Three heroes heard their cries and set off to rescue the daughters. The heroes came and fought the dragon and rescued the maidens. Then the heroes returned the daughters to their palace. When the Czar heard of the rescue, he rewarded the heroes.

Inferences When Comprehending "A dragon kidnapped the three daughters"

Superordinate Goal: The dragon wanted to eat the daughters.
Subordinate Goal/Action: The dragon grabbed the daughters.
Causal Antecedent: The dragon saw the daughters.
Causal Consequence: Someone rescued the daughters.
Character Emotion: The daughters were frightened.
State: The dragon had scales.

5. *Character emotion*: An emotion experienced by a character in response to an action, event, or state.
6. *State*: An ongoing state that is not causally linked to the episodes in the plot. These include character traits, properties of objects, and spatial relationships among entities.

We focus on these inferences because the online status of these six classes of inferences allows us to discriminate between alternative models of inference generation.

Knowledge-based inferences are furnished by generic and specific knowledge structures rather than domain-independent systems of formal reasoning. When researchers test whether inferences are generated online, therefore, they must ensure that readers have an adequate amount of world knowledge. This can be accomplished by collecting verbal protocols from a group of readers while they comprehend the text and observing whether potential inferences are expressed in these protocols. If readers can generate the inferences in these verbal protocols, they must have the prerequisite world knowledge. Knowledge-based inferences have been exposed in studies that collect think-aloud protocols (Trabasso & Suh, 1993), question asking protocols (Olson, Duffy, & Mack, 1985), and question-answering protocols (Graesser, 1981; Graesser, Robertson, & Anderson, 1981). The fact that an inference occurs in these verbal protocols during comprehension does not mean that the inferences are normally generated online. Therefore, the researcher needs to verify that the inferences are truly online by collecting time-based behavioral measures, such as reading times for text segments or latencies in a secondary task involving inference items (e.g., word naming, lexical decisions). Magliano and Graesser (1991) have advocated a *three-pronged method* that consists of (a) models of the discourse processing that make predictions about inference generation, (b) the collection of verbal protocols to expose potential inferences, and (c) the collection of temporal measures during reading to test the online status of each class of inferences. We have adopted this three-pronged method in our own research on inference generation, as is illustrated in the remainder of this section.

Prong 1: Alternative Models of Inference Generation

There are a number of theoretical components and assumptions that could be embraced by virtually any model of inference generation in discourse processing and cognitive psychology. The following components and assumptions are not particularly controversial:

1. *Multiple information sources*: Four major sources of information contribute to the generation of knowledge-based inferences: the explicit text, generic and specific knowledge structures, reader goals, and the pragmatic context of the message.

2. *Surface code, textbase, and situation model*: These three levels of representation are achieved as a result of comprehension (Kintsch, 1988; van Dijk & Kintsch, 1983). The surface code preserves the exact wording and syntax of a clause. The textbase and the situation model are part of the meaning representation, as discussed previously.

3. *Multiple memory stores*: The three memory stores are short-term memory, working memory, and long-term memory. The processing of the current clause resides in short-term memory, whereas working memory preserves the meaning of two or three sentences prior to the current clause and critical information from earlier in the text that is recycled in working memory.

4. *Focus of attention*: A small subset of information is constructed in the reader's focal attention. This information is sometimes called the discourse focus (e.g., mind's eye, consciousness).

5. *Learning and automaticity*: A knowledge structure is more quickly and successfully accessed if it is overlearned through repetition. An automatized knowledge structure is quickly activated as a single chunk of information and imposes minimal costs to working memory resources (Just & Carpenter, 1992).

6. *Convergence and constraint satisfaction*: Explicit clauses and inferences receive more activation if the knowledge units are activated by several information sources (i.e., there is convergence) and the units satisfy the conceptual constraints imposed by multiple sources of information (Golden & Rumelhart, 1991; Graesser & Clark, 1985; Kintsch, 1988; O'Brien, Shank, Myers, & Rayner, 1988; St. John, in press). In a connectionist architecture, for example, an inference is formed if it receives positive activation from multiple sources of information and negative, inhibitory activation from very few, if any sources.

These six assumptions have been adopted by all of the models discussed in this section.

We identified six models that make distinctive predictions about the online status of the six classes of inferences illustrated in Table 1.1. It is beyond the scope of this chapter to specify each model in detail (see Graesser, Singer, & Trabasso, 1993). Instead, we briefly sketch the highlights of each model and declare the predictions. Our preferred model is a constructionist model of inference generation. For present purposes, we simplify matters by discretely segregating inferences into an online versus an offline status. We acknowledge that there is a probabilistic continuum between online and offline that can be attributed to variability in reader goals, reader abilities, texts, inference samples, experimental tasks, and so on. When we claim that class A inferences are online and class B are offline, we mean that class A inferences have a higher activation or likelihood of being generated online than do class B inferences.

An *explicit textbase model* leads to the prediction that none of the six classes of inferences are normally generated online. According to this model, the explicit text is the primary content of the meaning representation for text. A small number of inferences are occasionally generated to patch local coherence breaks in the explicit text. For example, one class of patching inferences would be anaphoric references (e.g., *they* refers to "the daughters"). Early theories of text comprehension directly or indirectly adopted this model because the emphasis was on representing explicit text (Kintsch & van Dijk, 1978; Mandler & Johnson, 1977). This explicit textbase position is perhaps a strawman position from the standpoint of current research and theory, at least in the context of stories. However, this model is probably the most plausible model in the case of expository texts on topics that are unfamiliar to the reader (Britton et al., 1990).

A *minimalist model* has been proposed by McKoon and Ratcliff (1992) to account for inferences that are automatically (rather than strategically) encoded during comprehension. The automatic inferences are generated most consistently and therefore should be more strongly activated, and in more diverse reading contexts, than are the strategic inferences. According to this model, the reader generates online those inferences that are required to make the statements in the text locally coherent. Local coherence refers to structures and processes that organize adjacent clauses or short sequences of clauses that cooccur in working memory. The causal antecedent inferences are the only class of inferences that are needed to establish local coherence (among the six classes in Table 1.1).

A *current-state selection strategy* model (CSS) specifies how causal connections are constructed between clauses (Fletcher & Bloom, 1988). This CSS model is an augmentation of Kintsch and van Dijk's (1978) model of text comprehension, which relied heavily on noun-argument repetition as the foundation for establishing local text coherence. This CSS model is similar to Van den Broek's causal inference-maker model (Van den Broek, 1990; Van den Broek & Lorch, 1993) and other models that emphasize the importance of establishing causal coherence during story comprehension (Graesser & Clark, 1985; Trabasso & van den Broek, 1985; Trabasso & Suh, 1993).

A basic assumption of the CSS model is that the reader's attention is focused on a small set of clauses in short-term memory after each sentence is read. The time to comprehend the next incoming sentence is fast if a causal or noncausal connection can be formed between the new sentence and the clauses in short-term memory. However, if no connection can be found, the comprehender attempts to establish coherence by either reinstating a causal antecedent or superordinate goal from earlier in the story or constructing an explanatory inference (i.e., a causal antecedent or superordinate goal). Additional time is needed to construct these intertext connections and extratextual inferences. Sometimes the reader is unsuccessful in establishing coherence and must wait for more text to ascribe meaning to the new sentence. The CSS model leads to the prediction that explanation-based inferences (i.e., causal antecedent and superordinate goal inferences) are constructed during comprehension. These two classes of inferences are produced when people answer "why" questions about actions and events in stories (e.g., "Why did the dragon kidnap the daughters?"; Graesser, Lang, & Roberts, 1991; Graesser et al., 1981).

A *constructionist model* recently proposed by Graesser, Singer, and Trabasso (1993) embraces an *effort-after-meaning* principle (Bartlett, 1932; Berlyne, 1949). According to this principle, comprehenders have an inherent proclivity to ascribe meaning to text and perceptual input; that is, they construct meaning representations at the deepest and most global levels that can be supported by the text, their reading goals, and their background world knowledge. Only shallow levels of understanding can be achieved if (a) the text is inconsiderate (i.e., choppy, pointless), (b) the reader lacks prerequisite background knowledge (e.g., technical expository text on an unfamiliar topic), or (c) the reader has shallow reading goals (e.g., proofreading a manuscript for spelling errors). Deep, global levels of understanding are achieved when adults read most stories because the text is considerate, the background world knowledge is intact, and their goal is to read for understanding.

Graesser et al.'s (1993) constructionist model is based on two key assumptions that provide distinct predictions about which classes of inferences are online. The *explanation assumption* states that readers attempt to explain why actions, events, and states are mentioned in the text. The explanatory inferences concern causal antecedents and superordinate goals, as discussed previously in the context of the CSS model. The *coherence assumption* states that the reader attempts to construct a meaning representation that is coherent at both local and global levels. Causal antecedent inferences are needed for establishing local coherence (see the previous discussion of the minimalist model). Superordinate goal and character emotion inferences are critical for establishing global coherence according to theories that capture global levels of narrative representation (Dyer,

1983; Lehnert, 1981; Stein & Levine, 1991). For example, negative emotions occur when the main goals of characters are blocked by other characters with conflicting goals or by unexpected events in the world. The constructionist model, therefore, predicts that three of the six classes of inferences in Table 1.1 are generated online, namely, causal antecedent, superordinate goal, and character emotion inferences.

In contrast, inferences about causal consequences, subordinate goals, and states are not normally generated online. Subordinate goals and states involve elaborative details that rarely need to be inferred in the construction of explanations and coherent messages. Causal consequences are not normally inferred online because (a) there are too many hypothetical plots that could be forecasted, (b) most of the forecasted plots are not confirmed when the full story is known (Graesser, 1981; Kintsch, 1988), and (c) it requires substantial cognitive resources to forecast even a single hypothetical plot (Johnson-Laird, 1983).

A *prediction-substantiation model* leads to the assertion that reading is expectation-driven in addition to being driven by attempts to explain input and form coherent messages. According to this model, readers generate expectations about future episodes in the story plot and these expectations guide the comprehension of clauses in a top-down fashion (Bower, Black, & Turner, 1979; DeJong, 1979; Dyer, 1983; Graesser, Gordon, & Sawyer, 1979; Schank & Abelson, 1977). This model explains why the reading time for a clause is facilitated when it matches a prior expectation and is slowed down when it clashes with a prior expectation. Expectations are formed whenever a global knowledge structure, such as a script or a theme, is activated. For example, suppose that a *revenge* theme is activated when the reader discovers that a villain capriciously harmed a victim whom a hero loves. The reader would forecast that the hero will subsequently harm the villain. The prediction-substantiation model predicts that four of the six classes of inferences are normally generated online: causal antecedent, causal consequence, superordinate goal, and character emotion inferences.

A *promiscuous inference-generation model* predicts that all six classes of inferences are generated online provided that the reader has the prerequisite world knowledge. The reader essentially builds an elaborate lifelike situation model by fleshing out many of the details about characters, props, spatial layout, actions, and events. The meaning representation is akin to a fuzzy videotape of the narrative that includes detailed information about the mental states of characters. This is perhaps a strawman position because no one has seriously advocated that normal comprehenders construct this level of detail (unless the person is a movie director, an actor, or an author). However, researchers have occasionally claimed that a constructionist theory would embrace such a position (McKoon & Ratcliff, 1992). This model is at the opposite end of the continuum from the explicit textbase position.

Prong 2: Collection of Question Answering Protocols to Expose Inferences

In the second prong of the three-pronged method, verbal protocols are collected from a sample of readers while they comprehend a text, clause by clause. The content of the verbal protocols contains online and offline knowledge-based inferences. We can conclude that a population of readers has the prerequisite background knowledge for understanding a text and generating a particular class of inferences if the inferences are manifested in the verbal protocols.

Graesser (1981) collected question-answering protocols from a sample of readers while they read four short narrative texts, clause-by-clause. The Czar story in Table 1.1 was one of the four stories. After reading each explicit action, event, and state in the text, the participants answered questions about each clause. One group of participants answered "why" questions. According to Graesser et al. (1991), answers to "why" questions expose inferences about causal antecedents and superordinate goals. A second group answered "how" questions, which expose inferences about the subordinate goals and actions of explicit actions and the causal antecedents of explicit events. A third group of participants answered "what-happens-next" questions, which expose inferences about causal consequences, superordinate goals, and character emotions. State inferences were elicited by more than one of these question categories; participants occasionally mentioned states in order to provide elaborations and support content for the primary answers to the questions.

Graesser (1981) prepared a *constructive history chart* for each inference that was elicited in the question-answering protocols. The chart identified which explicit clauses in the text elicited a particular inference, the type of question that elicited it, and the proportion of participants who mentioned the inference at each point in the question-answering task. The first clause in the story that elicited the inference was particularly informative because that was the point at which the inference first emerged in the meaning representation. An inference was classified as a "new" inference in these instances. Constructive history charts were prepared for hundreds of knowledge-based inferences that were exposed by the question-answering task. These inference items were used subsequently in experiments that involved collecting time-based behavioral measures to determine whether a class of inferences was made online.

Graesser and Clark (1985) collected additional verbal protocol data on the same four narrative passages. They identified all of the nouns, adjectives, and main verbs words in each text. They used knowledge-engineering methods to extract information associated with each content word. One group of participants completed a free-generation task by listing the typical states, actions, and events associated with each content word. A second group of participants answered why and how questions about each item that was generated by at least two participants in the free-generation task. A typical content word had 166 statement nodes that were produced by at least two participants in either the free-generation task or the question-answering task. Graesser and Clark constructed a *conceptual graph structure* that organized the statement nodes stored under each content word. Each statement node also was scaled on a number of dimensions with respect to the content word; namely, typicality, necessity, importance, distinctiveness, structural centrality, and free-generation likelihood. These knowledge-engineering methods permitted Graesser and Clark to determine which content words (if any) produced the knowledge-based inferences associated with the stories. For example, the character emotion inference "the daughters were frightened" (see Table 1.1) matched one of the statement nodes stored under *kidnap* (i.e., "victim is frightened") and one of the statement nodes stored under *dragon* (i.e., "person is frightened"). The state inference "the dragon has scales" matched one of the statement nodes stored under *dragon*. Some knowledge-based inferences were novel situational inferences because they were not inherited from any of the content words. In summary, Graesser and Clark identified the information sources for each of the knowledge-based inferences that had been extracted in the Graesser (1981) study.

Prong 3: Collection of Time-Based Measures to Assess the Online Status of Inferences

Time-based behavioral measures need to be collected to test whether a class of inferences is truly made online. Therefore, Graesser and his colleagues conducted a number of studies that tested the online status of the inferences elicited by the verbal protocols. The time-based behavioral measures included word-reading times (Graesser, Haberlandt, & Koizumi, 1987), word-naming latencies (Long, Golding, & Graesser, 1992), and lexical-decision latencies (Long et al., 1992; Long & Golding, 1993; Long, Golding, Graesser, & Clark, 1990: Magliano, Baggett, Johnson, & Graesser, 1993; Millis, 1989).

Word-reading times were predicted to be longest for those words in the text that generate many online inferences. If there was no relationship between word-reading times and the number of new inferences within class *X*, it was concluded that class *X* inferences were not online; in contrast, if reading times were affected by the number of class *Y* inferences triggered by particular words in the text, then it was concluded that class *Y* inferences were online. For example, Graesser et al. (1987) reported that end-of-clause word-reading times were significantly affected by the number of causal antecedent and superordinate goal inferences generated by the end-of-clause words, but not by the number of state inferences, subordinate goal inferences, and causal consequence inferences. This outcome is compatible with the constructionist model and the CSS model, but not the other four models of inference generation described earlier.

In the word-naming and lexical-decision tasks, the reader received a test string on a computer screen shortly after reading each explicit clause in the text. As quickly as possible after the test string appeared, the participant named the word or decided whether the test string was a word (e.g., *barg*) or a nonword (e.g., *grab*). The critical test strings consisted of distinctive words that were extracted from the inference statements. For example, after reading the explicit clause *The dragon kidnapped the daughters*, they received one of the following test words that corresponded to the inferences in Table 1.1: *eat, grab, see, rescue, frighten*, or *scale*. Once again, these inferences (and test words) had been produced in the question-answering task reported by Graesser (1981); they were new inferences elicited by the explicit clause *n* and not in any of the question-answering protocols for clauses 1 to $n - 1$.

There was a control condition for each test word in which latencies were collected when the test word appeared in an unrelated passage context. This permitted the computation of an activation score, as depicted in Formula 3 (see, Kintsch, 1988; Till, Mross, & Kintsch, 1988).

$$\text{Activation score} = \text{Time(unrelated context)} - \text{Time(inference context)} \qquad (3)$$

An activation score was determined for each inference in this manner. Moreover, it was possible to measure the time-course of inference activation by varying the rate of text presentation (via rapid serial visual presentation, or RSVP) and by varying the amount of time between the onset of the last word in the clause and the onset of the text string (i.e., the stimulus onset asynchrony, or SOA). This methodology made it possible to impose yet additional control over the test words. Classes of inferences were matched on word length, word frequency, word class, the likelihood of generating the inference in the question-answering task, and the number of information sources (i.e., the number of content words in the target clause that contained a node that matched the inference).

The constructionist model and CSS model have received the most support from studies that involve naming latencies and lexical-decision latencies. Long conducted several experiments that contrasted superordinate goal inferences and subordinate goal/action inferences (Long et al., 1990; Long & Golding, 1993; Long et al., 1992). The patterns of activation scores for word naming and lexical decisions were as follows:

WORD NAMING: superordinate > subordinate = 0

LEXICAL DECISION: superordinate > subordinate > 0

Long also found that good comprehenders generated the superordinate goal inferences more quickly and consistently than did poor comprehenders. Magliano, Baggett, Johnson, and Graesser (1993) collected lexical-decision latencies to contrast causal antecedent and causal consequence inferences. The activation scores for these lexical-decision latencies indicated that causal antecedent inferences are generated online, but causal consequence inferences are not, as summarized in the following:

LEXICAL DECISION: causal antecedent > causal consequence = 0

Long et al. (1990) conducted a study that contrasted causal antecedent and state inferences, using a lexical-decision task, and found that the former inferences had higher activations than the latter, as indicated in the following:

LEXICAL DECISION: causal antecedent > state

When considered together, these results support the claim that the causal antecedent and superordinate goal inferences have higher activation scores than do causal consequence, subordinate goal/action, and state inferences (which in turn approach zero). These results are compatible with the word-reading time study conducted by Graesser et al. (1987).

There is an abundance of research outside of the Graesser laboratory that has investigated inference generation without using the three-pronged method (see review by Graesser, Singer, & Trabasso, 1993). These studies also support the prediction that inferences about superordinate goals and causal antecedents are generated online more consistently than inferences about subordinate goals/actions, causal consequences, and states. Thus, these studies also support the constructionist and CSS models. The critical class of inferences that distinguishes between these two models is that of character emotion inferences. Gernsbacher, Goldsmith, and Robertson (1992) collected naming latencies for emotion words that were interspersed in a story. For example, one story involved a main character stealing money from a store where his best friend worked and later learning that his best friend had been fired. Naming latencies were shorter for an appropriate test word (*guilt*) than an inappropriate test word (*pride*). These data indicate that character emotion inferences are generated online, which supports the constructionist model rather than the CSS model. Support has also been found for the constructionist model rather than the CSS model in an experimental paradigm that involved determining the conditions under which reinstatement searches were executed to establish global coherence (Dopkin, Klin, & Myers, 1993; Singer, in press; Suh & Trabasso, 1993; Van den Broek & Lorch, 1993).

In summary, the constructionist model provides the most accurate predictions about the classes of inferences that are generated online. This model predicts that inferences about superordinate goals, causal antecedents, and character emotions are generated online to a greater extent than inferences about subordinate goals/actions, causal consequences, and states. The three-pronged method provided clarity in identifying and testing the online status of knowledge-based inferences. The theoretical and empirical picture was much more murky before this method.

Currently, we are pursuing a number of directions that should shed further light on the generation of knowledge-based inferences. We are examining the exact time course of inference generation for each inference class. This involves varying the RSVP rates and SOA intervals at a fine-grained level. We also are investigating the extent to which inference generation varies for fast versus slow readers and good versus poor comprehenders. More attention needs to be devoted to global inferences, such as those concerning character emotions, complex plot configurations, attitudes of the author, and appropriate emotions of the reader. We also are examining whether inference-activation scores can be explained by the information sources that are resident in working memory during comprehension. For example, are the activation scores different for (a) novel inferences that are not inherited from the information stored under any content word in the explicit text, (b) inferences that are inherited from only one content word, and (c) inferences that are inherited from multiple content words? Hopefully, the field will converge on an adequate theory of inference generation during the next decade.

QUESTION ASKING DURING COMPREHENSION

Question asking is a litmus test for understanding. People ask good questions when they are capable of identifying gaps, contradictions, incongruities, anomalies, and ambiguities in their knowledge base. Good questions emerge when a person attempts to advance existing knowledge. It is well documented that the comprehension and retention of technical material substantially improves after people are trained to ask good questions (King, 1989; Palincsar & Brown, 1984; Pressley, Goodchild, Fleet, Zajachewski, & Evans, 1989; Singer & Donlan, 1982).

Researchers have proposed that question asking is as fundamental a component of cognition as is perception, memory, learning, decision making, and problem solving. It has been argued that question asking plays a central role in the comprehension of text and social behavior (Collins, Brown, & Larkin, 1980; Hilton, 1990; Olson et al., 1985), the learning of complex material (Collins, 1988; Miyake & Norman, 1979; Palincsar & Brown, 1984; Schank, 1986), problem solving (Klahr & Dunbar, 1988; Riesbeck, 1988), creativity (Sternberg, 1987), curiosity (Berlyne, 1960), self-control (Meichenbaum, 1971), and research (Campbell, Daft, & Hulin, 1982). In Schank's (1986) SWALE model, for example, learning occurs when an anomalous event is observed and questions are generated to guide the construction of an explanation for the event. Because of the pervasive role of question asking in the cognitive system, cognitive scientists recently developed computer interfaces that facilitate knowledge acquisition by making it extremely easy for the user to ask questions (Graesser, Langston, & Lang, 1992; Langston & Graesser, 1991; Schank, Ferguson, Birnbaum, Barger, & Greising, 1991: Sebrechts, & Swartz, 1991).

Despite the importance and virtues of question asking, it is well documented that people typically are not very good at it. Children ask very few questions in a classroom environment; approximately .2 questions per hr per student (Dillon, 1988). The incidence of questions increases to approximately 20 questions per hr in tutoring sessions, but the vast majority of these questions are shallow rather than deep questions (Graesser, Person, & Huber, 1993). Shallow questions address the content and interpretation of explicit material, whereas deep questions involve inference, application, synthesis, and evaluation (Bloom, 1984; Flammer, 1981). Tutoring studies have reported correlations near zero or negative correlations between the achievement level of students and measures of question asking, such as the total incidence of questions, the incidence of deep questions, and the incidence of genuine information-seeking questions (Fishbein, Eckart, Lauver, van Leeuwen, & Langmeyer, 1990; Graesser & Person, 1992). Moreover, there is no significant curvilinear relationship between achievement and question asking. These results are incompatible with the claim that good students ask good questions and with the broader theoretical claim that question asking is a fundamental cognitive activity.

There are at least three reasons why the incidence of question asking is low. First, there are numerous social costs and barriers to posing questions in a classroom setting (van der Meij, 1988). When a bad question is asked, the student exposes his or her ignorance and thereby loses status. When a good question is asked, the student has a high likelihood of interrupting the teacher or being irrelevant to the current context. Second, poor question asking can be attributed to cognitive deficits. It is well documented that people have trouble identifying their own knowledge deficits. Students frequently miss contradictions and inconsistencies in scientific texts, mathematical word problems, and other types of technical material (Glenberg, Wilkinson, & Epstein, 1982; Markman, 1979; Otero & Campanario, 1990). Most readers have trouble calibrating how well they are comprehending material (Glenberg & Epstein, 1987; Magliano, Little, & Graesser, 1993; Maki, Foley, Kajer, Thompson, & Willert, 1990; Weaver, 1990). There would be a slippery cognitive foundation for asking questions if both children and adults had trouble identifying their own knowledge deficits. Third, people are not exposed to good question-asking skills in most educational and social environments. Most teachers are poor role models for question asking because most of their questions (96%) are shallow questions (Kerry, 1987; Dillon, 1988). With rare exceptions, teachers do not ask information-seeking questions that reflect uncertainty and a genuine curiosity to learn something new. Teachers do not use sophisticated Socratic methods to expose the students' misconceptions and gaps in understanding (Collins, 1988; Graesser et al., in press). The mastery of effective question-asking skills requires substantial training that most students do not receive.

Surprisingly, there has been little psychological research on the cognitive processes involved in generating questions. Graesser, Person, and Huber (1992) identified four major question-generation mechanisms: (a) attempts to correct knowledge deficits, (b) monitoring the common ground between speech participants, (c) coordinating social activity, and (d) monitoring the flow of conversation. The first of these mechanisms is of primary interest in the present chapter. Knowledge-deficit questions are asked under one or more of the following conditions:

1. *An obstacle to achieving a goal*: When faced with an obstacle, a person seeks information from a good information source that removes or circumvents the obstacle. For example, when our computer malfunctions, we ask experts and friends how to correct the problem

2. *A contradiction, anomaly, or glitch in an explanation*: A question is asked in an effort to resolve a conceptual incompatibility. For example, there will be questions when a vendor claims he reimbursed your credit card, but the amount is not listed on your credit card bill.

3. *An obvious gap in knowledge*: A question is asked to fill in the gap. For example, when someone mentions an exotic word during conversation (e.g., *kitsch*), you might ask "What does kitsch mean?"

4. *Equally attractive alternatives*: A question is asked to gather new information that will break a tie between equivalent alternatives. For example, when you can't decide which of three dishes to order in a restaurant, you ask the waitress questions about the three dishes.

Although this taxonomy identifies the conditions under which questions are asked, it is not a satisfactory process model of the mechanisms of question asking.

Graesser and McMahen (1993) proposed a model for generating questions that attempt to correct knowledge deficits. The model has three highly interactive components: anomaly detection, question articulation, and social editing. The anomaly-detection process identifies obstacles, anomalies, knowledge gaps, and uncertainties, as specified in the taxonomy presented previously. The comprehender may or may not be successful in recognizing a knowledge deficit. The question-articulation process involves construction of a verbal code and question from a knowledge deficit that is detected. Individuals with low verbal abilities would have trouble encoding the knowledge deficits in words. The social-editing process involves assessment of the costs and benefits of asking a question in a particular social situation (see van der Meij, 1987, 1988). A potential question is not asked when the costs are too high or the benefits minimal. Each of these three components represents a potential barrier to asking a question.

Graesser and McMahen (1993) conducted experiments to the three-component model of question asking. College students attempted to solve a number of algebra word problems, statistics problems, and analytical brain teasers. There were five different versions of each problem. The *original* version was the complete original version of a problem, as presented in an algebra textbook, a statistics textbook, or a book with analytical brain teasers. The other four versions were slight transformations of the original version and introduced an anomaly. The *deletion* version omitted critical information that was needed to solve the problem. The *contradiction* version added a sentence or phrase that contradicted another piece of information in the problem. The *salient irrelevancy* version had an additional sentence or phrase that was obviously irrelevant, whereas the *subtle irrelevancy* version inserted a subtle piece of irrelevant information.

TABLE 2.1
Five Versions of an Algebra Word Problem from
Graesser and McMahen (1993)

Original

The Bears won 40 games and lost 24, while the Bulls won 32 games and lost 18. Which team had the higher percentage of wins?

Deletion

The Bears won 40 games and lost 24, while the Bulls won 32. Which team had the higher percentage of wins?

Contradiction

The Bears won 40 games and lost 24, while the Bulls won 32 and lost 18. *The Bulls won more games than the Bears.* Which team had the higher percentage of wins?

Salient Irrelevancy

The Bears won 40 games and lost 24, while the Bulls won 32 games and lost 18. *Several Bear team members were always getting into arguments with some members of the Bulls team.* Which team had the higher percentage of wins?

Subtle Irrelevancy

The Bears won 40 games and lost 24, while the Bulls won 32 games and lost 18. *Nearly 20% of the games almost resulted in ties.* Which team had the higher percentage of wins?

Table 1.2 presents the five versions of one of the algebra word problems. Graesser and McMahen investigated the likelihood that college students detected these anomalies and the likelihood that they asked questions that addressed a detected anomaly.

In one experiment, the participants were instructed to write down in a booklet all questions that came to mind while they solved the problems. Graesser and McMahen confirmed the obvious prediction that more questions would be generated in the four transformed versions than in the original versions of the problems. They also scored the likelihood that a participant asked at least one question that addressed an anomaly in the four transformed versions. The mean likelihood scores of asking a question about the anomaly were .50, .31, .31, and .23 for the deletion, contradiction, salient irrelevancy, and subtle irrelevancy versions, respectively. These scores differed significantly in this experiment, which involved "forced" question asking. The questions survived two barriers in this situation; namely, anomaly detection and question articulation. There was no social editing barrier because the participants were instructed to generate whatever questions came to mind.

Graesser and McMahen (1993) ran an experiment with the same materials, but under "self-induced" question-asking conditions. The participants were merely instructed to solve the problems. While presenting the instructions to the participants, the experimenter mentioned that she would be in an adjacent room and available if they had any questions. The experimenter tape-recorded all questions that the participants asked in this situation. It should be noted that a student would need to get up from a table (in front of four or five other students) and walk into the adjacent room to ask a question in this experiment. In this case, the likelihood of asking a question relevant to an anomaly was very low; .04, .08, .00, and .02 in the deletion, contradiction, salient irrelevancy, and subtle irrelevancy conditions, respectively. For all four types of anomalies combined, the likelihood of asking a question about an anomaly was .34 under forced question asking and only .04 under self-induced question asking. Thus, social editing substantially reduced the incidence of question asking. Only 10% of the questions that passed both the anomaly-detection process and the question-articulation process ended up passing the social-editing process.

Graesser and McMahen (1993) conducted another experiment to assess the likelihood that anomalies were detected. After attempting to solve each problem, the participants supplied a rating as to whether there was anything unusual about the problem on a 6-point Likert scale. This scale segregated "yes" responses (ratings of 4, 5, or 6) from "no" responses (ratings of 1, 2, and 3), so that the probability of participants giving a "yes" response could be computed. A baserate probability was computed for the original version to adjust for response biases. An anomaly-detection likelihood was computed according to Formula 4.

$$\text{Anomaly detection likelihood} = [p(\text{YES} \mid \text{anomaly}) - p(\text{YES} \mid \text{original})] \,/\, [1.0 - p(\text{YES} \mid \text{original})] \quad (4)$$

The mean anomaly detection scores were .47, .25, .00, and −.11 for deletions, contradictions, salient irrelevancies, and subtle irrelevancies, respectively. For deletions and contradictions, the likelihood of detecting an anomaly (.36) was similar to the likelihood of articulating a question (.41). The irrelevancies, however, apparently were not regarded as anomalies because their detection likelihoods were essentially zero. The participants apparently had no problem articulating questions about anomalies that were detected because the overall likelihood of generating a question about an anomaly (.34) actually exceeded the likelihood of detecting an anomaly in the rating task (.15). This suggests that some anomalies are not detected unless the participants are forced to ask questions.

In summary, the major barriers to question asking were linked to the process of detecting anomalies and the process of social editing. The barriers did not reside in the process of verbal coding and question articulation. Thus, attempts to improve question-asking skills should be devoted to enhancing sensitivity to anomalies and to removing potential social barriers. In contrast, little would be gained by training individuals how to express anomalies in words.

CLOSING COMMENTS

In this chapter we introduced several new models of comprehension that were designed to capture mechanisms at deep levels of understanding. Researchers in cognitive psychology and discourse processing were once enamored with the surface levels of comprehension because there were dozens of clearcut models that led to decisive predictions about variables that were easy to perceive and manipulate. In contrast, the mechanisms of deeper levels of comprehension were barely visible. Now the zeitgeist is changing in many circles. In this chapter, we presented new models of deep comprehension that make decisive predictions. We illustrated how these models can be rigorously tested. It appears that discourse processing researchers can venture into the deeper waters with minimal fear of drowning.

ACKNOWLEDGMENT

The research was funded by grants awarded to the first author by the Office of Naval Research (N00014-90-J-1492 and N00014-92-J-1826).

REFERENCES

Austin, J. L. (1962). *How to do things with words*. New York: Oxford, University Press.
Bach, K., & Harnish, R. M. (1979). *Linguistic communication and speech acts*. Cambridge, MA: MIT Press.
Bartlett, F. C. (1932). *Remembering: A study in experimental and social psychology*. New York: Cambridge University Press.
Berlyne, D. E. (1949). 'Interest' as a psychological concept. *British Journal of Psychology, 39*, 184–195.
Berlyne, D. E. (1960). *Conflict, arousal, and curiosity*. New York: McGraw-Hill.
Bloom, B. S. (1984). The 2 Sigma problem: The search for methods of group instruction as effective as one-to-one tutoring. *Educational Researcher, 13*, 4–16.
Bower, G. H., Black, J. B., & Turner, T. J. (1979). Scripts in memory for text. *Cognitive Psychology, 11*, 177–220.
Britton, B. K., van Dusen, L., Glynn, S. M., & Hemphill, D. (1990). The impact of inferences on instructional text. In A. C. Graesser & G. H. Bower (Eds.), *Inferences and text comprehension* (pp. 53–70). New York: Academic Press.
Brooks, R. A. (1991). How to build complete creatures rather than isolated cognitive simulators. In K. VanLehn (Ed.), *Architectures for intelligence* (pp. 225–239). Hillsdale, NJ: Lawrence Erlbaum Associates.
Bruner, J. (1986). *Actual minds, possible worlds*. Cambridge, MA: Harvard University Press.
Campbell, J. P., Daft, R. L., & Hulin, C. L. (1982). *What to study: Generating and developing research questions*. Beverly Hills, CA: Sage.
Clark, H. H., & Schaefer, E. R. (1989). Contributing to discourse. *Cognitive Science, 13*, 259–294.
Cleeremans, A., & McClelland, J. L. (1991). Learning the structure of event sequences. *Journal of Experimental Psychology: General, 120*, 235–253.

Collins, A. (1988). Different goals of inquiry teaching. *Questioning Exchange, 2*, 39–45.

Collins, A., Brown, J. S., & Larkin, K. M. (1980). Inference in text understanding. In R. J. Spiro, B. C. Bruce, & W. F. Brewer (Eds.), *Theoretical issues in reading comprehension* (pp. 385–407). Hillsdale, NJ: Lawrence Erlbaum Associates.

D'Andrade, R. G., & Wish, M. (1985). Speech act theory in quantitative research on interpersonal behavior. *Discourse Processes, 8*, 229–259.

DeJong, G. (1979). Prediction and substantiation: A new approach to natural language processing. *Cognitive Science, 3*, 251–273.

Dillon, J. T., (1988). *Questioning and teaching: A manual of practice*. New York: Teachers College Press.

Dopkins, S., Klin, C., & Myers, J. L. (1993). Accessibility of information about goals during the processing of narrative texts. *Journal of Experimental Psychology: Learning, Memory, and Cognition, 19*, 70–80.

Dyer, M. G. (1983). *In-depth understanding: A computer model of integrated processing for narrative comprehension*. Cambridge, MA: MIT Press.

Elman, J. L. (1990). Finding structure in time. *Cognitive Science, 14*, 179–211.

Fishbein, H. D., Eckart, T., Lauver, E., Van Leeuwen, R., Langmeyer, D. (1990). Learners' questions and comprehension in a tutoring setting. *Journal of Educational Psychology, 1*, 163–170.

Flammer, A. (1981). Towards a theory of question asking. *Psychological Research, 43*, 407–420.

Fletcher, C. R., & Bloom, C. P. (1988). Causal reasoning in the comprehension of simple narrative texts. *Journal of Memory and Language, 27*, 236–244.

Gernsbacher, M. A., Goldsmith, H. H., & Robertson, R. R. (1992). Do readers mentally represent character's emotional states? *Cognition and Emotion, 6*, 89–112.

Glenberg, A. M., & Epstein, W. (1987). In expert calibration of comprehension. *Memory of Cognition, 15*, 84–93.

Glenberg, A. M., Meyer, M., & Lindem, K. (1987) Mental models contribute to foregrounding during text comprehension. *Journal of Memory and Language, 26*, 69–83.

Glenberg, A. M., Wilkinson, A. C., & Epstein, W. (1982). The illusion of knowing: Failure in the self-assessment of comprehension. *Memory and Cognition, 10*, 597–602.

Goffman, E. (1974). *Frame analysis*. Cambridge, MA: Harvard University Press.

Golden, R. M., & Rumelhart, D. E. (1991). A distributed representation and model for story comprehension and recall. In *Proceedings of the Thirteenth Annual Conference of the Cognitive Science Society* (pp. 7–12). Hillsdale, NJ: Lawrence Erlbaum Associates.

Graesser, A. C. (1981). *Prose comprehension beyond the word*. New York: Springer-Verlag.

Graesser, A. C. (1992). *Questioning mechanisms during complex learning*. Memphis, TN: The University of Memphis. (ERIC Document Reproduction Service No. TM 020 505)

Graesser, A. C., & Bower, G. H. (Eds.). (1990). *Inferences and text comprehension*. New York: Academic Press.

Graesser, A. C., & Clark, L. F. (1985). *Structures and procedures of implicit knowledge*. Norwood, NJ: Ablex.

Graesser, A. C., Gordon, S. E., & Sawyer, J. D. (1979). Memory for typical and atypical actions in scripted activities: Test of a script + tag hypothesis. *Journal of Verbal Learning and Verbal Behavior, 18*, 319–332.

Graesser, A. C., Haberlandt, K., & Koizumi, D. (1987). How is reading time influenced by knowledge based inferences and world knowledge. In B. K. Britton & S. M. Glynn (Eds.), *Executive control processes in reading* (pp. 217–251). Hillsdale, NJ: Lawrence Erlbaum Associates.

Graesser, A. C., & Kreuz, R. J. (1993). A theory of inference generation during text comprehension. *Discourse Processes, 16*, 145–160.

Graesser, A. C., Lang, K. L., & Roberts, R. M. (1991). Question answering in the context of stories. *Journal of Experimental Psychology: General, 120*, 254–277.

Graesser, A. C., Langston, M., & Lang, K. L. (1992). Designing educational software around questioning. *Journal of Artificial Intelligence and Education, 3*, 235–241.

Graesser, A. C., & McMahen, C. L. (1993). Anomalous information triggers questions when adults solve problems and comprehend stories. *Journal of Educational Psychology, 85,* 136–151.

Graesser, A. C., & Person, N. K. (in press). Question asking during tutoring. *American Educational Research Journal.*

Graesser, A. C., Person, N., & Huber, J. (1992). Mechanisms that generate questions. In T. Lauer, E. Peacock, & A. Graesser (Eds.). *Questions and information systems* (pp. 167–187). Hillsdale, NJ: Lawrence Erlbaum Associates.

Graesser, A. C., Person, N., & Huber, J. (1993). Question asking during tutoring and in the design of educational software. In M. Rabinowitz (Ed.), *Cognitive science foundations of instruction* (pp. 149–172). Hillsdale, NJ: Lawrence Erlbaum Associates.

Graesser, A. C., Robertson, S. P., & Anderson, P. A. (1981). Incorporating inferences in narrative representations: A study of how and why. *Cognitive Psychology, 13,* 1–26.

Graesser, A. C., Singer, M., & Trabasso, T. (1994). Constructing inferences during narrative text comprehension. *Psychological Review, 101,* 371–395.

Hilton, D. J. (1990). Conversational processes and causal explanation. *Psychological Bulletin, 107,* 110–119.

Jacob, R. J. K. (1983). Using formal specifications in the design of human–computer interface. *Communications of the Association for Computing Machinery, 26,* 126–133.

Johnson-Laird, P. N. (1983). *Mental models.* Cambridge, MA: Harvard University Press.

Just, M. A., & Carpenter, P. A. (1992). A capacity theory of comprehension: Individual differences in working memory. *Psychological Review, 99,* 122–149.

Kahneman, D., Slovic, P., & Tversky, A. (1982). *Judgments under uncertainty: Heuristics and biases.* New York: Cambridge University Press.

Kerry, T. (1987). Classroom questions in England. *Questioning Exchange, 1,* 32–33.

King, A. (1989). Effects of self-questioning training on college students' comprehension of lectures. *Contemporary Educational Psychology, 14,* 366–381.

Kintsch, W. (1988). The role of knowledge in discourse comprehension: A constructive-integration model. *Psychological Review, 95,* 163–182.

Kintsch, W. (1993). Information accretion and reduction in text processing: Inferences. *Discourse Processes, 16,* 193–202.

Kintsch, W., & van Dijk, T. A. (1978). Toward a model of text comprehension and production. *Psychological Review, 85,* 363–394.

Klahr, D., & Dunbar, K. (1988). Dual search space during scientific reasoning. *Cognitive Science, 12,* 1–48.

Langston, M. C., & Graesser, A. C. (1992). Question asking during learning with a point and query interface. In *Proceedings of the Fourteenth Annual Conference of the Cognitive Science Society* (pp. 921–926). Hillsdale, NJ: Lawrence Erlbaum Associates.

Lehnert, W. G. (1981). Plots units and narrative summarization. *Cognitive Science, 5,* 293–331.

Long, D. L., & Golding, J. M. (1993). Superordinate goal inferences: Are they automatically generated during comprehension? *Discourse Processes, 16,* 55–74.

Long, D. L., Golding, J. M., & Graesser, A. C. (1992). The generation of goal related inferences during narrative comprehension. *Journal of Memory and Language, 31,* 634–647.

Long, D. L., Golding, J. M., Graesser, A. C., & Clark, L. F. (1990). Goal, event, and state inferences: An investigation of inference generation during story comprehension. In A. C. Graesser & G. H. Bower (Eds.), *The psychology of learning and motivation: Inferences and text comprehension* (pp. 89–102). New York: Academic Press.

Magliano, J. P., Baggett, W. B., Johnson, B. K., & Graesser, A. C. (1993). The time course of generating causal antecedent and causal consequence inferences. *Discourse Processes, 16,* 35–54.

Magliano, J. P., Little, L. D., & Graesser, A. C. (1993). The impact of comprehension instruction on the calibration of comprehension. *Journal of Reading and Instruction, 32,* 49–63.

Magliano, J. P., & Graesser, A. C. (1991). A three-pronged method for studying inference generation in literary text. *Poetics, 20*, 193–232.

Maki, R. H., Foley, J. M., Kajer, W. K., Thompson, R. C., & Willert, M. G. (1990). Increased processing enhances calibration of comprehension. *Journal of Experimental Psychology: Learning, Memory, and Cognition, 16*, 609–616.

Mandler, J. M. (1984). *Stories, scripts, and scenes: Aspects of schema theory*. Hillsdale, NJ: Lawrence Erlbaum Associates.

Mandler, J. M., & Johnson, N. S. (1977). Remembrance of things parsed: Story structure and recall. *Cognitive Psychology, 9*, 111–151.

Markman, E. M. (1979). Realizing that you don't understand: Elementary school children's awareness of inconsistencies. *Child Development, 50*, 643–655.

McKoon, G., & Ratcliff, R. (1992). Inference during reading. *Psychological Review, 99*, 440–466.

Mehan, H. (1979). "What time is it Denise?": Asking known-information questions in classroom discourse. *Theory into Practice, 18*, 285–294.

Meichenbaum, D. (1971). *Cognitive behavior therapy*. New York: Plenum Press.

Millis, K. K. (1989). *The time course of constructing bridging and expectation knowledge-based inferences during the comprehension of expository text*. Unpublished doctoral dissertation, Memphis State University.

Minsky, M. (1975). A framework for representing knowledge. In P. H. Winston (Ed.), *The psychology of computer vision*. New York: McGraw-Hill.

Miyake, N., & Norman, D. A. (1979). To ask a question, one must know enough to know what is not known. *Journal of Verbal Learning and Verbal Behavior, 18*, 357–364.

Morrow, D. G., Greenspan, S. L., & Bower, G. H. (1987). Accessibility and situation models in narrative comprehension. *Journal of Memory and Language, 26*, 165–187.

Nelson, K. (1986). *Event knowledge: Structure and function in development*. Hillsdale, NJ: Lawrence Erlbaum Associates.

O'Brien, E. J., Shank, D. M., Myers, J. L., & Rayner, K. (1988). Elaborative inferences during reading: Do they occur on-line? *Journal of Experimental Psychology: Learning, Memory, and Cognition, 14*, 410–420.

Olson, G. M., Duffy, S. A., & Mack, R. L. (1985). Question asking as a component of text comprehension. In A. C. Graesser & J. B. Black (Eds.), *The psychology of questions* (pp. 219–226). Hillsdale, NJ: Lawrence Erlbaum Associates.

Otero, J. C., & Campanario, J. M. (1990). Comprehension evaluation and regulation in learning from science texts. *Journal of Research in Science Teaching, 27*, 447–460.

Palincsar, A. S., & Brown, A. L. (1984). Reciprocal teaching of comprehension-monitoring activities. *Cognition and Instruction, 1*, 117–175.

Pressley, M., Goodchild, F., Fleet, J., Zajachewski, R., & Evans, E. (1987). The challenges of classroom strategy instruction. *The Elementary School Journal, 89*, 301–342.

Riesbeck, C. K. (1988). Are questions just functions calls? *Questioning Exchange, 2*, 17–24.

Rips, L. J. (1990). Reasoning. In M. R. Rosenzweig & L. W. Porter (Eds.), *Annual Review of Psychology* (Vol. 41, pp. 321–353). Palo Alto, CA: Annual Review, Inc.

Rumelhart, D. E., & McClelland, J. L. (1986). *Parallel distributed processing: Explorations in the microstructure of cognition* (Vol. 1). Cambridge: MIT Press.

St. John, M. F. (1991). The story gestalt: A model of knowledge intensive processes in text comprehension. In *Proceedings of the Thirteenth Annual Conference of the Cognitive Science Society* (pp. 25–30). Hillsdale, NJ: Lawrence Erlbaum Associates.

Schank, R. C. (1986). *Explanation patterns: Understanding mechanically and creatively*. Hillsdale, NJ: Lawrence Erlbaum Associates.

Schank, R. C. (1990). *Tell me a story: A new look at real and artificial memory*. New York: Scribner's.

Schank, R. C., & Abelson, R. (1977). *Scripts, plans, goals, and understanding: An inquiry into human knowledge structures*. Hillsdale, NJ: Lawrence Erlbaum Associates.

Schank, R. C., Ferguson, W., Birnbaum, L., Barger, J., & Greising, M. (1991). ASK TOM: An experimental interface for video case libraries. In *Proceedings of the 13th annual conference of the cognitive science society* (pp. 570–575). Hillsdale, NJ: Lawrence Erlbaum Associates.

Schegloff, E. A., & Sacks, H. (1973). Opening up closings. *Semiotica, 8*, 289–327.

Searle, J. R. (1969). *Speech acts*. Cambridge, England, Cambridge University Press.

Sebrechts, M. M., & Swartz, M. L. (1991). Question asking as a tool for novice computer skill acquisition. In S. Robertson (Ed.), *Proceedings of International Conference on Computer–Human Interaction* (293–297). New York: ACM.

Sell, M. A., Cohen, R., Crain, M., Duncan, M. K., MacDonald, C. D., & Ray, G. E. (1991, April). *The context of dyadic interactions: Communication as a function of task demands and social relationships*. Paper presented at the annual convention of the Society for Research on Child Development, Seattle, WA.

Singer, M. (1988). Inferences in reading. *Reading Research: Advances in Theory and Practice, 6*, 177–219.

Singer, M. (in press). Discourse inference processes. In M. A. Gernsbacher (Ed.), *Handbook of psycholinguistics*. New York: Academic Press.

Singer, H., & Donlan, D. (1982). Active comprehension: Problem solving schema with question generation for comprehension of complex short stories. *Reading Research Quarterly, 17*, 166–186.

Stein, N. L., & Levine, L. J. (1991). Making sense out of emotion: The representation and use of goal-structured knowledge. In W. Kessen, A. Ortony, & F. Craik (Eds.), *Memories, thoughts, and emotions: Essays in honor of George Mandler* (pp. 295–322). Hillsdale, NJ: Lawrence Erlbaum Associates.

Sternberg, R. J. (1987). Questioning and intelligence. *Questioning Exchange, 1*, 11–13.

Stevens, A. L., & Rumelhart, D. E. (1975). Errors in reading: Analysis using an augmented transition network model of grammar. In D. A. Norman & D. E. Rumelhart (Eds.), *Explorations in cognition* (pp. 136–155). San Francisco: Freeman.

Suh, S. Y., & Trabasso, T. (1993). Inferences during reading: Converging evidence from discourse analysis, talk-aloud protocols and recognition priming. *Journal of Memory and Language, 32*, 279–300.

Swamer, S. S., Graesser, A. C., Franklin, S. P., Sell, M. A., Cohen, R. & Baggett, W. B. (1993). A connectionist model of speech act prediction. In *Proceedings of the 15th Annual Cognitive Science Society* (pp. 994–999). Hillsdale, NJ: Lawrence Erlbaum Associates.

Till, R. E., Mross, E. F., & Kintsch, W. (1988). Time course of priming for associate and inference words in a discourse context. *Memory and Cognition, 16*, 283–298.

Trabasso, T., & Suh, S. Y. (1993). Using talk-aloud protocols to reveal inferences during comprehension of text. *Discourse Processes, 16*, 3–34.

Trabasso, T., & van den Broek, P. (1985). Causal thinking and the representation of narrative events. *Journal of Memory and Language, 24*, 612–630.

Turner, E. H., & Cullingford, R. E. (1989). Using conversation MOPS in natural language interfaces. *Discourse Processes, 12*, 63–90.

van den Broek, P. (1990). Causal inferences and the comprehension of narrative text. In A. C. Graesser & G. H. Bower (Eds.), *Inferences and text comprehension* (pp. 175–196). New York: Academic Press.

van den Broek, P., & Lorch, R. F. (1993). Network representations of causal relations of causal relations in memory for narrative texts: Evidence from primed recognition. *Discourse Processes, 16*, 169–180.

van der Meij, H. (1987). Assumptions of information-seeking questions. *Questioning Exchange, 1*, 111–117.

van der Meij, H. (1988). Constraints on question asking in classrooms. *Journal of Educational Psychology, 80*, 401–405.

van Dijk, T. A., & Kintsch, W. (1983). *Strategies of discourse comprehension.* New York: Academic Press.

Weaver, C. A. (1990). Constraining factors in calibration of comprehension. *Journal of Experimental Psychology: Learning, Memory, and Cognition, 16,* 214–222.

Whitney, P. (1987). Psychological theories of elaborative inferences: Implications for schema-theoretic views of comprehension. *Reading Research Quarterly, 22,* 299–310.

CHAPTER

2

A PREDICATION SEMANTICS MODEL OF TEXT COMPREHENSION AND RECALL

Althea Turner
NYNEX

Bruce K. Britton
University of Georgia

Paul Andraessen
Coral Gables, FL

Deborah McCutchen
University of Washington

The purpose of this chapter is to describe a predication semantics model of text comprehension and report an experiment that tested its predictions for recall. The model descended from models developed by Kintsch and his associates, particularly the Miller and Kintsch (1980) implementation of the theory described in Kintsch and van Dijk (1978). The present model differs from the Kintsch model in that it involves the use of semantic information from the predicates of the propositions to extract the gist of the text.

The model is similar to Kintsch's in that it simulates the reading process as a series of cycles. Each cycle has two phases: input and reduction. During the input phase, some of the text's propositions are read into working memory. There the propositions are related to each other and to earlier propositions by overlap of arguments, thus forming a connected network. During the reduction phase, the gist of that network is extracted, and the gist propositions are then held in working memory until the next cycle.

The most important differences between the Kintsch model and the predication semantics model are in the reduction phase. In both models, the reduction phase involves the selection of a small number of ideas from the previous text to "keep in mind" as the next segment of text is processed as input. Some ideas must be kept in mind so that the next part of the text can be connected to the earlier parts. Only a small number of ideas can be kept in mind because readers have only a limited working memory capacity.

The models differ in their conceptions of how readers decide which ideas to keep in mind. The Miller and Kintsch (1980) implementation of the Kintsch and van Dijk (1978) theory used an algorithm called the *leading edge strategy*. The leading edge strategy takes as input a hierarchical tree diagram representing the level and recency of each proposition in working memory. The tree is itself constructed from the overlap relations among the input propositions. In the leading edge algorithm, propositions are selected, starting with those at the highest level of the tree (with level height defined in terms of psychological importance). The most recent of these propositions are selected until working memory is full. These propositions are the ones held over in working memory.

In contrast, the predication semantics model uses a different algorithm, called the *reduction process*. The input to the reduction process is a network of propositions. As in the case of Kintsch's tree, the network is constructed from the overlapping relations among the input propositions. Unlike Kintsch's tree, which only relates each proposition to its direct superordinate and subordinate propositions, the network preserves information about the connections that each proposition has with every other proposition in working memory. The reduction process also differs from the leading edge strategy in that the connectedness information is combined with the recency information to yield a single value for each proposition, which we call its *strength value*. Strength values are used in the later phases of reduction.

Perhaps the most important difference between the models is that more semantic information is used by the reduction process of the predication semantics model than by the leading edge strategy. The semantic information is carried by the predicates of the text's propositions. A predicate specifies a relation between arguments. For example, in the following sentence the predicate is *hit*.

(1) John hit the ball with the bat in the park at noon

In Example 1, the predicate specifies the relations between John, the ball, the bat, the park, and noon. In general, the predicate *hit* has a standard semantics which includes the notions of the hitter, the hittee, the instrument, and often the location and time. We can represent the semantics of the predicate *hit* in a general predicate frame with standard slots:

(2) hitter, *hit*, hittee, instrument, location, time

In these frames, the slot (i.e., the *arguments* of the proposition of which *hit* is the predicate) are filled from Example 1 as follows:

(3) John, *hit*, ball, bat, park, noon

Included in the semantics of *hit* is the provision that some arguments are optional. The optional arguments for *hit* are the instrument, location, and time arguments. For example, no one would think it odd to say "John hit the ball" even though it leaves out the optional arguments. However, the semantics of *hit* also specifies that other arguments are obligatory. For example, we could not say "John hit . . ." without either the reader filling in the missing argument or noticing that something important is missing. This aspect of the model extends previous case grammar approaches (Fillmore, 1968; Gruber, 1965; Jackendoff, 1972).

How does the model use semantic information in the reduction process? The reduction process has two purposes. One purpose is to extract the gist of the text in working memory so that it can be held over for use in the next cycle. For the example of *hit*, the semantics is such that the obligatory arguments are most likely to be the gist. If something must be dispensed with, it should be the optional arguments because they will be the least likely elements needed for computing the necessary gist. Therefore, Example 1 would be reduced to "John hit the ball." The second purpose of the reduction process is to reduce the load on working memory. Reducing the number of arguments in the *hit* proposition would achieve this goal.

During the reduction phase, our model uses the semantics of 28 predicate classes, which are listed in Table 2.1. For each proposition with a predicate in one of those classes, information about the semantics of the predicate is combined with information about its connectedness, recency, and strength. This is the input to a later part of the reduction process, in which the propositions are prioritized in working memory. The highest priority propositions are those that the program is least likely to reduce in size or to eliminate from working memory; the lowest priority propositions are candidates for immediate reduction. The last part of the reduction process involves the reduction and elimination of propositions in priority order, until working memory is enough below capacity to provide sufficient capacity for the next part of the text to be input.

Throughout the reduction phase, information about the propositions in working memory is transferred to long-term memory. The long-term strength of each proposition determines its probability of recall, which permits us to make predictions about the recall of individual propositions.

In the remainder of this chapter, we describe the input phase briefly and the reduction phase in detail. We then describe how the long-term memory trace

TABLE 2.1
Class of Predicates Recognized and Reduced by the Simulation Model of Reduction Rules

cause	communication	composition	concession	conjunct	contrast
extent	hedge	identity	intensifier	intrinsic	location
manner	name	ncontrast	number	part	possess
process	purpose	qcontrast	qualify	quantify	range
reference	set	time	topic		

of the text is determined by the processing occurring in working memory. Next, we describe the results of an experiment in which we tested the predictions of the model for four texts. Finally, we discuss the results and various related issues.

THE MODEL

Input Phase

The present model differs from Miller and Kintsch (1980) in the way that it simulates the input phase. In Kintsch's model, deciding how many new propositions to read during each input cycle was done by the operator, with input usually suspended at a sentence or clause boundary. In the present model, the program has a set of rules that guide the input decisions. One basic rule is to look for the end of a connected unit of information. This is accomplished by using sentence and clause boundaries that are marked by punctuation. Because clause boundaries are not always marked by punctuation, the program also uses other types of information to decide when to suspend input. One type is the number of propositions accumulated so far in working memory. As more propositions are input, the number of propositions in working memory increases. For example, suppose we constrain the model's working memory to hold no more than 13 propositions temporarily at the end of any input phase, with the number to be reduced to no more than 7 at the end of the reduction phase. As the number of propositions in working memory approaches 13, the input program includes rules that make it increasingly receptive to various reasons for suspending the input. Psychologically, this corresponds to the introspection that one's working memory is approaching capacity, and the increasing sense that input will soon have to be suspended.

Decisions to suspend input also are influenced by whether all the new propositions form a connected chain. If they do not, the program continues accepting input until they do form such a chain, unless the working memory limit of 13 is near. The extent to which the new propositions form a connected chain is evaluated by the program as each new proposition is input. This involves looking for overlap between the arguments of each newly input proposition and the arguments of every other proposition in working memory. If there are overlapping arguments between a newly input proposition and another proposition, there is connectedness. At any point at which all the propositions in working memory form connected chains, the program becomes more receptive to the possibility of terminating input, especially if the input limit of working memory is being approached. Psychologically, this corresponds to the tendency to try to finish reading a connected chunk of the text before attempting to extract its gist (i.e., start the reduction phase).

Another factor that plays a role in decisions to suspend input is the internal completeness of each new proposition. For a proposition to be internally complete, all of its obligatory argument slots must be filled. For example, a proposition such as John, *hit* . . . has an unfilled slot, as explained previously. Such a proposition is internally incomplete. The input program tries to continue input until all the new propositions are internally complete.

The overall operation of the input program is controlled by a set of rules[1] which specify the conditions to be met for input to be suspended. For example, one rule can be stated as follows:

> *If* at least two new propositions have been read and *if* working memory is two-thirds full and all new propositions form a connected chunk and all propositions in working memory are complete *then* end this input phase.

Such rules automatically balance limits on the number of propositions held in working memory (Kintsch & Keenan, 1973; Miller, 1956) with clause boundary markers (Fodor, Bever, & Garrett, 1974) and internal completeness (de Beaugrande, 1980; Kintsch, 1988). The input program was designed to be similar to human input processes in that the program reads the text one word at a time. As each word is read, the program consults its proposition list to determine whether that word was used in a proposition and if it was, that part of the proposition is activated and the next word is processed.

Reduction Phase

Three parts of the reduction phase are described. First, we describe the role of the information on recency and connectedness that results from the input phase. This information is used to compute a strength value for each proposition, as mentioned previously. Second, we describe *predicate semantics rules* and their role in the reduction phase. Third, we describe how the model decides which propositions are to be reduced.

Recency, Connectedness, and Strength

The predication semantics model calculates a strength value for each proposition. The strength value is a function of the recency and connectedness of the proposition, as well as its strength from earlier processing cycles. The calculation of the strength value is based on a single initial value and two equations. The single initial strength value expresses the strength due to the mere occurrence of the proposition. One equation expresses the rate of increase in strength as a function of connectedness and the other equation expresses its decay. The

[1]The program is implemented in the C programming language, and is available from the first author.

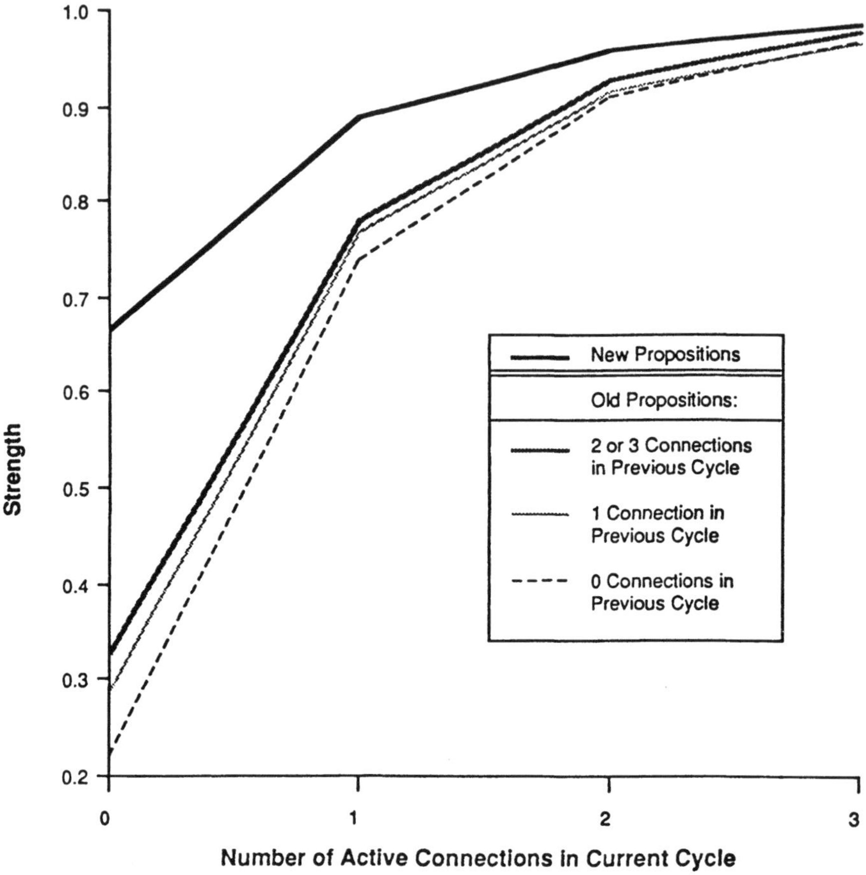

FIG. 2.1. Strength values based on recency and connectedness.

resulting strength values are depicted graphically in Fig. 2.1. In this figure, the initial strength value is shown on the solid line at the ordinate. This value is always assigned to the most recent propositions that are input during the current cycle and have no connectedness. For example, in Fig. 2.1 the initial strength value was set at two thirds of the maximum strength of 1, or .67. This value corresponds to the psychological intuition that a newly input proposition should have fairly substantial strength, but not so much as to prevent an increase in strength if it is highly connected.

The rest of the points in Fig. 2.1 are produced by applying one or both equations. The first equation is for determining the growth in strength with increased connectedness; it expresses the idea that each connection adds a fixed proportion of the remaining possible strength to the strength that the proposition had without the extra connection. Specifically, each additional connection adds .67 of the remaining possible strength. This can be expressed in Formula 1, where

S is the strength of a proposition and c is the number of connections of that proposition, with $c + 1$ signifying the addition of a connection:

$$S_{c+1} = S_c + .67\ (1 - S_c) \tag{1}$$

Thus, the strength value of a proposition with an additional connection (S_{c+1}) is equal to the strength it would have had without that connection (S_c) plus a fixed proportion (.67) of its remaining possible strength ($1 - S_c$).

For example, consider a new proposition with one connection. The strength it would have had without that connection would be subscripted as $c = 0$. The calculations would be:

$$S_{c+1} = S_{c=0} + .67\ (1 - S_{c=0})$$
$$S_{c+1} = .67 + .67\ (1 - .67)$$
$$S_{c+1} = .89$$

This point appears on the solid line of Fig. 2.1 above the abscissa for one active connection. The other points in the solid line of Fig. 2.1 can be calculated in the same way. This is a standard stochastic model.

By way of summary, a proposition gets .67 of its possible strength by virtue of its mere occurrence, which is supplemented by .67 more of its possible strength for each connection it has with other propositions. These strength values are used in the reduction process so that, other things equal, the higher a proposition's strength, the more likely it is to be held over. Psychologically, this expresses the intuition that newly mentioned propositions are likely to be useful if held over, especially if they have connections to other propositions. It also corresponds to the intuition that those text ideas that should be held over for use on the next cycle include those that occurred most recently (i.e., newly input ones) and those that have the greatest number of active connections. For our purposes, the present approach is superior to the leading edge strategy because the strength value can be combined with the predicate's semantic information during the reduction process, as shown in the next section.

The remaining points in Fig. 2.1 are produced by using the equation for decay. This equation expresses the intuition that, as propositions age, they are less likely to be useful. At the end of each cycle, the strength of each proposition decays by a fixed proportion. We set the decay value to 1 minus the initial strength value. If we set the initial strength value to .67, then after each cycle, each proposition decays to one third of its strength. This can be expressed as in Formula 2.

$$\begin{gathered}\text{new strength (i.e., strength on next cycle)}\\ = .33 \times \text{old strength (i.e., strength from previous cycle)}\end{gathered} \tag{2}$$

For example, for a proposition that had no active connections on the previous cycle, the old strength value would be .67 (left-most point on the solid line), and its strength on the next cycle would be .33 × .67, or .22. In Fig. 2.1, this is the lowest point on the ordinate. All points in Fig. 2.1 can be produced from Formulas 1 and 2 and the single initial value.

The Role of Predicate Semantics in the Reduction Phase

The goal of the reduction phase is to identify the gist propositions of the network, so they can be held over to the next cycle. We begin with an example of how a typical predicate is reduced. For some predicates, it is obvious that they are unlikely to be part of the gist. For example, *hedge* predicates are unlikely to be essential to most texts. Consider the following hedged assertion:

(4) The model accounts for about 10% of the variance.

Readers will lose little of importance if they remove the hedge word *about*, thereby leaving

(5) The model accounts for 10% of the variance.

That is, if a reader's working memory contained both *about* and the assertion that it hedged and was overloaded so that he or she had to delete some of the contents, what should be removed? If the reader removed the hedged assertion and kept the hedge word, that would leave only *about*, which would probably be of little use on the next cycle. If the reader instead removed the hedge word *about*, that would leave the assertion, which is most likely to be useful on later cycles.

We now formalize the rules for the *hedge* predicate and go on to describe rules for other typical predicates. The model uses three types of rules for reduction: *core, generalize*, and *simplify*.

Core Rules. Formally, the reduction rule for each predicate is stated as a rewrite rule. For *hedge*, the rule is to extract the *core* of the proposition. As an example, the *core* for the *hedge* predicate is written in general terms as follows:

(6) hedge word, *hedges*, hedged assertion

In example 3, the argument slots are filled as

(7) about, *hedges*, the model accounts for 10% of the variance.

The rule for reducing this proposition specifies that its core, which is the assertion, should be kept and the hedge word removed. This can be written more generally as the following (with the arrow read as "rewrite as"):

(8) core of (hedge word, *hedges*, hedged assertion) → hedged assertion

In the context of the example sentence, we have

(9) core of (about, *hedges*, the model accounts for 10% of the variance) → the model accounts for 10% of the variance.

Recall that the goals of the reduction process are to retain the gist while reducing the load on working memory. The result of the core rule for *hedges* is to remove the *hedge* proposition from working memory, leaving behind the assertion. Because the assertion is more likely to be the gist, this contributes to one goal of the reduction process: retention of the gist. Moreover, because the action taken by the core rule for *hedge* also removes the *hedge* proposition, the rule also contributes to the other goal of the reduction process: reduction of the load on working memory.

Most of the predicate reduction rules are of this core type. Another example is the *possess* predicate. The notion of possession has a standard meaning, which includes the motions of the possessor and the possessed. This can be expressed as:

(10) possessor, *possesses*, possessed object

Thus, a sentence such as:

(11) The world has wool.

can be expressed as:

(12) world, *possesses*, wool

To express the judgment that the core of this predicate is the possessed object, we can write the rule:

(13) core of (possessor, *possesses*, possessed object) → possessed object

Applying this rule to Example 6, we derive the following:

(14) core of (world, *possesses*, wool) → wool

It can be seen that such a reduction would be the most useful one if the passage was primarily about wool; that is, because the idea of wool is part of the gist, it probably would be used again on the next cycle. However, if the passage was instead about the world, rather than wool, it might not be the best reduction. In an attempt to deal with such cases, the predication semantics model has been constructed so that it can take this situation into account. The model does this by using the previously calculated strength information in the conditions of the rules. In this example, this takes advantage of the fact that if the passage were about the world and not wool, the concept "world" would have a high strength value, because it will have occurred recently and is connected to many recent propositions. The rule that takes this information into account can be written as follows:

(15) core of (possessor, *possesses*, possessed object) $\rightarrow$ best argument.

The *best argument* is the concept with the highest strength, as computed in the first part of the reduction process. Therefore, if the possessor *world* has greater strength by virtue of being used most recently or being most connected, it will be chosen as the core. In contrast, if the passage is about wool, the possessed object wool will be chosen as the core. If the two arguments have equal strength, the earlier rule about possession would be used, with the result being that the possessed object is chosen.

An example using somewhat more complex conditions is provided by the rule for reducing conjunctions with two arguments, such as *apples and oranges*:

> core of (Argument 1, *conjoined-with*, Argument 2) $\rightarrow$ if the arguments are not propositions, the core is Argument 1, unless that argument is not active (i.e., referred to in the current cycle), in which case the core is Argument 2; if the arguments are both propositions, the core is the argument with the highest strength.

Generalize Rules. Another class of reduction rules does not extract the core, but instead rewrites the proposition into a more generalized form, leaving out some information. The retained information is most likely the gist. These *generalize* rules retain the gist and reduce the load on working memory by omitting information. The *contrast* predicate is a good example of this kind of reduction rule. The sentence:

(16) Australia has more sheep than any other country.

describes a contrast (expressed by the words *more . . . than*) between one proposition ("Australia has sheep") and another proposition ("any other country than Australia"); that is, "Australia has sheep" is to be contrasted with an external standard (i.e., "any other country"). The predicate frame for *contrast* is:

> to-be-contrasted proposition, *contrasts-with*, standard it is contrasted with

If a working memory overload forces this proposition to be reduced, a generalize rule specifies how it is to be rewritten to express the idea in a more general form that retains the gist. Because one part of this proposition expresses a quantitative idea (i.e., "more sheep"), it can be expressed by the *quantify* predicate. Rewriting this proposition with the *quantify* predicate retains the general idea that there is an amount involved, but leaves out the standard to which it is compared. Thus, the standard can be removed from working memory, thereby changing Example 16 to:

(17) Australia has many sheep

Formally, in this case the rule can be expressed as follows:

generalization of (Argument 1 (to-be-contrasted proposition), *contrasts-with* ("more"), Argument 2 (standard) → change the predicate to QUANTIFY

and if the second argument is a proposition, *then* remove it from working memory unless it is embedded in another proposition; *and* add a second argument that is a quantitative value reflecting the contrasting relationship (e.g., if contrast is "more," a possible value is "many").

It should be noted that the last phrase of the rule must be implemented by the operator because the model does not have the linguistic knowledge necessary to decide that *many* is the appropriate word.

This rule captures the intuition that the gist of the *contrast* predicate is more likely to be the to-be-contrasted proposition than the standard against which it is contrasted. As regards the overload of working memory, if Argument 2 is a proposition, this rule removes it from working memory (unless it is embedded in another proposition) and thereby reduces the memory load.

According to the model, a series of rules is applied until working memory has sufficient spare capacity. We digress briefly here to illustrate this by describing the next reduction of this proposition. If it is later necessary to reduce the *quantify* predicate, a core rule applies:

core of (Argument 1, *quantified-by*, value) → Argument 1.

Thus, Example 17 would be reduced to:

(18) Australia has sheep.

Returning to our illustration of generalize rules, the same sort of generalize rule applied to *contrast* also can be applied to other quantitative predicates. For example, *extent-of* is a specific case of the general idea of *quantify* and can be generalized as:

generalization of (Argument 1, *extent-of*, Argument 2) → (Argument 1, *quantified-by*, quantitative value)

For example, in:

(19) 30% of the world's wool

Argument 1 is *world's wool* and Argument 2 is *30%*. If space in working memory is at a premium, this can be reduced to the less specific quantitative expression:

(20) some of the world's wool

and thereby dispensing with the idea of "30%" unless it is embedded in another proposition.

Simplify Rules. Besides the core and generalize rules, there is a class of *simplify* rules. In simplify rules an argument is removed from the propositions of the predicates. An example is removing the time and location arguments of HIT, as described previously (see Example 1 and the discussion subsequent to it).

Successive Operation of the Reduction rules. To clarify the predicate semantics component of the reduction process presented thus far, we gather the results of these examples together. Starting with:

(21) Australia has more sheep than any other country.

the *contrast* reduction rule applies to *more . . . than*, to produce:

(22) Australia has many sheep.

If further reduction is required, the *quantify* reduction rule applies to *many* to produce

(23) Australia has sheep.

Going on to our next sentence:

(24) Australia produces about 30% of the world's wool.

the *hedge* rule applies to *about*, to produce:

(25) Australia produces 30% of the world's wool.

Then the *extent-of* rule applies, to produce:

(26) Australia produces some of the world's wool.

Next, the *possess* rule applies, to *world's wool*, to produce.

(27) Australia produces some wool.

Thus, the text "Australia has more sheep than any other country. Australia produces about 30% of the world's wool." is reduced by the model to "Australia has many sheep. Australia produces some wool." Our claim is that readers are likely to reduce the text in similar ways.

Holding Over a Connected Network. Another feature of the reduction process is that it has a stronger tendency to hold over a connected propositional network than does the leading edge strategy. In part, this is the result of conditions (foreshadowed in the *contrast* rule above) that specify that a proposition cannot be removed from working memory if it is embedded in another proposition. This tends to lead to a connected network because propositions are retained if they are mentioned elsewhere. Other rule conditions handle cases in which a proposition is embedded in other propositions and is not eliminated, but is instead changed in form or reduced. Our reduction process replaces any other occurrences of that proposition with the core of the reduced proposition. For example, suppose a *hedges* proposition is embedded in another proposition in working memory. When the *hedges* proposition is reduced to its core assertion, the reduction process inserts the core assertion in place of all later mentions of the proposition. Because this ensures that other propositions in working memory do not mention a proposition that is no longer in working memory, it maintains a connected representation as reduction proceeds.

In contrast, the leading edge strategy considers only a proposition's level in the tree and its recency. Because it has no provisions for detecting the embeddings of to-be-eliminated propositions, the leading edge strategy cannot use this information in its decisions. It is possible, therefore, for this strategy to hold over propositions that are unconnected to any of the other propositions that have been held over. Our reduction process is consistent with our introspection that readers try to retain a connected gist.

How the Model Decides Which Propositions to Reduce

At the beginning of each reduction phase, the model prioritizes the propositions in working memory according to their likely importance to the ongoing gist of the text. The priority of each proposition is based primarily on the semantics of the predicate, and secondarily on the proposition's activity, strength, and recency. The predicates listed in Table 2.1 are divided into three broad classes based on importance. A class of low importance includes the predicates *hedge, intensifier* (e.g., *very*), and *reference* (e.g., *she, he*) because they are least likely to be central to the gist. If working memory is overloaded, propositions with these predicates are likely to be reduced soonest.

The class of predicates of highest importance includes three groups of predicates. One group includes predicates such as *cause, purpose, topic, location, time,* and *contrast.* Propositions with these predicates are most likely to link together large sets of propositions that are remote from each other in the text; for example, pairs of sentences, sets of sentences, paragraphs, or larger chunks of the text. This class of predicates is referred to as *remote coordinators.* The word token of a remote coordinator often appears within one set of its to-be-coordinated ideas but long before the others. That is, when a remote coordinator first appears, some of the propositions that it will coordinate may not yet have appeared. It is useful, therefore, to retain the remote coordinator in working memory for some time, expecting that the to-be-coordinated part of the text will appear later.

The second class of predicates of highest importance includes two subgroups. The first subgroup within this class is composed of predicates that are most often useful locally, that is, within their own sentence or clause (e.g., *qualify, quantify, extent, number,* and *range*). Such local predicates are usually of high importance on their first input cycle because they relate to ideas in the remainder of the input sentence. However, because their scope is often within their own sentence, the importance of local predicates for holdover drops quickly on the next cycle unless they are again referenced by new input propositions. If they are referred to again, however, they should be held over. This pattern is ensured by placing local predicates in the highest importance class on their first cycle (if they have even one active connection), but quickly reducing their importance level on the next cycle if they fall below their initial strength value. Psychologically, this corresponds to the intuition that propositions that are locally important should only be retained in working memory on later cycles only as long as there is evidence that they are still important.

The second subgroup within the second class of predicates is of intermediate importance. Included here are predicates that represent those moderately complex structures that often relate whole propositions to each other or which extend across sentence boundaries (e.g., *part, possess, composition*). These are of somewhat less immediate usefulness than the local predicates, but may need to be retained somewhat longer, until they encounter the propositions to which they relate.

The third class of predicates of highest importance includes predicates we do not cover in our model. Because the model includes many of the most common predicates, those omitted tend to be among the more rarely used predicates. This class also includes predicates for which the semantics are more complex than those covered in this chapter. Our inclusion of them among the highest importance predicates, in part, reflects our generalization that rare or complex predicates are likely to be important. For present purposes, we call this third class *special* predicates. Finally, the lowest priority of all is assigned to redundant propositions.

The predication semantics model reduces and prioritizes predicates according to a combination of their semantics and their strength values. To this point, we have used an illustrative initial strength value of .67, with the increase in strength due to an additional connection being .67 of the remaining strength and the decay of strength from one cycle to the next set at 1 minus .67. That value can also be used as an illustrative value for the point at which a proposition drops from the third, fourth, or fifth reduction categories to lower ones, which we could set to .67. In the appendix, we provide an example (with an alpha .67) of the processing for the passage about raising sheep in Australia.

We can generalize the model by treating the initial strength value and the related values as a parameter (*alpha*) of the model. In the examples to this point, alpha has been .67. In our computer simulations of the model, we used three different values of alpha: .1, .4, and .7. Different values of alpha produced different sets of predictions about which propositions would be reduced and which propositions would be recalled. In Table 2.2, we formally describe the algorithm that the program used to prioritize propositions for reduction, with alpha as the parameter.

How Long-Term Memory Traces Are Determined by Processing in Working Memory

The long-term memory traces are entirely the product of the processing that occurs in working memory. The traces are constructed as follows:

1. At the end of each input phase, the network in working memory is transferred intact to long-term memory, along with a long-term memory value associated with each proposition.

2. The long-term memory value associated with each proposition is determined jointly by the amount of working memory resources available at the time the proposition is stored in long-term memory, and the strength value of the proposition in working memory at the time of storage. As regards the role of working memory resources, the more resources available at the time the proposition is stored in long-term memory, the higher is its long-term memory value on that storage occasion. The amount of working memory resources available on any storage occasion is determined by the load on working memory at that time; the more propositions that are present in working memory, the fewer resources available for storage of the propositions in long-term memory. Psychologically, one thing is stored in long-term memory on each storage occasion—namely, the network from working memory. However, the working memory

TABLE 2.2
How the Reduction Program Prioritizes Propositions

1. Assign lowest priority to redundant propositions (those that exactly duplicate propositions already in working memory).
2. Assign next lowest priority to propositions with *hedge, intensifier,* and *reference* predicates.
3. Assign next lowest priority to propositions with local predicates with no active connections and a strength value less than alpha.
4. Assign next lowest priority to remote coordinators, intermediate coordinators, and special predicates with no active connections and a strength value less than one minus alpha.
5. Assign next lowest priority to intermediate coordinators with at least one active connection and a strength value greater than one minus alpha.
6. Assign highest priority to remote coordinators and special predicates with strength values greater than one minus alpha, and local predicates with strengths greater than alpha.
7. In each category, if there is more than one such proposition, assign highest priority to the proposition with the larger strength value. If the strength values are tied, assign highest priority to the proposition with the largest number of connections. If the number of connections is also tied, assign the highest priority to the most recently input proposition.

resources available for that storage occasion must be distributed over the entire to-be-stored network. If the network is very small, each proposition receives a substantial proportion of the available resources; if the network is very large, each proposition gets a smaller proportion of the same available resources.

The role of the proposition's strength value in working memory is simple: a portion of it is stored in long-term memory. Formally, the model implements this idea by dividing the strength of each proposition in working memory by the total number of propositions in working memory at the time of storage. The result is the long-term memory value for that proposition on that storage occasion. Thus, if the to-be-stored network is large, the number of propositions in working memory is large, and each proposition gets relatively less storage resources. Propositions in smaller networks have their strengths divided by a smaller total and thus, they acquire larger long-term memory values.

3. The long-term memory values for each proposition accumulate each time that the proposition is transferred again to long-term memory.

4. Whenever a proposition is altered within a cycle, the altered version is transferred to long-term memory and adds its long-term memory value to the previous version of that proposition.

5. If a proposition is eliminated from the network during a cycle, it accumulates no further long-term memory value after its elimination.

6. In graphic terms, the successively transferred networks are superimposed on each other in long-term memory. Propositions with more layers of superimposition have been transferred more often (i.e., they were less likely to be reduced and more likely to be part of the gist) and thus, they have more depth or weight in memory.

At the completion of text processing, long-term memory contains three variables for each proposition and its connections. One variable is the number of entries in long-term memory for the proposition. These entries include not only those for the original proposition, but also those for its various reduced forms. The second variable is the total of the long-term memory values for all the entries of that proposition. Derived from these is the third value; the average long-term memory value of that proposition, which is the total value divided by the number of entries.

Effects of Serial Position in the Texts

Two additional variables were included in the reduction phase of the model. Although their numerical values were taken from our input phase, the rationale for including them was derived not from the model, but from the results of previous research. These variables index the serial position of propositions in the text: the serial position within the paragraph and the serial position within the text as a whole. For example, the three propositions read in the initial input phase received values of 1 for both variables, those read on the second input phase received 2, and so on until the end of the first paragraph; at which time, the count for serial position within the second paragraph began again, while the count for serial position within the whole text continued. These variables were included because previous research had shown that readers frequently remember more information from early in the passage, presumably because that is where the theme is introduced, and from early in each paragraph, presumably because topic sentences usually occur there (Kieras, 1978; Mandler, 1978; Mandler & Johnson, 1977; van Dijk & Kintsch, 1983).

THE EXPERIMENT

Method

Subjects

Sixty-four students in an undergraduate introductory psychology course at the University of Colorado volunteered to participate in fulfillment of a course requirement. Sixteen were replaced because they wrote abbreviated protocols and, thus, did not follow the instructions to write down as much as they could remember. Protocols with word counts in the bottom 20th percentile of words recalled for a given text were considered abbreviated protocols. If a participant gave abbreviated recalls for two or more texts, he or she was replaced. (Analyses of both the full 64 and the 48 participants are reported subsequently in the Results section.)

Materials

Four passages were selected from ones that had previously been propositionalized. The passage about sheep raising in Australia was taken from a junior high school social studies text; a passage about continental drift was taken from a trade book on geology (106 propositions); a passage about the history of San Francisco was excerpted from a city guidebook (90 propositions); and a passage about breathing as an example of a biological feedback mechanism was taken from a 10th-grade biology textbook (87 propositions). Each passage included three paragraphs and, after editing for length, each was 210 words long. A slightly shorter passage about the history of paint was selected to use as a practice text but was not analyzed.

Procedure

The order in which the participants read and recalled the four texts was counterbalanced using six Latin squares. Participants were randomly assigned to one of the 24 possible orders. Each order was read by two participants.

Participants were given booklets containing the practice text and the four experimental texts. They were instructed to read for comprehension, but not to memorize verbatim. They read at their own pace. After they had read each passage, they turned to the next page and wrote in their own words as much as they could remember from the passage. Participants then rated the extent of their previous knowledge about the topic of the passage. They also rated it in terms of how interesting they found it to be.

Parameterization in the Simulations

In the simulations, the size of the working memory parameters were varied along with the strength parameter alpha. The working memory parameters were the maximum number of propositions brought in during the input cycle, the maximum number at the end of the reduction cycle, and the minimum number at the end of reduction. Four sets of working memory parameters were examined: *large* (with bounds of 21, 11, and 5 propositions for the input maximum, the reduction end maximum, and the reduction end minimum, respectively), *moderate–large* (with bounds of 17, 9, and 4), *moderate* (with bounds of 13, 7, and 3), and *small* (with bounds of 9, 5, and 2). Alpha was set at .1, .4, or .7.

Results

Each recall protocol was propositionalized. The resulting propositions were compared to the original list of propositions from the target passages. Latin square analyses were performed on the number of propositions recalled for each passage, the times to read and recall them, the participants' self-rated prior knowledge, and ratings of interest.

Proportion of Propositions Recalled and Reading Times

The written protocols obtained from the 48 participants ranged from 1 to 55 propositions in length, with a mean of 25.65 ($SD = 11.17$), which does not include the 2% of propositions produced that were judged as irrelevant to the text. The amount recalled was dependent on the passage, $F_{(3,36)} = 18.02$, $PRE = 0.27$, $p < 0.001$. More was recalled from the Australian Sheep passage ($M = 31.96$ propositions) than from the other passages, whereas recall for Continental Drift passage was midway between the others ($M = 25.46$) and the least was recalled from the Biological Feedback and San Francisco passages ($M = 22.46$ and $M = 22.38$, respectively). The order in which a text was read only approached significance, $F_{(3,72)} = 2.4$, $PRE = 0.04$, $p = 0.07$. In contrast to the results for proposition recall, no differences were found for reading times for the four texts.

Prior Knowledge of Topic

After reading each text, the participants indicated how much they knew about the topic of the passage on a 5-point scale (1 = *very little*; 5 = *quite a lot*). People perceived that they knew more about some topics than others, $F_{(3,72)} = 23.72$, $PRE = 0.32$, $p < 0.0001$. People believed that they knew more about the Biological Feedback and Continental Drift passages, and least about the San Francisco and Australian Sheep passages ($M = 2.79$, 2.61, 1.77, 1.59, respectively). The correlations between rated prior knowledge and the number of words and propositions recalled were not significant.

Related Interestingness

Participants also rated how interesting they found each passage on a 5-point scale (1 = *not at all*; 5 = *quite a bit*). No differences in interest were found among the texts (overall mean = 2.67). The participants' interest was affected by the order of the texts ($F_{(3,72)} = 3.58$, $PRE = 0.07$, $p < 0.018$). The first text read after the practice text was rated less interesting ($M = 2.41$) than was the second ($M = 2.76$) and the third ($M = 2.97$). A drop of interest was observed for the fourth text ($M = 2.56$). The amount of interest a participant indicated for a passage had a small correlation with the amount recalled ($r = 0.28$) and the time taken to recall ($r = 0.29$). In addition, participants who were more interested in a topic tended to know more about it ($r = 0.30$).

Comparison of the Simulations with Recall

The serial position variables were entered into a multiple regression analysis which indicated that they accounted for about 19% of the variance in recall. The three predictor variables from the model were then used to account for the residual variance in a multiple regression. This analysis indicated that they accounted for about 11% of the variance. Table 2.3 presents the results for each

TABLE 2.3
Percent Variance Accounted for by the Predication Semantics Model for Each Text at all Parameter Values

		Text Passages				
Working Memory Parameters	*Alpha*	*Sheep*	*Continental Drift*	*Breathing*	*San Francisco*
Large (21-11-5)[a]	.1	.09*	.06	.04	.11*
	.4	.13*	.14*	.08*	.01
	.7	.22	.19*	.09*	.03
Moderately Large (17-9-4)[a]	.1	.13*	.11*	.04	.13*
	.4	.14*	.14*	.16*	.04
	.7	.21*	.25*	.14*	.03
Medium (13-7-3)[a]	.1	.14*	.12*	.08*	.10*
	.4	.11*	.14*	.11*	.05
	.7	.18*	.15*	.08*	.01
Small (9-5-2)[a]	.1	.08*	.12*	.07*	.12*
	.4	.08*	.07*	.07*	.07*
	.7	.14*	.15*	.08*	.04

[a]These values refer to the maximum number of propositions brought in during the input cycle, the maximum number at the end of the reduction cycle, and the minimum number at the end of reduction, respectively.

*$p < .05$.

passage at each combination of the parameter values. These results support the model. For three of the four passages, the model's best performance occurred with moderately large memory parameters. Figure 2.2 shows the observed and predicted recall for each proposition in the sheep passage. (These results were for the 48 participants for whom we had a fully balanced design. Regression analysis for the full set of 64 participants demonstrated that the serial position variables accounted for 20% of the variance and the predictor variables for 11% of the variance.)

GENERAL DISCUSSION

Evaluation of the Predication Semantics Model

Predication Semantics

The present model uses semantic information in its processing. The success of the Miller and Kintsch (1980) model showed that significant progress could be made without much use of semantic information. But there was good reason to expect that additional progress could be made by adding semantic information, because semantics is the essence of language use: both the author and the reader are primarily concerned with the semantic representation of the text.

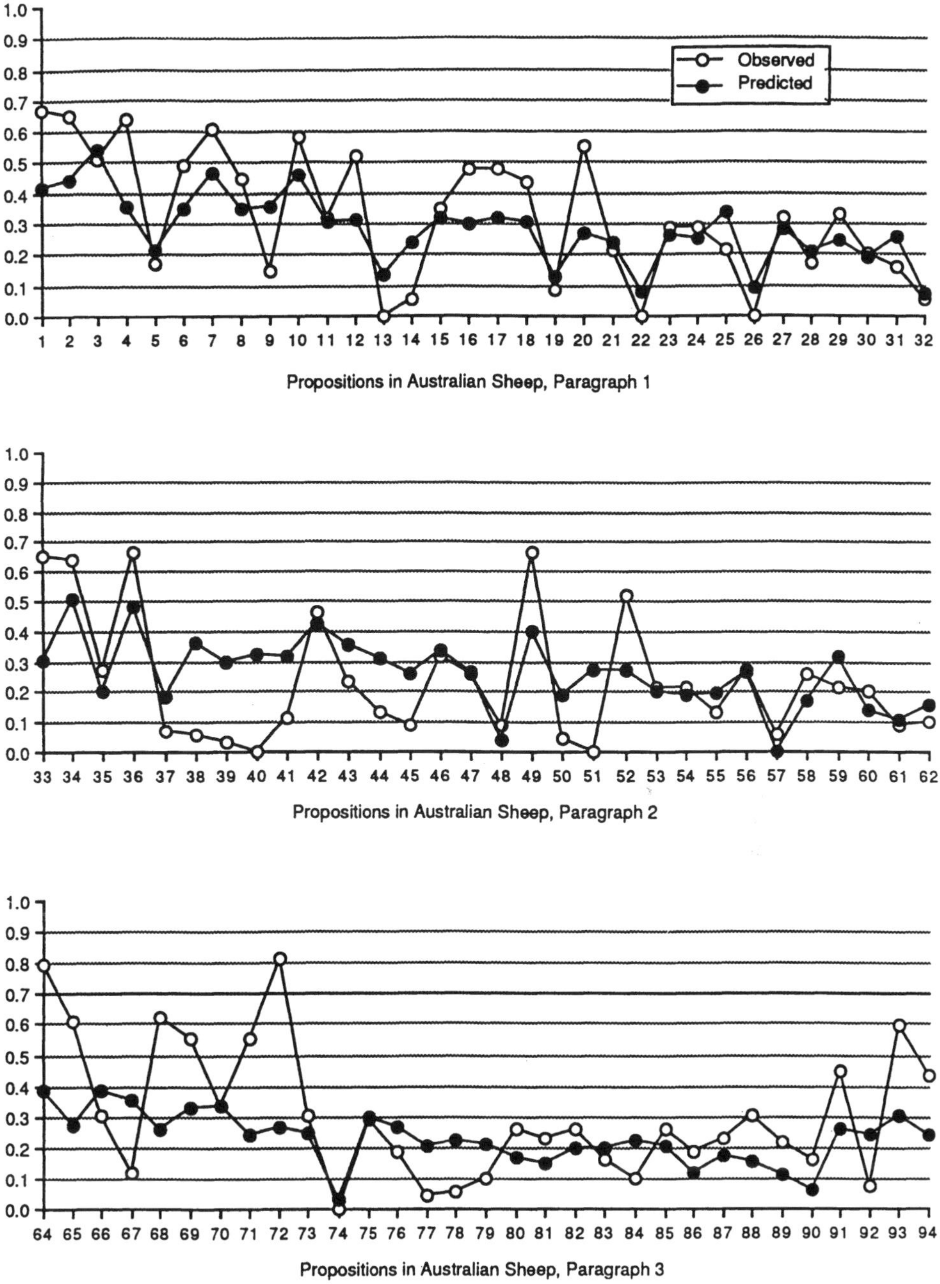

FIG. 2.2. Observed and predicted recall scores for "Australian Sheep" passage.

For this reason, a model which correctly incorporated aspects of meaning seemed likely to be more successful.

The results of our experiment demonstrated that the predication semantics model accounted for a significant part of the recall variance. This was achieved with a relatively modest amount of semantics; our rules use only a small fraction of the semantic information in the English language. Specifically, the 28 predicate classes for which we used semantic rules are only a subset of all English predicates and the class of all predicates is itself only a small subset of the semantics associated with the rest of the 50,000–200,000 lexical items in English.

The semantics that we used for each predicate was only a subset of its full semantics. Specifically, we used only that part of the semantics that could be formulated while abstracting from any specific class of text situations; we did not include any of the semantics associated with the predicate's uses in specific subject matter domains or text genres. As an illustration of how domain-specific semantics might be incorporated, consider again:

(28) John, *hit*, ball, bat, park, noon

A domain-independent and genre-independent predicate semantics, as used in our model, would always consider the location and time arguments as optional. However, in the context of a police investigation, or in the courtroom-trial schema or detective-story genre, the fact that John was in the park at noon might be critical to the gist (e.g., for establishing whether he had the opportunity to commit a crime). In contrast, the hitting of the ball might be of no importance at all. Therefore, in such situations, schemas, and genres, the exclusion of the time and location arguments would lead to an inappropriate reduction. Incorporating domain-specific and genre-specific predicate reduction rules might have the effect of substantially increasing the fit of the model in those domains and genres. It should be noted that a different and arguably more complete predicate semantics can be found in Graesser and Clark (1985) and Altermann (1985).

Sources of the Reduction Rules

Macrorules. The idea for using rules of this type came from the macrorules proposed by Kintsch and van Dijk (1978). The original Kintsch and van Dijk (1978) theory described macrorules that produced macropropositions that expressed the gist of the text. These macrorules were not implemented in the Miller and Kintsch (1980) model.

The reduction process we used in the predication semantics model can be viewed as a partial implementation of some aspects of Kintsch and van Dijk's (1978) macrorules. Two of their macrorules were:

1. *Deletion.* A proposition that is neither a direct nor an indirect interpretation condition of a subsequent proposition may be deleted.

2. *Generalization.* A sequence of propositions may be replaced by the general proposition denoting an immediate superset (Kintsch & van Dijk, 1978).

In our reduction process, a partial counterpart for the deletion macrorule is seen in the elimination of propositions that are not connected to any other propositions. A partial counterpart for the generalization macrorule is seen in our generalization rules.

Experience in Scoring Free Recall. The rules used in the model were formulated by the first author from more than a decade's worth of experience in propositionalizing texts and scoring free recall (Turner, 1987; Turner & Greene, 1978). They represent generalizations from that experience.

Readers' Language Experience. Our reduction rules successfully simulated reader behavior. Presumably, this reflected the fact that they expressed true generalizations about reader behavior in our population. If readers followed the same rules as the model, it was either because (a) they had learned them, (b) the rules are built into the human cognitive system, or (c) some combination of these. Although it appears that the model's success is partly due to built-in aspects of the human cognitive system (i.e., the working memory limitation), we have no reason to think that the specific predication reduction rules are built in rather than learned. Language experience is the most likely source of this learning. Our language experience comes from others' writing and speaking, as well as our own. Thus, the rules probably are learned because they are experienced frequently in the text and speech we encounter. For example, repeated experience with *hedge* predicates could lead to the empirical generalization that a *hedge* word is less likely to be useful later than is the assertion which is hedged. This could lead to formulation of the psychological equivalent of our rule. With extensive practice, this rule might become automatized and no longer accessible to consciousness.

Other Aspects of the Model

The model also introduced innovations in the input phase, the network representation of connectedness, and the processing of recency and connectedness information.

Input Phase. The face validity of the input phase is somewhat improved over previous simulations. Instead of the operator controlling the input, the program itself decides the size of each input chunk, based on the types of information that readers take into account, such as punctuation marks, working memory limitations, internal completeness of each proposition, and connectedness between propositions. As empirical evidence accumulates on human input processes (e.g., Magliano, Graesser, Eymard, Haberlandt, & Gholson, 1993) these rules can be modified accordingly. Although our input phase itself is automatic, it takes as input a propositional representation that is derived by people, not automatically. This limits the scope of our model.

Network Representation. A second innovation is the model's internal representation of the text. A network representation was used instead of the hierarchical tree of Kintsch and van Dijk (1978) and Miller and Kintsch (1980). This network is used in two ways: in working memory, to represent the building of the text base during the process of its construction; and in long-term memory, to represent the long-term memory strength and interconnections of the propositions.

Our arguments for the network representation over the hierarchical tree are based on the former's greater generality and psychological plausibility. As regards generality, every tree can be represented as a suitably constrained network, but not every network can be represented as a tree. Networks can also represent structures other than trees. This difference in the representations' generality leads to differences in the psychological plausibility of the representations for many texts. The hierarchical tree representation requires that all propositions be connected to each other in a hierarchical manner, and all must be connected to a single root node, either directly or indirectly, through other propositions. Some texts clearly have been written to have this hierarchical tree structure, often following the hierarchical structure of the author's conception of the subject matter. Such a representation is psychologically plausible for texts with hierarchical structures. However, many texts have a more complex, less constrained structure that can be represented better as a network. The greater generality of the network representation ensures that both types of text can be represented as networks, with the former network constrained to be a tree.

The second advantage of the network representation over the hierarchical tree representation implemented in Miller and Kintsch (1980) is that, in the latter, the root node was selected by the operator, based partly on argument overlap and based partly on intuition. The network representation has nothing corresponding to a root node; this obviates the need for operator intervention.

Recency and Connectedness. In the predication semantics model, the recency and connectedness of each proposition is considered within a module whose output was a strength value. This strength value is then used as one input to the reduction process. One consequence of this modularity is that the role of recency and connectedness can be separated easily from the rest of the model. In contrast, in the Miller and Kintsch (1980) simulation, the role of recency and connectedness was embedded in the operation of the model and could not be separated. This modularity of our model may be useful in future modeling efforts.

Limitations of the Predication Semantics Model

As a model of the human comprehension process, our model has several limitations. These include the following: there is no mechanism for constructing propositions from the words of the text; the model's procedural prior knowledge needs to be supplemented; more semantic prior knowledge should be incorporated; and individual differences must be considered.

Constructing Propositions

There are several sources of evidence that the proposition is the unit of language processing and that propositions are constructed online by the reader. The more propositions contained in a text of a fixed length, the longer it takes to read the text (Kintsch & Keenan, 1973). If the number of words and propositions is held constant, the more new arguments a text contains, the longer it takes to read (Kintsch, Kozminsky, Streby, McKoon, & Keenan, 1975; Manelis & Yekovich, 1976). In memory, arguments from the same proposition are more closely associated than arguments from different propositions (Ratcliff & McKoon, 1978). Models using propositions as the unit of analysis have been quite successful, as shown by the results of Kintsch (1988), Kintsch and van Dijk (1978), Miller and Kintsch (1980), Fletcher (1986), and the present study.

If the proposition is the unit of language processing, human readers may construct propositions as they read. A complete model of human language processing would include a mechanism for constructing propositions. When the predication semantics model was first developed, the components needed for a more automatic proposition construction mechanism were not available in computational form. However, enough components are available now to make feasible a partly automatic proposition constructor. One currently available component includes an online dictionary that provides information about the possible parts of speech of a word, its meanings, and its relations to other words (Miller, Beckwith, Fellbaum, Gross, & Miller, 1990). Another component is a parser that provides a diagram of the grammatical role of a sentence's constituents and the syntactic relations to each other (e.g., Kieras, 1989). Information about the grammatical role of each word can be used in deciding whether it is a predicate or an argument. Once a predicate is identified, information from its lexical entry then could be used to identify the case roles associated with it. An examination of the lexical entries of nearby words could be used to help establish whether they are arguments that fit any of the roles. Output from the parser also can help to decide which argument fits which role.

However, both the dictionary and the available parsers are still limited in their coverage. The components needed for a fully automatic proposition constructor are presumably available to skilled human readers. This includes much more complete lexicons and parsers, but also a large amount of world knowledge. The latter will be considered further in the next section.

Procedural Prior Knowledge

Prior knowledge plays an important role in text comprehension. A great deal of one type of prior knowledge already has been incorporated into the predication semantics model; namely, procedural knowledge. For example, in the input phase, the model decides when to end input by using procedural rules that incorporate prior knowledge about its own working memory limitations and the typical textual features that signal when an input chunk is complete. Presumably, readers also use such prior knowledge about their own working memory limitations and about the typical textual features that signal completed chunks. This knowledge is probably embedded in procedures rather than available declaratively, as is the case in our model.

In its reduction phase, the model uses prior knowledge about the classes of predicates, their relative priority, the relative importance of the case roles in particular predicates, and procedures for reformulating the information (e.g., by taking its core, generalizing it, or making it more specific). This prior knowledge also is expressed as procedural rules, and it appears likely that some counterpart exists in human readers. There also is procedural prior knowledge about storing information in long-term memory both in the model and in humans.

Our experience with the model suggests additions that could profitably be made in the model's procedural prior knowledge. For example, the present model does not incorporate the knowledge that the frequency of mention of a concept in a discourse is typically related to the concept's importance in the discourse. Procedurally, this could be incorporated by adding a rule that specifies that when a concept appears more than once in the text, its strength is increased. Such a change could also affect reinstatement; those concepts with higher strength values might be searched first during attempted reinstatements, thereby accounting for the ease of reinstatement of topical information (Lesgold, Roth, & Curtis, 1979). This would allow a concept to be reinstated at its increased value after lapses in its use have resulted in its being purged from working memory.

In some cases, the results of our test of the model provided some evidence that procedural prior knowledge needed to be added. For example, the predication semantics rules for *time:when* predicates could be altered to increase their priority, reflecting the fact that our subjects recalled specific dates more often than the model predicted. This may have occurred because, after years of academic testing, they place particular emphasis on dates in their reading strategies for history passages. It seems likely that other reading strategies could be incorporated as well, in the form of procedural prior knowledge about useful ways for dealing with text.

World Knowledge

The most conspicuous limitation of the model is the paucity of its world knowledge, including semantic knowledge. We mentioned that the lexical part of semantic memory is very sparse in the model, including the 28 predicate classes that are in procedural form. The semantics of the rest of the lexicon is not represented at all. However, this shortcoming of the model was foreseen and, thus, the model was designed to accept the addition of a semantic memory. Even a minimal semantic memory could be used easily by the model. A fairly minimal semantic memory would include only the concepts mentioned in the text, along with an a priori strength value for each concept derived from a normative familiarity index that reflects its pre-experimental strength. When a concept occurred in the text, working memory would draw a token of that concept from semantic memory, taking with it the current strength level from semantic memory. This would ensure that the strength value of a concept in working memory would reflect not only its frequency of mention within the particular text, but also its pre-experimental familiarity. This would account for our finding that people recall the name of the bay when it is San Francisco Bay (a familiar concept), but forget the name of the lake when it is Laguna de los Dolores.

This minimal semantic memory could deal with some aspects of expert-novice differences. For example, a simulation of a baseball expert could include higher a priori strength values for concepts crucial to the game-goal hierarchy, such as those related to moving players around the bases, scoring runs, making outs, etc. (Spilich, Vesonder, Chiesi, & Voss, 1979). Other goal hierarchies could be handled in a similar way (Dahlgren, 1988). It should be noted that a minimal semantic memory could accomplish this without including any information about the relations between concepts.

If the semantic memory concepts were arranged in a relational network so that activation could be passed among them, it is likely that there would be further improvements in the model's coverage. If whole clusters of concepts could be activated in groups, schemas, scripts, and plans could be activated and used to guide reduction processes. Further expansion to include word meanings within semantic memory is feasible with available components (Miller et al., 1990). Finally, going beyond semantic knowledge of the meanings of words and their relations, prior knowledge about real world events and relations could be incorporated, as in, for example, Graesser and Clark (1985).

The model is designed to accept such semantic memory and prior knowledge augmentation at several points in processing. For example, the contribution from prior world knowledge could be activated during the input phase. If this were done, the initial network would contain not only the text information but also the prior world knowledge activated by it, which then would be subject to reduction along with the text. This corresponds to the flood of prior knowledge which is sometimes activated by a text. Alternatively, just the minimal semantic memory contribution could be activated during the reduction process. In this case, the result would be to alter the strength values of certain concepts so that they are less likely to be reduced. As yet another alternative, both the world knowledge and semantic memory contribution could be activated together after reduction has been completed. The latter alternative would have the advantage of summoning less world knowledge because only the propositions remaining after reduction could activate this knowledge. This would avoid the potential computational explosion when memory retrieval is unconstrained (Reiger, 1975). Semantic memory augmentation at any of these points could draw so much added information into working memory that further reduction would be needed to free resources for the next cycle. Psychologically, this corresponds to what happens when we encounter a situation about which we have a large amount of prior knowledge: our processing resources are temporarily overloaded (Britton & Tesser, 1983).

A related limitation of the model, which is shared with its predecessors, is the inability to make the inferences which are so often required to fill gaps in the course of creating a coherent representation of a text, and whose absence is devastating to the mental representations of those readers who fail to make them (Britton & Gulgoz, 1991; Britton, Van Dusen, Glynn, & Hemphill, 1990). The reduction processes already included in the model could contribute here because the processing resources freed by the decreased working memory storage demands could be reallocated to other processes, including inferencing. The augmentation of the semantic memory component would provide a potent source of the knowledge external to the text that is so often necessary to make appropriate inferences. Finally, ordering text concepts in terms of strength values (at whatever stage of processing) would make it possible for the model to make predictions about the probability of useful inferences for each concept: inferences should be more likely for concepts with high strength values. This would allow an inferencing component to restrict its attention to the more likely concepts, reducing the potential for the combinatorial explosion which would be threatened if inferencing was unconstrained (Reisbeck, 1975).

Individual Differences

Finally, in our model we have focused on processes that operate automatically and consistently in the course of understanding discourse and ignored individual differences in such things as working memory capacity, reduction abilities, long-term memory abilities, and reading strategies. Such individual differences can be temporary, corresponding to changes in state within an individual from time to time based on, among other things, physiological changes, emotional reactions, and goals, or they can be more lasting, corresponding to relatively enduring ability differences. An individual's reading strategies could be modeled by modifying the procedural prior knowledge of the model. Differences in reduction abilities are a particularly interesting case. Our model was designed to reduce while maintaining a fully connected representation. Some readers may be less able to do this, which would lead to predictable consequences.

ACKNOWLEDGMENTS

The research was supported in part by a grant from the Air Force Human Resources Laboratory, Learning Abilities Measurement Project (LAMP), under Air Force Training Command Contract F41689-89-D-0251 to the second author, and by support from the Institute for Behavioral Research and the Artificial Intelligence Program at the University of Georgia.

APPENDIX: AN EXAMPLE OF THE FULL PREDICATION SEMANTICS MODEL

How the model works is illustrated here with a simple example. The text is shown in full in Table 2.A1 and its propositions are listed in Table 2.A2. (In Table 2.A2 the predicate is first in each proposition. In the present example, the predicates were made more English-like and placed between their arguments to make them easier to read.) Parts of this text were used for many of the examples we presented previously, and the full text was one of the four texts used in the experiment. Alpha was set at .67, and the input maximum, reduction maximum, and reduction minimum were set at 13, 7, and 3, respectively.

The simulation began with the first input phase. In this case, the input stopped when the program encountered the period at the end of the first sentence. The product of the first input phase is shown in list format in Table 2.A3. The numbers in the first column at the right of Table 2.A3 are the number of active connections on the current cycle for each proposition. The program noticed these during the input phase because, as the input program input each proposition, it determined whether that proposition was part of a connected chain and, therefore, when to stop input. It did this by looking for matches between the arguments of each newly input proposition and arguments of each other proposition in working memory.

In this case, it found that each proposition was connected to two other propositions: P1 was mentioned as an argument of P2, and its argument "Australia"

TABLE 2.A1
"Australia Sheep" Passage

Australia has more sheep than any other country. It produces about 30% of the world's wool. The part of Australia where the largest number of sheep are raised is in the region receiving 10 to 20 inches of rain a year. This semiarid region covers fully one third of Australia. Most of Australia's sheep are in the eastern part of the continent, but some are also in the southwest.

Three fourths of Australia's sheep are pure merinos. They are popular because of the large amount of semiarid land. The Merino thrives on the grasses and low bushes which grow on semiarid plains. They are known for their heavy fleeces of fine quality wool which bring a high price from textile manufacturers. Merinos were introduced into Australia only 5 years after the first settlement and have been important ever since.

The remaining one fourth of Australia's sheep are of mixed breeds which are raised both for meat and wool. The crossbreeds are raised especially in the moist regions where pastures are planted in good grass. The lambs are fattened and sold to meat packers. Some of the mutton is exported, but much is sold in markets in Australia. The wool, which is coarser than merino wool, is sold to carpet manufacturers.

TABLE 2.A2
Propositions of the "Australia Sheep" Passage

P1	possess [australia, sheep]
P2	contrast:more [P1, P3]
P3	any-other [country, australia]
P4	produce [australia, P7]
P5	hedge [P6, about]
P6	number-of [percent, thirty]
P7	extent-of [P8, P5]
P8	possess [world, wool]
P9	part-of [australia, part]
P10	location:where [P11, P9]
P11	contrast:most [P12]
P12	raise [sheep]
P13	reference [P10, P14]
P14	part-of [australia, P18]
P15	receive [region, P17]
P16	range-of [inches, ten, twenty]
P17	extent-of [rain, P16]
P18	time:during [P15, year]
P19	reference [P20, P13]
P20	qualify [region, semiarid]
P22	intensify [P23, fully]
P23	number-of [thirds, one]
P24	extent-of [australia, P22]
P25	contrast:most [P27, P26]
P26	possess [australia, sheep]
P27	location:in [sheep, P28]
P28	part-of [continent, east]
P29	but-also [P27, P31]
P30	quantify [P26, some]
P31	location:in [P30, P32]
P32	part-of [continent, southwest]
P33	number-of [fourths, three]
P34	extent-of [P35, P33]
P35	possess [australia, sheep]
P36	consist-of [P34, P37]
P37	intensify [merinos, pure]
P38	qualify [P37, popular]
P39	cause [P38, P40]
P40	quantify [P41, large]
P41	qualify [P41, large]
P42	thrive-on [merinos, P43]
P43	conjunct:and [grass, P44]
P44	quantify [bushes, low]
P45	grow [P43]
P46	location:on [P45, 47]

(Continued)

TABLE 2.A2
(Continued)

P49	possess [merinos, P51]
P50	quantify [fleeces, heavy]
P51	consist-of [P50, P52]
P52	qualify [wool, fine-quality]
P53	sell [P49, P54, P55]
P54	quantify [price, high]
P55	manufacture [textile]
P56	introduce-into [merino, australia]
P57	intensify [P58, only]
P58	number-of [years, five]
P59	time:after [P56,P60,P57]
P60	qualify [settlement,first]
P61	conjunct:and [P59,P63]
P62	qualify [merinos,important]
P63	time:ever-since [P62,P65]
P64	remaining [P66,P34]
P65	number-of [fourths,one]
P66	extent-of [P67,P65]
P67	possess [australia,sheep]
P68	consist-of [P64,P69]
P69	mix [breeds]
P70	raise [P69]
P71	conjunct:both-and [meat,wool]
P72	purpose-of [P70,P71]
P73	raise [crossbreeds]
P74	intensify [P75,especially]
P75	location:in [P73,P76]
P76	qualify [regions,moist]
P77	location:where [P78,P76]
P78	plant [pastures,P79]
P79	qualify [grass, good]
P80	fatten [lambs]
P81	conjunct:and [P80,P82]
P82	sell [lambs,P83]
P83	pack [meat]
P84	quantify [mutton,some]
P85	export [P84]
P86	concession [P85,P89]
P87	quantify [mutton,much]
P88	sell [P87]
P89	location:in [P88,P90]
P90	location:in [markets,australia]
P91	contrast:coarser [wool,P92]
P92	possess [merinos,wool]
P93	sell [P91, P94]
P94	manufacture [carpet]

TABLE 2.A3
Mental Representation After Input Phase 1

Propositions	*Number of Active Connections on Current Cycle*	*Strength*
P1: Australia, *possesses*, sheep	2	.96
P2: P1, *contrast:more*, P3	2	.96
P3: country, *any-other-than*, Australia	2	.96

Represents: Australia has more sheep than any other country.
Working Memory Contents: 3 propositions
Average Strength: .96
No reduction is required because: working memory contents are between 3 and 7 propositions; average strength > .84.
Proceed to next cycle.

was mentioned in P3; P2 mentioned P1 and P3; P3 was mentioned in P2, and its argument "Australia" was mentioned in P1. Thus, the strength values were all .96, which can be read from Fig. 2.1. The next step was to decide if any reduction was required. Because three propositions are well within working memory capacity, no reduction was required. Thus, the program ended the cycle by decrementing each strength value by multiplying it by .33, before proceeding to the next cycle.

The results are shown in Table 2.A4. Again, the first step was to look for connectedness between the propositions. Beginning with the newly input propo-

TABLE 2.A4
Mental Representation After Input Phase 2

Propositions	*Number of Active Connections on Current Cycle*	*Strength*
P1: Australia, *possesses*, sheep	3	.97
P2: P1, *contrast:more*, P3	0	.32
P3: Country, *any-other-than*, Australia	3	.97
P4: Australia, *produces*, P7	3	.98
P5: P6, *hedged-by*, about	2	.96
P6: percent, *number-of*, thirty	1	.89
P7: P8, *extent-of*, P5	3	.98
P8: world, *possesses*, wool	1	.89

Represents: Australia has more sheep than any other country. It produces about 30% of the world's wool.
Working Memory Contents: 8 propositions
Average Strength: .87
Reduction is required because working memory contents are > 7 propositions.
Reduction Order: 5, 2, 6, 8, 1, 3, 4, 7

sitions, P4 and P7 were connected to three other propositions and received the appropriate strength value from the top line in Fig. 2.1. P5 was connected to two other propositions, and received an intermediate strength value. P6 and P8 were connected to only one, and thus, each received a lower strength value.

P1, P2, and P3 received different treatment because they were old propositions. All were decremented by .33 at the end of cycle one, but arguments of P1 and P3 were both referred to by propositions either newly active or still active in the second input cycle, (i.e., for P1 by P2, P3, and P4 and for P3 by P1, P2, and P4) and thus, their strength was increased by .67 of the remaining strength, as shown in Fig. 2.1. However, P2 was not referred to again by any other active proposition, nor were its arguments, so its strength value was left decremented by one third.

The next step was to decide if any reduction was required. Because we had set the reduction end maximum parameter at 7 propositions, and 8 propositions exceeds the capacity that can be held over in working memory by one, reduction was required. To decide which proposition should be reduced, the program prioritizes the propositions. None of the propositions appeared before and thus, category 1 in Table 2.2 was not used. The *hedge* proposition P5 was the only one in category 2 of Table 2.2, and thus, it was lowest in priority. Next lowest was the *contrast* proposition (P2), which, as an intermediate coordinator, was in category 4 of Table 2.2 because it had no active connections and a strength value less than .33. The rest of the propositions were in category 6 of Table 2.2 because their strengths were still high at this point. Within category 6, they were prioritized by strength value and recency: P6 and P8 both had the lowest strengths of .89, but because P6 was older it had lower priority; P1 and P3 had the next highest strengths but P1 was oldest; of P4 and P7, P4 was oldest and thus, P7 had the highest priority. (The prioritization order is shown at the line labeled "Reduction Order" at the bottom of Table 2.A4.)

This left P5 as the first candidate for reduction. The core of P5 is the proposition to be hedged, which is P6; the part to be removed is the hedge word *about.* When the core:*hedge* rule was applied, only the core remained, which is P6. Because P5 appeared in P7, it was replaced with its core, P6. The result is shown in Table 2.A5.

At this point, only 7 propositions remained in working memory, and the average strength was .84 and, therefore, no further reduction was required. The simulation proceeded to the next cycle.

In Input Phase 3, the input maximum working memory capacity of 13 propositions was not large enough to hold both the 7 propositions held over and the 10 new propositions of the second sentence. No helpful punctuation marks were present and, thus, the model used the rule shown in the Input Phase section. The resulting working memory contents are shown in Table 2.A6. The connectedness, strength values, and prioritization were determined as previously.

When the program began to reduce P2, this entailed the side effect of reducing P3. This is explained in the rule on *contrasts-with* in the section on The Role of

TABLE 2.A5

Mental Representation After First Reduction After Input Phase 2

Propositions	*Number of Active Connections on Current Cycle*	*Strength*
P1: Australia, *possesses*, sheep	3	.97
P2: P1, *contrast:more*, P3	0	.32
P3: country, *any-other-than*, Australia	3	.97
P4: Australia, *produces*, P7	3	.98
P5:	–	–
P6: percent, *number-of*, thirty	1	.89
P7: P8, *extent-of*, P6	3	.98
P8: world, *possesses*, wool	1	.89

Represents: Australia has more sheep than any other country. It produces 30% of the world's wool.

Working Memory Contents: 7 propositions

Average Strength: .84

No reduction is required because: working memory contents are between 3 and 7 propositions; average strength > .84.

Proceed to next cycle.

Note. Rules applied were:

HEDGED-BY Rule: CORE (assertion, HEDGED-BY, hedge word) → assertion.

Applied to P5: CORE-OF P5: (P6, HEDGED-BY, about) → P6.

Result of Reducing P5.

TABLE 2.A6

Mental Representation After Input Phase 3

Propositions	*Number of Active Connections on Current Cycle*	*Strength*
P1: Australia, *possesses*, sheep	5	.99
P2: P1, *contrast:more*, P3	0	.11
P3: Country, *any-other-than*, Australia	4	.99
P4: Australia, *produces*, P7	1	.97
P6: percent, *number-of*, thirty	1	.76
P7: P8, *extent-of*, P6	1	.77
P8: World, *possesses*, wool	1	.76
P9: *part-of*, Australia	4	.99
P10: P11, *location:where*, P9	3	.98
P11: *contrast:most*, P12	1	.89
P12: *raise*, sheep	2	.96

Represents: Australia has more sheep than any other country. It produces 30% of the world's wool. The part of Australia where the largest number of sheep are raised . . .

Working Memory Contents: 11 propositions

Average Strength: .84

Reduction is required because working memory contents are > 7 propositions.

Reduction Order: 2, 6, 8, 7, 11, 9, 12, 4, 10, 3, 1.

Predicate Semantics in the Reduction Phase; briefly, because the second argument of the *contrast* (here P3) is a proposition, it was removed from working memory. The rest of the rule for reducing *contrast* was applied, resulting in a generalized version of P2. The result is shown in Table 2.A7. A side effect of removing P3 was that the connectedness of P4 and P9 were changed because P3's argument "Australia" was no longer contributing a connection to them at this time. This made a visible difference in the strength of P4, reducing it from .97 to .92 but, for P9, the connectedness was still too high, at this point, for the change to make a visible difference at two decimal places. The consequence of P4's decreased strength was that its priority changed; although in Table 2.A6 it had higher priority than P12 because its strength was higher, in Table 2.A7 its lowered strength value puts it below P2 in priority.

Because working memory still contained more than seven propositions at this point, more reduction was required. P2 was again the first candidate, and

TABLE 2.A7
Mental Representation After First Reduction After Input Phase 3

Propositions	*Number of Active Connections on Current Cycle*	*Strength*
P1: Australia, *possesses*, sheep	4	.99
P2: P1, *quantified-by*, indefinite value: many	0	.11
P3:	—	—
P4: Australia, *produces*, P7	2	.92
P6: percent, *number-of*, 30	1	.76
P7: P8, *extent-of*, P6	1	.77
P8: world, *possesses*, wool	1	.76
P9: *part-of*, Australia	1	.98
P10: P11, *location:where*, P9	3	.98
P11: *contrast:most*, P12	1	.89
P12: *raise*, sheep	2	.96

Represents: Australia has many sheep. It produces 30% of the world's wool. The part of Australia where the largest number of sheep are raised . . .
Working Memory Contents: 10 propositions
Average Strength: .81
Reduction is required because working memory contents are > 7 propositions.
Reduction Order: 2, 6, 8, 7, 11, 9, 4, 12, 10, 1

Note. Rules applied were:

CONTRAST Rule: GENERALIZATION: (to-be-contrasted proposition, CONTRASTS-WITH, standard). Change the predicate to QUANTIFIED-BY and if the second argument is a proposition, then remove it from working memory, unless it is embedded in another proposition; and add a second argument that is an indefinite quantitative value reflecting the contrasting relationship (e.g., if contrast is "more," a possible value is "many").

Applied to P2: GENERALIZATION of P2: (P1, CONTRAST:MORE, P3) → P2: (P1, QUANTIFIED-BY, indefinite value:many) and remove P3 from working memory.

Result of Reducing P2.

TABLE 2.A8
Mental Representation After Second Reduction After Input Phase 3

Propositions	*Number of Active Connections on Current Cycle*	*Strength*
P1: Australia, *possesses*, sheep	3	.97
P2:	–	–
P4: Australia, *produces*, P7	2	.92
P6: percent, *number-of*, thirty	1	.76
P7: P8, *extent-of*, P6	1	.77
P8: world, *possesses*, wool		.76
P9: *part-of*, Australia	3	.98
P10: P11, *location:where*, P9	3	.98
P11: *contrast:most*, P12	1	.89
P12: *raise*, sheep	2	.96

Represents: Australia has sheep. It produces 30% of the world's wool. The part of Australia where the largest number of sheep are raised . . .
Working Memory Contents: 9 propositions
Average Strength: .89
Reduction is required because working memory contents are > 7 propositions.
Reduction Order: 6, 8, 7, 11, 9, 4, 12, 1, 10.

Note. Rules applied were:
Reduce P2
QUANTIFY Rule: CORE-of (Argument 1, QUANTIFIED-BY, value) → Argument 1
Applied to P2: CORE of P2: (P1, QUANTIFIED-BY, indefinite value: many) → P1

this time the core of *quantify* rule applied. The result is shown in Table 2.A8. The only side effect was that the connections of P1 were reduced from 4 to 3, reducing its strength from .99 to .97, and reversing its prioritization with P10.

P6 was the next candidate for reduction, but because P6 was embedded in P7, the conditions for the *number-of* rule could not be met unless P7 was reduced first. Specifically, because the *number-of* proposition was embedded in a context (i.e., P7) that requires a number (as the *extent-of* proposition does), we had to change the context so that it no longer required a number before we could remove the number. Otherwise, the resulting representation would have had something missing, like the previous "John hit . . ." example. This was done using the generalization:*extent-of* rule, changing P7 in much the same way as P2 was changed by its generalization rule, and then eliminating P6. The result is shown in Table 2.A9.

Finally P8 was reduced by taking its core, which was then placed as the first argument of P7. The result is shown in Table 2.A10. Because, at this point, working memory contained only 7 propositions and the average strength was above .84, the model proceeded to the next input cycle.

TABLE 2.A9
Mental Representation After Third Reduction After Input Phase 3

Propositions	*Number of Active Connections on Current Cycle*	*Strength*
P1: Australia, *possesses*, sheep	3	.97
P4: Australia, *produces*, P7	2	.92
P6:	–	–
P7: P8, *quantified-by*, indefinite value:much	1	.77
P8: world, *possesses*, wool	1	.76
P9: *part-of*, Australia	3	.98
P10: P11, *location:where*, P9	3	.89
P11: *contrast:most*, P12	1	.89
P12: *raise*, sheep	2	.96

Represents: Australia has sheep. It produces much of the world's wool. The part of Australia where the largest number of sheep are raised . . .
Working Memory Contents: 8 propositions
Average strength: .91
Reduction is required because working memory contents are > 7 propositions.
Reduction order: 8, 7, 11, 9, 4, 12, 1, 10

Note. Rules applied were:

Reduce P6

NUMBER-OF Rule: because P6 is embedded in P7, the conditions of this rule cannot be met unless P7 can be reduced.

Reduce P7

EXTENT-OF rule:

Generalization of: (Argument 1, EXTENT-OF, Argument 2) → change the predicate to QUANTIFIED-BY and if the second argument is a proposition, then remove it from working memory unless it is embedded in another proposition and add a second argument that is an indefinite quantitative value reflecting the extent of relationship (e.g., if extent-of is large, a possible value is "much").

Applied to P7:

GENERALIZATION-of P7: (P8, EXTENT-OF, P6) → P7: (P8, QUANTIFIED-BY, indefinite value: much) and remove P6 from working memory.

TABLE 2.A10
Mental Representation After Fourth Reduction After Input Phase 3

Propositions	*Number of Active Connections on Current Cycle*	*Strength*
P1: Australia, *possesses*, sheep	3	.97
P4: Australia, *produces*, P7	2	.92
P7: Wool, *quantified-by*, indefinite value: much	1	.77
P8:	–	–
P9: *part-of*, Australia	3	.98
P10: P11, *location:where*, P9	3	.98
P11: *contrast:most*, P12	1	.89
P12: *raise*, Sheep	2	.96

Represents: Australia has sheep. It produces much wool. The part of Australia where the largest number of sheep are raised . . .
Working Memory Contents: 7 propositions
Average strength:
No Reduction is required because: Working Memory Contents are between 3 and 7 propositions.
Average strength > .84.
Proceed to next input cycle.

Note. Rules applied were:
Reduce P8
POSSESSED Rule: CORE-OF (possessor, POSSESSES, possessed object) → possessed object
Applied to P8: CORE-of P8: (world, POSSESSES, wool) →
Result of Reducing P8: –

REFERENCES

Alterman, R. (1985). A dictionary based on concept coherence. *Artificial Intelligence, 25*, 153–186.

Britton, B. K., & Gulgoz, S. (1991). Using Kintsch's computational model to improve instructional text: Effects of repairing inference calls on recall and cognitive structures. *Journal of Educational Psychology, 83*, 329–345.

Britton, B. K., & Tesser, A. (1983). Effects of prior knowledge on use of cognitive capacity in three complex cognitive tasks. *Journal of Verbal Learning and Verbal Behavior, 26*, 421–436.

Britton, B. K., Van Dusen, L., Glynn, S. M., & Hemphill, D. (1990). The impact of inferences on instructional text. In A. C. Graesser & G. H. Bower (Eds.), *The psychology of learning and motivation* (Vol. 25, pp. 53–70). New York: Academic Press.

Dahlgren, K. (1988). *Naive semantics for natural language understanding*. Boston: Kluwer.

de Beaugrande, R. (1980). *Text, discourse, and process*. Hillsdale, NJ: Lawrence Erlbaum Associates.

Fillmore, C. J. (1968). The case for case. In E. Bach and R. T. Harms (Eds.), *Universals of linguistic theory* (pp. 1–88). New York: Holt, Rinehart & Winston.

Fletcher, C. R. (1986). Strategies for the allocation of short-term memory during comprehension. *Journal of Memory & Language, 25*, 43–58.

Fodor, J. A., Bever, T. G., & Garrett, M. F. (1974). *The psychology of language*. New York: McGraw-Hill.

Graesser, A. C., & Clark, L. F. (1985). *The structures and procedures of implicit knowledge*. Norwood, NJ: Ablex.

Gruber, J. (1965). *Studies in lexical relations*. Unpublished doctoral dissertation, Massachusetts Institute of Technology, Cambridge.

Jackendoff, R. (1972). *Semantic interpretation in generative grammar*. Cambridge, MA: MIT Press.

Kieras, D. E. (1989). An advanced computerized aid for the writing of comprehensible technical documents. In B. Britton & S. Glynn (Eds.), *Computer writing environments: Theory, research and design* (pp. 143–168). Hillsdale, NJ: Lawrence Erlbaum Associates.

Kieras, D. E. (1978). Good and bad structure in simple paragraphs: Effects on apparent theme, reading time, and recall. *Journal of Verbal Learning and Verbal Behavior, 17*, 13–28.

Kieras, D. E. (1989). An advanced computerized aid for the writing of comprehensible technical documents. In B. Britton, & S. Glynn (Eds.), *Computer writing environments: Theory, research and design* (pp. 143–168). Hillsdale, NJ: Lawrence Erlbaum Associates.

Kintsch, W. (1988). The role of knowledge in discourse comprehension: A construction-integration model. *Psychological Review, 95*, 163–182.

Kintsch, W., & Keenan, J. M. (1973). Reading rate as a function of the number of propositions in the base structure of sentences. *Cognitive Psychology, 5*, 257–274.

Kintsch, W., Kozminsky, E., Streby, W. J., McKoon, G., & Keenan, J. M. (1975). Comprehension and recall of text as a function of content variables. *Journal of Verbal Learning and Verbal Behavior, 14*, 196–214.

Kintsch, W., & van Dijk, T. A. (1978). Toward a model of text comprehension and production. *Psychological Review, 85*, 363–394.

Lesgold, A. M., Roth, S. F., & Curtis, M. E. (1979). Foregrounding effects in discourse comprehension. *Journal of Verbal Learning and Verbal Behavior, 18*, 291–308.

Magliano, J. P., Graesser, A. C., Eymard, L. A., Haberlandt, K., & Gholson, B. (1993). Locus of interpretive and inference processes during text comprehension: A comparison of gaze durations and word reading times. *Journal of Experimental Psychology: Learning, Memory & Cognition, 19*, 704–709.

Mandler, J. M. (1978). A code in the node: The use of the story schema in retrieval. *Discourse Processes, 1*, 14–35.

Mandler, J. M., & Johnson, N. S. (1977). Remembrance of things parsed: Story structure and recall. *Cognitive Psychology, 9*, 111–151.

Manelis, L., & Yekovich, F. R. (1976). Repetition of propositional arguments in sentences. *Journal of Verbal Learning and Verbal Behavior, 15*, 301–312.

Miller, G. A. (1956). The magical number seven, plus or minus two: Some limits on capacity for processing information. *Psychological Review, 63*, 81–97.

Miller, G. A., Beckwith, R., Fellbaum, C., Gross, D., & Miller, K. (1990). *Five papers on WordNet* (CSL Report 43). Princeton, NJ: Cognitive Science Laboratory.

Miller, J. R., & Kintsch, W. (1980). Readability and recall of short prose passages: A theoretical analysis. *Journal of Experimental Psychology: Human Learning and Memory, 6*, 335–354.

Ratcliff, R., & McKoon, G. (1978). Priming in item recognition: Evidence for the propositional structure of sentences. *Journal of Verbal Learning and Verbal Behavior, 17*, 403–418.

Reiger, C. (1975). Conceptual analysis. In R. C. Schank (Ed.), *Conceptual information processing* (pp. 157–288). Amsterdam, North Holland.

Spilich, G. J., Vesonder, G. T., Chiesi, H. L., & Voss, J. F. (1979). Text processing of domain-related information for individuals with high and low domain knowledge. *Journal of Verbal Learning and Verbal Behavior, 18*, 275–290.

Turner, A. A. (1987). *The propositional analysis system, version 1.0* (Tech. Rep. No. 87-02). Boulder: University of Colorado, Institute of Cognitive Science.

Turner, A., & Greene, E. (1978). Construction and use of a propositional text base. *Journal Supplement Abstract Service Catalogue of selected documents in psychology* (MS 1713).

van Dijk, T. A., & Kintsch, W. (1983). *Strategies of discourse comprehension*. New York: Academic Press.

CHAPTER

3

EXTENDING CAPACITY-CONSTRAINED CONSTRUCTION INTEGRATION: TOWARD "SMARTER" AND FLEXIBLE MODELS OF TEXT COMPREHENSION

Susan R. Goldman
Sashank Varma
Nathalie Coté
Vanderbilt University

Research on, and theorizing about, language, discourse, text comprehension, and memory have demonstrated that (a) there are complex interactions among learner, text and task characteristics, and (b) limitations on cognitive resources lead to competition among various processing, storage, and retrieval activities, as well as strategies for accomplishing them (e.g., Goldman & Saul, 1990a; Just & Carpenter, 1992; Kletzien, 1991; Lee-Sammons & Whitney, 1991; Whitney, Ritchie, & Clark, 1991; Yochum, 1991). In this chapter, our primary interest is in models of text comprehension that have the potential to deal with interactions among learner, text, and task characteristics that have implications for resource allocation in working memory.

Text comprehension involves processing at multiple levels of language (e.g., word, sentence, discourse). In a capacity-constrained environment, resource-demanding processes associated with a specific language level might compete for resources with other language levels; hence, the impact of resource-intensive processing could cascade throughout the system, affecting the quality and timing of all processing activities. Models of text comprehension have often addressed issues related to working memory by assuming a parameter that captures the size of the working memory buffer with respect to a fixed number of propositions (e.g., Kintsch & van Dijk, 1978; Spilich, Vesonder, Chiesi, & Voss, 1979). However, some computer architectures have made it feasible to model comprehension within a working memory environment in which there is an overall capacity constraint that applies to available resources (Just & Carpenter, 1992). The amount of information that can be processed, stored, or recalled depends not on the buffer size, but on what else is competing for working memory resources. As long as the demands on resources are less than the overall amount of resources available, there are no negative consequences for processing. One such architecture is that developed by Just and Carpenter (1992): Capacity-Constrained Collaborative Activation Based Production System (3CAPS). They used this architecture to model processing of sentences with potentially ambiguous syntactic structures.

In this chapter, we describe the evolution of our thinking about a comprehensive model of text comprehension for non-narrative texts. Simulation models of comprehension play a central role in our thinking. We find this modeling effort useful precisely because of the multifaceted nature of the factors that influence what an individual understands and remembers from a text. Modeling efforts are informative from two perspectives. First, in building a simulation model that successfully predicts or matches behavioral data, new insights are gained into what human cognitive activity might be like. Second, when simulation modeling does not match the behavioral data, understanding where and why the model "misses" also can be revealing about the nature of human cognitive activity. Such misses naturally lead to hypotheses that direct subsequent theoretical and empirical research. As will be evident, our research on comprehension by adults and children has been informed by both perspectives on the role of simulation models.

Our chapter begins with a brief overview of models of text comprehension. Our focus is on the seminal work of Kintsch and colleagues on models of text comprehension (e.g., Kintsch, 1974; Kintsch & van Dijk, 1978; van Dijk & Kintsch, 1983). These models include the Construction-Integration (CI) model, which makes weak assumptions about top-down guidance of comprehension (Kintsch, 1988, 1992; Kintsch, Britton, Fletcher, E. Kintsch, Mannes, & Nathan, 1993; Kintsch & Welsch, 1991). We then describe the major characteristics of 3CAPS and its precursor CAPS. In the second section, we summarize our own efforts to extend the CI model by embedding it in the 3CAPS architecture. Our initial efforts provided distinct advantages over a fixed-buffer size model, but also revealed some important limitations of CI models (Goldman & Varma, 1995). We report additional modeling efforts that use our capacity-constrained CI model (3CI). These efforts further delineate the strengths and weaknesses of the CI class of models. The limitations suggest specific directions for a "smarter" model of text comprehension and we describe the conceptual design of such a model in the final section of the chapter.

MODELS OF TEXT COMPREHENSION

The Kintsch and van Dijk Model

Kintsch, often in collaboration with van Dijk, has been responsible for stimulating the bulk of the modeling work in the area of comprehension of non-narrative text (cf. Kintsch, 1974, 1988; Kintsch & van Dijk, 1978; van Dijk & Kintsch, 1983).[1] These models propose that two distinct kinds of representations are formed from the sentences of the text: the *textbase* and the *situation model* (cf. van Dijk, 1987; van Dijk & Kintsch, 1983). Textbase representations are relatively faithful to the presented passage. They consist of propositions derived from the input sentences of the text, plus a small set of "necessary" inferences.[2] The textbase can undergo reduction to produce a macropropositional textbase, a representation that emphasizes the more important information from the text. (See van Dijk, 1987, or van Dijk & Kintsch, 1983, for a discussion of macropropositional derivation.)

Situation model representations integrate text information with readers' prior knowledge. The situation model is a representation of the world reflected in the text and its relationship to the learner's prior knowledge about the world. Situation, or mental model, representations often blur the distinction between what was exactly stated in a text and what ought to be true of the world described by the text. Situation models support problem solving and serve as the basis for updating and modifying what an individual knows (van Dijk, 1987; van Dijk & Kintsch, 1983). Kintsch's earlier models of comprehension relied on schema-driven, top-down processing for purposes of building situation models. In 1988, Kintsch proposed that such methods were not adaptive to new contexts and were quite inflexible (Kintsch, 1988; Kintsch et al., 1993). He proposed an alternative in the form of the Construction-Integration model, a class of models that relies on relatively weak methods to account for the role of prior knowledge.

Kintsch's Construction-Integration Model (CI)

The CI model (e.g., Kintsch, 1988, 1992) is a simulation that models how text representations are constructed, understood, and integrated with the reader's knowledge. During the construction phase a semantic network-like coherence matrix is created in which input propositions define the nodes. Links between nodes are created if they share arguments (i.e., *argument overlap*) or if one proposition is embedded in another (i.e., *propositional embedding*). All propositions and their links are given initial activation (usually one unit). The representation is fine-tuned through an integration process that uses a connectionist algorithm. Integration operates until the network *settles*; that is, until changes in

[1]In the area of story comprehension, the recursive network model of Trabasso and colleagues (Trabasso & Sperry, 1985; Trabasso & van den Broek, 1985) has been highly influential. There also have been applications of the Kintsch and van Dijk (1978) model to stories (e.g., Fletcher & Bloom, 1988; van den Broek, 1989, 1990).

[2]When and which inferences are made is an ongoing controversy. For our purposes, it is sufficient to note that anaphoric references are assumed to occur in the construction of a textbase. Bridging inferences such as those based on category membership are likely to be made on a probabilistic basis. In our work, we have taken a conservative position on inferences in the textbase and restrict them to inferences made to satisfy referential coherence.

the activation vectors resulting from successive cycles are less than some criterion.

A central assumption of the CI model (Kintsch, 1988) is that only those things that reside in working memory simultaneously can be connected. Typically, the propositions constituting a single sentence are input in a cycle. If the sentence is not the first sentence of a passage, some input from the previous cycle is "carried over," and processed along with the new input. The number of propositions carried over is given by parameter *s*, and the *s* most highly activated propositions are held over. The parameter *s* depends on assumptions about a fixed-capacity buffer. Frequently, buffer size is set at two propositions (e.g., Kintsch, 1988; Kintsch & van Dijk, 1978), but other values are possible (e.g., Tapiero & Denhiére, in press). Propositions not held over are transferred to long-term storage and are retrievable through reinstatement searches.

The final activations, or strengths, in working memory predict various short-term memory phenomena (e.g., Kintsch, 1988, 1992; Kintsch & Welsch, 1991; Kintsch, Welsch, Schmalhofer, & Zimny, 1990). The final activation values can be used to compute strength in long-term memory and these long-term memory activations have been found to satisfactorily predict behavioral recall data (e.g., Kintsch, 1992; Kintsch, McNamara, Songer, & Kintsch, 1992). Additional research has demonstrated the usefulness of this model for furthering our understanding of a host of phenomena, including memory retrieval, text comprehension, conceptual relatedness, and mathematical word problems (cf. Kintsch et al., 1993).

Comprehension in a Capacity-Constrained CAPS Environment

As developed by Just and Carpenter (1987, 1992), the CAPS architecture is a hybrid environment, containing both symbolic characteristics and connectionist characteristics. Two features of the architecture reflect its hybrid nature. First, the *collaborative* aspect of CAPS results from its elimination of conflict resolution between productions; instead, all matched productions are simultaneously fired. Second, *activation* plays several roles in CAPS that make it different from traditional production system architectures. Most importantly, preconditions of productions can exist at *levels* of activation rather than being either present or absent. For a precondition to match, it must be consistent in form and have an activation greater than some threshold. The primary action of productions is to copy activation from elements matched on their preconditions to elements specified in the action part of the production. Most often, this results in activation being directed from one element to another. These two features lend a connectionist flavor to CAPS processing: Productions fire in parallel, gradually changing the activations of working memory elements by an amount proportional to the activations of other elements.

Recently, Just and Carpenter (1992) embellished the CAPS model with the assumption that there exists an activation limit on working memory, sometimes referred to as the *cap*. This new capacity-constrained architecture is called 3CAPS, and it differs from typical production system environments in an important way. According to the *capacity-constraint assumption*, the total amount of activation available for working memory elements is capped. If fired productions request more activation than is available, the cap is reached. The requests and the activation currently assigned to working memory elements are scaled back an amount proportional to their activation relative to other working memory elements. Because productions iteratively fire until their goals are met, processing at the cap results in an overall system slowdown and the gradual loss of working memory elements that are not participating in processing. If elements fall below a minimum level, they are no longer functional in working memory and cannot participate in processing.

EMBEDDING THE CONSTRUCTION INTEGRATION MODEL IN 3CAPS: CAPACITY-CONSTRAINED CONSTRUCTION INTEGRATION MODEL (3CI)

Our own work modeling comprehension of informational text has examined the value added by embedding CI in the 3CAPS environment. In so doing, we replaced a fixed-buffer working memory with a capacity-constrained system that permits more dynamic determination of the semantic network of propositions that are formed through the construction and integration processes. We call our simulation model Capacity-Constrained CI (3CI). Goldman and Varma (1995) discuss several advantages of a 3CI class of models, the most important of which is that 3CI permits greater latitude in assumptions about the disposition of previously processed propositions. In CI, a fixed buffer of size *s*, in conjunction with final activation values on each processing cycle, determine which propositions are held over. The process can operate more dynamically in 3CI in that working memory functioning determines which and how many propositions remain active for the next input cycle. On some input cycles, all previous propositions might remain active; on others, only one or two might remain active. This is a potentially important difference between CI and 3CI because if more propositions are held over in working memory, there is a greater potential for links to be formed between the propositions that are held over and the propositions reflecting the next input sentence. This situation would result in a more highly interconnected semantic network. Moreover, assuming that interconnectedness reflects the coherence of the information, there should be corresponding increases in the predictive ability of the dynamic working memory model.

Additional advantages discussed by Goldman and Varma (1995) are that the 3CAPS architecture provides an environment for exploring interactions among text processing, prior knowledge, and strategic reading processes. We return to these issues when we consider the implications of our current modeling efforts.

Comparison of the Operation of CI and 3CI Models

Goldman and Varma (1995) describe in some detail the similarities and differences between the operation of CI and 3CI. We have summarized these similarities and differences in Table 3.1. As indicated in the table, the input for both models is a list of propositions that have been created by the researcher to reflect some text. The propositions are grouped into cycles, with each cycle containing the propositions of one sentence. However, other cycle sizes are possible. Figure 3.1 provides the parsed input for the first few sentences of a passage that describes various types of distance. The network formed after the second cycle is shown in the lower half of the figure. During the construction phase, the propositions of the current cycle are combined with selected propositions from the previous cycle(s), and links are formed on the basis of argument overlap or propositional embedding (e.g., p7 in Fig. 3.1). The propositions define the nodes, whereas the connections define the links in a semantic network-like representation. In CI, multiple overlaps and/or embeddings between two propositions do not increment the weight of the link between propositions. In 3CI, however, the link weights can vary depending on the number of overlapping arguments or embeddings between two nodes. As processing through the text proceeds, the network undergoes changes in the number and strengths of the nodes and links.

During integration, activation is spread through the propositional network. In CI, this is done using a connectionist post-multiplication scheme, whereas 3CI depends on the constrained activation environment of 3CAPS. When the network settles (defined as a minimal change, specified in advance, in the distribution

TABLE 3.1
Comparison of Construction-Integration (CI) and Capacity-Constrained CI (3CI) Models

Dimension	*Common to Both*	*CI only*	*3CI only*
Input	Parsed propositions		
Connection rules	Argument overlap and propositional embedding	Multiple overlaps/embeddings *are not* counted	Multiple overlaps/embeddings *are* counted
Integration		Connectionist postmultiplication algorithm	Distributes activation in a capacity-constrained environment
Long-term memory update	Integrated activation values are accumulated for each proposition and each link		
Carry-over rule		*s* most active propositions	All above-threshold propositions at their integrated activation levels

Sentence/Cycle 1:

Distance is the space between points.

p1 is[distance,space]
p2 is^between[space,points]

Sentence/Cycle 2:

When measured with a standard unit, the result is called absolute distance and is what persons think of when they think of distance.

p3 measure[someone1,distance,standard^unit]
p4 time[p5,p3]
p5 type^of[distance,absolute]
p6 and[p5,p7]
p7 think[persons,p8]
p8 is^equal[distance,p5]

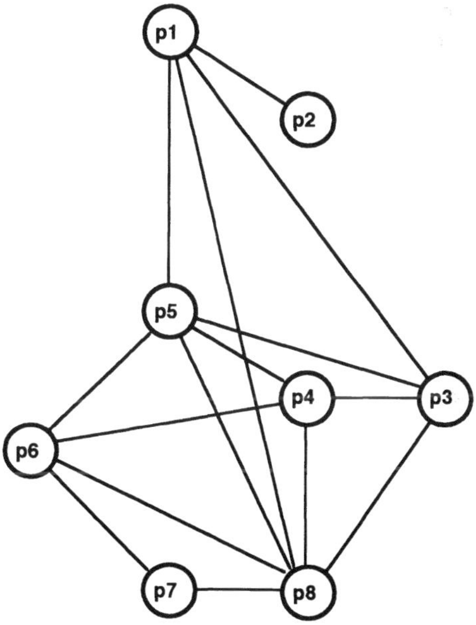

FIG. 3.1. Propositional input and network representation for the first two sentences of the Distance passage.

of activations on consecutive iterations), the final activation values are used to update the long-term memory trace of each proposition and propositional link. In CI, the final activations also are used to determine which propositions are carried over for processing with the next cycle. The number carried over is a parameter (s) and often is set at two propositions. In 3CI, all propositions whose final activations exceed some threshold are carried over at their settled activation levels.

In summary, CI and 3CI differ on three dimensions: whether they count multiple overlaps or embeddings; how they do integration; and how propositions are selected for carry over. These differences derive from 3CI's reliance on the dynamic working memory model of 3CAPS instead of the fixed-buffer scheme of CI. Elsewhere we have demonstrated that the working memory model is the crucial difference between CI and 3CI (Goldman & Varma, 1995).

Application of the Simulation Models

Several phenomena are considered in our evaluation of the simulations that we conducted with CI and 3CI. First, we look at whether the two models produce results that are correlated with one another. In other words, when modeling comprehension of a passage, in what ways do the two models agree and disagree? Second, we compare the models to behavioral recall data to examine the predictive ability of each. Previously, we reported the results of these comparisons based on one passage, "Distance" (Goldman & Varma, 1995). We summarize those results here and describe the results for three additional passages, one with a content structure similar to the Distance passage, and two with more complex content structures. As discussed subsequently, for the passage with the content structure similar to the Distance passage, we replicated our previous findings: 3CI predicted the behavioral data more adequately than did CI. For the passages with the more complex content structures, all of the simulation models predicted the behavioral data less adequately. However, there were some aspects of the simulations that matched the behavioral data. The pattern of matches and mismatches of the CI class of models on the more complex content structures is particularly revealing of the types of information needed by a "smarter" class of models that would be more comprehensive with respect to the comprehension of informational text. We consider such a class of models in the final section of the chapter.

The "Distance" Passage. The Distance passage is a descriptive, informational passage the full text of which is presented in Appendix A. The passage begins by providing a general definition of distance and then defines two types of distance: absolute and relative. The remainder of the passage provides descriptive information about five types of relative distance, each of which is introduced (sentences 5, 8, 11, 14, 17) and then elaborated by two sentences. In our analysis of the passage, we considered the topic of *distance* to be the superordinate theme of the passage and the different types of distance to be the main points of the passage. In the passage presented to the adult participants, sentences 1, 4, 8, 11, 14, and 17 were the first sentences of the six paragraphs in the passage.

Goldman and Varma (1995) found that the 3CI-Dynamic model produced long-term memory propositional node and link strengths that, although correlated with those of the CI model, diverged in interesting ways.[3] In particular, 3CI's divergences from CI corresponded with 3CI placing stronger weighting on the main point nodes of the Distance passage than did CI. The 3CI model also produced stronger link strength values for these sentences. Comparisons between CI and a fixed-buffer 3CI (3CI-Mimic) indicated that the only difference between CI and 3CI that could account for these patterns was the use of the dynamic working memory model in 3CI. Recently, we also ran a modified version of CI to explicitly test whether 3CI-Dynamic's counting of multiple overlaps and embeddings was responsible for its superior performance. The modified version of CI also counted multiple overlaps and embedding; its node and link strength predictions were virtually identical to those of the CI model run without the multiple links rule ($r = .99$, $p < .01$, $df = 17$).

Thus, our results on the Distance passage indicated that allowing propositional carry-over to operate dynamically in response to working memory constraints produced a pattern of weights consistent with intuitions about the relative importance of the various sentences in the passage. The results also were consistent with a great deal of prior research on main point identification in expository passages (e.g., Kieras, 1980, 1981, 1982; Lorch, 1989; Vipond, 1980).

In terms of predicting behavioral recall data, the 3CI model accounted for more variance than did the CI model. Figure 3.2 shows recall data for adults plotted as a function of the long-term memory link-strength measures that were produced by the 3CI simulation. The R^2s for the 3CI model were substantially greater than for the CI model, accounting for 60% or more of the variance in the adults' recall data in Fig. 3.2. In contrast, the CI model accounted for 28% to 37% of the variance across these three studies.

The "Nationalism" Passage: A Replication of "Distance." We tried to replicate the effects we had found on the Distance passage on additional passages to assure ourselves that the performance characteristics of 3CI were not passage-specific. We had previously collected adult behavioral recall data from a similarly structured passage, "Nationalism" (Goldman & Saul, 1990b, 1994). We simulated CI and 3CI using the same parameters that we had used on the Distance passage; that is, 3CI was given an activation capacity of 20 units, a value sufficient to permit processing of a sentence of average length without exceeding capacity.

The content structure of the Nationalism passage corresponds to that of Distance and is shown in Fig. 3.3, with the text corresponding to the sentence numbers provided in Table 3.2. The initial paragraph introduces the concept of national consciousness, its importance to the formation of a nation and nationalism, and the time course of the development of national consciousness. The

[3]Goldman and Varma (1995) ran two versions of 3CI: one, 3CI-Mimic, utilized the fixed-size buffer characteristic of CI, and the other, 3CI-Dynamic, utilized the constrained activation characteristic. Our use of 3CI in the present chapter corresponds to 3CI-Dynamic reported in Goldman and Varma (1995).

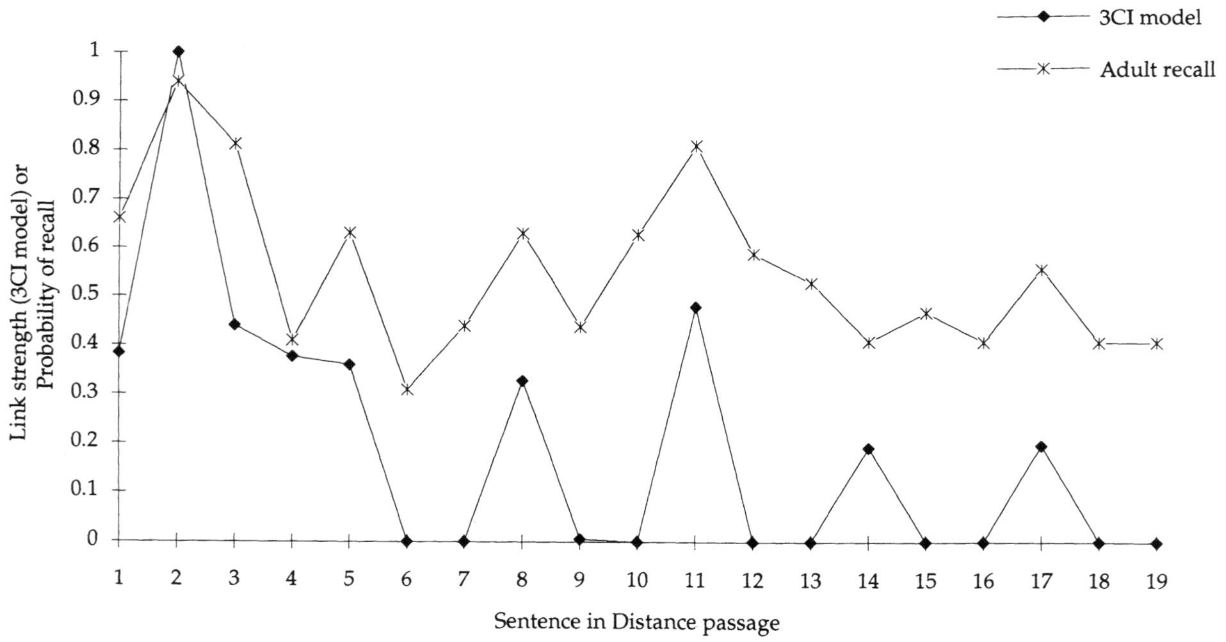

FIG. 3.2. Comparison of adult recall data and the long-term memory link strengths resulting from the 3CI-Dynamic simulation on the Distance passage.

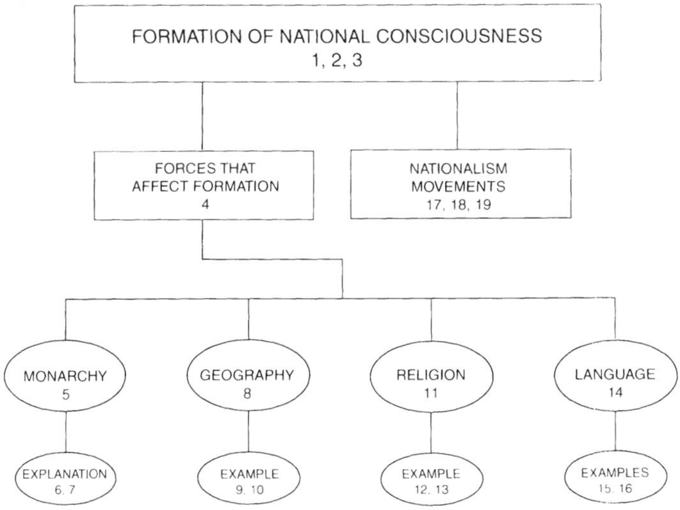

FIG. 3.3. Schematic content structure for the Nationalism passage. (Numbers refer to sentences listed in Table 3.2.)

remainder of the passage, except for the last three sentences, describes factors affecting the formation of national consciousness. Each factor is introduced (sentences 5, 8, 11, and 14 in Table 3.2) and subsequently is explained or exemplified (e.g., sentences 6, 7, 9, 10, 12, 13, 15, 16). The final paragraph discusses the need for popular support for nationalist movements (sentences 17, 18, 19 of Table 3.2). The main-point sentences of the passage are those that introduce the factors creating national consciousness (i.e., 5, 8, 11, and 14 in Table 3.2). The superordinate theme for the passage is a semantic field around the concept of *nation*, including the ideas of *nationalism*, *national consciousness*, *national idea*, and *nationalists*. When constructing the propositional parses of the sentences in this text, we represented the concepts according to these underlying semantic relationships. Additional descriptive information about the Nationalism passage is provided in Table 3.3.

The simulations we conducted produced long-term memory strengths for the input dispositions. From these, we constructed the two measures of importance in the present chapter. First, there was the sentence node strength, which was computed by averaging the strengths of each of the atomic-proposition nodes that comprised the complex proposition. Second, there was a link strength for each sentence, which was defined as the total strength of the links between the complex proposition and propositions in other sentences. It should be noted that the node and link-strength measures were normalized, and ranged between 0 and 1.

The first issue to consider is whether CI and 3CI produced the same pattern of activations across the 19 sentences of the Nationalism passage. Correlations

TABLE 3.2
Sentences in the Nationalism Passage

1. Modern history has been concerned with the events that lead to the forming of a nation and national consciousness.
2. Although you can have a nation without nationalism, you cannot have nationalism without national consciousness.
3. National consciousness often arises through a long and gradual process, but sometimes it arises in a quick and violent manner.
4. There are a variety of forces that exert impetus for the formation of national consciousness.
5. In older nations, states were created and run by monarchies.
6. A territorial nucleus was organized under a monarch, who expanded his authority to a wider area.
7. The resulting monarchical state was the original focus of its subjects' loyalty.
8. Geography has been decisive in forming national consciousness in cases where a fledgling nation is physically separate from its mother nation.
9. The American colonists' struggle for independence provides an example of this influence.
10. Their economic conflict and eventual war with Great Britain resulted from such geographic factors as physical separation and differences in natural resources, climate, and terrain.
11. In nations where the rulers and the ruled have been of different faiths, religion has played an important role.
12. This was especially clear in the case of Christians under Turkish rule in Eastern Europe, and Muslims under British rule in North-West Africa.
13. As these people began to express objection to foreign rule, religion was the essence of their feeling of being different.
14. Language has been a factor influencing national consciousness in many countries.
15. The people who used to be called "Balkans" broke up into Greeks, Serbs, Romanians, and Bulgarians, according to their languages.
16. The idea that all those whose language was Arabic were one nation was the decisive factor in the case of Arab nationalism.
17. Nationalist movements become effective when they have mass support.
18. But nationalism cannot even begin until there is an elite of convinced nationalists expressing the national idea.
19. The national idea becomes a rallying point that is often exploited by the elite to gain popular support.

TABLE 3.3
Structure and Content Information About the Nationalism, Fat, and Sugar Passages

	Theme		
	Nationalism	*Fat in Our Diet*	*Sugar in Our Diet*
Number of sentences/processing cycles	19	28	29
Number of sentences containing superordinate concept	12	27	21
Number of propositions	103	97	84
Difficulty level (grade equivalent)	12	6.6	6.0

between the models indicated that neither node strength nor link strength were correlated across models. Within each model, these two measures were significantly correlated, although the correlations were lower than those observed for the Distance passage.[4] Figure 3.4 depicts the link-strength measure for 3CI and CI. This figure indicates that the activations diverged in much the same way as on the Distance passage: 3CI shows differentiation of the main-point sentences from the elaborations of main points, with peaks occurring at sentences 5, 8, 11, and 14. The 3CI simulation also produced higher activations for the first two sentences relative to the other sentences in the passage than did CI. The first two sentences establish *nationalism* as a passage theme, or superordinate for the remainder of the passage. Activation rapidly accrued to these propositions and a relatively tight network was formed around them. Subsequent propositions containing arguments in the *nation* semantic field had the opportunity to form links to this network. The main point sentences were the ones that shared arguments with the *nation* semantic field. A similar pattern of activations occurred for the node-strength measure in the 3CI simulation.

In contrast to 3CI, due to CI's carry-over rule of selecting the two most highly activated propositions, processing tends to be locally driven and, thus, there are fewer opportunities for sentences later in the passage to form connections with propositions early in the passage. In fact, of the 36 opportunities to carry-over propositions, only 3 were carried over on more than a single successive processing cycle. Thus, CI produced more localized peaks than 3CI. The longer "history" allowed 3CI to form a global structure around the superordinate concept.

For the Nationalism passage, comparisons of each of the simulation models with the adult recall data were not as clear cut as for the Distance passage. Across all 19 sentences, the correlations between node-strength measures and recall and between link-strength measures and recall were positive but statistically nonsignificant for both simulation models. When we looked at the graphs of the adult probability of recall data against the simulation results, it was clear that the pattern of activations produced by the 3CI simulation was quite similar to the pattern of adult recall. The exception was the first sentence, which adults tended to recall at much lower levels than predicted by 3CI (see Fig. 3.5). Other than sentence 1, the general increases and decreases were fairly consistent. In fact, we computed the correlation without sentence 1 and obtained significant correlations for the 3CI model link-strength ($r = .73$, $p < .01$, $df = 16$) and node-strength measures ($r = .54$, $p < .05$, $df = 17$).

There was no such similarity in the patterns for adult recall and the CI model, as indicated in Fig. 3.6. For example, CI peaked on sentences 6, 14, and 15 and had several segments of text where there was no differentiation among the sentences (e.g., sentences 8–13). This pattern was at variance with the recall performance.

---

[4]Correlations of node strength and link strength were $r = .54$ for CI and $r = .90$ for 3CI, $p < .05$, $df = 17$. Correlations of each measure across models ranged between .02 and .29.

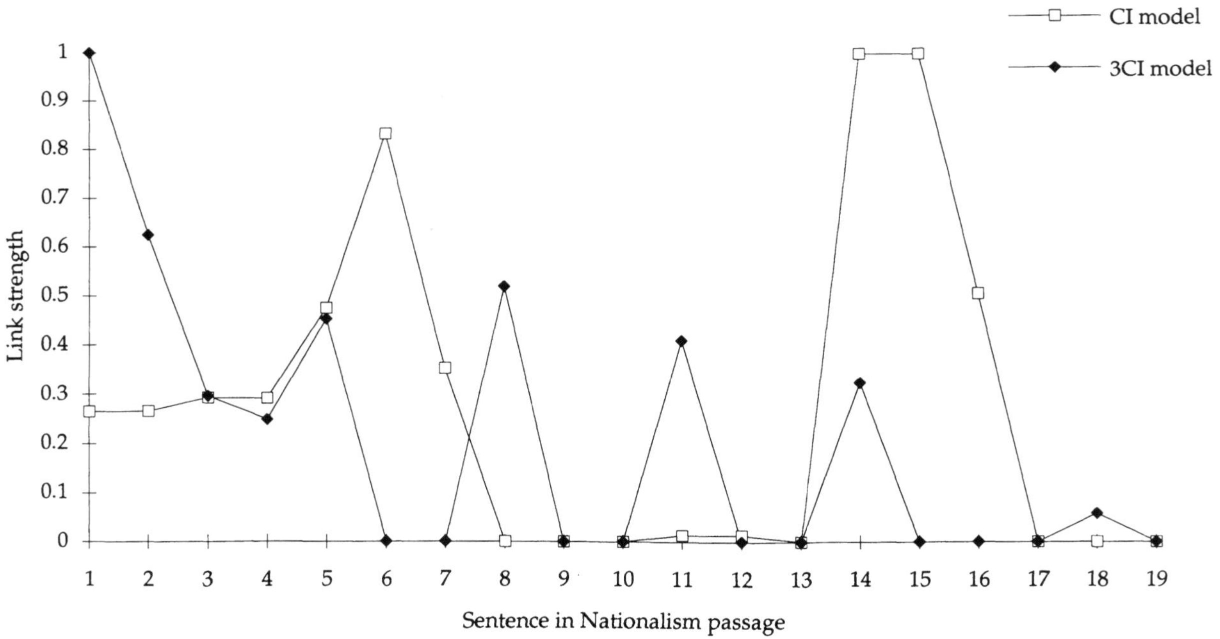

FIG. 3.4. Comparison of long-term memory link strengths resulting from the 3CI- and the CI-simulation runs on the Nationalism passage.

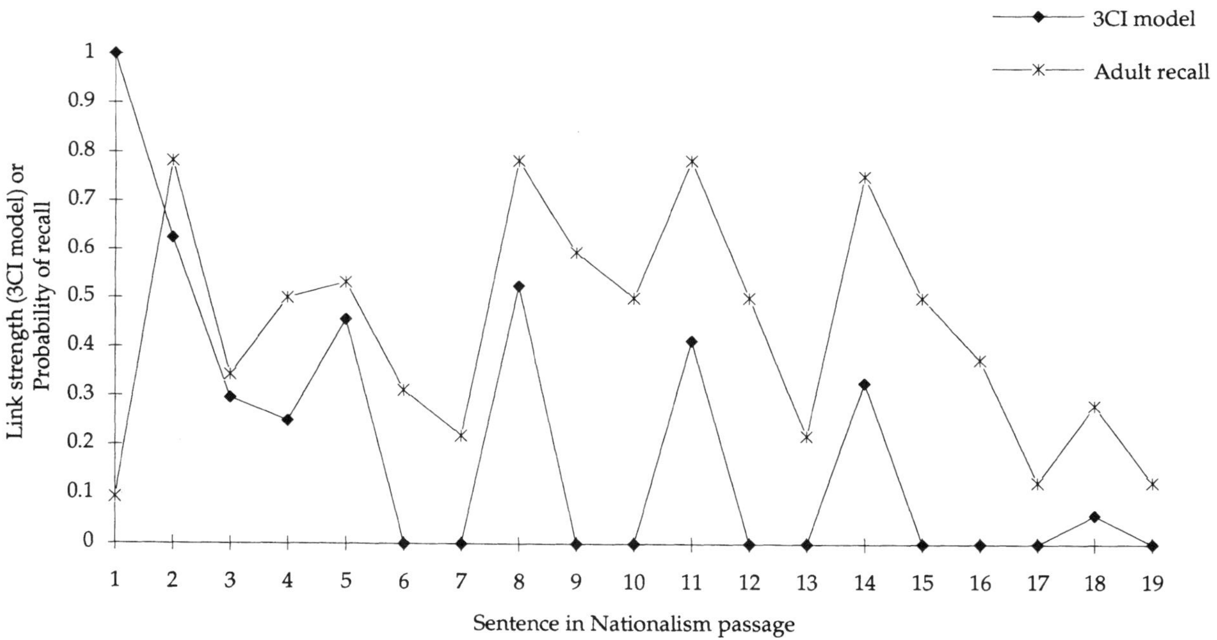

FIG. 3.5. Comparison of adult recall data and 3CI link strength on the Nationalism passage.

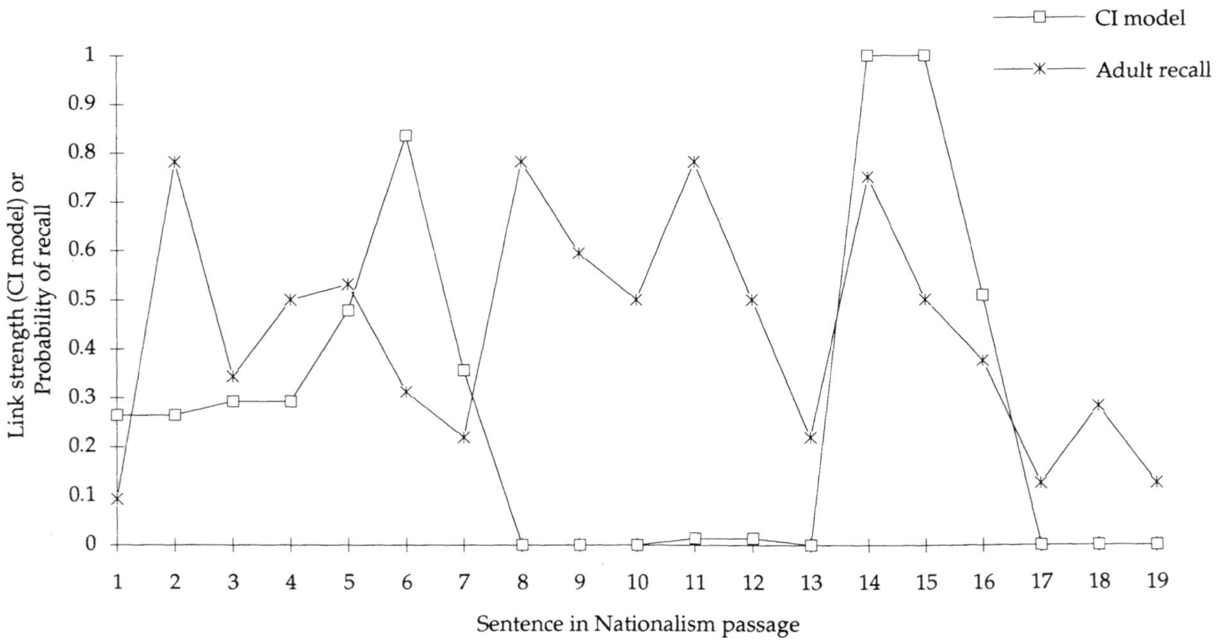

FIG. 3.6. Comparison of adult recall data and CI link strength on the Nationalism passage.

In summary, the simulations of the Nationalism passage replicated the results we had obtained for the Distance passage. The dynamic working memory model of 3CI produced long-term memory strengths that were more predictive of adult recall than were those derived from the fixed-buffer model. Using the connection mechanisms of argument overlap and propositional embedding, 3CI was able to construct a superordinate concept and a global structure that reflected the linking of the main points in the passage to the superordinate. The CI model seemed to have been driven by more local semantic overlap and, as a consequence, failed to generate long-term memory patterns that reflected the global structure of the passage.

As indicated previously, the content structures of the Distance and the Nationalism passages are quite similar and could be described as *description–example*. In both passages, the superordinate theme is introduced in the first paragraph and the remainder of the passage systematically introduces main points related to the theme. These points are elaborated and exemplified, but the elaboration sentences do not contain arguments that overlap with the other main point sentences or with the superordinate theme. These two passages were modified from the original source material (i.e., introductory, college-level textbooks) to conform to this content structure. The content itself was relatively unfamiliar and abstract to the adults who participated in the studies. To extend our test of the 3CI model, we simulated two additional passages that had more complex content structures, but which were about information that was more likely to be familiar to readers. We report the results of these efforts in the next section.

Extension of the 3CI Model to Other Content Structures

We developed informational passages on topics in nutrition. We collected comprehension and memory data from adults and elementary school-age students. The passages were actually designed for a think-aloud study in which we examined readers' (a) detection and resolution of comprehension problems, (b) activation of prior knowledge and connection of it with text content, including inconsistencies between prior knowledge and text content (Coté, Goldman, Gjellstad, Keeton, & Millican, 1994), and (c) use of enumeration (e.g., *first, second*) and paragraphing as markers of importance and global text structure. As a result, we created passages that were open to multiple interpretations at several points and in which there were multiple possibilities for the superordinate concepts and main points. Both were about nutrition topics, one about fat and one about sugar.

Simulation modeling was conducted using the same parameters as those used on the Distance and Nationalism passages. The long-term memory node-strength and link-strength measures produced by 3CI and CI were intercorrelated and used to predict recall of each of the nutrition passages. Recall data were collected from groups of 16 adults, 18 fourth-grade students, and 16 sixth-grade students after they had read each passage while concurrently giving a think-aloud protocol.

Descriptive information about the passages is provided in Table 3.3. In terms of traditional readability indices, as well as our evaluation of the content, these should have been easy passages for adults. We consider each passage in turn.

The "Fat" Passage. The text of the Fat passage is given in Table 3.4, and the schematic content structure is shown in Fig. 3.7. In contrast to the Nationalism schematic (Fig. 3.3), there are three clusters of information in the Fat passage (i.e., importance, sources, and ways it is harmful), as well as three types of fats that are compared on the harmfulness continuum. There are also implicit comparisons of types and sources of fats. In contrast to the Nationalism passage, there are a number of cross-connections between the clusters and more explicit connections among the individual sentences. There also is an embedded enumerated structure that begins at sentence 13 in the Fat passage, but it is connected to the idea that fats are harmful (in contrast to enumerated structures

TABLE 3.4
Sentences of the Fat Passage

1. Fats in Our Diet
2. Fats are an important part of our diet.
3. They provide twice as much energy as carbohydrates and proteins.
4. Our bodies contain layers of fat that protect some delicate body organs from injury.
5. In addition, fats add flavor and texture to food.
6. People in the United States eat a lot of foods with fats in them.
7. But our bodies only need a very small amount of fat to be healthy.
8. If we eat more than our bodies need, the extra can be harmful.
9. If we know which foods contain fats, it will be easier for us to eat less of them.
10. There are three different kinds of fats; some are less harmful than others.
11. Foods that come from animals usually contain the harmful ones.
12. Plant foods usually have less harmful kinds of fats.
13. There are three kinds of fats: saturated, polyunsaturated, and monounsaturated.
14. Saturated fat is the most harmful.
15. Saturated fat is found mostly in red meat and in many dairy products like butter and whole milk.
16. Some vegetable oils, which are made from plants, also have it.
17. If we eat too much of it, it will slowly clog the walls of our blood vessels.
18. Eventually, eating too much saturated fat can lead to heart attacks, strokes, and other serious illnesses.
19. Polyunsaturated fat is less harmful than saturated fat.
20. It can still damage the blood vessels and the heart if we eat too much of it.
21. Most vegetable oils and fish oils are polyunsaturated.
22. Monounsaturated fat is the least harmful to the body.
23. It may even reduce the risk of getting blocked blood vessels.
24. Monounsaturated fats, as well as polyunsaturated, are found in vegetables, many types of nuts, and fish like salmon and mackerel.
25. Most of the monounsaturated fat that we eat comes from olive oil.
26. Animal foods are the major source of fat in the American diet.
27. We can safely reduce the amount of animal foods in our diets.
28. We can get the fat we need from many plant foods.

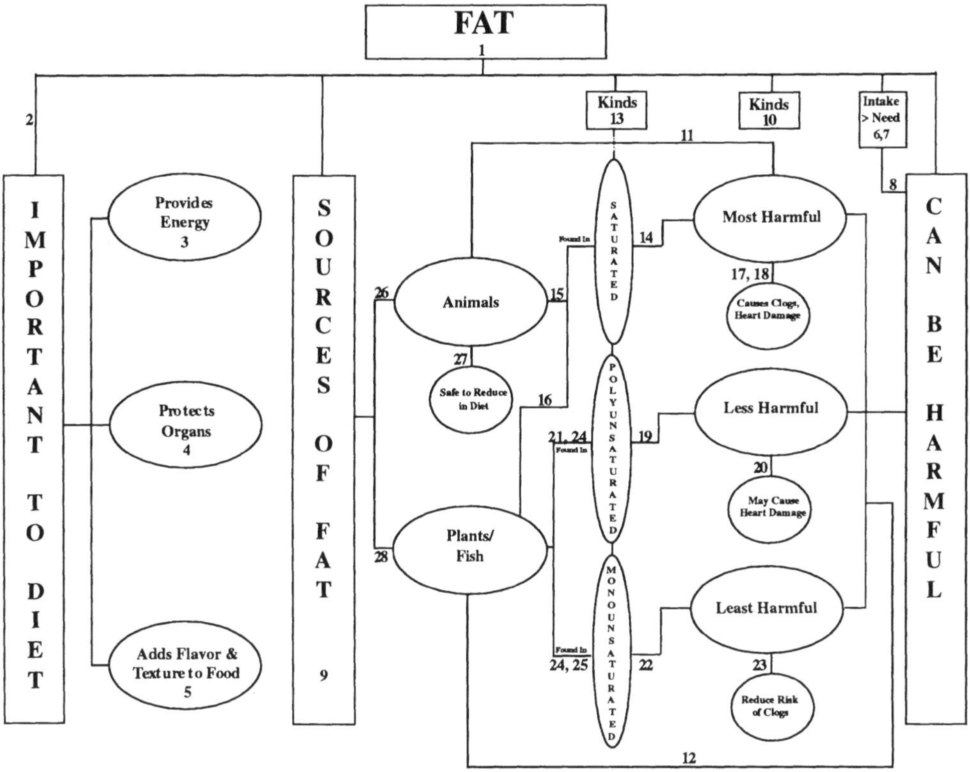

FIG. 3.7. Schematic content structure for the Fat passage. (Numbers refer to sentences listed in Table 3.4.)

in the Nationalism and Distance passages). In short, there were a number of ideas about fat that were introduced in this passage. Argument overlap was far more ubiquitous than in the Nationalism or Distance passages.

As to the results, the simulations demonstrated that the node-strength and link-strength measures were significantly intercorrelated for the 3CI model ($r = .53$, $p < .01$, $df = 26$) but not for the CI model ($r = .19$). However, across models, each of the long-term memory measures were correlated significantly, $r = .60$, $p < .01$ for node strength and $r = .72$, $p < .01$ for link strength. These correlations indicate a general consistency in the patterns of long-term memory strength across the models. Figure 3.8 shows these patterns for the node-strength measure. The overall patterns for the two models are quite consistent, with the exception of the first sentence. Sentences receiving relatively high activation in both models included those mentioning the positive functions of fat (sentences 4, 5 in Table 3.4), that eating too much fat is harmful (sentences 6 and 8 in Table 3.4) and that there are three kinds of fat (sentence 13 in Table 3.4). The major difference between the models is that the 3CI model showed a general downward

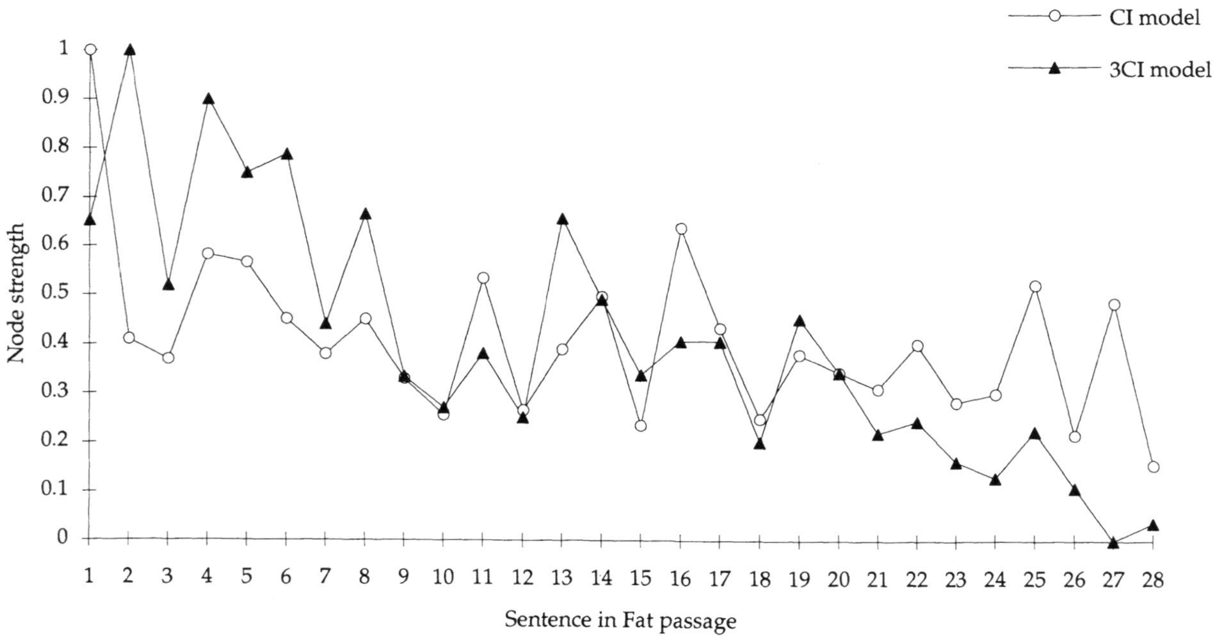

FIG. 3.8. Comparison of long-term memory node strengths resulting from the 3CI and the CI simulation runs on the Fat passage.

trend in the strengths, consistent with the method by which it holds propositions in working memory: those occurring earlier in the passage had a greater probability of participating in more cycles than did those occurring later in the passage. As a result, only two of the three kinds of fat received particularly high activations (sentences 14 and 19 but not 22 in Table 3.4) even though these sentences seemed to be main points. The CI model, because of its carry-over method, was less prone to the tendency toward lower activations for sentences later in the passage and it gave relatively high activation to the three types of fat. However, three other sentences that seem more like elaborations than main points also were relatively strong (sentences 16, 25, and 27; see Table 3.4).

The simulation models agreed with one another, but prediction of the recall data by each model was less satisfactory than their prediction for the Nationalism and Distance passages. The node-strength measure for the 3CI model correlated significantly with the adult recall data, but at a lower level than that obtained for Nationalism and Distance, $r = .42$, $p < .05$, $df = 26$. Neither of the CI measures were significantly correlated with adult recall; nor was 3CI's link-strength measure. Examination of the node strengths produced by 3CI graphed against the adult recall data (Fig. 3.9) indicated that there were two sentences on which the model predictions were very much out of line (sentences 16 and 24 in Table 3.4), and the relative ordering of the first three sentences was inaccurate. Besides these exceptions, the relative pattern of node strengths produced by 3CI was a reasonable match to the pattern observed in the recall data;[5] the removal of sentences 16 and 24 from the correlation increased it to $r = .56$, $p < .01$, $df = 24$.

Why did the 3CI model miss so badly on sentences 16 and 24 (see Table 3.4)? The model overpredicted sentence 16, which states that saturated fats are found in vegetable oils, because this sentence contains the superordinate concept *fat*, and it is a central node in the network active in working memory. There are two quite plausible reasons that none of the adults ever recalled this information. First, sentence 16 is inconsistent with other information in the passage (refer to Table 3.4, sentences 12, 19, 27, and 28). In addition, it is quite likely that this information contradicts adult readers' prior knowledge about saturated fat and healthy foods. In contrast, the model underpredicted sentence 24. Virtually all the adults recalled the specific information about the sources of the less harmful fats (e.g., salmon, mackerel, nuts, and vegetables). Again, we think that there are two reasons for the model's underpredictions. At this point in the passage, the nodes and links in this sentence compete for activation with a highly interconnected network that has been formed in processing the previous 23 sentences. For a new sentence to receive very high strength at this point, it would have to overlap on multiple arguments with many of the active nodes in the

[5]Note also that our qualitative examination (i.e., the relative patterns) indicated a very poor match of the recall and CI node-strength data. In general, node strengths for elaboration points were higher than those for the main points.

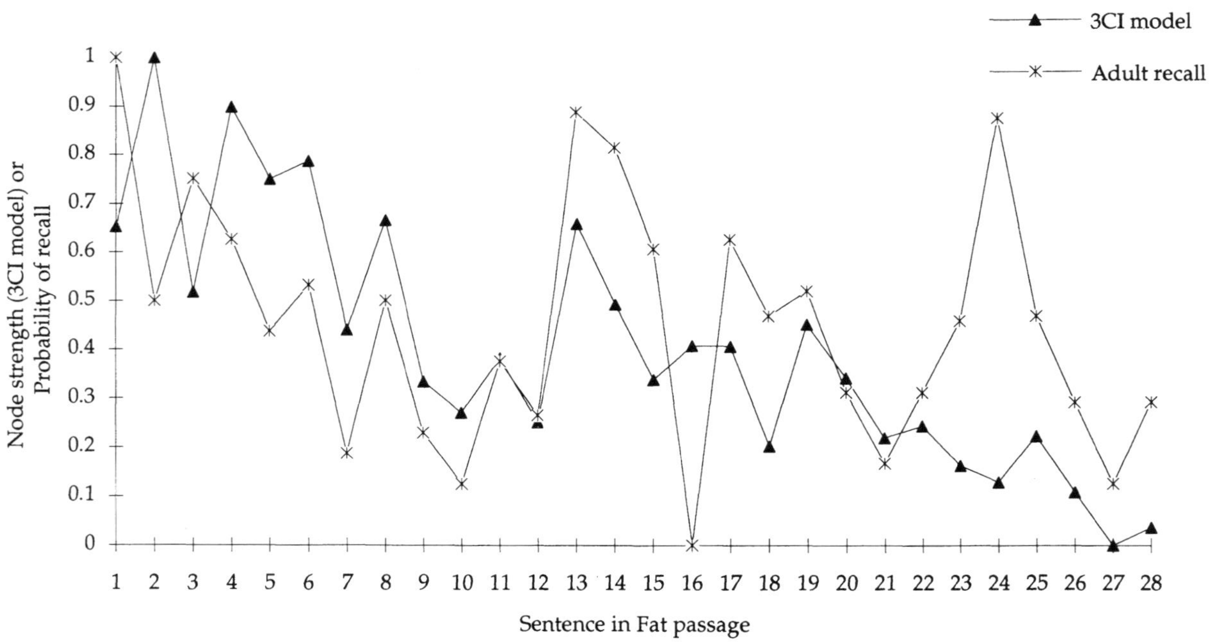

FIG. 3.9. Comparison of adult recall and long-term memory node strengths resulting from the 3CI simulation of the Fat passage.

network. There was insufficient overlap with the active nodes for the nodes in sentence 24 to achieve more than moderate activation. Second, the 3CI model has no prior knowledge and no basis for recognizing concrete or familiar events, locations, or objects. However, familiarity and concreteness are probably the reasons that the ideas in this sentence were recalled so well.

The failure of the model on sentences 16 and 24 points out the need for two mechanisms that are absent from 3CI. First, there needs to be a mechanism for detecting contradictions or inconsistencies in the information in a passage. Second, 3CI needs a way to appropriately activate prior knowledge, a limitation previously discussed by Goldman and Varma (1995).

The CI model predicted the children's recall data better than did the 3CI model, although the correlations were again relatively low. CI node strength and probability of recall by the children were correlated $r = .39$, $p < .05$, $df = 28$. CI link strength and the 3CI measures were not correlated with children's recall. The CI model also had been better at predicting children's recall of the Distance passage (see Goldman and Varma, 1995, for details). We attribute this to the bias that CI has for local processing. Children may retain less of the overall text structure than do adults; hence, a model that utilizes a more local, buffer-clearing procedure produces a better fit to the data than one that is based on a dynamic working memory model. Despite the level of the correlations, when we examined the patterns of node strength for the CI model and for the 3CI model against the children's recall (not shown), there were sections of the text for which the patterns of recall and node strengths were relatively similar.

The "Sugar" Passage. As did the Fat passage, the Sugar passage contains multiple structures and potential superordinate concepts. A schematic of the content structure for the Sugar passage is shown in Fig. 3.10 and the sentences are given in Table 3.5. The initial part of the passage discusses the relationship between sugar, energy, and carbohydrates and introduces two types of sugar. The latter half of the passage discusses three ways in which processed sugar can be harmful to the body. Two of these ways are explained by relatively long causal chains. Elements within the causal chains overlap with some of the concepts mentioned in the beginning part of the passage.

The results of the simulations of the Sugar passage were similar to those for the Fat passage. The long-term memory measures for CI and 3CI were correlated with one another ($r = .42$, $p < .05$ for node strength, and $r = .78$, $p < .01$ for link strength). In addition, within each model the two long-term memory measures were significantly correlated ($r = .64$, $p < .01$ for CI, and $r = .89$, $p < .01$ for 3CI). The 3CI model nodes with the greatest strength, or whose node strengths were most differentiated from those of neighboring sentences, were those (a) from the beginning of the passage and (b) naming the harmful effects of processed sugar (i.e., sentences 13, 14, 18, 19, 25 from Table 3.5). Furthermore, sentences 16, 17, and 26 (see Table 3.5) had high node strengths relative to their neighboring sentences

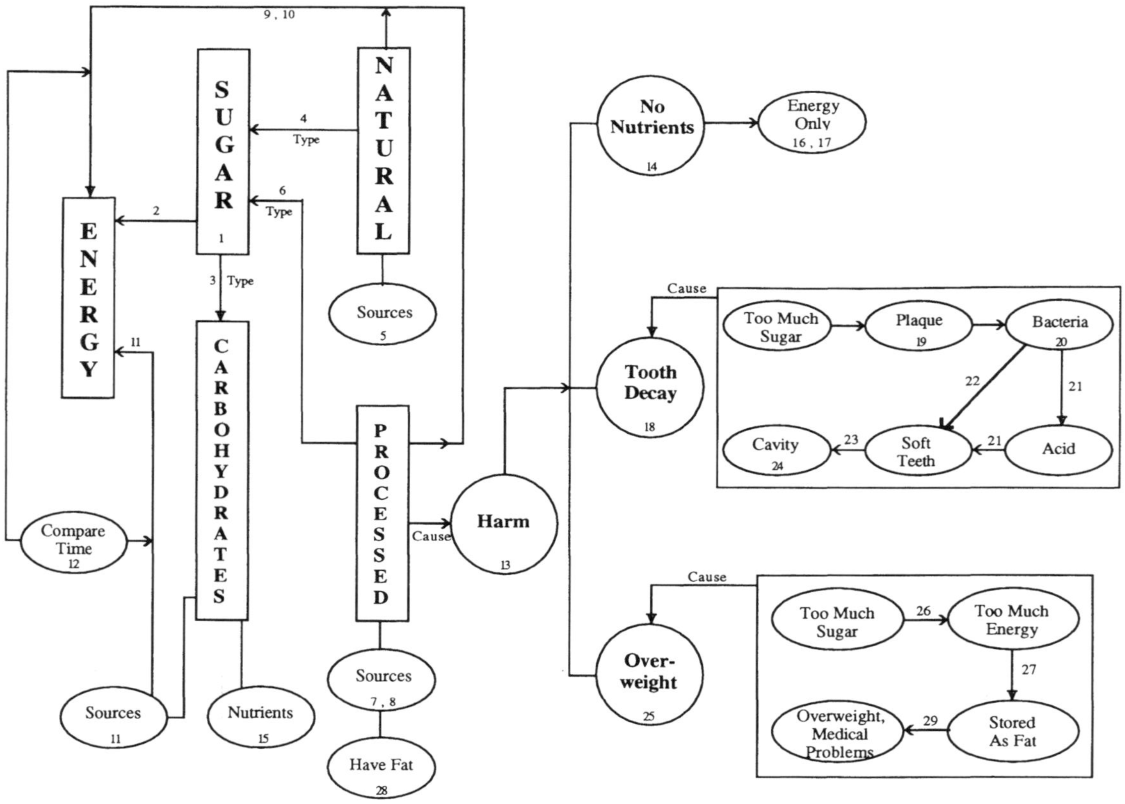

FIG. 3.10. Schematic content structure for the Sugar passage. (Numbers refer to sentences listed in Table 3.5.)

TABLE 3.5
Sentences of the Sugar Passage

1. Sugar in Our Diet
2. Sugar is an important part of our diet because it supplies energy.
3. It is a member of the group of food substances called carbohydrates.
4. There are many natural sources of sugar in the foods we eat.
5. Apples, carrots, and raisins all have a lot of sugar in them.
6. Many foods have another kind of sugar in them called processed sugar.
7. Some cereals, like Frosted Flakes and Cocoa Puffs, have processed sugar added to them.
8. Soft drinks and cookies also have a lot of processed sugar in them.
9. Natural sugar and processed sugar both provide us with energy almost as soon as we eat them.
10. But the energy we get from sugar does not last very long.
11. We also get energy from other kinds of carbohydrates such as those found in pasta, bread, and potatoes.
12. It takes us longer to feel the energy from these foods, but it lasts longer than the energy we get from sugar.
13. Eating too much processed sugar can be harmful to our health in three ways.
14. First, processed sugar does not contain any nutrients or vitamins.
15. Other kinds of carbohydrates, such as starch, do provide nutrients.
16. Sugar only supplies energy.
17. It is called an "empty" food.
18. Eating processed sugar causes tooth decay.
19. This is because it helps form plaque, a coating that builds up on the outside of our teeth.
20. Bacteria that are present in plaque feed on the sugar in food.
21. The bacteria produce acid and the acid softens the teeth.
22. Then the bacteria can get into the tooth.
23. Once inside, they eat away at the tooth and make a cavity or hole.
24. It must be fixed by a dentist.
25. Eating too much sugar can lead to being overweight.
26. When we eat too much sugar, we get more energy than we need.
27. Our bodies store the extra energy in the form of extra fat.
28. In fact, many foods that have a lot of processed sugar also contain fat.
29. Storing too much fat can lead to being overweight, heart disease, diabetes, and high blood pressure.

due to overlap with both *energy* and *sugar*, concepts central to the active network. For the most part, sentences in the causal chains that explained the harmful effects were not very strong. The node strength patterns for CI were similar, although CI showed a peak on one of the harmful effects (sentence 14) and the nodes in the causal chain for tooth decay were stronger than in the 3CI model.

Although 3CI and CI agreed with one another, they did not predict the recall data of either the adults or the children. Moreover, the patterns of node or link strengths were not qualitatively similar to the patterns of recall data. Examination of the recall pattern of the adults and children (see Fig. 3.11) indicated that the peaks in recall tended to be on very specific pieces of information, some with intuitively high affect value. Of the sentences that adults recalled most frequently (sentences 1, 5, and 24 in Table 3.5), the first was the title and the

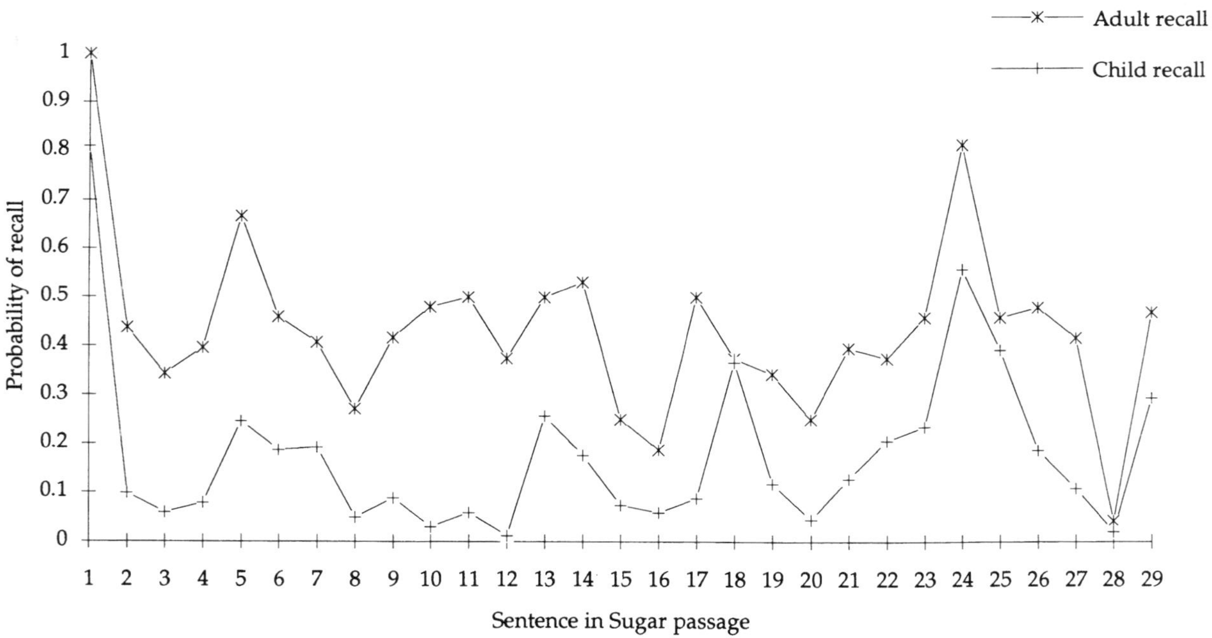

FIG. 3.11. Recall pattern for adults and children on the Sugar passage.

other two mentioned very specific and concrete objects and events (e.g., *Apples, carrots, and raisins contain a lot of sugar* and *Dentists have to fix cavities*). From the perspective of the 3CI simulation, the dentist and food-item sentences are elaborations of the main points having to do with tooth decay and sources of natural sugar, respectively. Due to the argument structure of the active network and the argument structure of the input propositions, the information in sentences 5 and 24 is viewed as rather unrelated to the main thrust of the passage, is not well-integrated with the previous propositions in the network, and thus receives very little activation. For adults and children, in contrast, the information in these sentences is highly salient perhaps because it is surprising (i.e., we don't usually think of fruit as containing sugar) or because the event is highly aversive (i.e., going to the dentist). As indicated in our discussion of the Fat passage, both models are clearly at a disadvantage in predicting recall of such a passage without having a way to capitalize on prior knowledge.

Evaluation of the Results of the Simulation Modeling

As we indicated earlier, simulation models are informative from two perspectives: The first is what they tell you when they do predict behavioral data and the second is what they tell you when they don't predict behavioral data. In terms of our simulation modeling to date, we found that embedding CI in a dynamic working memory model provided certain advantages over a fixed-buffer model of working memory. In particular, the dynamic model formulates a superordinate concept (or set of concepts) early in the passage if at all possible. This superordinate drives further processing and formation of the network: As new propositions enter working memory, those that connect with the identified superordinate node are more centrally incorporated into the network than those that do not overlap. The consequence is that for passages with certain content structures, the model is capable of generating a macrostructure or global discourse structure that has fidelity to that which human readers may be creating. The kind of content structure from which 3CI can generate a global discourse structure is one in which there is a clear hierarchical structure to the information (e.g., a *description–example* relationship among many of the sentences) and a principled occurrence of the superordinate concept. As content structures begin to include nonhierarchically organized topics that are interconnected and connected to a superordinate concept, it becomes increasingly difficult for 3CI to isolate a global discourse structure. In contrast, in the fixed-buffer CI model where there is no mechanism for keeping a longer passage "history" in working memory, even crude global discourse structures are not constructed, and local overlaps tend to dominate processing.

There is a clear down side to the way that 3CI constructs the network in terms of the effects that the early network has on processing of the subsequent text. The stronger and more coherent the initial network becomes, the harder it is for any new information to enter the network. Consequently, information later in a passage tends to receive lower activation than does information that is temporally earlier in the passage. The four passages that we analyzed are not terribly long in comparison to the universe of informational text. It somehow seems unrealistic that the kind of primacy bias that our current 3CI environment exerts is correct. In contrast, CI with a fixed buffer is driven almost completely by local processing and, thus, makes fewer strength differentiations among propositions. Therefore, for texts with a nonhierarchical content structure, the fixed buffer may lead to a better fit with the data.

The need to provide other capabilities beyond those of 3CI is clear. For example, one reason 3CI predicted recall of the nutrition passages so poorly was that the human data indicated high recall of very specific and concrete details, reminiscent of the phenomena observed by Garner and dubbed the *seductive detail effect* (e.g., Garner, Gillingham, & White, 1989). The CI class of models discussed here, including 3CI, is very unsophisticated with respect to semantic information, prior knowledge, and strategies for linking propositions. Argument overlap and propositional embedding are the mechanisms for generating connections and network structures. The limitations of relying solely on these are apparent. There have been efforts to augment these linking mechanisms by including causal structure as a strategy in constructing the connection matrix for narratives (e.g., Kintsch, 1992). The addition of the causal strategy has improved prediction of the data, but the causal propositions have to be coded by hand by the researchers; there are no simulation models that can automatically generate the causal propositions. Furthermore, the models are provided with propositionalized input and, therefore, do not deal with word- or sentence-level processing. Hence, the interactions of processing at those levels with processing at the network-construction level (i.e., formation of the textbase) cannot be examined. These are issues that must be dealt with by a comprehensive model of text comprehension. (See Goldman & Varma, 1995, for further discussion of the limitations of the 3CI class of models.)

In the next section of the chapter, we discuss in more detail limitations of the current CI class of models. Based on these limitations, we suggest a conceptual design for a "smarter" model of comprehension and learning from informational text. The conceptual design is a sketch of a system comprised of five modules, four of which are language-processing modules, whereas the fifth is an executive that we call the Strategy Competition module. The four language-processing modules operate autonomously and interactively, as described later.

TOWARD A "SMARTER" MODEL OF COMPREHENSION AND LEARNING FROM INFORMATIONAL TEXT

Several capabilities must be added to "smarten up" our current class of CI models. These capabilities begin to bring back some of the mechanisms previously proposed as elements of a model of comprehension (cf. Kintsch & van Dijk, 1978; van Dijk & Kintsch, 1983). They also are consistent, however, with conceptual elements introduced into other CI-class models (e.g., Mannes & Kintsch, 1991). These capabilities include (a) access to prior knowledge in the domain of the passage, (b) knowledge of discourse and conventions for signaling different types of discourse structure, and (c) strategies for monitoring comprehension and responding flexibly to comprehension problems (cf. Goldman & Saul, 1990a; Lorch, 1989; Lorch & Chen, 1986; Lorch & Lorch, 1986). Because of advances in research on syntactic processing (see Perfetti & Britt, 1995), there is now sufficient information available to tackle parsing and the derivation of propositions from the surface structure of the text.

Our conceptual design for a "smarter" model includes four major language-processing modules (i.e., the lexical, syntactic, textbase, situation model modules) and a Strategy Competition module that acts as a general executive. These modules are necessary to deal with processing at multiple levels of language and make it possible to examine the impact of difficulties experienced at one level of language on processing and comprehension at other levels. This interaction, or competition for limited capacity resources, probably exerts a powerful effect on comprehension and learning from text by human readers. Models that do not provide a way to address these interactions and their effects in a capacity-constrained environment will come up short in terms of simulating the actual processing of textual information.

The Strategy Competition module regulates processing and allocation of resources to different processing activities, including allocation to its own activities. Each module provides information to the Strategy Competition module, which acts as the general executor. In this role, it uses knowledge of discourse structure; strategies for detecting and resolving comprehension problems, including gaps in coherence; and heuristics for redistributing working memory resources. One feature that our conceptual design permits is rereading. We think rereading is an important feature of a smarter model, in part because readers do a lot of rereading when they are not constrained by external conditions to read each sentence once, in forward order (cf. Goldman & Saul, 1990a). However, current CI class models have no mechanism to flexibly respond to comprehension demands. The Strategy Competition module is necessary to implement rereading and other forms of flexibility. The rationale for our smarter model of text comprehension is based on three limitations of the current CI models: reliance on propositionalized input, lack of prior knowledge, and inflexibility in reading strategies. These limitations are discussed in the context of our conceptual design for a smarter model following a discussion of some assumptions common to the language-processing modules.

General Assumptions That Underlie the Language Processing Modules

Each language processing module generates multiple candidate representations that compete with one another. The one for which there is the most evidence survives. Sources of evidence are other consistent elements within the module as well as consistent candidate representations being developed in other modules. The assumption of a relatively sloppy process of generating candidate representations from which a winner emerges contrasts with models that attempt to deterministically select the one correct interpretation. It is, however, consistent with the style of processing found in CI-class models. Our assumption of evidential, competitive processing may enable us to avoid many of the problems that plague more rigid, deterministic language-processing models.[6]

The language-processing modules function in a capacity-constrained environment. Each module has access to a unique and limited set of resources to support its processing needs and the representations it creates. A module's procedural knowledge specifies how new linguistic input and the emerging representations within it and in other modules trigger the creation of new representations. Representations within each module continuously compete for resources based on the evidence for their usefulness or validity. Because resources are limited, representations with consistently stronger evidence will draw resources away from competing representations in the module that have weaker support. Processing within a module strongly resembles processing in CI. Across modules, there is a strong interactive flavor reminiscent of the Reader and Capacity-Constrained Reader (CCReader) models developed by Just and Carpenter (1987, 1992): Representations in one module direct resources to consistent, and possibly supporting representations in other modules.

Given this processing blueprint for the language modules, the 3CAPS architecture becomes an ideal development environment. Limited processing resources map onto the capacity-constrained working memory of 3CAPS. In support of the division of resources between modules, 3CAPS includes the ability to partition working memory into separately constrained pools. The procedural knowledge which constructs and weights the representations of each module can be coded as productions.

There are two additional reasons to implement the language modules in 3CAPS. First, it is known to be capable of supporting major language models with similar architectural demands, notably Reader and CCReader (Just & Carpenter, 1987, 1992). In fact, the textbase module for our "smarter" model has been prototyped in 3CAPS in the form of 3CI. The second advantage of using 3CAPS is the recent addition of an architectural feature that most nonconnectionist architectures lack, namely, a settling criterion. In many production systems and in previous versions of 3CAPS, new input was processed until all productions completed their work and no longer satisfied their preconditions. This is a discrete stopping criterion. In contrast, 3CI forced us to develop a new stopping mechanism for 3CAPS: New input is processed until the total change

[6]The competition among candidate representations is similar to the Pandemonium model (Selfridge & Neisser, 1960). However, because the pandemonium is generated by competition among representations within a limited-capacity system and is managed by the Strategy Competition Model, the "smarter" model is more than a pandemonium model.

in activation across all working memory elements falls below some threshold. This is a graded stopping criterion because processing stops when its impact on working memory becomes minimal. The addition to 3CAPS of the settling mechanism was a crucial step toward implementing our "smarter" model and the CI, connectionist style of processing we believe important.

Generating the Textbase From the Surface Text: Lexical, Syntactic, and Textbase Modules

The current class of CI models operates on parsed, propositionalized input and has no mechanisms for generating those parses (e.g., Goldman & Varma, 1995; Kintsch, 1988; Kintsch & van Dijk, 1978; van Dijk & Kintsch, 1983). By finessing the issue of the derivation of the propositional representation (but see Kieras, 1989), this class of model fails to capture an important source of comprehension difficulty. Protocol data from adults and children indicate that approximately 75% of comprehension problems occur at pre-propositional levels, that is, at word and surface-structure phrase levels (Goldman, Coté, & Saul, in preparation; Saul, Coté, & Goldman, 1993). Readers often are strategic in their efforts to deal with these problems. Sometimes they reread the sentence but other times they read on in the text. They may reason about how information within the sentence is connected or about how the sentence relates to other information in the text. Predicting processing time will require that a smarter model have a mechanism that takes this level of language processing into account.

One implication of capacity-constrained comprehension models (e.g., Just & Carpenter, 1992) is that processing at lexical and syntactic levels can affect processing at the propositional and situation model levels in important ways (cf. MacDonald, Just, & Carpenter, 1992). Previous models of comprehension have focused on one or two levels of language, but rarely on the interactive effects of processing at all levels in a complete model of comprehension and representation of text, even if those effects occur late in the process (e.g., Gernsbacher, 1990; Just & Carpenter, 1992; Kieras, 1982; Kintsch, 1988; Kintsch & van Dijk, 1978; van Dijk & Kintsch, 1983). A major issue that bears investigation is how resources are allocated to processing at the various levels of language, and the impact of difficulties at one level on processing at the other levels.

The conceptual design of the lexical, syntactic, and textbase modules is consistent with the CI and connectionist processing style that characterizes our current 3CI simulation model. Specifically, the lexical module would operate similarly to the lexical portions of Reader and CCReader (Just & Carpenter, 1987, 1992), except that the lexicon would be organized in terms of semantic fields (cf. Barsalou, 1992). Multiple senses of a word could be activated and compete with each other. Sense selection could be influenced by other modules. For instance, the textbase and situation model modules could prime certain semantic fields in the lexicon, depending on the semantic content of their representations.

Similarly, the syntax module would generate multiple structural representations for the input string, operating in a manner roughly corresponding to a bottom-up chart parser (Allen, 1987). In a limited capacity environment, these representations would compete with one another for resources, based on the respective evidence for them. Evidence could come from developing representations in the syntax module and from developing representations in other modules.

In general, resource availability governs the life of alternative interpretations. In a situation in which few resources are available, the correct syntactic structure of a sentence could be displaced by another interpretation. Subsequently, a breakdown in local coherence would occur. This breakdown would be detected by the Strategy Competition module, which would then select the most appropriate repair strategy to rectify the problem.

In our smarter model, the current 3CI textbase-processing module would be enhanced by having available to it productions from the Strategy Competition module that would be responsible for bridging inferences (Haviland & Clark, 1974) and resolving anaphoric referents (see Singer, 1990, for a review). Propositional derivation would begin as soon as candidate lexical and syntactic interpretations of a sentence emerged. The possible phrase structures proposed by the syntax module would combine with the semantic features (e.g., animacy, verb tense) of the active lexical senses of each phrase head to produce a propositional representation.

Important interactions between the textbase module and the lexical and syntactic modules could occur. Propositions could direct activation to the lexical senses and syntactic phrases that supported them. Thus, if a proposition were reinforced by many other propositions through argument overlap and propositional embedding, the activation it directed to supporting lexical and syntactic representations could sustain them even in the face of contradictory new words. This top-down feedback would work in the other direction as well: As lexical and syntactic interpretations gained or lost activation, depending on whether they could accommodate future words in the sentence, activations of the propositions that represented them would fluctuate.

Issues of Prior Knowledge: Implications for Processing and Representation

As we indicated earlier, CI class models are provided with only weak, associative methods for bringing prior knowledge to bear on comprehension (e.g., activation of high associates to the concepts reflected in the input propositions). Those associates that have high overlap with the set of propositions from the text being processed survive the integration process. Propositional networks (and coherence) are established through argument overlap and propositional embedding. Unless synonymy is coded by hand, CI and 3CI models will not recognize it. Furthermore, the applicability and success of argument overlap and propositional embedding as the sole determinants of coherence varies depending on the structure of the text, as illustrated by the work reported in this chapter, as well as the work of others. Hand coding causal propositions and introducing them into the network or hand selecting certain propositions to receive additional activation because they are important or have some other special status in the text (Otero & Kintsch, 1992) often increases the predictive ability of the models (see Goldman & Varma, 1995; Kintsch, 1992; Tapiero & Denhière, 1995). However, because these elements are introduced by the researcher, the impact of them on the actual processing and utilization of working memory resources remains hidden.

If they are to address the knowledge problem, smarter models also will need to take advantage of (a) knowledge of discourse structure and rhetorical predicates that signal it (Goldman & Saul, 1990a, 1994; Lorch, 1989; Meyer, 1975), and (b) strategies for monitoring and repairing comprehension problems when comprehension falters, including methods for differentiating acceptable from unacceptable breaks in coherence. As noted previously, the symbolic architecture of 3CAPS supports the plausible operation of linking rules based on competition among structures for different kinds of informational text.

The operation of all four language-processing modules is affected by assumptions about prior knowledge and how it operates in processing text and constructing organized memorial representations. For example, the propositions that are connected in the textbase depend on how the lexicon is organized and what overlap is recognized. Based on our experiences in hand coding propositions, we anticipate that the lexicon will need to be organized in terms of families of grammatically and conceptually related lexical items, consistent with semantic field notions (cf. Barsalou, 1992), as mentioned earlier. The importance of particular propositions will be affected by what is known about discourse structure. The module most affected by assumptions about prior knowledge undoubtedly will be the module that constructs a situation model. Although it is clear that a smarter model needs to be capable of constructing a situation model, at this point in our work we have only begun to consider how situation model construction might occur. We offer only a few speculations about this module here.

Situation Model Module. The primary mechanism for constructing the situation model will likely be an inferential one, with inferences being made on the basis of activated prior knowledge and the textbase. These inferences might include summaries across propositions in the textbase that are based on rules such as those proposed by van Dijk and Kintsch (1983), as well as propositions from prior knowledge that have become activated during processing. Once inferences are made, they would activate or be activated by other inferences consistent with them. Over time, mutually activating clusters of inferences would form and singular ones would be displaced. In making these inferences between prior knowledge and the textbase, our smarter model would rely on knowledge in the domain and knowledge of discourse structures, including surface text cues to these structures.

Our smarter model would need to "know" some set of passage-relevant and passage-irrelevant content structures, as well as discourse structures.[7] The process of using the discourse knowledge might proceed as follows: Productions of the situation-model module could activate the discourse structures that appear relevant to the content of the text being read. Activation would be based on rhetorical devices, including the title, and key words that signal description, causality, comparison, and so forth. If a fragment of the text triggers one of these productions, discourse structures would be instantiated for the specific passage to the degree possible in the segment of working memory available for the situation model. Other productions would attempt to fill other slots in the developing global passage structure with propositions from the textbase (see Graeser, Singer, & Trabasso, 1994).

A similar process might occur with content structures: Productions in the situation model module could examine the propositions of the textbase and the active discourse structures, and use knowledge of rhetorical devices to instantiate activated content structures or activate new content structures as appropriate. The Strategy Competition module would regulate the search for cues and evaluate the evidence for particular structures. Our conceptual design ameliorates issues of inflexibility in the use of prior knowledge through the mechanism of activation of multiple content structures and their competition with one another.

The textbase and situation model modules would interact when propositions reinforced the activations of the structures in which they filled slots. Similarly, the structures would reinforce the activations of propositions that satisfy slot values. Because the pool of working memory resources available for the situation model is constrained, content and discourse structures that are unable to fill more than a few of their slots would lose activation to those that are maximally consistent with propositions of the textbase and other structures.

Although we have no demonstration proof for the viability of our speculations about how a situation model module might operate in either a smarter simulation model or in a human reader, we are convinced that the specification of such a module is necessary for a comprehensive model. It is difficult to imagine a comprehensive model that does not have a way to deal with the acquisition of new information and formation of updated knowledge structures as a result of reading informational text. In the next section, we consider some additional issues related to the acquisition of new information and the need for a module that acts as executive for our smarter model.

The Strategy Competition Module: CEO of a "Smarter" Model

We conceptualize the Strategy Competition module as having two important sets of functions. The first set of functions relates to comprehension monitoring,

---

[7]We use the term *structure* here in as neutral a way as possible with respect to the type of structure. At this point, we are not partial to any of the more specific terms that might be used in its place, such as *frame* or *schema*.

the use of prior knowledge, and interactions among the language-processing modules. The second set was mentioned in our descriptions of the language processing modules; namely, the redistribution of working memory resources in response to (a) demands from the different modules and (b) evaluation of competing senses, parses, representations, and inferences generated by the lexical, syntactic, propositional textbase, and situational modules, respectively.

The first set of functions implements the Strategy Competition Model proposed by Goldman and Saul (1990a) to account for individual flexibility in reading. In accounting for this flexibility, the Strategy Competition Model includes several components that are involved in comprehension: (a) knowledge of rhetorical devices for signalling topic change, importance, and global organization; (b) knowledge of discourse schemata for achieving global coherence; (c) processes to achieve local coherence, including those that repair detected comprehension problems; and (d) monitoring and evaluation processes. These components generate a variety of comprehension strategies that compete with one another. Monitoring and evaluation processes regulate thresholds for determining the strategies for which there is sufficient evidence to "fire." (See Goldman & Saul, 1990a, for additional details.)

The intent is for the Strategy Competition module to implement the foregoing components as a set of productions. Thus, these productions "know about" rhetorical devices for signaling topic change and importance; detect comprehension problems at the lexical, syntactic, and propositional levels, including fragmentation of the textbase; implement repair strategies that correct these problems; and evaluate the performance of these repair strategies.

Here we provide an extended example of how such a module might function. If the propositions generated by the current sentence do not overlap well with the existing textbase, different productions in the Strategy Competition module would assess the cause of the problem. Productions that make bridging inferences, check for anaphoric reference, and look for synonymy relations are examples of the kinds of problems and resolutions that would be relevant. Productions that interpret structural cues in the input could also be activated by the nonoverlap in the textbase. For example, if the current sentence began a new paragraph, its propositions might discuss a different topic than did propositions that had already been read. In this case, a production would fire and increase the activation of a *continue reading* strategy, the goal of which is to connect the propositions of the current sentence (i.e., the topic sentence) with the propositions of the remaining sentences in the paragraph. (See Goldman, Varma, & Ortega, 1992, for a first approximation to such a system.) Another production could suggest connecting the current sentence with the propositions of the thesis sentence of the passage, because each paragraph should relate to this sentence. This could be done by skimming to the thesis sentence, rereading it, and returning to the paragraph. Extensive rereading might be necessary if the thesis sentence could not be located easily. Other strategies could also suggest solutions to a lack of coherence in the textbase: reread the sentence in case the propositions extracted the first time were incorrect; reread the previous sentence if its propositions were no longer present in working memory; and so on. The strategy with the most evidence (as measured by the activation of its condition elements) would be executed. Other productions would monitor its progress and suggest alternative strategies if it fails.

The redistribution of working memory resources by the Strategy Competition module may be important for dealing with a problem we mentioned in discussing the results of the simulation modeling: 3CI has a tendency for initial propositions in the passage to accrue large amounts of activation, making it difficult for new input to survive the settling process. If a set of propositions occurring at the beginning of the passage has a large degree of argument overlap, a fairly tightly knit network of propositions results. This network tends to pull activation toward it and away from new input. Only new input that has high overlap with the network can break through and become part of the network. Whereas the relationship between a tightly connected set of propositions and new input may account for the frequently observed primacy effects, it has serious implications for incorporating prior knowledge in text processing. Prior knowledge is likely to reflect a tightly connected network of associates. Therefore, there is the danger that this prior knowledge will swamp the new information, creating a situation in which, regardless of what a text says, updating fails to occur. Such a situation may account for the fact that what people read often fails to affect misconceptions or prior beliefs.

We discussed previously the tendency of tightly connected networks to lock out new input. We think that a reasonable solution to this problem is to adjust the amount of working memory resources allocated to maintaining a network as compared to processing new input. We have manipulated the allocation biases, but these manipulations were quite simplistic in that differential allocation parameters were applied through the entire simulation. The results of these simulations have been encouraging in that more of the information later in the passage accrued greater strength, but the improvement in predictability of behavioral recall data was not substantial. A smarter model will need to deal with changing allocation biases over the course of the entire passage. This will require executive control strategies such as monitoring and evaluation. These control strategies would regulate the allocation of capacity to new and old information, shifting priorities in response to factors such as comprehension problems or particularly difficult sections of text. In this manner, we will be able to establish a working memory that is responsive to fluctuating needs of the comprehension system.

SUMMARY AND CONCLUSIONS

In this chapter, we provided evidence of the advantages of embedding the Construction-Integration model in a capacity-constrained environment, creating 3CI. The effect of embedding CI in a resource-limited working memory architecture is that the model retains more of a history of the passage as it comprehends successive sentences. This difference leads 3CI to produce a pattern of node and link strengths that identifies superordinate concepts relatively early and maintains them throughout subsequent processing of the passage. The 3CI model (and for that matter the CI model) predicts behavioral recall data best for hierarchically structured passages in which the superordinate concept has something of a privileged occurrence in the main points of the passage. The passages on which the simulation models performed best were about somewhat abstract concepts that readers might be expected to know relatively little about.

For passages with more complex content structures and with the same concepts occurring in many of the sentences, the 3CI model was able to predict qualitative features of recall. That is, the relative pattern of node strengths for the Fat passage matched the adult recall data, whereas the CI model was not able to do so. The CI model did, however, predict children's recall data better than the 3CI, a phenomenon that we think is due to children processing the text at a more local level than do adults. Finally, simulations were run on a fourth passage, Sugar, that had a complex content structure but relatively familiar information. Recall by adults and children appeared to be driven by prior knowledge and content familiarity. On this passage, the simulation models yielded poor predictions.

The results of these simulations, both the positive and the negative, shed light on the strengths and limitations of the current 3CI class of models. Based on the limitations suggested by the results of the modeling, as well as related research, we proposed the conceptual design of a smarter class of models that will be able to more adequately simulate comprehension and learning. The smarter class of models assumes a capacity-constrained working memory environment. The limitations of the current 3CI class of models suggest the need to introduce prior knowledge and mechanisms for deriving propositional textbases from the input text. A primary motivation for the proposal of a CI model was the apparent rigidity of schema-driven processing and its failure to respond adequately to new contexts (Kintsch, 1988; Kintsch et al., 1993). To avoid such rigidity and introduce prior knowledge, our conceptual design postulates a mechanism that allows for activation of multiple knowledge structures, as well as multiple syntactic, lexical, textbase, and situation model structures. The multiple representations compete with one another for resources; they also can provide mutually facilitative evidence across modules. This process is monitored and evaluated by a Strategy Competition module, a primary goal of which is to regulate the allocation of resources to different language activities and ensure flexibility in the processing of informational text.

APPENDIX: SENTENCES IN THE DISTANCE PASSAGE

1. Distance is simply the space between two points.
2. Measured with a standard unit such as the kilometer or mile, the result is called absolute distance and is what most persons probably think of when they think of distance.

3. However, there is also something called relative distance, which is when absolute distance is influenced by other factors.
4. There are a number of factors that affect distance measurement.
5. Economic distance is measured in relation to the cost of movement from one place to another.
6. There is a cost involved in any movement, in terms of either money or energy.
7. The cost of shipping something by water is usually about one-tenth the cost over land, despite the fact that land routes are usually shorter.
8. Distance can be measured relative to time.
9. Maps that use travel time instead of mile markers as the units of measure distort the usual spatial relations among locations.
10. Travel time from a single point, such as the central business district, to a location 10 miles north may be the same as travel time to a location 30 miles south.
11. Psychological distance is measured relative to our perceptions, which may vary.
12. What may seem like a long trip to some individuals may seem short to others.
13. Even the same route going and coming can seem different to a single traveler, depending on road conditions, time of day, or anticipation of the end of the trip.
14. Distance can be measured relative to direction of movement.
15. When 2 points are located at different elevations, movement from point A to point B may not be as easy as from B to A.
16. The mileage between the points may be equal but uphill movement is harder than downhill.
17. Distances in geographic space can seem longer due to friction with obstacles.
18. For example, large crowds or heavy traffic are considered friction because they slow down our movement.
19. Often we are willing to travel farther in order to reduce friction, such as when we go to a suburban mall rather than to a downtown store to avoid traffic and crowds.

REFERENCES

Allen, J. (1987). *Natural language understanding.* Menlo Park, CA: Benjamin/Cummings.

Barsalou, L. W. (1992). Frames, concepts, and conceptual fields. In A. Lehrer & E. F. Kittay (Eds.), *Frames, fields, and contrasts: New essays in semantic and lexical organization* (pp. 27–74). Hillsdale, NJ: Lawrence Erlbaum Associates.

Coté, N., Goldman, S. R., Gjellstad, L., Keeton, J., Millican, C. (1994, November). *Children's use of prior knowledge and experience in understanding informational text on nutrition*. Paper presented at the annual meeting of the MSERA, Nashville, TN.

Fletcher, C. R., & Bloom, C. P. (1988). Causal reasoning in the comprehension of simple narrative texts. *Journal of Memory and Language, 27*, 235–244.

Garner, R., Gillingham, M. D., & White, C. S. (1989). Effects of "seductive details" on macroprocessing and microprocessing in adults and children. *Cognition and Instruction, 6*, 41–57.

Gernsbacher, M. A. (1990). *Language comprehension as structure building*. Hillsdale, NJ: Lawrence Erlbaum Associates.

Goldman, S. R., Coté, N., & Saul, E. U. (in preparation). *Flexibility in the repair of comprehension problems*. Manuscript in preparation. Nashville, TN: Vanderbilt University.

Goldman, S. R., & Saul, E. U. (1990a). Flexibility in text processing: A strategy competition model. *Learning and Individual Differences, 2*, 181–219.

Goldman, S. R., & Saul, E. U. (1990b, November). *Paragraphing and task effects on reading strategies*. Paper presented at the meetings of the Psychonomics Society, New Orleans, LA.

Goldman, S. R., & Saul, E. U. (1994). *Effects of paragraphing and task on comprehension*. Manuscript submitted for publication.

Goldman, S. R., & Varma, S. (1995). CAPping the construction-integration model of discourse comprehension. In C. Weaver, S. Mannes, & C. Fletcher (Eds.), *Discourse comprehension: Models of processing revisited* (pp. 337–358). Hillsdale, NJ: Lawrence Erlbaum Associates.

Goldman, S. R., Varma, S., & Ortega, J. (1992). *Application of CAPS modeling to strategy competition and flexibility in discourse comprehension*. Final Report to Cognitive Science Program, Office of Naval Research. Nashville, TN: Vanderbilt University.

Graesser, A. C., Singer, M., & Trabasso, T. (1994). Constructing inferences during narrative text comprehension. *Psychological Review, 101*, 371–395.

Haviland, S. E., & Clark, H. H. (1974). What's new? Acquiring new information as a process in comprehension. *Journal of Verbal Learning and Verbal Behavior, 13*, 512–521.

Just, M. A., & Carpenter, P. A. (1987). *The psychology of reading and language comprehension*. Boston: Allyn and Bacon.

Just, M. A., & Carpenter, P. A. (1992). A capacity theory of comprehension: Individual differences in working memory. *Psychological Review, 99*, 122–149.

Kieras, D. E. (1980). Initial mention as a signal to thematic content in technical passages. *Memory and Cognition, 8*, 345–353.

Kieras, D. E. (1981). The role of major referents and sentence topics in the construction of passage macrostructure. *Discourse Processes, 4*, 1–15.

Kieras, D. E. (1982). A model of reader strategy for abstracting main ideas from simple technical prose. *Text, 2*, 47–18.

Kieras, D. E. (1989). An advanced computerized aid for the writing of comprehensible technical documents. In B. Britton & S. Glynn (Eds.), *Computer writing environments: Theory, research, and design* (pp. 143–168). Hillsdale, NJ: Lawrence Erlbaum Associates.

Kintsch, E., McNamara, D. S., Songer, N., Kintsch, W. (1992). *Revising the coherence of science texts to improve comprehension and learning I: Traits of mammals* (Tech. Rep. No. 92–03). Boulder: University of Colorado, Institute of Cognitive Science.

Kintsch, W. (1974). *The representation of meaning in memory*. Hillsdale, NJ: Lawrence Erlbaum Associates.

Kintsch, W. (1988). The role of knowledge in discourse comprehension: A construction-integration model. *Psychological Review, 95*, 163–182.

Kintsch, W. (1992). How readers construct situation models for stories: The role of syntactic cues and causal inferences. In A. F. Healy, S. M. Kosslyn, & R. M. Shiffrin (Eds.), *From learning theory to connectionist theory: Essays in honor of William K. Estes, Vol. II* (pp. 261–278). Hillsdale, NJ: Lawrence Erlbaum Associates.

Kintsch, W., Britton, B. K., Fletcher, C. R., Kintsch, E., Mannes, S. M., & Nathan, M. J. (1993). A comprehension-based approach to learning and understanding. In D. L. Medin (Ed.), *The psychology of learning and motivation: Advances in research and theory* (Vol. 30, pp. 165–214). NY: Academic Press.

Kintsch, W., & van Dijk, T. A. (1978). Toward a model of text comprehension and production. *Psychological Review, 85*, 363–394.

Kintsch, W., & Welsch, D. M. (1991). The construction-integration model: A framework for studying memory for text. In W. E. Hockley & S. Lewandowsky (Eds.), *Relating theory and data: Essays on human memory* (pp. 367–385). Hillsdale, NJ: Lawrence Erlbaum Associates.

Kintsch, W., Welsch, D., Schmalhofer, F., & Zimny, S. (1990). Sentence memory: A theoretical analysis. *Journal of Memory and Language, 29*, 133–159.

Kletzien, S. B. (1991). Strategy use by good and poor comprehenders reading expository text of differing levels. *Reading Research Quarterly, 26*, 67–86.

Lee-Sammons, W. H., & Whitney, P. (1991). Reading perspectives and memory for text—an individual differences analysis. *Journal of Experimental Psychology, 17*, 1074–1081.

Lorch, R. F., Jr. (1989). Text signaling devices and their effects on reading and memory processes. *Educational psychology review* (Vol. 1, pp. 209–234). NY: Plenum.

Lorch, R. F., & Chen, A. H. (1986). Effects of number signals on reading and recall. *Journal of Educational Psychology, 78*, 263–270.

Lorch, R. F., & Lorch, E. P. (1986). On-line processing of summary and importance signals in reading. *Discourse Processes, 9*, 489–496.

MacDonald, M. C., Just, M. A., & Carpenter, P. A. (1992). Working memory constraints on the processing of syntactic ambiguity. *Cognitive Psychology, 24*, 56–98.

Mannes, S. M., & Kintsch, W. (1991). Planning routine computing tasks: Understanding what to do. *Cognitive Science, 15*, 305–342.

Meyer, B. J. F. (1975). *The organization of prose and its effects on memory.* Amsterdam: North-Holland Publishing.

Otero, J., & Kintsch, W. (1992). Failures to detect contradictions in a text: What readers believe versus what they need. *Psychological Science, 3*, 229–235.

Perfetti, C. A., & Britt, M. A. (1995). Where do propositions come from? In C. Weaver, S. Mannes, & C. Fletcher (Eds.), *Discourse comprehension: Models of processing revisited* (pp. 11–34). Hillsdale, NJ: Lawrence Erlbaum Associates.

Saul, E. U., Coté, N., & Goldman, S. R. (1993, April). *Students' strategies for making tests make sense.* Paper presented at the annual meeting of the American Educational Research association, Atlanta.

Selfridge, O. G., & Neisser, U. (1960). Pattern recognition by machine. *Scientific American, 203*, 60–80.

Singer, M. (1990). *Psychology of language.* Hillsdale, NJ: Lawrence Erlbaum Associates.

Spilich, G. J., Vesonder, G. T., Chiesi, H. L., & Voss, J. F. (1979). Text processing of domain-related information for individuals with high and low domain knowledge. *Journal of Verbal Learning and Verbal Behavior, 18*, 275–290.

Tapiero, I., & Denhière, G. (1995). Simulating recall and recognition by using Kintsch's Construction-Integration Model. In C. Weaver, C. Fletcher, & S. Mannes (Eds.), *Discourse comprehension: Strategies and processing revisited* (pp. 211–232). Hillsdale, NJ: Lawrence Erlbaum Associates.

Trabasso, T., & Sperry, L. (1985). Causal relatedness and importance of story events. *Journal of Memory and Language, 24*, 595–611.

Trabasso, T., & van den Broek, P. W. (1985). Causal thinking and the representation of narrative events. *Journal of Memory and Language, 24*, 612–630.

van den Broek, P. (1989). Causal reasoning and inference making in judging the importance of story statements. *Child Development, 60*, 286–297.

van den Broek, P. (1990). The causal inference maker: Towards a process model of inference generation in text comprehension. In D. A. Balota, G. B. Flores d'Arcais, & K. Rayner (Eds.), *Comprehension processes in reading* (pp. 423–445). Hillsdale, NJ: Lawrence Erlbaum Associates.

van Dijk, T. (1987). Episodic models of discourse processing. In R. Horowitz & S. J. Samuels (Eds.), *Comprehending oral and written language* (pp. 161–196). San Diego: Academic Press.

van Dijk, T., & Kintsch, W. (1983). *Strategies of discourse comprehension*. New York: Academic Press.

Vipond, D. (1980). Micro- and macroprocesses in text comprehension. *Journal of Verbal Learning and Verbal Behavior, 19*, 276–296.

Whitney, P., Ritchie, B. G., & Clark, M. B. (1991). Working memory capacity and the use of elaborative inferences in text comprehension. *Discourse Processes, 14*, 133–145.

Yochum, N. (1991). Children's learning from informational text: The relationship between prior knowledge and text structure. *Journal of Reading Behavior, 23*, 87–108.

CHAPTER

4

Effects of Prior Knowledge on Text Comprehension: A Simple Modeling Approach

Suzanne Mannes
Marie St. George
University of Delaware

Prior knowledge vitally affects everything we do, from perceiving and imaging to text comprehension and creative problem solving. It should not be surprising to find, therefore, that the organization of this knowledge from long-term memory has a great influence on the outcome of our experiences. The importance of this a priori organization, or the ability to organize thoughts as they are encountered, has been well documented in the text comprehension literature.

In a classic study, Bransford and Johnson (1972) demonstrated that providing a thematic title to participants prior to reading an ambiguous passage has dramatic effects on later recall. In their study, those who read the titles recalled approximately twice as much as those who read the ambiguous passage without the benefit of its title. This highlighted the power of a schema to activate relevant knowledge prior to the reading of a text and thereby produce better comprehension of that text.

Anderson and Pichert (1978) showed how prior knowledge can influence what readers choose to recall about a text. Texts were presented which had two different interpretations. In one text, the main character could be a prisoner or a wrestler, whereas in the second text, an event could be interpreted as a card game or a music concert. Anderson and Pichert showed the paragraphs to groups of wrestlers and music students, and found that their subsequent recall was based on the interpretation they chose while reading the passage. The music students interpreted the first text as being about a prisoner and the second text as being about a music concert. In contrast, the wrestlers interpreted the first text as being about a wrestler and the second text as being about a card game. Clearly, comprehension of a text depends upon the prior knowledge of the reader.

Van Dijk and Kintsch (1983) have proposed a theory of text comprehension in which the role of prior knowledge is explicit. According to their theory, the reader tries to acquire three levels of internal representation during comprehension. The reader is viewed as taking an active role in the comprehension process, allocating different amounts of his or her limited resources to the construction of one or more of these levels of representation.

The most basic level is the *verbatim representation*, which is derived directly from the surface structure of the text. If this representation is present, the reader will be highly successful at discriminating between similar statements which may or may not be from the text. This virtual mirror image of the text content is subject to rapid decay (Sachs, 1967).

The *textbase representation* is a more stable copy of the textual information. It is based on the concepts and meanings of the text, and contains both a *microstructure* and *macrostructure*. The microstructure reflects the semantic details of the text, whereas the macrostructure reflects the main ideas that tie together larger sections of the text.

The final level of representation is referred to as the *situation model*. This representation is not solely textbased, but rather is a combination of prior knowledge, including the goals and attitudes of the reader, and text information. The situation model reflects the successful integration of new information with old information. This type of representation is useful in situations that require problem solving or divergent thinking; however, when a precise replication of the previously read text is required, the situation model may not be helpful. The textbase and verbatim representations contain purely textbased information, which is good for recall tasks, whereas the situation model contains information regarding what the text is about. Therefore, with the situation model, the lines that separate new information from old information can be blurred.

These different levels of representations have been supported by behavioral data (e.g., Kintsch, Welsch, Schmalhofer, & Zimny, 1990; Mannes & Kintsch, 1987; Schmalhofer & Glavanov, 1986). By providing different goals for readers, Schmalhofer and Glavanov (1986) affected the nature of the information comprehended and later recalled by readers. Readers who were told that they would have to summarize the passage after reading it had better verbatim and textbase representations than did those readers who were told that they should read the passage to acquire knowledge. The knowledge acquisition readers, although performing poorly on tasks requiring verbatim and textbase representations, performed well on tasks requiring a situation model. Thus, the group that was told that they would be summarizing the passage excelled in tasks requiring memory retrieval, whereas the group that was told to read for knowledge acquisition excelled in tasks requiring complex problem solving. Therefore, the instructions given before reading a passage can serve as a type of prior knowledge, and the text representation constructed and subsequent performance can differ substantially as a function of this knowledge.

It has been shown that by manipulating the structure of the information provided prior to the reading of a text, while keeping the content of the information constant, remarkable differences in both memory for the text and creative problem-solving abilities emerge (Mannes & Kintsch, 1987). Participants were shown advance organizers in the form of an outline prior to reading a text about the use of microbes in industry. One group studied an outline that was consistent in structure with the text, whereas another group studied an outline that was inconsistent with the structure of the text. It is important to note that the information in both of these outlines was the same; only the order of the information was changed. The consistent outline presented the information in an order that was consistent in perspective with the order in which the information would appear in the text. The inconsistent outline was organized according to an encyclopedia entry on the characteristics of microbes. After studying one of the outlines and reading the text, participants were given two groups of tests. Participants were asked to summarize the text, verify the truth of a number of statements from the text, and recall a particular paragraph from the text. These three tasks comprised the memory retrieval group of tests. Participants also were asked to verify inferences based on the text content, suggest how to solve a serious problem that had been highlighted in the text, and rank alternative experimenter-generated solutions to this problem. These three tasks made up the problem-solving portion of the tests. Participants who studied the consistent outline excelled at the tasks requiring memory retrieval, whereas the participants who studied the inconsistent outline excelled at the tasks requiring inferences and problem solving.

These results can be interpreted in the context of the levels of representation proposed by van Dijk and Kintsch (1983). The group who read the inconsistent outline had to reconcile the new perspective of the text with the old information that they read in the outline and modify their situation model accordingly. As a result, few resources remained for strengthening the memory trace for the textbase information. In contrast, the group who read the consistent outline had resources available to strengthen their textbase representation because the text information was readily integrated into the existing, text-appropriate, situation model. Hence, during reading of the text, construction of the situation model received proportionately more resources for the inconsistent outline group resulting in higher performance on the problem-solving tasks, whereas the textbase representation received proportionately more resources for the consistent outline group resulting in higher performance on the direct memory-retrieval tests.

One interpretation of these findings is that the nature of the outline read prior to the text affected the organization of the information in the network of long-term memory. Depending on the way in which information is presented, different patterns of activation or interconnectivity between concepts may result. Perhaps because the inconsistent outline group had more work to do integrating the perspective of the outline with that of the text, this resulted in a greater number of connections between concepts. These different patterns of interconnectivity may have been what was reflected in the performance differences between the inconsistent and consistent outline groups.

EXPERIMENTAL INVESTIGATION

In an attempt to garner support for the theoretical interpretation proposed by Mannes and Kintsch (1987), two subsequent studies were performed by Mannes (1994). The studies involved the same learning materials as did the Mannes and Kintsch studies; that is, the article on the use of microbes in industry and two outlines that presented the same content from either the same perspective as the text (i.e., the consistent outline) or from a perspective different from the text (i.e., the inconsistent outline). In each of these studies, after reading the outline and the text, the participants completed certain tests.

Study 1

After studying one of the two outlines (or no outline for a control group) and reading the text, participants in this study completed three tests: a summarization of the article task, a cued-response task, and a network task. Summaries were completed first and the order of the other two tasks was counterbalanced. For the cued-response task, the participants were asked to write down the first thing that came into their minds after reading a cue. There were 10 cues, and each cue was a simple statement representing an idea from the experimental materials (e.g., *Wild microbes are healthy*). This task was designed to assess whether the participants receiving the different outlines had constructed qualitatively different domain representations.

In the network task, participants were presented with a piece of paper containing five circles. They were instructed to write the five most important things that they had learned in the experiment, one in each circle. Following this, they were instructed to draw lines between the circles or ideas that they thought were related and to label the lines with a number between 0 (*not very related*) and 2 (*very related*) to indicate the degree of relatedness between the items. This task also was designed to gauge differences, specifically with respect to differential degrees of connectivity in the underlying domain representations of the different outline groups.

Participants' responses to the summarization task were evaluated both quantitatively (i.e., in terms of how many propositions were produced) and qualitatively (i.e., in terms of the types of propositions that were produced and how well the essay was written). Summaries from all groups contained approximately the same number of text propositions. The summaries were equally well written and contained approximately the same number of main ideas from the text, regardless of outline condition. The summaries of the participants in the inconsistent outline condition, however, were more likely than the others to contain intrusions of material from the outline, which suggests that they had integrated the outline and text material to a greater extent.

In Mannes and Kintsch (1987), participants reading the inconsistent outline produced summaries that were structurally inferior to those of the participants reading the consistent outlines. However, one of the ways in which the summaries in that study were scored was by determining the degree to which the summary adhered to the same organization as the text. Understandably, those participants with the consistent outline produced summaries that more closely resembled the text organization. Because a good summary might not follow the text organization, that method of scoring was replaced with a scoring procedure that was designed to evaluate the quality of the summary, without considering the extent to which it represented the structure of the text. As a consequence of this change in scoring procedure, the results of the present study showed no differences in summary quality as a result of outline condition. This suggests that although additional resources might have been required to reconcile the new perspective of the text with the already existing situation model when it followed an inconsistently structured outline, all participants still were able to grasp the gist of the text. In fact, Mannes and Kintsch found that, on an immediate test, all participants produced approximately the same number of Level 1 propositions, regardless of outline condition. These are precisely the propositions that could be considered to be macropropositions and upon which an effective summary depends. Also, in accordance with the Mannes and Kintsch findings, the inconsistent outline participants in the current study were more likely to produce outline intrusions in their summaries than were the consistent outline participants.

The responses to the cued-response task were categorized as being one of three types: a *metastatement*, a *restatement*, or an *elaboration*. For example, consider the cue *Microbes are different sizes*. A response was scored as a metastatement if it had no direct, semantic relationship to the experimental materials (e.g., *That's interesting.*). A response was scored as a restatement if it was merely a repetition of a cue or a comment that added trivial details to the provided cue, (e.g., *Small and large microbes exist.*). A response was scored as an elaboration if it served to piece together ideas ulterior to the cue and from distinct locations in the experimental materials (e.g., *We can use strainers to separate different sized microbes.*). An analysis of the frequency with which these different statement types were produced by participants in the different outline conditions showed that participants in the inconsistent outline condition produced more elaborative responses than the average of the other two groups (i.e., the consistent and no outline conditions).

The responses from each group of participants were then examined with a sorting procedure in which, for each outline condition, a unique number of response classes was determined for each cue. Analyses showed that the participants reading the inconsistent outline produced more unique classes of responses than did the other two groups, on average.

The data from the network task were first scored in a quantitative manner to determine the number and strength of the links that had been drawn. There were no differences between the groups in terms of the number of links drawn between circles or the total or average weights that these links were assigned. Next, the responses to the network task were scored qualitatively in terms of their actual content. The responses contained within the nodes were divided into two classes: those that could be attributed to the text (text items), and those that only occurred in the outline (nontext items). Analyses showed that the inconsistent outline group produced a significantly greater number of nontext ideas than did both the consistent outline and no outline groups. Moreover, the former drew a larger number of links between text and nontext ideas than did both the consistent outline and no outline groups. This was true when the number of text-to-outline links was considered in absolute terms (i.e., the total number of links that were drawn from text to outline nodes), as well as when they were considered as a proportion of the total number of links drawn.

The cued-response and network data are consistent with the hypothesis that readers in the inconsistent outline group produced more varied connections between ideas in memory than did the consistent outline group and that the former participants had effectively integrated the text about the industrial use of microbes and the outline about the characteristics of microbes. The variety and idiosyncratic nature of the participants' responses in the network and cued-response tasks precluded a precise analysis of the differing degrees of relationship drawn between the text and outline material in the two outline groups. The second study, in which pairs of simple statements were presented to the participants in a relatedness task, was designed to permit this type of investigation.

Study 2

In a second experiment, Mannes (1994) investigated the quantitative nature of the links in readers' long-term memories. Participants were given a relatedness task after studying an outline (either consistent or inconsistent) and reading the text. The relatedness task involved judging the relatedness of pairs of simple statements presented on the computer screen by using values from 1 (*very unrelated*) to 6 (*very related*). Twenty items were chosen from the experimental materials: half represented the "characteristics" perspective by explicitly mentioning microbes and a related characteristic, whereas the other half represented the "industry" perspective by mentioning industrial processes and applications. These 20 items were presented randomly in all possible pairs (190) to participants who were asked to judge the relatedness of each pair quickly and without deliberation.

The observed relatedness ratings of the participants showed a reliable effect of outline condition. The inconsistent outline group rated the pairs as more related than did the consistent outline group. The average relatedness ratings for the pairs of statements was 3.52 for the inconsistent outline group compared to an average of 2.99 for the consistent outline group. Two relatedness values then were computed for each participant: one based on the responses to pairs in which both statements represented the same perspective (*within-perspective* pairs), and the other based on responses to pairs in which each statement represented one of the two perspectives (*between-perspectives* pairs). An analysis of these two relatedness values by outline condition showed a reliable interaction in which the inconsistent outline participants rated both types of pairs as equally related, but the consistent outline participants rated the within-perspectives pairs as more related than the between-perspective pairs.

This result lends support to the suggestion that those who read the inconsistent outline prior to the text made more interconnections between the microbes and industry information than did those who read the consistent outline. Those in the inconsistent outline condition rated the between-perspectives pairs as more related than did those in the consistent outline condition. In addition, the former failed to rate these pairs as less related than the within-perspectives pairs. Recall that this is consistent with the Mannes and Kintsch (1987) finding that readers who saw the inconsistent outline were better at integrating new information with old and solving problems that required divergent thinking. In that study, students who read the inconsistent outline were more likely than those who read the consistent outline to include facts about characteristics of microbes in their answers to the open-ended industry question they were asked. That this integration of perspectives took place during comprehension of the text in the current study, rather than at the time of testing, is supported by the fact that the inconsistent outline group made their relatedness judgments more rapidly than the consistent outline group.

Thus, those who read the inconsistent outline had more work to do when reading and studying the text material, however, this effort typically pays off. When readers are exposed to different organizations of some domain-related material, these multiple perspectives are integrated and provide a richer knowledge base for the reader.

THE GENERAL MODEL

A simulation based upon the Construction-Integration theory (Kintsch, 1988) was used to model the relatedness data from Study 2. In this simulation, long-term memory was represented as a network of interrelated statements, and spreading activation was used to activate and deactivate certain portions of the network. As described subsequently, different networks were constructed to represent the long-term memories of participants in the two outline conditions. The spread of activation was begun at identical locations in each of the networks, and, once the networks settled, the resulting patterns of activity were examined.

The relatedness data modeled are suggestive of a more interconnected network of the domain material for the inconsistent outline participants than for the consistent outline participants. The former rated all pairs of statements as more related, on average, than did the latter. We inferred that this meant that any given statement in long-term memory was directly related to more statements for the inconsistent outline participants than for the consistent outline participants. This forms the basis for our first prediction which, given our methods of determining the links between nodes in the simulation, suggests that there will be a larger number of connections among domain-related statements in the inconsistent outline participants' long-term memory network than in the consistent outline participants'.

This difference in perceived relatedness formed the basis for the second prediction in that once the spread of activation has begun, the network of the inconsistent outline participants should have, at any given point in time, more active nodes than that of the consistent outline participants. Moreover, the fact that the inconsistent outline participants made their judgments more quickly than the consistent outline participants, forms the basis for the third prediction, in that we expected the spreading activation phase of the simulation (i.e., the time it takes for a network to settle) to be shorter for the inconsistent outline than the consistent outline network.

Lastly, the reliable sentence-pair type (within- versus between-perspective pairs)-by-outline interaction provides the basis for the fourth prediction. Here, one would expect that, for the consistent outline network, the statements that become active would depend upon the place in the network in which the spread of activation was begun, but for the inconsistent outline network, the initial point of activation should not differentially activate within—versus between—perspectives nodes. For example, if the spread of activation is begun at a statement communicating the industry perspective within the consistent outline network, more industry (within-perspectives statements) than characteristics statements (between-perspectives statements) should become active. However, with the same starting point for activation spread, nodes representing both perspectives should be equally likely to become active in the inconsistent outline network.

A simulation (Mannes, 1990) based upon the Construction-Integration model of Kintsch (1988) was used to match the four predictions derived from these data. In this version of the model, it is assumed that a reader approaches a text, sentence-by-sentence, propositionalizing the text content as he or she proceeds. As subsequent sentences are encountered, the reader keeps in a short-term buffer some number of propositions that have been deemed important, and propositions that simultaneously occupy the buffer have the opportunity for relationships among them to be derived by the reader. These propositions, and the relationships among them, are then stored in long-term memory for future use. Propositions are added to the buffer, and relationships are derived, until the reader attempts to add an additional proposition to the buffer and finds that it is full. When this occurs, the new proposition replaces one of the earlier ones currently in the buffer, and reading continues. The resulting text representation stored in long-term memory is assumed to take the form of an associative network.

In this network, the nodes are representative of propositions that can be expressed as simple statements communicating one idea (e.g., *Microbes have shapes*), and the links are representative of the strength of the relationship between pairs of propositions. The links between the nodes are bidirectional. The links are not typed, but simply represent the degree of relationship between node contents. Because all the information contained within the experimental materials is internally consistent (i.e., there are no inherent contradictions or disaffirmations), all links are excitatory in nature.

In our model of the relatedness data, the nodes in the associative network consisted of the short statements that had served as the stimuli in the relatedness task. These were represented in a propositional format, with each proposition having a single predicate and two or more arguments. There were 20 nodes corresponding to the 20 statements, with a possible 190 links between them. These links were determined by the use of two different methods. First, as has been used extensively in past research with this class of model (e.g., Doane, Kintsch, & Polson, 1989; Mannes & Kintsch, 1987, 1991), the metric of *argument overlap* was used. Thus, all node pairs that shared a reference to a common argument were linked.

The second method of determining connectivity, *contiguity*, follows directly from our theoretical assertion that items that simultaneously occupy the short-term buffer may become related to each other. The notion of association based upon temporal contiguity is one of the fundamental laws of association and receives much support from past research claiming the importance of contiguity in determining associative relations among items (e.g., Bower, 1972). This method is described in detail subsequently.

For each prediction, sets of simulations were run in which different memory representations, one for each of the two outline-plus-text combinations, were first constructed. These were derived by using the connectivity processes described previously and took the form of associative networks. Next, four sets of simulations, one for each prediction, were run with each of the outline-plus-text networks. Each simulation consisted of 20 runs, such that the spread of activation was started at each of the 20 nodes once, and activation was allowed to flow throughout the network until it stabilized. The resulting activation values for each of the 20 nodes were then interpreted with respect to the four described predictions. The manner in which each of the individual networks was created is described in the following section.

Network Construction

Each statement from the relatedness task was represented in an extended, or complex, propositional format. Because these statements were generally simple sentences, this representation format resulted in propositions with a single predicate and two or more arguments. For example, the statement *Bacteria renew their own resources* could be represented as "renew bacteria resources." The connectivity among these propositions was determined, first by argument overlap, and then by contiguity. In determining connectivity based upon argument overlap, each proposition pair was searched for instances of shared arguments and, if they were found, a link was formed between the two nodes sharing a reference to the common argument. The determination of relationship based upon contiguity required substantially more steps.

First, the location of each proposition representing a statement from the relatedness task was identified in each of the outlines and in the text. Connectivity based upon contiguity was then determined by identifying situations in which one proposition followed another in each source. This resulted in two different sets of contiguity relationships: one based upon contiguity in the text, which was the same for both networks, and one based upon contiguity in the outline, which was different for each network. Thus for each outline-plus-text combination, any pair of propositions could have occurred contiguously in 0 (never following each other), 1 (following each other in either the text or the outline), or 2 (following each other in both the text and outline) instances.

Two parameters were associated with the derivation of these relationships, *contiguity persistence* and *instance*. Contiguity persistence reflects how far away from each other, in text distance, two propositions might occur but still have an opportunity to simultaneously occupy the short-term buffer and thus, become related to each other. This variable was intended to simulate short-term buffers of different sizes because the larger the buffer is hypothesized to be, the more likely it is to be simultaneously occupied by distant propositions.

Instance refers to how the strength of relationship is determined for two propositions that have been involved in a contiguous relationship more than once. For example, in the consistent outline and text, because they presented the microbes material from the same perspective, certain pairs of ideas followed each other (i.e., had a contiguous relationship) in both the outline and the text. One might argue that each occasion on which the two propositions simultaneously occupy the short-term buffer is equally important to the reader in developing their representation of the domain material. Alternatively, it might be argued that the degree of cognitive processing in which a reader engages when first encountering a relation between two propositions differs from the processes engaged during subsequent encounters (e.g., Ellis, Parente, & Walker, 1974). Thus, when contiguity between two propositions was experienced on two different occasions, two different parameter values could be used in deriving the strength of the relation between those propositions: one for the first instance of contiguity and another for the second instance. These parameter values were set as equal or unequal depending upon the simulation.

Because the method of argument overlap for determining relations between propositions is not sensitive to presentation order (all possible pairs of propositions are examined for occurrences of argument overlap), it results in the same set of connections for both outline-plus-text combinations. This is not true for contiguity persistence. This method of determining relationship strength is sensitive to presentation order and the surrounding context in which a proposition is encountered. As a consequence, it produces a different set of connections for each of the outline-plus-text combinations.

We report in the following sections the results from four sets of simulations in which two different levels of contiguity persistence (one paragraph and two paragraphs) and two levels of instance (equal and unequal) were varied.

Activation Spread

Activation is spread throughout the associative network via standard vector-matrix multiplication procedures. These procedures have been used extensively in the past (e.g., Doane, Kintsch, & Polson, 1989; Kintsch, 1988; Mannes & Kintsch, 1991) and entail multiplying an initial activation vector by a matrix of values that represent the degree of relation between all possible pairs of statements in the associative network. In these sets of simulations, the initial activation vector was always comprised of a single one and 19 zeros, and, in each of the 20 simulations for each set, the spread of activation was started at a different node. Each multiplication results in a new activation vector and unchanged matrix. The resulting vector is normalized (i.e., all values are transformed proportionally such that they add to one) and it is compared element by element to the vector by which the matrix has just been multiplied. If the change in vector values is substantial, indicating continued activity flow, the new vector is used for the next vector-matrix multiplication cycle. This cycle repeats itself until the change in vector values from one multiplication to the next reaches a criterion set by the user, at which time the network is considered settled or stable.

Different aspects of the network can be interpreted during and after activation spread. For example, one may observe the number of multiplications that were necessary for the network to settle. Although there is not one-to-one mapping between settling time and judgment time, one can infer that faster judgments from participants are modeled by networks that settle faster. One also can observe the number of active nodes, both during the spread of activation and in the settled network, and infer that a greater number of active nodes is the simulation's way of representing overall greater perceived relatedness. In addition, one can identify the statements that those active nodes are intended to represent, and see whether the particular set of active nodes for each outline-plus-text network varies as a function of the node at which the spread of activation was begun.

Predictions

The following predictions are based on both the experimental data and the theoretical interpretation that was developed to account for them. First, the processes used to determine connectivity were expected to result in more interconnections in the inconsistent outline network than in the consistent outline network. This is the characteristic of the mental representation that is hypothesized to have led to the superior problem-solving capabilities for the students with an inconsistent outline in past studies and to the more uniform relatedness ratings from such students in Study 2.

Second, once the spread of activation has been started from a given node, it was expected that there would be a larger number of other nodes activated in the inconsistent outline network than in the consistent outline network. This prediction is based on the assumptions that a) the inconsistent outline network has more interconnections among its items, b) the flow of activation is uniform across all links emanating from any one node, and c) nodes can become activated through first-, second-, and third-hand links. For example, if node A is linked to node B, but not to node C, but node B is linked to node C, then if A is activated, C will receive secondary activation from A through B.

Third, the inconsistent outline participants made their judgments more rapidly and, thus, if readers base their relatedness judgments on settled networks, the inconsistent outline networks should settle more quickly (in a fewer number of multiplications) than do the consistent outline networks.

Fourth, there should be a statement-pair type-by-outline interaction as was observed in the relatedness data. That interaction showed that all pairs, regardless of their type, were rated as equally related by the inconsistent outline group, but that within-perspective pairs were judged as more related than between-perspectives pairs by the consistent outline group. In the simulation, this interaction was expected to be evidenced by different patterns of activation among nodes for the inconsistent outline and consistent outline networks, depending on where the spread of activation is started. For the inconsistent outline network, regardless of the node at which the spread of activation is begun, nodes representing both types of statements (characteristics and industry) should become activated. For the consistent outline network, the node at which activation is spread is begun should differentially activate nodes such that more within- than between-perspectives nodes become active.

SIMULATIONS

A series of simulations were run in which the values for each of the model's parameters were varied, though the full parameter space was not systematically explored. In particular, for each prediction four separate sets of simulations were run: two in which all connectivity parameters (including argument overlap, and first and second instances of contiguity) were *equal* (EQ), and two in which

TABLE 4.1
Mean Number of Connections in Each Network as a Function of Outline and Contiguity Persistence

	Contiguity Persistence	
Outline	*EQ-CP1*	*EQ-CP2*
Consistent	.70	1.10
Inconsistent	1.15	1.55

the parameters were *not equal* (NEQ). When the parameters were equal, they were all set to .5.

The parameter values used in the NEQ simulations were .7 for the first instance of contiguity, .3 for the second instance of contiguity, and .1 for argument overlap.[1] These values were chosen for the following reasons. First, it was reasoned that because the text and outline dealt with such a well circumscribed domain, with many repetitions and cross references to the same topics, argument overlap might not play as strong a role in determining connectivity as it does in other circumstances, and contiguity might play a more prominent role. Second, as mentioned previously, after two topics have been encountered together once, subsequent encounters of the same pair may not be as salient. Therefore, the second derivation of a relation between two items might not strengthen the connection between those items in an additive manner.

For each of these pairs of simulations, one simulation was run in which the contiguity persistence parameter was set to 1 (the EQ-CP1 and NEQ-CP1 simulations), and the other was run with the contiguity persistence parameter set to 2 (the EQ-CP2 and NEQ-CP2 simulations). With the contiguity persistence parameter set to 1, items can become related to each other by means of contiguity only if they occur in the same or adjacent paragraphs in the text or in the same or adjacent sections of the outline. With the parameter set to 2, the possibilities for relationships based upon contiguity are more far-reaching, extending for two paragraphs (or outline sections).

Variation in the contiguity-persistence parameter was intended to simulate the likely outcome of short-term buffers of varying sizes, and to lend an idea about the portion of text over which something such as a contiguity metric might have its effect. If the buffer is small (CP1), items occurring far from each other are unlikely to simultaneously occupy the buffer, and thus, are unlikely to become related. As the buffer grows in size, item turnover will be slower and the likelihood of relationships based upon contiguity increases. The results for each of these four simulations (EQ-CP1, EQ-CP2, NEQ-CP1, and NEQ-CP2) are discussed in the follow-

[1]Previous investigations with this simulation have shown that fairly drastic changes in the parameter values change the results little, provided that the relative relationships among the values remain the same.

ing sections in relation to the ability of each to match the aforementioned four predictions.

Prediction 1: Connections

It was possible to evaluate the ability of each simulation to match our first prediction immediately after network construction and before the spread of activation. The number of interconnections for each outline-plus-text combination is independent of the actual connectivity parameters that serve to specify link strength, assuming each is set to some value greater than zero. The number of interconnections is, however, affected by the parameter value for contiguity persistence, with a larger parameter value producing more possible interconnection opportunities for both outline-plus-text combinations. Thus, to evaluate our ability to meet this prediction only two simulations were necessary, EQ-CP1 and EQ-CP2.

In an attempt to determine the extent of interconnectivity and whether the number of connections differ reliably for the two outline-plus-text combinations, each of the 20 items was used as the unit of analysis, and the numbers of other items to which it was connected in the consistent outline versus the inconsistent outline networks were subject to matched *t*-tests. Table 4.1 shows the average number of interconnections per statement for the two networks as a function of the contiguity persistence parameter.

Setting the contiguity persistence parameter to 1 (EQ-CP1) resulted in reliably more connections per statement for the inconsistent outline-plus-text network than for the consistent outline-plus-text combination, $t(19) = 2.93$, $p < .01$. With the contiguity persistence parameter set to 2 (EQ-CP2), the inconsistent outline-text combination still resulted in more connections per node than did the consistent outline-text combination, $t(19) = 3.33$, $p < .005$. In addition, as would be expected, increasing the contiguity-persistence parameter from 1 to 2, simulating an enlarged short-term buffer, resulted in a greater number of connections per node for both the consistent outline-text condition, $t(19) = 2.99$, $p < .01$, and the inconsistent text-outline condition, $t(19) = 3.56$, $p < .01$.

Although increasing the parameter for contiguity persistence resulted in an increased number of connections per node for both outline-text combinations, both values for contiguity persistence produced more connections per node for the inconsistent outline than the consistent outline network. Thus, it is not possible to distinguish which parameter value for contiguity persistence is more appropriate for modeling these data based upon the prediction regarding number of connections in the network.

Prediction 2: Active Nodes

The superior problem-solving ability of the students receiving an outline that was inconsistent in structure from the to-be-read text, together with their ability to integrate the text and outline material to a greater extent than those having received the consistent outline, led us to hypothesize that for any particular idea that had been learned, the spread of activity in the inconsistent outline-plus-text representation would be more encompassing. Thus, it was expected that when an attempt was made to model these data with the current simulation, at a given point in time (as measured by multiplication cycles) more nodes would be activated for the inconsistent outline than for the consistent outline network. In the relatedness task, the students were told to make their relatedness decisions quickly and without deliberation. An early stopping point in the spread of activity was utilized to emulate their performance.

Four simulations (EQ-CP1, EQ-CP2, NEQ-CP1, and NEQ-CP2) were run varying the contiguity-persistence parameter and setting the connectivity parameters to be equal or unequal. The first two simulations used a connectivity parameter of .5 for all methods of determining connectivity among pairs of statements, as well as varying contiguity persistence (EQ-CP1 and EQ-CP2). That is, argument overlap and first and second contiguity instances were all weighted equally such that if two statements shared arguments or occurred contiguously, the strength of the connection between them was incremented by .5.

The spread of activation was started at each statement, and each network was examined after two vector-matrix multiplications. Table 4.2 presents the mean number of nodes active in these simulations after two multiplication cycles. For both the EQ-CP1 and EQ-CP2 simulations, the inconsistent outline network had more active nodes than did the consistent outline network, $t(19) = 3.39$, $p < .01$, and, $t(19) = 3.18$, $p < .01$, respectively.

In the second pair of simulations, both the connectivity and contiguity-persistence parameters were manipulated (NEQ-CP1 and NEQ-CP2). Again, the inconsistent outline network had more active nodes than the consistent outline network. Surprisingly, when the spread of activation was stopped at this early stage, changing the parameter values used to determine connectivity had no effect on the number of nodes that was active. That is, at two iterations, the same number of nodes were active in the inconsistent outline network regardless of whether parameter values for all types of connectivity were equal or unequal, as described previously (i.e., the number of active nodes in EQ-CP1 was the same as in NEQ-CP1) and, the same was true for the consistent outline network. As with the connections simulations, increasing the contiguity parameter from

TABLE 4.2
Mean Number of Active Nodes in the Networks After Two Multiplication Iterations as a Function of Outline and Parameter Values

	Parameter Combinations			
Outline	*EQ-CP1*	*EQ-CP2*	*NEQ-CP1*	*NEQ-CP2*
Consistent	10.60	12.30	10.60	12.30
Inconsistent	12.60	13.70	12.60	13.70

1 to 2 did increase the number of active nodes in each of the networks by roughly the same amount, $t(19) = 2.40$, $p < .05$ and $t(19) = 3.53$, $p < .01$ for the inconsistent outline and consistent outline networks, respectively. These results also are shown in Table 4.2.

Prediction 3: Settling

The more uniform relatedness ratings of the inconsistent outline than the consistent outline participants would seem to indicate that their spread of activation was more encompassing and more constant. In addition, the inconsistent outline participants made their judgments more quickly than did the consistent outline participants. As a consequence of these findings, one would expect that in the simulation, activation would spread more rapidly in the inconsistent outline network, and as a result, that network would settle in fewer vector-matrix multiplication cycles (i.e., iterations) than would the consistent outline network.

For each simulation (EQ-CP1, EQ-CP2, NEQ-CP1, and NEQ-CP2) for the two outline-plus-text networks, the spread of activation was started at each of the 20 nodes, and the number of multiplication cycles required for the network to settle was observed. The number of iterations required for each network to settle when the spread of activation was started at each of the nodes was analyzed with matched *t*-tests. Table 4.3 contains the mean number of vector-matrix multiplications required for each of the networks to settle. In the first two sets of simulations, all parameters were equal. When the contiguity persistence parameter was set to one (EQ-CP1), there was no reliable difference in the number of iterations taken for the different outline-plus-text networks to settle, $t(19) < 1$. When the contiguity persistence parameter was set to two (EQ-CP2), again there was no reliable difference between the number of iterations taken for the different outline-plus-text networks to settle, $t(19) = 1.75$, $p > .05$, although in both cases the means were in the predicted direction, with the inconsistent outline networks settling in slightly fewer cycles than the consistent outline networks.

As mentioned previously, we reasoned that the different types of connectivity might not play equally important roles in our students' development of the mental representations of the domain. When the connectivity parameters were not equal, there was no reliable difference between the number of iterations for the different

TABLE 4.3
Mean Number of Vector-Matrix Multiplications Required for the Networks to Settle as a Function of Outline and Parameter Values

	Parameter Combinations			
Outline	*EQ-CP1*	*EQ-CP2*	*NEQ-CP1*	*NEQ-CP2*
Consistent	4.00	4.10	3.85	3.80
Inconsistent	3.90	3.85	4.45	4.35

TABLE 4.4
Mean Number of Activated Within- Versus Between-Perspectives Pairs as a Function of Outline and Contiguity Persistence

	Contiguity Persistence			
	CP1		*CP2*	
Outline	*WITHIN*	*BETWEEN*	*WITHIN*	*BETWEEN*
Consistent	6.95	3.65	7.40	4.90
Inconsistent	7.20	5.40	7.30	6.40

outline-plus-text networks to settle for contiguity persistence of 1 (NEQ-CP1), $t(19) = 1.67$, $p > .05$, or 2 (NEQ-CP2), $t(19) = 1.76$, $p > .05$, although now the direction of the means is opposite to that which was predicted, with the consistent outline networks settling slightly faster than the inconsistent outline networks.

Prediction 4: Types of Nodes

The last aspect of the experimental data that remains to be addressed has to do with the differential relatedness of the statement pairs, as perceived by the participants in the two outline conditions. The inconsistent outline group rated all pairs of statements, both within- and between-perspectives, as nearly equally related, whereas the consistent outline participants rated the within-perspective pairs as more related than the between-perspectives pairs. Thus, in the simulations, the statement at which the spread of activation is begun should have no effect on the number or type of other items that become active in the inconsistent outline network. However, it should have an effect on the number or type of other items that become active in the consistent outline network.

After each simulation run, the number of within- and between-perspectives nodes that had become active were counted. For example, when the networks had settled after the spread of activation was begun at a node representing the characteristics perspective, the number of active characteristics nodes (within-perspective) and the number of active industry nodes (between-perspectives) were counted. Table 4.4 contains the mean number of items of each type activated for the consistent and inconsistent outline networks.

Matched *t*-tests were run for each of the four networks[2] using each cue (the node from which activation spread was begun) as the item of analysis, and the numbers of within- and between-perspectives nodes it activated as the dependent measures. When the contiguity persistence parameter was set to 1 (EQ-CP1),

[2]Investigations of the simulation results showed no differences in the activity of different nodes based on the (in)equality of the connectivity parameters. Hence, only simulations in which the contiguity persistence parameter was varied (EQ-CP1 and EQ-CP2) are reported here.

the inconsistent outline network showed no reliable difference between the number of active within- versus between-perspectives nodes, $t(19) = 1.95$, $p > .05$. Consistent with the experimental data, approximately the same number of nodes of both types became active regardless of the node at which the spread of activation was started. This also was true when the contiguity persistence parameter was set to 2 (EQ-CP2), $t(19) = 1.03$, $p > .05$. In addition, the small, unreliable difference between the number of activated within- versus between-perspectives nodes became even smaller (7.2 versus 5.4 for EQ-CP1, and 7.3 versus 6.4 for EQ-CP2).

For the consistent outline networks, the comparison between the number of active nodes of a within- versus between-perspectives nature was reliable. For contiguity persistence set to 1 (EQ-CP1), $t(19) = 3.45$, $p < .01$, and for contiguity persistence set to 2 (EQ-CP2), $t(19) = 2.86$, $p = .01$. As for the inconsistent outline networks, increasing the contiguity persistence parameter from 1 to 2 for the consistent outline networks makes the difference between the number of activated within- versus between-perspectives nodes smaller (6.95 versus 3.65 for EQ-CP1, and 7.4 versus 4.9 for EQ-CP2), which is almost certainly due to the extended nature of the activity flow when the size of the short-term buffer used to derive the networks was increased. Thus, even though the model is able to match Prediction 4 concerning types of nodes, it does not give us information about which setting for contiguity persistence is the better one.

DISCUSSION

Data have been presented that are consistent with our hypothesis regarding the cognitive processes readers apply when reading a target text under conditions of varying background-knowledge structure. A simple model was presented to simulate various aspects of the experimental data. In this discussion, the data and their relationship to past research is reviewed. This is followed by a description of the proposed model, a brief review of the simulation findings, and possible future modifications of the model. The section concludes with a consideration of the implications for a model of knowledge integration.

The Data

In accordance with previous research from our laboratory, the performance of the participants in the two studies described is consistent with the claim that more highly interconnected networks arise from exposure to an outline that differs in structure from a to-be-read text. In contrast, readers receiving an outline that is structured similarly to the to-be-read text show a different pattern of results suggesting fewer, although stronger, interconnections among ideas.

As evidenced in the first study, participants with an inconsistent outline produced a greater number of elaborations and unique responses to a set of cues than participants with a consistent outline. The inconsistent outline readers also included more outline ideas as important in their summaries and networks, and they integrated these with text information to a greater degree than did the consistent outline readers. In the second study, this interconnectivity was evidenced by pairs of statements perceived as more related, on average, by the inconsistent outline participants than the consistent outline participants. These ratings were more uniform for the former than for the latter participants, and they were made more quickly.

Although the findings from the present study may seem counterintuitive, in that increased comprehension difficulty results in a more flexible representation of the domain, they are consistent with previous data from similar studies. The current results are best understood in light of other research concerned with the roles of prior knowledge and violations of readers expectancies on memory.

A surprising finding has been reported by Amster, Brooks, Lucas, and Özyörük-gee (1992). During list learning, participants in their studies were better able to recall members of weakly associated pairs than strongly associated pairs. This finding can be called the *expectation-violation effect* and can be explained as follows. When a reader is presented with a pair of words to learn, the cognitive processes involved in committing that pair to memory will vary depending upon the strength of the relationship that already exists in long-term memory (i.e., prior knowledge). If the presented pair is strongly related (i.e., a relation already exists in long-term memory), the episodic activation from the current context activates this relation and there is no need for further elaboration. If one cannot come up with an immediate relation between two items (as might be the case when presented with a weakly associated pair of words), the reader is surprised, his or her expectancies about what items should occur together are violated, and he or she actively seeks a relation. This process results in greater elaboration and more retrieval paths and cues for the weakly associated pairs.

Our interpretation of the cognitive processes utilized by the students in our different outline conditions is in accordance with this explanation. We postulate that the outline sets up for the reader a set of expectations about which topics are related and the temporal sequence of topics that is appropriate for the material. When consistent outline readers encounter the text, these expectancies are not violated. The experience of seeing two items in a close temporal relationship serves to reactivate and perhaps strengthen the already existent long-term memory connection between them, and further elaboration is not required. Inconsistent outline readers have a different experience when confronting the text. These readers are surprised by the ordering of topics and by the relationships communicated by the text; their expectancies are violated. These readers activate their representation of the current ideas in long-term memory, and then search actively for a way in which to integrate this new relationship with what they already know. This elaboration often leads to the derivation of a new link, which in turn provides an additional retrieval path.

Other findings supporting the impact of this expectancy violation on performance have been provided by, among others, O'Brien and Myers (1985) and Ellis, Parente, and Walker (1974). O'Brien and Myers observed superior recall memory for unpredictable words placed within the context of a passage. Ellis, Parente, and Walker found enhanced recall for words presented in varied lists (i.e., the same words, but organized differently) when compared to recall for lists of words presented in the same organization on successive presentations. Thus, the present results are in accordance with an already existing body of literature.

The Model

We chose to test the model on the degree of its match to four predictions that were based primarily on the relatedness data from the second study described. In simulating these data, a simple model founded upon the Construction-Integration model of Kintsch (1988) was presented. A network representation of the experimental materials was constructed for each of the outline-plus-text conditions, and then activation, started at different points within each network, was allowed to spread. The spread of activity served to integrate the network by satisfying constraints set up by the interrelations of nodes in each of the networks.

This model did not use a sophisticated method of determining the nodes that would become related to each other in the different representations of the domain. Instead, we capitalized on the sharing of arguments among node contents and their temporal contiguity. By varying the persistence of this contiguity (to simulate short-term buffers of different capacities) and the relative impact of contiguity and argument overlap, we were able to produce results that were compatible for the most part, with the experimental data.

Simulation Results

First, it was predicted that the inconsistent outline network, constructed via these simple mechanisms, would contain more interconnections among nodes than the consistent outline network. This prediction was based on both the high number of pairs of statements that were rated as being related by the inconsistent outline group in Study 2, and indirectly on the greater number of elaborations this group produced to the cues in the cued-response task. This was referred to as the connections prediction. Second, it was predicted that during the spread of activation, the inconsistent outline network would show more nodes activated by a particular cue than would the consistent outline network. This prediction follows from the fact that, in Study 2, the inconsistent outline participants rated all pairs, on average, as more related than did the consistent outline participants. Only if many other ideas in their domain representations were made active by a cue, would we expect them to experience greater perceived relatedness. This prediction was referred to as the active nodes prediction. The third prediction follows from the fact that the inconsistent outline participants made their relatedness judgments more quickly than did the consistent outline participants, and states that the inconsistent outline network should take a shorter period of time to settle during integration than the consistent outline network. This was referred to as the settling prediction. Fourth, it was predicted that the pattern of active nodes would vary depending upon the type of cue from which activation flow was started for the consistent outline network, but not for the inconsistent outline network. That is, because the inconsistent outline participants rated both within- and between-perspective pairs of statements as equally related, any given cue must activate items representing both perspectives (i.e., industry and characteristics). In contrast, the consistent outline participants rated the within-perspectives pairs as more related than the between-perspectives pairs, and as a result, each cue should activate more items from within the same perspective than from the other perspective. Thus, for the inconsistent outline network, we expected no difference in the number of within- versus between-perspectives nodes activated, but we expected there to be a difference between the number of within- versus between-perspectives nodes activated for the consistent outline network. This was referred to as the *types of nodes prediction*. The ability of the model to match these four predictions under the different possible parameter settings is summarized in Table 4.5.

As can be seen from Table 4.5, none of the parameter settings were able to accommodate all four predictions with statistical reliability. All of the simulations met the connections prediction, and the difference in the number of connections for the two outline-plus-text networks was the same regardless of contiguity persistence or connectivity equivalence.

Those simulations in which contiguity persistence was set to 1 (EQ-CP1 and NEQ-CP1), indicating a smaller short-term buffer, came closer to matching the active node prediction than did the simulations in which the parameter was set to 2 (EQ-CP2 and NEQ-CP2), because it is in those simulations that the difference in number of active nodes for the two outline-plus-text combinations was largest. Again, whether or not the connectivity parameters were equal (EQ versus NEQ), the simulations produced the same difference in active nodes for the two outline-plus-text networks.

None of the parameter combinations could match the settling prediction with statistical reliability, although when the parameter values were equal (EQ-CP1 and EQ-CP2) the means were in the predicted direction, and when they were unequal (NEQ-CP1 and NEQ-CP2) the pattern was opposite the predictions. Also, the difference in settling rates for the two outline-plus-text networks was larger in the EQ-CP2 than in the EQ-CP1 simulation. Note that this is the only prediction for which the EQ and NEQ simulations produced different results.

For all four simulations, the difference in the number of active nodes of different types (within- versus between-perspectives) was, as predicted, never significant for the inconsistent outline network, but always significant for the con-

TABLE 4.5
Predictions Met by Simulations Based on the Parameter Settings Used

	Prediction			
Simulation	*Connections*[a]	*Active Nodes*[b]	*Settling*[c]	*Type of Nodes*[d]
EQ-CP1	**inconsistent > consistent*** **Δ = .45**	**inconsistent > consistent*** **Δ = 2.00**	inconsistent < consistent Δ = .10	inconsistent Δ = 1.80 consistent* Δ = 3.30
NEQ-CP1	**inconsistent > consistent*** **Δ = .45**	**inconsistent > consistent*** **Δ = 2.00**	inconsistent > consistent Δ = .60	inconsistent Δ = 1.80 consistent* Δ = 3.30
EQ-CP2	**inconsistent > consistent*** **Δ = .45**	inconsistent > consistent* Δ = 1.40	**inconsistent < consistent** **Δ = .25**	**inconsistent Δ = .90** **consistent* Δ = 2.50**
NEQ-CP2	**inconsistent > consistent*** **Δ = .45**	inconsistent > consistent* Δ = 1.40	inconsistent > consistent Δ = .55	**inconsistent Δ = .90** **consistent* Δ = 2.50**

*indicates the difference (Δ) is reliable at the .05 level. The simulation that best meets each prediction is printed in boldface type.

[a]Connections: There should be more connections in the inconsistent than in the consistent network. Δ is the difference in number of connections for the inconsistent versus consistent network.

[b]Active Nodes: There should be more nodes active in the inconsistent than in the consistent network. Δ is the difference in number of active nodes for the inconsistent versus consistent network.

[c]Settling: The inconsistent network should take less time to settle than the consistent network. Δ is the difference in number of iterations to settle for the inconsistent versus consistent network.

[d]Type of Nodes: The same number of pairs of both types (within- and between-perspectives) should be active in the inconsistent network, but not in the consistent network. Δ is the difference between the average number of within- versus between-perspectives pairs activated.

sistent outline network. Further, although the difference in the number of activated within- versus between-perspectives nodes decreased for both networks when contiguity persistence was increased (from CP1 to CP2), this decrease occurred to a lesser extent for the consistent outline network.

Thus, although none of the present combinations of short-term buffer size (i.e., contiguity persistence) and connectivity equivalence can match all the predictions, that in which the short-term buffer is relatively larger and in which the different methods of connectivity are given equal weight appears best. The implications of these findings are discussed in the following section.

Implications for a Theory of Knowledge Integration

Although a systematic exploration of the parameter space was not undertaken, several speculative claims about knowledge integration can be offered. First, it appears that in terms of establishing relationships for important domain concepts, based upon contiguity, the size of the short-term buffer is not severely limited. In producing simulation results that were qualitatively similar to the relatedness ratings of participants, it was possible to derive relationships based on contiguity for items occurring as far away from each other as two text paragraphs. This may have been due to participants utilizing a relatively enlarged short-term buffer when reading well written extended expository text of an interesting nature. Alternatively, it may have been due to the focused essence of the text, such that even though readers' short-term buffers remained relatively small, the topic-centered nature of the text made clear which propositions were to be kept in the short-term buffer from one processing cycle to the next. Future research focussed on the number and type of active concepts present in the short-term buffer under such naturalistic reading conditions should shed light on which of these alternative is most likely.

When the connectivity parameter values were equal, the simulation modeled the relatedness data more successfully than when the parameter values were not equal, although settling was the only prediction on which this variable produced qualitatively different results. This suggests that argument overlap may be as important in determining connectivity among ideas as is temporal contiguity. Thus, mentioning the same idea repeatedly, each time in a different context, may be an effective method for cueing readers to establish relations between disparate pieces of knowledge.

It is interesting to note that, because all the parameter values were equal, the second encounter of a relationship might be as important in establishing the domain representation as is the first. This would account for the strong textbase representations that are held by participants in conditions analogous to the consistent outline conditions used here. They experience instances of contiguity for the same item pairs on multiple occasions, and each time they do, the link between those items is reinforced in memory. The result is a stable structure that reflects the perspective and temporal organization of both the outline and the text. Inconsistent outline readers, in contrast, have an opportunity to create a new link between a pair of items each time a unique pair is experienced in a contiguous relationship. Thus, during reading of the text, consistent outline readers may most often engage the processes involved in strengthening existing relationships, whereas inconsistent outline readers may engage those processes involved in creating new relationships, as well as strengthening some existing ones.

In determining whether these different hypothesized processes (i.e., primarily strengthening for the consistent outline participants, but strengthening and creating for the inconsistent outline participants) occurred during the reading of the text, an additional post hoc investigation of the relatedness ratings from Study 2 was conducted. The ratings from each of the two outline groups were separately factor analyzed. Based on the scree plots produced by each analysis, it appears that to account for the same proportion of variance in the relatedness ratings of the two different outline groups, different numbers of factors are required. Consistent with our hypothesis regarding the more complex processing of the inconsistent outline group, more factors were required to account for their ratings than for the ratings of the consistent outline group. This adds credence to the speculation that readers possessing prior knowledge that is different in perspective from a target text may engage cognitive processes during reading that are different or more extensive than those of readers whose prior knowledge is the same in perspective from the target text.

Given the sparse nature of the model, the observed ability to fit the data is encouraging. Future modifications to the model might include additional methods for determining connectivity based on, for example, metrics such as causal relatedness and category membership. Varying the importance of connections already present in long-term memory (i.e., links based on the perspective presented in the outline) and those currently being processed (i.e., links based on the perspective presented by the text), as well as including connections derived in a probabilistic rather than a deterministic manner, loom as potential alterations in the model, alterations that will improve our understanding of the integration of knowledge from different sources.

REFERENCES

Amster, H., Brooks, C., Lucas, S., & Özyörük-gee, N. (1992, November). *The expectation-violation effect and the role of semantic relatedness in an episodic task.* Paper presented at the 33rd Annual Meeting of the Psychonomic Society, St. Louis, MO.

Anderson, R. C., & Pichert, J. W. (1978). Recall of previously unrecallable material following a shift in perspective. *Journal of Verbal Learning and Verbal Behavior, 17*, 1–12.

Bower, G. H. (1972). A selective review of organizational factors in memory. In E. Tulving & W. Donaldson (Eds.), *Organization of memory* (pp. 93–134). New York: Academic Press.

Bransford, J. D., & Johnson, M. K. (1972). Contextual prerequisites for understanding: Some investigations of comprehension and recall. *Journal of Verbal Learning and Verbal Behavior, 11*, 717–726.

Doane, S. M., Kintsch, W., & Polson, P. G. (1989). Action planning: Producing UNIX commands. In *Proceedings of the Eleventh Annual Conference of the Cognitive Science Society* (pp. 458–465). Hillsdale, NJ: Lawrence Erlbaum Associates.

Ellis, H. C., Parente, F. J., & Walker, C. W. (1974). Coding and varied input versus repetition in human memory. *Journal of Experimental Psychology, 102*, 284–290.

Kintsch, W. (1988). The role of knowledge in discourse comprehension: A construction-integration model. *Psychological Review, 95*, 163–182.

Kintsch, W., Welsch, D., Schmalhofer, F., & Zimny, S. (1990). Sentence memory: A theoretical analysis. *Journal of Memory and Language, 29*, 133–159.

Mannes, S. (1990). *Using KOTO to create connectivity matrices and spread activation through them* (program documentation). Unpublished manuscript.

Mannes, S. (1994). Strategic processing of text. *Journal of Educational Psychology, 86*(4), 577–588.

Mannes, S. M., & Kintsch, W. (1987). Knowledge organization and text organization. *Cognition and Instruction, 4*, 91–115.

Mannes, S. M., & Kintsch, W. (1991). Routine computing tasks: Planning as understanding. *Cognitive Science, 15*, 305–342.

O'Brien, E. J., & Myers, J. L. (1985). When comprehension difficulty improves memory for text. *Journal of Experimental Psychology: Learning, Memory, and Cognition, 11*, 12–21.

Rumelhart, D. E., & McClelland, J. L. (1986). *Parallel distributed processing: Explorations is the microstructure of cognition: Vol. 1. Foundations*. Cambridge, MA: MIT Press.

Sachs, J. D. (1967). Recognition memory for syntactic and semantic aspects of connected discourse. *Perception and Psychophysics, 2*, 437–442.

Schmalhofer, F., & Glavanov, D. (1986). Three components of understanding a programmer's manual: Verbatim, propositional and situational representations. *Journal of Memory and Language, 25*, 279–294.

van Dijk, T. A., & Kintsch, W. (1983). *Strategies of discourse comprehension*. New York: Academic Press.

CHAPTER

5

A MODEL OF NARRATIVE COMPREHENSION AND RECALL

Charles R. Fletcher
Paul van den Broek
Erik J. Arthur
University of Minnesota

To a skilled reader, comprehension is a simple, even enjoyable, process. However, underlying this intuitively simple activity is a complex interaction of basic cognitive processes. In order to deal with this complexity, researchers have concentrated on some aspects of comprehension and ignored others. Consider, for example, the model of comprehension proposed by Kintsch and van Dijk (1978; van Dijk & Kintsch, 1983). This model focuses on the role of long- and short-term memory in comprehension, but ignores the fact that understanding a text is largely a problem-solving task. In contrast, Trabasso and van den Broek (1985; Trabasso & Sperry, 1985; van den Broek, 1988) have developed a model of comprehension that emphasizes the role of problem solving and ignores the constraints imposed by long- and short-term memory. The result is two models of comprehension that are intuitively appealing and have generated substantial empirical support, but that have so little in common that they are sometimes viewed as competing alternatives.

Fletcher and Bloom (1988) argued that both models are "correct" and proposed a hybrid model of narrative comprehension that is simultaneously consistent with Kintsch and van Dijk's assumptions concerning the role of long- and short-term memory in comprehension and Trabasso and van den Broek's assumptions about the role of problem solving in understanding a narrative text. In achieving this synthesis, Fletcher and Bloom needed to make an additional assumption: namely, that the use of long- and short-term memory during narrative comprehension mirrors their use in other problem-solving situations (see, e.g., Newell & Simon, 1972; Greeno & Simon, 1988). As a result, the model proposed by Fletcher and Bloom can be viewed as a synthesis of three separate lines of research.

To test their model, Fletcher and Bloom (1988) used it to predict free recall probabilities for each proposition in eight simple narrative texts. In general, they found that the model accounted for more of the variance in college students' free recall protocols than did the earlier models of Kintsch and van Dijk (1978) or Trabasso and van den Broek (1985). Fletcher and Bloom assumed that this success reflected a correspondence between the processes the participants in their study used to encode a text and those assumed by their model. Unfortunately, this assumption may have been incorrect because free recall data reflect the influence of *both* encoding and retrieval processes (cf. Bloom, Fletcher, van den Broek, Reitz, & Shapiro, 1990; Fletcher, Hummel, & Marsolek, 1990). Another shortcoming of Fletcher and Bloom's model, is its inability to predict the order of free recall. Both of these problems can be traced to a single underlying cause, the fact that the model lacks an explicit retrieval component.

The research reported in this chapter had four interrelated goals. The first goal was to extend the comprehension model of Fletcher and Bloom (1988) by reformulating it within the model of human memory proposed by Shiffrin and his colleagues (Gillund & Shiffrin, 1984; Raaijmakers & Shiffrin, 1980, 1981), thereby achieving a further synthesis of previously independent theories. The second goal was to use that same framework to add a free recall component to the model. The third goal was to evaluate the model by implementing it as a computer program and testing its ability to predict both what people recall and when they recall it. The fourth goal was to explore the degree to which the model's success results from its ability to describe how a text is encoded rather than how it is retrieved. In pursuing these goals, we hoped to improve our understanding of the complex interaction of processes that underlie the seemingly simple act of understanding and remembering a story.

CONSTRAINTS ON THE MODEL

As we have noted, the model of narrative comprehension and recall proposed here represents a confluence of four independent theories. In formulating this model, we attempted to deviate from these theories as little as possible, treating their major assumptions as theoretical constraints. It is useful to review those constraints, and their origins, before describing the details of our own model.

A Problem-Solving Model of Narrative Comprehension

According to the model proposed by Trabasso and van den Broek (1985; Trabasso & Sperry, 1985; van den Broek, 1988), the meaning of a narrative text is represented in long-term memory as a network. The nodes of this network represent the individual clauses of the text, whereas the links represent causal and enabling relations among those clauses. Consider, for example, the text in Table 5.1. The network representing this text is shown in Fig. 5.1. In the model, a link is assumed from Clause A to Clause B if (a) the event described by A occurs before the event described by B; (b) A is still operative when B occurs; and (c) in the circumstances described in the text, B would not have occurred in the absence of A (i.e., A is necessary for B). Thus, Fig. 5.1 shows a link from Clause 2 to Clause 1 because: Danny saw the bike before he wanted it, seeing the bike was still affecting Danny's behavior when he decided that he wanted the bike, and if Danny had not seen the bike, he would not have wanted it. These criteria are discussed in detail by Trabasso, van den Broek, and Suh (1989) and by van den Broek (1990a). A reader's ability to discover the causal connections in a text by applying these criteria to all possible pairs of clauses is clearly limited by processing constraints. As a result, the representation in Fig. 5.1 is best thought of as an ideal representation and Trabasso and van den Broek's model is best thought of as a model of the ideal understander (van den Broek, 1990b).

This model assumes that comprehension is a problem-solving process. Understanding an individual clause requires that the reader discover its causal antecedents and consequences (using the criteria described earlier). Under-

TABLE 5.1
Text of "Danny's New Bike"

Clause Number	*Statement*
1.	Danny wanted to have the red bike
2.	that he saw in the window of the neighborhood bike shop.
3.	Danny knew that first he had to have $50
4.	to buy the bike.
5.	He asked his parents if they would give him the money.
6.	His parents denied his request.
7.	They suggested that Danny earn the money himself
8.	by getting a job.
9.	Danny was mad at his parents
10.	for not giving him the money,
11.	but he was determined to get the $50 somehow.
12.	He knew he would have to find a job,
13.	so he called the newspaper
14.	and asked for a paper route.
15.	He started delivering papers in his neighborhood the next week
16.	and earned $10 a week.
17.	With this job,
18.	Danny had $50 within a few weeks.
19.	He took his hard-earned money to the shop,
20.	bought the bike,
21.	and happily rode home.

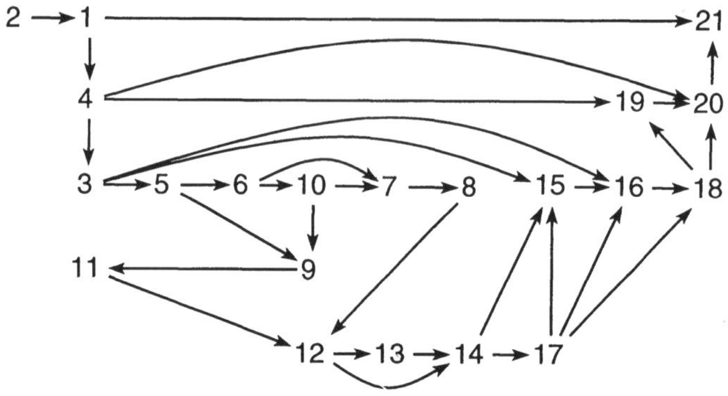

FIG. 5.1. Causal structure of *Danny's New Bike*. (An arrow from Clause 2 to Clause 1 indicates that the former causes the latter.)

standing the text as a whole requires that the reader find a causal path that links its opening (clause 2 in Table 5.1) to its final outcome (clause 21 in Table 5.1). Similar arguments have been made by Black and Bower (1980) and by Schank (1975) and are preserved in the model proposed here. These arguments are supported by data showing that (a) clauses with many causal connections are recalled better and rated as more important than are clauses with few causal connections, and (b) with the number of connections held constant, clauses on a causal path connecting the opening of a text to its outcome are recalled better and considered more important than clauses not on such a path (see, e.g., Black & Bower, 1980; Trabasso & Sperry, 1985; Trabasso & van den Broek, 1985; van den Broek, 1988).

A Cyclical Model of Comprehension

Kintsch and van Dijk (1978; van Dijk & Kintsch, 1983) also assumed that the meaning of a text is represented as a network. In contrast to Trabasso and van den Broek (1985), they assumed that the nodes of this network are propositions (see Table 5.2) and that the connections are based on co-reference. These assumptions are supported by probe recognition experiments, which reveal greater priming between concepts from the same proposition than from different propositions, and greater priming between propositions separated by few referential links than between propositions separated by many referential links (McKoon & Ratcliff, 1980; Ratcliff & McKoon, 1978).

Because of the limited capacity of short-term memory, Kintsch and van Dijk (1978) argued that this representation is constructed in cycles. During each cycle, the propositions corresponding to a single sentence are added to short-term memory. Connections are then established between pairs of propositions that are embedded (as P02 is embedded in P01 in Table 5.2) or that share an argument (as P02 and P03 share the argument BIKE in Table 5.2). After all possible

TABLE 5.2
Propositional Analysis of "Danny's New Bike," the Relationship Between Clauses and Propositions, and the Predicted and Observed Free Recall Probabilities for Each Proposition

			Probability of Free Recall	
ID	*Proposition*	*Clause*	*Predicted*	*Observed*
P00	(IS TITLE DANNY'S-NEW-BIKE)	0		
P01*	(WANT DANNY P2)	1	.76	.83
P02*	(POSSESS DANNY BIKE)	1	.79	.75
P03	(MOD BIKE RED)	1	.33	.29
P04*	(SEE DANNY BIKE)	2	.64	.59
P05*	(LOC BIKE WINDOW)	2	.64	.50
P06	(POSSESS NEIGHBORHOOD BIKE-SHOP)	2	.28	.21
P07*	(POSSESS BIKE-SHOP WINDOW)	2	.62	.33
P08*	(KNOW DANNY P11)	3	.41	.17
P09	(TIME P10 FIRST)	3	.07	.04
P10*	(POSSESS DANNY $50)	3	.48	.33
P11	(REASON P10 P12)	4	.09	.25
P12*	(BUY DANNY BIKE)	4	.24	.29
P13*	(ASK DANNY PARENTS P15)	5	.66	.96
P14*	(POSSESS DANNY PARENTS)	5	.68	.92
P15*	(GIVE PARENTS MONEY DANNY)	5	.65	.92
P16	(POSSESS DANNY PARENTS)	6	.12	.25
P17*	(DENY PARENTS REQUEST)	6	.45	.71
P18	(MAKE DANNY REQUEST)	6	.13	.17
P19*	(SUGGEST PARENTS P20)	7	.15	.58
P20*	(EARN DANNY MONEY)	7	.12	.42
P21	(MEANS P20 P22)	8	.05	.17
P22*	(GET DANNY JOB)	8	.33	.46
P23*	(MAD-AT DANNY PARENTS)	9	.15	.54
P24	(POSSESS DANNY PARENTS)	9	.09	.25
P25	(REASON P23 P26)	10	.05	.25
P26*	(NEG P27)	10	.07	.29
P27*	(GIVE PARENTS MONEY DANNY)	10	.15	.25
P28	(BUT P23 P29)	11	.00	.38
P29*	(DETERMINED-TO DANNY P30)	11	.44	.38
P30*	(GET DANNY $50)	11	.46	.17
P31	(MOD P30 SOMEHOW)	11	.05	.00
P32*	(KNOW DANNY P33)	12	.18	.04
P33*	(HAVE-TO DANNY P34)	12	.21	.04
P34*	(FIND DANNY JOB)	12	.20	.08
P35	(REASON P32 P36)	13	.05	.04
P36*	(CALL DANNY NEWSPAPER)	13	.22	.75
P37*	(ASK-FOR DANNY PAPER-ROUTE)	14	.37	.63
P38	(START DANNY P39)	15	.10	.25
P39*	(DELIVER DANNY PAPERS)	15	.24	.50
P40	(LOC P39 NEIGHBORHOOD)	15	.03	.13
P41	(POSSESS DANNY NEIGHBORHOOD)	15	.11	.08
P42	(TIME P38 NEXT-WEEK)	15	.00	.04

(Continued)

TABLE 5.2
(Continued)

			Probability of Free Recall	
ID	*Proposition*	*Clause*	*Predicted*	*Observed*
P43*	(EARN DANNY $10)	16	.57	.96
P44*	(RATE-OF P43 PER-WEEK)	16	.43	.92
P45*	(WITH JOB P46)	17	.18	.21
P46*	(POSSESS DANNY $50)	18	.57	.79
P47*	(WITHIN P46 FEW-WEEKS)	18	.55	.92
P48*	(TAKE-TO DANNY MONEY BIKE-SHOP)	19	.28	.29
P49	(POSSESS DANNY MONEY)	19	.24	.04
P50	(MOD MONEY HARD-EARNED)	19	.09	.04
P51*	(BUY DANNY BIKE)	20	.67	.75
P52*	(MOD P53 HAPPILY)	21	.46	.25
P53*	(RIDE DANNY HOME)	21	.59	.46

*Propositions that play an essential causal role.

links are established, the entire structure is stored in long-term memory. Attention then shifts to a subset of the propositions in short-term memory. These remain available and are reprocessed along with the propositions that enter during the next cycle. All remaining propositions are lost from short-term memory before the next cycle begins. This model is supported by research demonstrating that propositions that (hypothetically) remain in short-term memory for multiple processing cycles are recalled better than otherwise equivalent propositions that are processed only once (Kintsch & van Dijk, 1978; Miller & Kintsch, 1980). The model also has been found to predict probe-recognition times (Fletcher, 1981), the contents of think-aloud protocols (Fletcher, 1986), and readability differences between texts (Fletcher, 1986; Kintsch & Vipond, 1979; Miller & Kintsch, 1980). Our model preserves the basic outline of Kintsch and van Dijk's model, and their assumption that co-reference increases the coherence of a text's representation in memory.

For a model such as Kintsch and van Dijk's (1978) to have any predictive power, it must be possible to specify the process that determines which propositions remain in short-term memory when a sentence boundary is reached. Research on arithmetic word problems (Fletcher, 1985; Kintsch & Greeno, 1985), police interrogations (Clark, Stephenson, & Rutter, 1986), and descriptions of baseball games (Spilich, Vesonder, Chiesi, & Voss, 1979) suggest that this process differs from one genre of text to another and is guided by the reader's goals. Along with Fletcher and Bloom (1988), we assume that when the text in question is a narrative, the selection process maximizes the reader's ability to discover its causal structure. As did van Dijk and Kintsch (1983), we assume that the selection process has two parts. The reader first identifies a single clause as most likely to have an appropriate semantic relationship to the following sentence. Next, the reader identifies the important propositions in that clause and holds them in short-term memory. In this context, important propositions are those that allow the clause to serve its semantic role in the text.

State-Space Search Models of Problem Solving

Human problem solving is often described as a search process (see, e.g., Greeno & Simon, 1988; Newell & Simon, 1972). The problem itself is thought of as a network, or *state space*, in which the nodes represent possible problem states and the arcs represent allowable transitions from one state to another. Thus, the state space for playing chess would include one node for each possible configuration of pieces on the chess board; arcs would connect all pairs of configurations that differed by a single, legal move. The search process begins at a *start state* (the opening board position) and finishes when it reaches a *solution state* (checkmate). The path that the process takes through the state space (when it is successful) is referred to as the *solution path*. Because of the limited capacity of short-term memory, the problem solver is aware of no more than a few states at a time. To overcome this limitation, attention is continuously focused on one particular state, called the *current state*. Initially, the current state is the same as the start state. The states connected to the current state by arcs are examined and a heuristic evaluation process is used to determine which of these is closest to the goal state and, thus, the most likely next step in the solution path. The state selected becomes the new current state. Attention is shifted to it and the process repeats until the goal state is reached. The evaluation process that determines the new current state differs from one type of problem to another. Occasionally, this process leads to a deadend, a state off the path that connects the start state to the goal state. If this happens, the problem solver "backs up" to a previous state. Experienced problem solvers use evaluation heuristics that minimize this occurrence. Both Greeno and Simon (1988) and Newell and Simon (1972) present specific state-space search models for a variety of problem-solving tasks. They also demonstrate the ability of these models to reproduce the behavior of people engaged in those tasks.

We assume that the causal structure of a narrative text is analogous to a state space. This suggests that the limited capacity of short-term memory is overcome during comprehension by focusing attention on some analogue of the current state. Fletcher and Bloom (1988) have suggested that such an analogue (a) should be the most likely causal antecedent to the next sentence in the text, and (b) should maximize the number of causal connections in the text that can be discovered without "backing up." They argue that these conditions are best met by the most recent clause that has antecedents, but no consequences, in the preceding text. This clause represents the "end" (thus far) of the causal path connecting the text's opening to its outcome, and that causal path is the obvious analogue of a solution path. Therefore, we assume that, for narratives, the selection process described by Kintsch and van Dijk (1978, van Dijk & Kintsch, 1983) always focuses a reader's attention on the last clause entered into short-term memory that has antecedents but not consequences. We assume that, during free recall, a reader attempts to reconstruct the causal path through the text, and that achieving this goal requires the same type of search process used during comprehension. The difference between the two is that, during comprehension, potential successors to the "current state clause" are provided by the text, whereas, during recall, they have to be generated by the reader.

The SAM Model of Human Memory

Shiffrin and his colleagues (Gillund & Shiffrin, 1984; Raaijmakers & Shiffrin, 1980, 1981) developed a model of human memory referred to as SAM (Search of Associative Memory). In this model, long-term memory is represented as a network of "images," where an image can be any psychologically meaningful unit, such as a word, a picture, or (for present purposes) a proposition. Further, the connections in this network are assumed to vary in strength. Each image is assumed to have connections to (a) itself, (b) a special image called CONTEXT, and (c) all the other images in long-term memory. The strength of the connection between an image and itself reflects the average strength of association among its component parts, such as the predicate and the arguments that comprise an individual proposition. The strength of the connection between an image and CONTEXT reflects the average strength of association between the image and the psychological and physical contexts in which it has been encountered previously. The longer an image is studied (i.e., the longer it remains in short-term memory) the stronger its connections to itself and CONTEXT become. The strength of the connection between two images is assumed to increase in proportion to the time the images remain in short-term memory together.

Retrieval of this structure in long-term memory is conceptualized as a probabilistic search process involving two states. In the first stage, a strategic process selects a set of retrieval cues from the images in short-term memory. In the second stage, an automatic process uses those cues to search long-term memory. The latter stage includes two probabilistic sub-processes: sampling of an image from long-term memory and, subsequently, recovering the information in the sampled image. Given a set of cues Q_1 through Q_M, the probability of sampling image I_i is equal to:

$$P_S(I_i \mid Q_1, Q_2 \ldots Q_M) = \frac{\prod_{j=1}^{M} S_T(Q_j, I_i)}{\sum_{k=1}^{N} \prod_{j=1}^{M} S_T(Q_k, I_i)} \tag{1}$$

where $S_T(Q_j, I_i)$ is the strength of the connection between cue Q_j and image I_i and N is the total number of images in long-term memory. Thus, the likelihood of sampling any particular image is increased if (a) it is strongly associated with all of the retrieval cues, or (b) other images are weakly associated with any of the retrieval cues. Exactly one image is sampled each time long-term memory is searched. Once an image has been sampled, the probability of recovering the information in it is:

$$P_R(I_i \mid Q_1, Q_2 \ldots Q_M) = 1 - \exp\{-\sum_{j=1}^{M} S_T(Q_j, I_i)\} \quad (2)$$

Thus, the probability of recovering the information in an image depends only on the strength of its connections to the retrieval cues. In contrast to the sampling process, the recovery process can fail, in which case nothing is recalled.

Fitting this model to a set of free recall data requires that a researcher specify an encoding strategy, a retrieval strategy, and values for six free parameters (as summarized in Table 5.3). The encoding strategy determines how long each to-be-remembered item remains in short-term memory during the study phase of an experiment. Together with the four strength parameters (a, b, c, and d), the encoding strategy determines the contents of long-term memory. The retrieval strategy controls the choice of retrieval cues during the recall and operates in conjunction with the parameters $L_{\max}$ and $K_{\max}$. The retrieval strategy selects new retrieval cues after $L_{\max}$ retrieval failures occur with the old cues (hereafter, *local* failures), and terminates after $K_{\max}$ failures have accumulated (hereafter, *total* failures). A retrieval failure occurs whenever the model fails to recover the information in a sampled image or when it samples and recovers the image of a previously recalled item.

SAM provides the architecture within which our model was developed. SAM was selected for two reasons. First, similar to each of the theories discussed

TABLE 5.3
Parameters Needed to Fit Free Recall Data with SAM

Parameter	*Description*
a	Strength of association between CONTEXT and an image that remains in short-term memory for time t
b	Strength of association between images that remain in short-term memory together for time t
c	Strength of association between an image and itself after the image remains in short-term memory for time t
d	Strength of association between images that never co-occur in short-term memory
$L_{\max}$	Number of local failures allowed before new retrieval cues are chosen
$K_{\max}$	Number of total failures allowed before the model halts

previously, it assumes that information is represented in memory as a network of semantically interpretable symbols. This shared assumption makes an integrated model feasible. Second, SAM accurately describes performance in an impressive array of list-learning paradigms (see e.g., Gillund & Shiffrin, 1984; Raaijmakers & Shiffrin, 1980, 1981; Ratcliff, Clark, & Shiffrin, 1990) and has been successful (with some modification) in predicting recognition memory for words (Ratcliff & McKoon, 1988) and sentences (Kintsch, Welsch, & Schmalhofer, & Zimny, 1990) encountered while reading a meaningful text.

THE MODEL

Overview

Comprehension Component. During comprehension, our model adds propositions to short-term memory one at a time. As each proposition is added, associative links are created to the proposition itself, the context, and all other propositions in short-term memory. The link that each proposition has to the context is assigned a strength of a. Links to other propositions are assigned a strength of b_O. In addition, if two propositions are from the same clause, the strength of their association is incremented by b_S. If the propositions share a referent, or if one of them is embedded in the other, their strength of association is increased by b_r. If the propositions belong to causally related clauses (i.e., an antecedent and consequent pair), and each is essential to the semantic role played by its clause, the strength of their association is increased by b_C. We consider a proposition essential if one or more causal connections would be lost without it. Each proposition's associative link to itself is assigned a strength of c. As this structure is created, it is simultaneously stored in long-term memory, with pairs of propositions that never co-occur in short-term memory being assigned a residual associative strength of d, regardless of the semantic relationship between them.

As propositions are added to short-term memory, the model focuses its attention on the propositions that are essential to the causal role played by the most recent clause that has causal antecedents, but no consequences, in the preceding text. When a sentence boundary is reached, all propositions that are not essential to this current state clause are dropped from short-term memory to make room for the following sentence. At the same time, the associative strengths connecting the current state propositions to one another, the context, and to themselves are incremented. The flow of propositions through short-term memory in this model and in the model described by Fletcher and Bloom (1988) is the same.

As an example of how the model works, consider the first sentence of "Danny's New Bike" (see Fig. 5.2 and the proposition list in Table 5.2). Just before the sentence boundary is reached, short-term memory contains the context, the title

(a) Before Sentence Boundary:

		PROPOSITIONAL IMAGES IN LTM						
		P01	***P02***	***P03***	***P04***	***P05***	***P06***	***P07***
	CONTEXT	*.21*	*.21*	*.21*	*.21*	*.21*	*.21*	*.21*
	P00 (TITLE DANNY'S-NEW-BIKE)	*.12*	*.12*	*.12*	*.12*	*.12*	*.12*	*.12*
S	***P01 (WANT DANNY P02)***	*.16*	*.58*	*.57*	*.16*	*.15*	*.12*	*.15*
T	***P02 (POSSESS DANNY BIKE)***	*.58*	*.16*	*.58*	*.16*	*.16*	*.12*	*.15*
M	***P03 (MOD BIKE RED)***	*.57*	*.58*	*.16*	*.13*	*.13*	*.12*	*.12*
	P04 (SEE DANNY BIKE)	*.16*	*.16*	*.13*	*.16*	*.58*	*.57*	*.57*
	P05 (LOC BIKE WINDOW)	*.15*	*.16*	*.13*	*.58*	*.16*	*.57*	*.58*
	P06 (POSSESS NEIGHBORHOOD BIKESHOP)	*.12*	*.12*	*.12*	*.57*	*.57*	*.16*	*.58*
	P07 (POSSESS BIKESHOP WINDOW)	*.15*	*.15*	*.12*	*.57*	*.58*	*.58*	*.16*

(b) After Sentence Boundary:

		PROPOSITIONAL IMAGES IN LTM						
		P01	***P02***	***P03***	***P04***	***P05***	***P06***	***P07***
S	***CONTEXT***	*.42*	*.42*	*.21*	*.21*	*.21*	*.21*	*.21*
T	***P01 (WANT DANNY P02)***	*.32*	*1.16*	*.57*	*.16*	*.15*	*.12*	*.15*
M	***P02 (POSSESS DANNY BIKE)***	*1.16*	*.32*	*.58*	*.16*	*.16*	*.12*	*.15*

FIG. 5.2. The state of the model (a) just before and (b) just after the first sentence boundary of *Danny's New Bike* is encountered. Each matrix shows the strength of association between the images available in short-term memory and all the propositional images that have been processed thus far (assumes that $a = .21$, $b_o = .12$, $b_s = .45$, $b_r = .01$, $b_c = .03$, and $c = .16$).

of the text (which we treat as a separate proposition, namely, P00), and the first seven propositions (i.e., P01 through P07). Each of the propositions is connected to itself, context, and the title. The strengths of these connections vary according to the values of the strength parameters. At this time, the model's attention is focused on propositions P01 (WANT DANNY P02) and P02 (POSSESS DANNY BIKE). These two propositions are essential to the causal role played by the first clause of the sentence. Because this clause is enabled by Clause 2, it is the last clause having antecedents but no consequences thus far in the text. After processing the sentence boundary, the model's short-term memory includes only P01, P02, and the context, but the links among these remaining images are strengthened. At this point, the model is ready to begin processing the second sentence of the text.

After the model has processed an entire text, long-term memory includes a completely interconnected network of propositions, plus the title of the text and the context in which it was studied. This network is then made available to the free recall component of the model. Clauses and sentences are represented in this network only as strongly associated clusters of propositions.

Free Recall Component. Our model treats free recall as a problem-solving task that involves retrieval of a causal path linking the text's opening to its final outcome. To accomplish this goal, the model attempts, at all times, to identify a cluster of propositions that together form a clause that is the most likely causal antecedent to the next step in the causal path. These propositions (which constitute the model's current state), along with the context in which the text was studied, are used as retrieval cues. Once the cues are chosen, they are used to sample and recover new propositions from long-term memory until L_{max} retrieval failures occur (i.e., the model either fails to recover the information in a sampled image or it samples and recovers a previously recalled image L_{max} times). Next, the model adds any newly recalled propositions to a list of recalled propositions, chooses a new set of cues, and attempts to sample and recover more propositions. This process is repeated until a total of K_{max} retrieval failures have accumulated.

In the model, three heuristics are used to choose retrieval cues. First, the model determines whether any of the recalled propositions form a causal consequence of the current state. If they do, and if those propositions have not been used as retrieval cues previously, they are selected as cues and the clause they form becomes the new current state. If this fails, the model checks for newly recalled propositions from the old current state. If any are found that are essential to the causal role of the current state clause, they are added to the previous set of retrieval cues. If this also fails, the model attempts to "back up," and the most recently recalled propositions that form a causal antecedent for the current state clause become the new current state. Moreover, the propositions from this cluster (plus context again) become the new set of retrieval cues.

For the model to work consistently, clauses at the beginning of the causal path through the text (such as Clause 2 in "Danny's New Bike") must be treated as if they were consequences of the context. This has two major effects. First, at the beginning of a free recall task, we assume that the title of the text (which we treat as a separate proposition, P00) and the context are used as retrieval cues. The causally important propositions from the first clause in the causal chain will be most strongly associated with these cues. As a result, they are usually recalled first and become the new current state. Second, if the model is forced to back up past the beginning of the text, context becomes the only retrieval cue. When this happens, none of the selection heuristics described above applies. After sampling and recovering with context alone, the model identifies the most recent set of propositions that are causally significant, form a clause, and have not been used previously as retrieval cues; these become the new current state.

In summary, the free recall component of the model attempts to retrieve a causal path linking the opening of a text to its final outcome. This is accomplished by using a probabilistic search process that always selects, as retrieval cues, the propositions at the end of the causal path conducted to that point. When this process reaches a causal dead end, it backs up through the causal structure of the text before proceeding forward again. The output of this process is an ordered list of recalled propositions. Because the model's sampling and recovery processes are probabilistic, the contents of the list will vary if the model processes the same text more than once.

The Simulation

To facilitate the testing of our model, we implemented it in a computer program called TeXT.[1] The program was written in Common Lisp and runs on a NeXTstation computer. It was implemented as a simple production system (Anderson, 1983; Newell, 1973) and includes three parts: a rule interpreter; a set of comprehension rules; and a set of free recall rules. Each of TeXT's rules includes a set of conditions, which typically are tests on the contents of short-term memory, and a set of actions, which usually alter the contents of short-term memory. The interpreter works by scanning an ordered set of rules until it finds one whose conditions are all true. The actions associated with that rule are then carried out (which usually makes another rule's conditions true). After that, the interpreter returns to the first rule in the set and the process repeats itself. The interpreter halts when no rule can be found whose conditions are all true. The comprehension component of the model is implemented by just five rules. English approximations to each of these rules are shown in Appendix A. The free recall component of the model is implemented by the nine rules shown in Appendix B. The program takes as input (a) a list of propositions, as shown in the first two columns of Table 5.2, (b) a list of the propositions that play an essential role in the causal function of each clause (also shown in Table 5.2), and (c) a list of the causal antecedents to each clause (i.e., the same information provided by Fig. 5.1). As output, it produces an ordered list of "recalled" propositions.

AN EMPIRICAL TEST OF THE MODEL

Predicting Free Recall

Free Recall Data. In a test of the model, we collected free recall protocols from 24 undergraduate psychology students at the University of Minnesota. Each participant was asked to read and recall five short narrative texts (including the text in Table 5.1). All texts were of approximately equal length and difficulty. Participants were presented one text per page in preassembled test booklets. The first text in each booklet was used for practice, four test texts followed in

[1]Copies of the TeXT program are available from the authors.

a random order. Participants were encouraged to read at their normal speed. They were aware that they would be tested on the texts, but did not know the nature of that test. Free recall instructions encouraged participants to write down as much of each text as they could remember. Each protocol was written on a separate sheet of paper that had the title of the to-be-remembered text printed at its top. The order of the test pages in each booklet was the same as the order in which the texts were presented.

Each free recall protocol was scored by two judges using criteria recommended by both Turner and Greene (1978) and Bovair and Kieras (1985). A participant was credited with recalling a particular proposition only if it (or a close paraphrase) was explicitly present in the protocol. The two judges agreed on 96% of their judgments and all disagreements were resolved through discussion. These judgments were then used to calculate an observed free recall probability for each proposition in the four test texts. As an example, the last column of Table 5.2 shows the observed free recall probabilities for each proposition in "Danny's New Bike." To determine the reliability of these data, the participants were randomly separated into two groups of 12 and free recall probabilities were calculated separately for each group. The squared correlation between these two sets of free recall probabilities, $r^2 = .69$, represents the upper limit on the proportion of variance in the data that could be accounted for by any model. To examine the order of free recall, we calculated the probability that a pair of recalled propositions are recalled in the correct (i.e., input) order, for each subject. The resulting mean of .99 and standard deviation of .02 indicate that the participants recalled the order of propositions in the stories almost perfectly.

Fitting the Model to the Free Recall Probabilities. The model was fit to the free recall data from each of the four texts separately. For each text, a set of values for the nine model parameters (a, b_0, b_s, b_r, b_c, c, d, L_{max}, and K_{max}) was chosen at random (from within a specified range) and the TeXT program was run 100 times. The results of these simulations were used to calculate a predicted free recall value for each proposition. The sum of squared deviations of the predicted free recall values from the observed values for the text was used to measure of the goodness-of-fit of the model to the free recall data.[2] One of the parameters then was chosen and incremented by a small, predetermined amount. Another 100 runs of the program was used to determine if this change produced an improvement in the fit of the model to the data; if it did, additional increments were made until no further improvements were observed, otherwise, the value of the parameter was adjusted downward until the best possible value was found. After all nine parameters had been adjusted in this fashion, the process was repeated until no further improvement was observed in the fit

[2]More common goodness-of-fit measures such as minimum chi-square or maximum likelihood ratio could not be used with these data because several of the observed free recall probabilities zero.

between the predicted and observed free recall probabilities. The fourth column of Table 5.2 shows the predicted free recall probabilities obtained with the best fitting parameter values for "Danny's New Bike."

Table 5.4 summarizes the results of this model fitting procedure. It reveals a high degree of consistency across the four texts. On average, the model accounted for 37% of the variance in our participants' free recall data, ranging from a high 51% to a low of 29% across texts. In addition, there was little variation in the best fitting parameter values across texts.

Predicting the Order of Free Recall. With all parameters set as their optimal values, the probability that a pair of propositions recalled by the model (during 100 simulation runs per text) were recalled in their input order was .73. Thus, the ability of the model to recall propositions in correct order lies midway between the chance value of .50 and the almost perfect value of .99 observed for our participants. Single group *t*-tests reveal that the model's performance is significantly better than chance for each of the four test texts (see Table 5.5).

Separating the Effects of Comprehension and Retrieval Strategies

To what extent is the success of our model due to its ability to describe how a text is encoded versus how it is retrieved? To answer this question, we created two alternative versions of the model. In one version, the influence of the comprehension strategy was removed by replacing it with a strategy that (on average) holds the same number of propositions in short-term memory whenever a sentence boundary is reached, but chooses those propositions randomly. In the other version, the influence of the retrieval strategy was negated by replacing it with a strategy that (on average) selects the same number of cues each time

TABLE 5.4
Best Fitting Parameters and Variance Accounted for (r^2) by the Model

Parameter	*Danny's New Bike*	*Farmer and the Donkey*	*Rick's New Job*	*Terry's Light*
a	.21	.18	.19	.21
b_0	.12	.20	.27	.28
b_s	.45	.70	.47	.48
b_r	.01	.02	.01	.05
b_c	.03	.03	.03	.08
c	.16	.19	.21	.17
d	.02	.02	.02	.03
L_{max}	6	7	1	2
K_{max}	114	119	109	110
r^2	.51***	.33***	.29***	.34***

***$p < .001$

TABLE 5.5
Probability That the Model Recalls a Pair of Propositions in Their Correct (i.e., Input Order)

	Probability of Correct Order	*t(99)*[a]
Danny's New Bike	.75	19.61***
Farmer and the Donkey	.88	38.03***
Rick's New Job	.71	8.22***
Terry's Light	.60	19.80***

[a]One-tailed t-tests evaluate the null hypothesis that the associated probability is not reliably greater than the chance value of .5.
***$p < .001$

L_{max} retrieval failures occur, but selects them at random. We then repeated the model fitting and evaluation procedures described earlier. The results of these computational experiments[3] are summarized in Fig. 5.3. The model's ability to predict which propositions were recalled was diminished by 32% when its comprehension strategy was replaced by a random process, but by only 11% when its retrieval strategy was similarly replaced. This suggests that the success of the model is due primarily to an ability to mimic how a text is encoded. However, a different picture emerged when we examined its ability to predict when propositions were recalled; here, the model's performance was diminished by 23% when the retrieval strategy was replaced by a random process but by only 5% when the comprehension strategy was replaced. Taken together, these results reveal that both of the model's components are essential to its success: the comprehension strategy allowed it to predict which propositions our participants recalled and the retrieval strategy allowed it to predict the order of their recall.

CONCLUSIONS

A number of important findings emerged from this research. First, we have shown that the comprehension model proposed by Fletcher and Bloom (1988) can be embedded in the architecture of Raaijmakers and Shiffrin's (1980, 1981; Gillund & Shiffrin, 1984) model of human memory. This represents a significant generalization of both models. It also permitted us to extend the comprehension model by adding a free recall component. Second, we have shown that the model is consistent and detailed enough so that it can be implemented as a computer program. This also facilitates the task of evaluating the model. Third, we have demonstrated that the model can account for more than one third of the variance

[3]The same pattern of results was observed across the four test texts and, thus, only aggregate results are discussed.

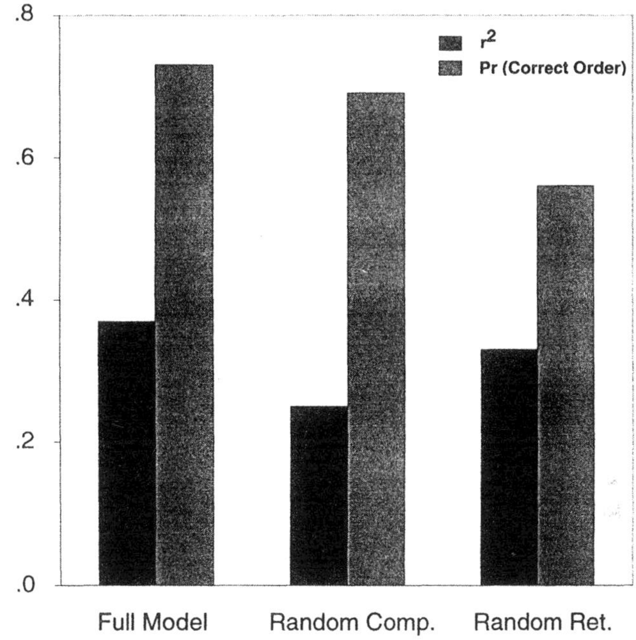

FIG. 5.3. Variance accounted for in free recall probabilities (r^2) and probability of recalling a pair of propositions in the correct order for all three versions of the model.

in college students' free recall protocols. This represents strong empirical support both for our model and for the earlier models from which it was derived. Fourth, we were able to go beyond most contemporary models of narrative comprehension by successfully predicting when propositions would be recalled. Again, this represents strong support both for our model and for its predecessors. Finally, we isolated the contributions of the model's encoding and retrieval strategies by showing that the comprehension strategy allows it to predict what will be remembered, whereas the retrieval strategy allows it to predict when.

The model described here has some clear limitations; however, each of these represents an opportunity for future research on the interaction of basic cognitive processes in narrative comprehension and recall. One limitation is the absence of reinstatement searches in the model. Van den Broek (1990a) has argued that when the causal antecedents of an event that are available in short-term memory are not sufficient for the event to occur, a reader will attempt to retrieve sufficient information from long-term memory. Initial support for this position has been provided by Bloom et al. (1990), but a number of unanswered questions remain: What are the retrieval cues? What other conditions initiate a search of long-term memory? Do all readers search long-term memory under the same circumstances? We believe that our model will facilitate the search for answers to these questions.

Another limitation of our model is that it makes no use of discourse structure as it encodes and retrieves a story (see, e.g., Mandler & Johnson, 1977; Rumelhart, 1977; Stein & Glenn, 1979). Yekovich and Thorndyke (1981) have argued that readers use such knowledge to retrieve the type of statement (goal, event, outcome, etc.) that should occur next in a story during free recall. This suggestion could be evaluated by adding knowledge of story structure to the model and determining whether its performance improves when the retrieval strategy uses the expected category of the next statement as an additional retrieval cue. This knowledge could also be used in place of L_{max} and K_{max} to determine when the model is to select new retrieval cues and when it is to halt (Stein & Glenn, 1979; van den Broek, 1988). We believe that the model proposed here will be a useful tool for exploring the use of discourse structure in narrative comprehension and recall.

A third limitation of our model is that it is unable to make bridging inferences. Recent research (e.g., Keenan, Baillet, & Brown, 1984; Myers, Shinjo, & Duffy, 1987) has shown that when one or more steps in a causal sequence are missing from a text, a reader will attempt to fill them in. Van den Broek (1990a) has argued that Kintsch's (1988) construction-integration model, in conjunction with the problem-solving procedures included in our model, offers a mechanism for making these inferences. This suggests the possibility of incorporating such a mechanism into our model. If this proves to be feasible, it will represent yet another step toward a unified theory of text comprehension and recall.

ACKNOWLEDGMENT

This research was supported in part by the Center for Research in Learning, Perception, and Cognition at the University of Minnesota, by Project Woksape, and by grant AFOSR-86-0280 to the first author. We are grateful to Ben Stiegler and Kurt Krebsbach for their programming assistance and to Bruce Britton, Art Graesser, and the members of the Minnesota Text Comprehension Research Group for their many helpful comments.

APPENDIX A: COMPREHENSION RULES

Rule C1. Sentence Boundary:

If the end of a sentence has been reached,
then purge everything except CONTEXT and the propositions in CURRENT-STATE from SHORT-TERM MEMORY,
increment the strength of association between CONTEXT and each proposition in SHORT-TERM MEMORY by a,

increment all connection strengths between the propositions remaining in SHORT-TERM MEMORY by $b_0 + b_s$,
increment all connection strengths among referentially related propositions in SHORT-TERM MEMORY by b_r,
increment the strength of association of each proposition in SHORT-TERM MEMORY to itself by c.

Rule C2. Make Links:

If SHORT-TERM MEMORY contains a proposition not linked to anything,
then create a link between the new proposition and CONTEXT and assign that link a strength of a,
create links of strength b_0 between the new proposition and all other propositions in SHORT-TERM MEMORY,
increment all connection strengths between the new proposition and propositions from the same clause in SHORT-TERM MEMORY by b_s,
increment all connection strengths between the new proposition and referentially related propositions in SHORT-TERM MEMORY by b_r,
increment all connection strengths between the new proposition and causally related propositions in SHORT-TERM MEMORY by b_c,
create a link of strength c between the new proposition and itself.

Rule C3. Enhance Current-State:

If a proposition in SHORT-TERM MEMORY is not part of the CURRENT-STATE,
the proposition is from the same clause as the CURRENT-STATE, and
the proposition is causally relevant,
then add the proposition to the CURRENT-STATE.

Rule C4. New Current-State:

If a proposition in SHORT-TERM MEMORY is not part of the CURRENT-STATE,
the proposition is causally relevant,
the proposition has causal antecedents in SHORT-TERM MEMORY, and
the proposition has no consequences in SHORT-TERM MEMORY,
then set the CURRENT-STATE equal to the proposition plus CONTEXT.

Rule C5. Next Input:

If the text contains additional propositions,

then add the next proposition to SHORT-TERM MEMORY and LONG-TERM MEMORY.

APPENDIX B: FREE RECALL RULES

Rule R1. Add to List:

If SHORT-TERM MEMORY contains a proposition not on RECALLED-LIST and
TOTAL-FAILURES is less than K_{max},
then add the item to RECALLED-LIST.

Rule R2. Recovery Failure:

If SHORT-TERM MEMORY contains RECOVERY-FAILURE and
TOTAL-FAILURES is less than K_{max},

then remove RECOVERY-FAILURE from SHORT-TERM MEMORY,
increment TOTAL-FAILURES by one,
increment LOCAL-FAILURES by one.

Rule R3. Sampling Failure:

If SHORT-TERM MEMORY contains two instances of the same proposition and
TOTAL-FAILURES is less than K_{max},
then delete one instance of the proposition from SHORT-TERM MEMORY,
increment TOTAL-FAILURES by one,
increment LOCAL-FAILURES by one.

Rule R4. New Current-State:

If SHORT-TERM MEMORY contains a proposition caused by the propositions in CURRENT-STATE and
this proposition has not been used as a retrieval cue,
then set CURRENT-STATE equal to this proposition,
mark the proposition as having been used as a retrieval cue.

Rule R5. Onward from Context:

If CURRENT-STATE is set to CONTEXT,
SHORT-TERM MEMORY contains a proposition with causal antecedents

this proposition has not been used as a retrieval cue,
LOCAL-FAILURES is greater than L_{max}, and
TOTAL-FAILURES is less than K_{max},

then set SHORT-TERM MEMORY equal to the proposition plus CONTEXT,
set CURRENT-STATE equal to the proposition,
mark the proposition as having been used as a retrieval cue,
reset LOCAL-FAILURES to zero.

Rule R6. Enhance Current-State:

If SHORT-TERM MEMORY contains a proposition not in CURRENT-STATE,
the proposition has the same causes and consequences as the propositions in CURRENT-STATE, and
TOTAL-FAILURES is less than K_{max},

then add the proposition to CURRENT-STATE,
mark the proposition as having been used as a retrieval cue.

Rule R7. Backtrack:

If LOCAL-FAILURES is greater than L_{max},
TOTAL-FAILURES is less than K_{max},
CURRENT-STATE contains at least one proposition, and
the propositions in CURRENT-STATE have causal antecedents on RECALLED-LIST.

then reset CURRENT-STATE to the most recent direct antecedents of CURRENT-STATE on RECALLED-LIST,
reset SHORT-TERM MEMORY to CONTEXT plus the new value of CURRENT-STATE,
reset LOCAL-FAILURES to zero.

Rule R8. Backtrack to Context:

If LOCAL-FAILURES is greater than L_{max} and
TOTAL-FAILURES is less than K_{max},

then reset CURRENT-STATE to CONTEXT,
reset SHORT-TERM MEMORY to CONTEXT,
reset LOCAL-FAILURES to zero.

Rule R9. Probe Long-Term Memory

If LOCAL-FAILURES is less than L_{max} and
TOTAL-FAILURES is less than K_{max},

then probe LONG-TERM MEMORY using CONTEXT and the contents of CURRENT-STATE as retrieval cues, add the recovered item (potentially "RECOVERY-FAILURE") to SHORT-TERM MEMORY.

REFERENCES

Anderson, J. R. (1983). *The architecture of cognition*. Cambridge, MA: Harvard University Press.

Black, J. B., & Bower, G. H. (1980). Story understanding as problem solving. *Poetics, 9*, 223–250.

Bloom, C. P., Fletcher, C. R., van den Broek, P., Reitz, L., & Shapiro, B. P. (1990). An online assessment of causal reasoning during comprehension. *Memory & Cognition, 18*, 65–71.

Bovair, S., & Kieras, D. E. (1985). A guide to propositional analysis for research on technical prose. In B. K. Britton & J. B. Black (Eds.), *Understanding expository text* (pp. 315–362). Hillsdale, NJ: Lawrence Erlbaum Associates.

Clark, N. K., Stephenson, G. M., & Rutter, D. R. (1986). Memory for complex social discourse: The analysis and prediction of individual and group recall. *Journal of Memory and Language, 25*, 295–313.

Fletcher, C. R. (1986). Strategies for the allocation of short-term memory during comprehension. *Journal of Memory and Language, 25*, 43–58.

Fletcher, C. R. (1985). Understanding and solving arithmetic word problems: A computer simulation. *Behavior Research Methods, Instruments, & Computers, 17*, 565–571.

Fletcher, C. R. (1981). Short-term memory processes in text comprehension. *Journal of Verbal Learning and Verbal Behavior, 20*, 564–574.

Fletcher, C. R., & Bloom, C. P. (1988). Causal reasoning in the comprehension of simple narrative texts. *Journal of Memory and Language, 27*, 235–244.

Fletcher, C. R., Hummel, J. E., & Marsolek, C. J. (1990). Causality and the allocation of attention during comprehension. *Journal of Experimental Psychology: Learning, Memory, and Cognition, 16*, 233–240.

Gillund, G., & Shiffrin, R. M. (1984). A retrieval model for both recognition and recall. *Psychological Review, 91*, 1–68.

Greeno, J. G., & Simon, H. A. (1988). Problem solving and reasoning. In R. C. Atkinson, R. J. Herrnstein, G. Lindzey, & R. D. Luce (Eds.), *Stevens' handbook of experimental psychology: Vol. 2. Learning and cognition* (rev. ed., pp. 589–672). New York: Wiley.

Keenan, J. M., Baillet, S. D., & Brown, P. (1984). The effects of causal cohesion on comprehension and memory. *Journal of Memory and Language, 23*, 115–126.

Kintsch, W. (1988). The role of knowledge in discourse comprehension: A construction-integration model. *Psychological Review, 95*, 163–182.

Kintsch, W., & Greeno, J. G. (1985). Understanding and solving arithmetic word problems. *Psychological Review, 92*, 109–129.

Kintsch, W., & van Dijk, T. A. (1978). Toward a model of text comprehension and production. *Psychological Review, 85*, 363–394.

Kintsch, W., & Vipond, D. (1979). Reading comprehension and readability in educational practice and psychological theory. In L. Nilsson (Ed.), *Perspectives on memory research* (pp. 329–365). Hillsdale, NJ: Lawrence Erlbaum Associates.

Kintsch, W., Welsch, D., Schmalhofer, F., & Zimny, S. (1990). Sentence recognition: A theoretical analysis. *Journal of Memory and Language, 29*, 133–159.

Mackie, J. L. (1980). *The cement of the universe: A study of causation*. Oxford, England: Clarendon.

Mandler, J. M., & Johnson, N. S. (1977). Remembrance of things parsed: Story structure and recall. *Cognitive Psychology, 9*, 111–151.

McKoon, G., & Ratcliff, R. (1980). Priming in item recognition: The organization of propositions in memory for text. *Journal of Verbal Learning and Verbal Behavior, 19*, 369–386.

Miller, J. R., & Kintsch, W. (1980). Readability and recall of short prose passages: A theoretical analysis. *Journal of Experimental Psychology: Human Learning and Memory, 6*, 335–354.

Myers, J. L., Shinjo, M., & Duffy, S. A. (1987). Degree of causal relatedness and memory. *Journal of Memory and Language, 26*, 453–465.

Newell, A. (1973). Production systems: Models of control structures. In W. G. Chase (Ed.), *Visual information processing* (pp. 463–526). New York: Academic Press.

Newell, A., & Simon, H. A. (1972). *Human problem solving*. Englewood Cliffs, NJ: Prentice-Hall.

Raaijmakers, J. G. W., & Shiffrin, R. M. (1980). SAM: A theory of probabilistic search of associative memory. In G. H. Bower (Ed.), *The psychology of learning and motivation* (Vol. 14, pp. 207–262). New York: Academic Press.

Raaijmakers, J. G. W., & Shiffrin, R. M. (1981). Search of associative memory. *Psychological Review, 88*, 93–134.

Ratcliff, R., Clark, S. E., & Shiffrin, R. M. (1990). List-strength effect: I. Data and discussion. *Journal of Experimental Psychology: Learning, Memory, and Cognition, 16*, 163–178.

Ratcliff, R., & McKoon, G. (1978). Priming in item recognition: Evidence for the propositional structure of sentences. *Journal of Verbal Learning and Verbal Behavior, 17*, 403–417.

Ratcliff, R., & McKoon, G. (1988). A retrieval theory of priming in memory. *Psychological Review, 95*, 385–408.

Rumelhart, D. E. (1977). Understanding and summarizing brief stories. In D. LaBerge & S. J. Samuels (Eds.), *Basic processes in reading: Perception and comprehension* (pp. 265–304). Hillsdale, NJ: Lawrence Erlbaum Associates.

Schank, R. (1975). The structure of episodes in memory. In D. G. Bobrow & A. M. Collins (Eds.), *Representation and understanding: Studies in cognitive science* (pp. 237–272). New York: Academic Press.

Spilich, G. J., Vesonder, G. T., Chiesi, H. L., & Voss, J. F. (1979). Text processing of domain-related information for individuals with high and low domain knowledge. *Journal of Verbal Learning and Verbal Behavior, 18*, 275–290.

Stein, N. L., & Glenn, C. G. (1979). An analysis of story comprehension in elementary school children. In R. O. Freedle (Ed.), *New directions in discourse processing* (Vol. 2, pp. 53–120). Hillsdale, NJ: Lawrence Erlbaum Associates.

Trabasso, T., & Sperry, L. L. (1985). Causal relatedness and importance of story events. *Journal of Memory and Language, 24*, 595–611.

Trabasso, T., & van den Broek, P. (1985). Causal thinking and the representation of narrative events. *Journal of Memory and Language, 24*, 612–630.

Trabasso, T., van den Broek, P., & Suh, S. Y. (1989). Logical necessity and transitivity of causal relations in stories. *Discourse Processes, 12*, 1–25.

Turner, A., & Greene, E. (1978). Construction and use of a propositional text base. *Journal Supplement Abstract Service catalogue of selected documents in psychology* (MS 1713).

van den Broek, P. (1988). The effects of causal relations and hierarchical position on the importance of story statements. *Journal of Memory and Language, 27*, 1–22.

van den Broek, P. (1990a). Causal inferences and the comprehension of narrative texts. In A. C. Graesser & G. H. Bower (Eds.), *The psychology of learning and motivation* (Vol. 24, pp. 175–196). New York: Academic Press.

van den Broek, P. (1990b). The causal inference maker: Towards a process model of inference generation in text comprehension. In D. Balota, G. Flores d'Arcais, & K. Rayner (Eds.), *Comprehension processes in reading* (pp. 423–445). Hillsdale, NJ: Lawrence Erlbaum Associates.

van Dijk, T. A., & Kintsch, W. (1983). *Strategies of discourse comprehension*. New York: Academic Press.

Yekovich, F. R., & Thorndyke, P. W. (1981). An evaluation of alternative functional models of narrative schemata. *Journal of Verbal Learning and Verbal Behavior, 20*, 454–469.

CHAPTER

6

A "LANDSCAPE" VIEW OF READING: FLUCTUATING PATTERNS OF ACTIVATION AND THE CONSTRUCTION OF A STABLE MEMORY REPRESENTATION

Paul van den Broek
Kirsten Risden
Charles R. Fletcher
Richard Thurlow
University of Minnesota

Reading comprehension is one of the most complex and uniquely human of cognitive activities. During reading, the successful comprehender connects the various events, persons, and objects that he or she encounters so that the text appears to be a coherent whole rather than a random list of facts and events. Frequently, the relations between parts of a text are implicit and, therefore, must be inferred. If all goes well, the result of inferential processing is a mental representation of the text that is relatively stable and that can be accessed at a later point in time to answer questions, retell the story, and so forth.

A considerable amount of research has been devoted to the online inferential processes that are involved in the establishment of relations between text elements. In addition, properties of the memory representation of texts have enjoyed the attention of investigators in psychology, education, and even anthropology for years. Much less is known, however, about the relation between the online processes and the memory representation. On the one hand, the reader's goal of building a coherent memory representation may influence which of various types of inferences he or she will generate. On the other hand, the inferences that are generated during reading somehow must lead to the representation of the text in memory.

In this chapter, we propose a theoretical model of reading comprehension that describes both the inferential processes that take place during reading and the way in which these processes form the basis for a stable memory representation of the text. In doing so, we combine aspects of earlier models of reading

(Kintsch & van Dijk, 1978; van Dijk & Kintsch, 1983) with findings from recent research on the relation between comprehension processes and memory (e.g., Graesser & Bower, 1990; Graesser & Kreuz, 1993; Kintsch, 1988; McKoon & Ratcliff, 1992; Trabasso & Suh, 1993; van den Broek, 1994; van den Broek & Lorch, 1993).

READING AS A LANDSCAPE OF INFERENCES AND FLUCTUATING ACTIVATIONS

Reading for comprehension poses quite a challenge: Readers attempt to maintain coherence as they proceed through the text, but they must do so within the constraints of limited attentional resources. The standards for coherence that readers employ vary across, as well as within, individuals as a function of factors such as reading ability, motivation, reading task, pragmatic concerns, and so forth (see Singer, Graesser, & Trabasso, 1994; McKoon & Ratcliff, 1992; van den Broek, Fletcher, & Risden, 1993; van den Broek, Risden, & Husebye-Hartmann, 1995). Two types of coherence have received particular attention and seem to be involved in a wide range of reading situations, however: *anaphoric clarity* and *causal explanation*. Anaphoric clarity is obtained when the reader has identified clearly the referents for the objects, persons, and so forth in the sentence that is currently being read. Thus, if we read:

(1) The lady gave the waiter $10. He returned to give her the change.

anaphoric clarity is established when we recognize that *he* refers to *the waiter* and *her* refers to *the lady* (Gernsbacher, 1990; Kintsch & van Dijk, 1978; Kintsch, 1988; O'Brien & Albrecht, 1991). Causal coherence is established when, in the eyes of the reader, the current sentence is sufficiently explained. In Example 1, the fact that the lady gave the waiter $10 does not provide sufficient explanation for the waiter returning with change unless the reader also infers that the lady gave too much money to the waiter (Trabasso, Secco, van den Broek, 1984; van den Broek, 1990; van den Broek, Rohleder, & Narvaéz, in press).

The process of maintaining coherence would be relatively easy if the reader could keep all the information encountered in the text available for access during comprehension of later sentences. Unfortunately, readers are limited in their attentional or short-term memory resources and, as a result, can activate only a small subset of the information gleaned from the text at any point during reading (Kintsch & van Dijk, 1978). When a new statement is encountered, a new reading cycle starts, and the information in attention or short-term memory may be updated. The concepts that are activated at any particular point in the text come from three sources. One source of activation is the current sentence. Concepts that are explicitly mentioned in the sentence will become activated, as will concepts that are strongly associated with the explicit concepts in semantic or episodic memory (Kintsch, 1988). A second source of activation is the previous reading cycle. Concepts from the previous cycle may be retained into the current reading cycle. Among the concepts that are likely to be carried over from the previous reading cycle are those that were explicitly mentioned in the preceding sentence (Kintsch, 1988), concepts that were referentially prominent (cf. the *leading edge strategy*, Kintsch & van Dijk, 1978), concepts that describe the protagonist's goal (Trabasso & Suh, 1993), and concepts that describe events that have antecedents but no consequences (Fletcher & Bloom, 1988).[1]

If information from these two sources provides anaphoric clarity and a causally sufficient explanation for the current event, coherence is quickly and relatively effortlessly achieved. Thus, reading is smooth if the current event is so common that its associates readily establish anaphoric clarity and causal explanation, or if the current sentence is a direct continuation (referentially and causally) of the previous sentence. In these cases, the reader continues to the next sentence in the text without the need for additional processing.

A third source of activation is the reinstatement of concepts from the prior text. If the activated information does not provide anaphoric or causal coherence, more effortful and time-consuming processes ensue to restore the missing coherence. In these cases, coherence can be derived from two sources. First, the reader can reactivate or reinstate information that was encountered during earlier reading cycles. Second, the reader can draw on his or her background knowledge to fill in the missing anaphoric or causal content (Golden & Rumelhart, 1993; Graesser & Clark, 1985; van den Broek et al., 1993).

The search through the reader's memory or knowledge base and the mechanism for the assessment of coherence can take a number of forms. One possibility is that the knowledge base is accessed in two stages (Smith, Shoben, & Rips, 1974; van den Broek & Lorch, 1993). In the first stage, a quick assessment is made to determine whether the reader's memory for the text or general knowledge base contains information that may provide the missing cause or anaphor. If the assessment in this first stage is positive, a second, slower stage follows in which the desired information is retrieved. If the initial assessment is negative, the search may be expanded (for example, by a further spread of activation), or the reader may suspend comprehension in anticipation that subsequent text will provide a resolution. Which of these two paths is taken depends on factors such as the reader's motivation, the available time, and so forth. This model is similar to the Resonance-Followed-by-Retrieval model proposed by Huitema, Dopkins, Klin, and Myers (1993), and Myers, O'Brien, Albrecht, and Mason (1994). There is some evidence that retrieval in reading is a two-stage process. For example, readers frequently do not slow their reading when a coherence break occurs and the prior text does not provide a resolution. Readers do slow, how-

[1]Maintenance of these types of information contributes to the likelihood of establishing anaphoric and causal coherence. The fact that readers employ these strategies attests to the psychological validity of the standards of anaphoric clarity and causal explanation.

ever, if subsequent text fails to provide the missing information (O'Brien, 1980; van den Broek & Thurlow, 1990).[2] A second possibility for the reader's search process is that activation spreads uniformly until a certain degree of resonance or harmony, as defined by anaphoric or causal compatibility, occurs between the information that is retrieved and the information in the current sentence (Britton & Eisenhart, 1993; Smolensky, 1986). At this point, the inferential process terminates without explicit retrieval necessarily taking place.

Regardless of the mechanisms that underlie coherence-building inferences during reading, breaks in anaphoric or causal coherence are likely to initiate reinstatements or recruitment of background knowledge. Furthermore, the information that is reinstated or retrieved from background knowledge will tend to provide the missing anaphoric or causal information.[3]

This account of coherence-driven inferential processes has received extensive empirical support. On the one hand, sentences are read more slowly if they require reinstatement of prior text or access to background knowledge to establish anaphoric or causal coherence than if they do not require such inferencing (e.g., Gernsbacher, 1989; O'Brien, 1987; van den Broek & Thurlow, 1990). In addition, information that restores coherence is more readily available to the reader after it has been required for comprehension than before (Dopkins, Klin, & Myers, 1993; McKoon & Ratcliff, 1980; Potts, Keenan, & Golding, 1988; Thurlow, 1991). On the other hand, readers are less likely to activate background knowledge or engage in reinstatement if local relations provide a sufficient explanation than if local relations do not supply such an explanation. Thus, readers find it difficult to generate concepts that bridge two statements if the antecedent provides full sufficiency for the consequent (Myers, Shinjo, & Duffy, 1987; cf. van den Broek et al., 1995). For example, readers are very slow to generate an event that would fit between:

(2) Jimmy's big brother beat him up.

and

(3) The next day he was covered with bruises.

and the events that they do generate tend to be either simple restatements of the first sentence (e.g., "Jimmy was hit by his brother") or complete alternative

---

[2]We thank Jerry Myers for suggesting the parallels between the two-stage and Resonance-Followed-by-Retrieval models.

[3]It is important to emphasize that although a break in anaphoric or causal coherence increases the likelihood that a particular inference will be generated, a break in itself is neither necessary nor sufficient for inferential activity to take place. There is ample evidence that inferences frequently are generated even when local coherence is present and, conversely, that it is possible to create situations in which coherence breaks do not evoke inferences (see Graesser, Singer, & Trabasso, 1994; McKoon & Ratcliff, 1992; van den Broek, 1994).

explanations (e.g., "Jimmy must have fallen off his bike"). Similarly, readers are less likely to perform a reinstatement search for distant causal antecedents if a local antecedent provides full sufficiency for the consequent than if it does not (Thurlow, 1991). For example, imagine reading the following sentence in the middle of a text:

(4) The papers got all wet.

This event is adequately explained when preceded by:

(5) She dropped the papers in a puddle.

but not when preceded by:

(6) The wind blew open the folder.

This latter condition is more likely to precipitate a reinstatement search. Indeed, in a study by Thurlow (1991), reading of Example 4 was slower, and concepts from potential antecedents mentioned earlier in the text (e.g., *rain* from *It was raining hard*) were more available, following this statement in the latter situation than in the former situation.

Findings such as these indicate that readers frequently engage in inferential activity to attain adequate coherence (cf. Graesser, Singer, & Trabasso, 1994; Singer et al., 1994; van den Broek, 1994). Thus, the presence or absence of anaphoric clarity and causally sufficient explanation influences both when different types of inferences (i.e., connecting, reinstatement, elaborative) will occur and what the functional content of the resulting inference is likely to be.

Anaphoric clarity and causal explanation arguably are the best known standards of coherence but they certainly are not the only ones that readers employ. If we were to read a manual, for example, we might employ a pragmatic standard of coherence, such as whether we feel that we can reproduce the actions described in the text. Regardless of the exact standards that a reader employs in a particular reading situation, however, the result is that the activations of various concepts and events fluctuate throughout the text.

Consider, for example, the "Knight" story in Table 6.1 (adapted from van den Broek & Trabasso, 1986). The right-hand column indicates the major concepts in each statement, with each concept approximately corresponding to a major proposition (see Turner & Greene, 1978). One concept that features prominently in the text is "dragon." At several points in the text, the dragon is explicitly mentioned (e.g., statements 3, 4, 7, and 10), it sometimes is referred to by a pronoun (e.g., statement 8), and sometimes it is required for causal coherence (e.g., statement 9). At other points, the dragon is neither mentioned nor required

TABLE 6.1
The "Knight" Story

Reading Cycle	*Statement*	*Constituent Concepts*
1.	A young knight rode through the forest.	knight/rode/forest
2.	The knight was unfamiliar with the country.	knight/unfamiliar/country(forest)
3.	Suddenly a dragon appeared.	dragon/appeared
4.	The dragon was kidnapping a beautiful princess.	dragon/kidnapping/princess
5.	The knight wanted to free her.	knight/wanted-free/her(princess)
6.	The knight wanted to marry her.	knight/wanted-marry/her(princess)
7.	The knight hurried after the dragon.	knight/hurried-after/dragon
8.	They fought for life and death.	they(knight/dragon)/fought-for/life-death
9.	Soon, the knight's armour was completely scorched.	knight's-armour/scorched
10.	At last, the knight killed the dragon.	knight/killed-dragon
11.	He freed the princess.	he(knight)/freed/princess
12.	The princess was very thankful to the knight.	princess/thankful/knight
13.	She married the knight.	she(princess)/married/knight

for anaphoric or causal coherence (e.g., statements 1, 2, 13). As a result, its activation fluctuates as one proceeds through the text.

The fluctuations in activation during reading can be illustrated by the application of a set of simple, but plausible, rules to the concepts in the Knight story.[4] First, it is assumed that explicitly mentioned concepts result in the highest activation. These concepts are assigned a 5 on a 5-point scale. Second, concepts that are required to restore anaphoric coherence are given activation strengths of 4. Third, concepts that contribute to the causal explanation of the current statement fall into two categories: *causes*, which provide a sufficient explanation for an event, and *enablements*, which are preconditions that are necessary but not sufficient for the current event (Trabasso, van den Broek, & Suh, 1989). For example, "Striking a match" would be a *cause* for "The match lit," whereas "There was oxygen" is only *enabling*. Causes receive values of 4, whereas enablements are given a value of 3. Fourth, statements may elicit associative elaborations, that is, inferences that are drawn from background knowledge but that do not contribute to the anaphoric or causal coherence of the text (e.g., "trees," "love," and "sword" for the Knight story). These elaborative inferences are assigned an activation value of 2.

Unless an activated concept is repeated or reinstated, its activation will return to zero. There are three possible ways in which this can happen. One possibility is that reading a new sentence overwrites all information from the preceding reading cycle. A second possibility is that some concepts decline, whereas others remain activated. (See the findings about maintenance of concepts reviewed previously.) A third possibility is that the activation of concepts gradually declines over subsequent cycles. For the purpose of illustrating the model, we assume that activations asymptotically decline to zero unless they are reinstated or reactivated by the new statement. This is approximated here by reducing the activation value of concepts that do not receive additional activation in the subsequent reading cycle to half of their original value, and to zero in the third cycle.

Two trained judges applied these rules to the concepts in the Knight story. Following Kintsch and van Dijk (1978), each reading cycle was taken to contain one statement. The resulting activations values for each concept in each reading cycle are displayed in Table 6.2.

When activation of all the concepts is considered over time, the result is a landscape of fluctuating patterns of activation. The activation level of a particular concept during the processing of a sentence is a function of the informational constraints in the text and the inferential processes that take place to establish anaphoric and causal coherence for that sentence. Such a landscape for the

---

[4]At this point our concern is with illustrating the model's assumptions about different sources of activation and different strengths associated with each source. The particular values chosen for each type of activated information are arbitrary.

TABLE 6.2
Activation of Concepts in the Knight Story

Concept	Reading Cycle 1	2	3	4	5	6	7	8	9	10	11	12	13	Total activation
Knight	5	5	2.5	0	5	5	5	4	4	5	4	5	5	54.5
Rode	5	3	1.5	0	0	0	0	0	0	0	0	0	0	9.5
Horse	2	1	0	0	0	0	0	0	0	0	0	0	0	3
Forest	5	4	2	0	0	0	0	0	0	0	0	0	0	11
Trees	2	1	0	0	0	0	0	0	0	0	0	0	0	3
Unfamiliar	0	5	3	1.5	0	0	0	0	0	0	0	0	0	9.5
Country	0	5	3	1.5	0	0	0	0	0	0	0	0	0	9.5
Dragon	0	0	5	5	3	1.5	5	4	3	5	2.5	0	0	34
Appeared	0	0	5	3	1.5	0	0	0	0	0	0	0	0	9.5
Kidnapping	0	0	0	5	3	1.5	0	0	0	0	0	0	0	9.5
Beautiful	0	0	0	5	2.5	3	1.5	0	0	0	0	0	0	12
Princess	0	0	0	5	4	4	2	0	0	0	5	5	4	29
Want-Free	0	0	0	0	5	2.5	3	3	1.5	0	3	1.5	0	19.5
Want-Marry	0	0	0	0	0	5	3	1.5	0	0	0	0	3	12.5
Love	0	0	0	0	0	4	2	0	0	0	0	0	0	6
Hurried-After	0	0	0	0	0	0	5	3	1.5	0	0	0	0	9.5
Fought	0	0	0	0	0	0	0	5	3	3	1.5	0	0	12.5
Life-Death	0	0	0	0	0	0	0	5	2.5	3	1.5	0	0	12
Armor	0	0	0	0	0	0	0	0	5	2.5	0	0	0	7.5
Scorched	0	0	0	0	0	0	0	0	5	2.5	0	0	0	7.5
Fire	0	0	0	0	0	0	0	0	3	1.5	0	0	0	4.5
Killed	0	0	0	0	0	0	0	0	0	5	3	1.5	0	9.5
Sword	0	0	0	0	0	0	0	0	0	2	1	0	0	3
Freed	0	0	0	0	0	0	0	0	0	0	5	3	1.5	9.5
Thankful	0	0	0	0	0	0	0	0	0	0	0	5	3	8
Married	0	0	0	0	0	0	0	0	0	0	0	0	5	5

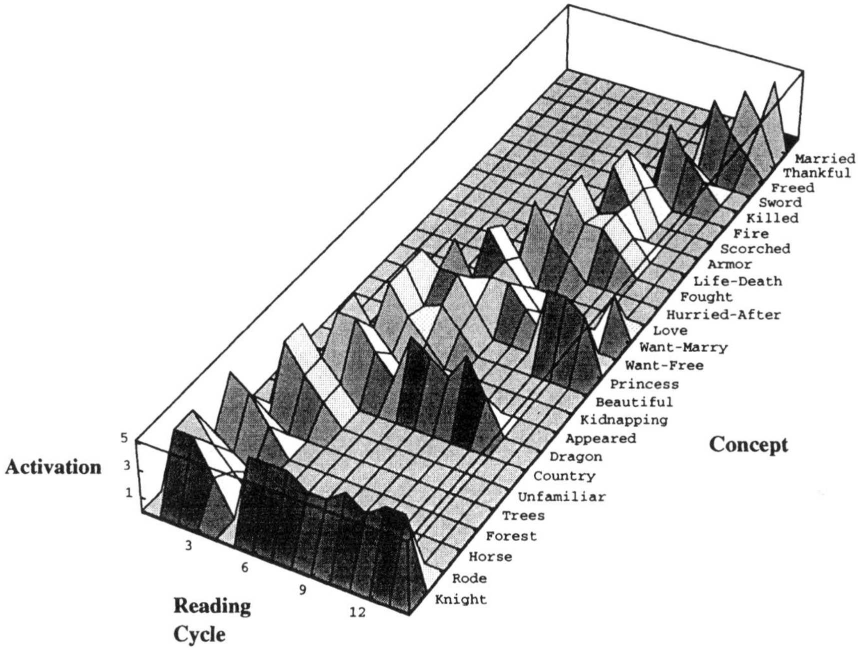

FIG. 6.1. Landscape of activation for the Knight story.

Knight story is depicted in Fig. 6.1.[5] Cross-sections of the landscape across reading cycles reflect the pattern of activation for individual concepts over the course of the story. Conversely, a cross-section of the landscape for a reading cycle across concepts shows all concepts that were activated concurrently at that cycle.

Testing the Model: Do Activations Fluctuate as a Function of Anaphoric and Causal Reinstatements?

The model's predictions about activations during reading were compared to those reported by naive readers. Two texts were used, the Knight story (described previously) and the "Tiger's Whisker" (adapted from Stein & Glenn, 1978). The two judges who had scored the Knight story also applied the model's criteria of anaphoric clarity and causal sufficiency to the second text. As before, they used the rules to determine the activations for the concepts at each reading cycle. The interrater agreement on the judgments for both stories was high. The result was two matrices of activations such as the one displayed in Table 6.1.

[5]The activation values in Fig. 6.1 are identical to those in Table 6.2. Representing these values in a table allows us to connect online processes to the memory representation of the text in subsequent sections of the chapter, whereas the graphic representation communicates the "landscape" nature of the activation patterns.

The model's predictions for the activations of concepts were tested by having each story read by 7 naive participants. Subjects read their story sentence by sentence. At each reading cycle (i.e., at each statement), participants were presented with a scoring sheet that listed propositions and concepts that were explicitly mentioned in, or closely associated with, the text. Participants had been instructed to indicate on a 5-point scale how strongly each statement made them think of each concept. No further instructions were given, and no reference was made to causal or anaphoric coherence. Thus, the readers were naive to the theoretical notions of coherence. For each participant, an activation matrix similar to the theoretical one displayed in Table 6.1 was obtained.

We determined whether the naive readers generally agreed on the activations of concepts by computing correlations between their matrices of activations. The average correlation between the participants' ratings for each cell in the matrix was high, .79. Thus, there was strong consistency among the naive readers with respect to the activations of each concept at each reading cycle. The reliability of the naive readers' ratings was $.79^2 = .624$. This constitutes the upper boundary of the variance that any predictor variable could account for in these data.

Given the high agreement among the naive readers, it was possible to test the validity of the model's predictions. In fact, the theoretically derived activations corresponded very well with those given by the naive readers: The correlation between predicted activations and the average activations produced by the participants was .73, and the proportion of variance that was accounted for by the model was .533. The latter is very close to the maximum amount of explained variance that is allowed by the reliability of the naive participants' ratings.

For purposes of comparison, the same correlations were computed for a second model. In this model, activations due to referential and causal reinstatements were removed. The correlations for this "impoverished" model was considerably lower, .46. This pattern of results provides strong evidence that information from the prior text is activated when such information is required for referential and causal coherence.

In summary, the activation of concepts and events during reading results from a dynamic interplay between information in the current sentence and the reader's requirements for coherence. The landscape approach provides a graphical representation of the dynamics of comprehension. The framework is based on the notion that the reading process is characterized by fluctuating patterns of activation. When a reader encounters a sentence, various concepts are activated as a result of the comprehension process. These concepts include the ideas, events, objects, persons, and so forth that are described in the sentence, but these concepts also can include information from the prior text or from background knowledge. As the reader proceeds through the text, attention shifts: Some concepts increase in their activation, others decrease, and still others remain relatively stable. The fluctuating patterns of activation for each of the individual concepts together constitute, as it were, a *landscape* of activations. This landscape of fluctuating activations forms the basis for the construction of a stable representation in memory.

COHERENCE AND THE REPRESENTATION OF THE TEXT IN MEMORY

Considerable research has demonstrated that a successfully comprehended text is represented in memory as a coherent structure. The conventional way of thinking of this structure is in terms of a network of linked nodes, such that the links reflect causal and anaphoric relations between concepts. The psychological validity of the notion that these links form the basis of the memory representations of texts has been demonstrated empirically. For example, presentation of one member of a pair of related sentences primes recognition of the other member (Trabasso & Suh, 1993; van den Broek & Lorch, 1993). Furthermore, the strength of the relation between statements influences how well they are remembered. Myers et al. (1987), for example, found better memory for sentence pairs that were related via a strong causal connection than for sentence pairs that were related via a weak causal connection. Interestingly, these authors also found that memory for sentence pairs related via causal connections of moderate strength were remembered even better than those sharing a strong causal relation. Myers and Duffy (1990) suggested that the addition of explanatory concepts and their connections to the representation of these moderately related sentence pairs not only establishes coherence, but provides multiple retrieval routes that facilitate memory for these sentences. This effect of number of connections on memory for statements has been demonstrated elsewhere as well. For example, statements with many connections to other statements in a text are recalled more frequently (Graesser & Clark, 1985; Miller & Kintsch, 1980; Trabasso et al., 1984; Trabasso & Sperry, 1985), more easily accessed (O'Brien & Myers, 1987) and rated more important (van den Broek, 1988) than are statements with few connections. Thus, both the strength and the number of connections associated with a given statement determine the likelihood that it will be remembered. These and other findings attest to the psychological validity of the memory representation of a text as a coherent network structure founded on anaphoric and causal links between concept nodes.

From Fluctuating Patterns of Activation to Stable Representations in Memory

The landscape representation combines dynamic features of online processing with the assumption of causal and referential relational structure in memory. In the model, the fluctuating pattern of activation reflects the reader's attempt to maintain referential and causal coherence. The question, then, is how patterns of activation during reading result in a relatively permanent memory representation of a text. Two structural features of the landscape of activations allow one to conceptualize how properties of online processing determine and correspond to properties of the memory representation. First, by tracing the course of activation for each individual node or concept in the text as the reader proceeds, one can identify the overall amount of activation that each node has received by the end of the story. The right-hand column in Table 6.2 provides the sum of the activation values that each concept in the Knight story received across reading cycles. According to the model, comparison of these values across concepts reflects the relative importance of the concepts in the story.

Second, as Fig. 6.1 illustrates, at any given point during reading, some concepts will be activated simultaneously. Prior research has demonstrated that concepts that are activated simultaneously tend to be connected in memory (Fletcher & Bloom, 1988; Fletcher, Chrysler, van den Broek, Deaton, & Bloom, 1995; Kintsch & van Dijk, 1978). In the current model, we extend this notion and propose that the strength of the relation between two concepts in episodic memory depends on two properties of the online activations: the frequency with which two concepts are simultaneously activated and the amount of activation that each concept receives during each reading cycle in which they co-occur. More specifically, we propose that the strength of the relation between two concepts is a multiplicative function of the activations of the individual concepts at each reading cycle. Such a function can take various forms, but for purposes of illustration we use the following simplification:

$$S(x,y) = \sum_{i=1}^{I} A_{x_i} A_{y_i} \tag{1}$$

in which $S(x,y)$ refers to the strength of the final relation between concepts x and y, i refers to the number of the current reading cycle in the text, I refers to the total number of reading cycles, and A_{xi} and A_{yi} refer to the activations of concepts x and y at reading cycle i, respectively. The strength of the relation between each concept and every other concept is represented by a cross products matrix that was calculated by multiplying the matrix in Table 6.2 (excluding the marginal sums) by itself. Table 6.3 provides the resulting matrix. The diagonal and the duplicate half of the matrix are omitted for purposes of clarity.

In summary, according to this model, the relational memory structure for a text emerges through simultaneous activation of concepts. Two features of the landscape of activations, the total activation that an individual concept receives and the strength of its relatedness to the remainder of the text, capture the centrality of a concept in the memory representation. These two features can be represented graphically. This is illustrated in the partial memory representation of the Knight story in Fig. 6.2. In this figure, the size of the circle for each concept is proportional

TABLE 6.3
Cross-Products of Activation for Concepts in the "Knight" Story

	Kn	*R*	*H*	*Fo*	*T*	*U*	*Co*	*D*	*A*	*Ki*	*B*	*P*	*WF*	*WM*	*L*	*HA*	*F*	*LD*	*Ar*	*Sc*	*Fi*	*K*	*Sw*	*Fr*	*Th*	*M*
Knight		44	15	50	15	33	33	123	20	23	35	115	90	61	30	43	53	51	33	33	20	45	14	43	40	25
Rode			13	40	13	20	20	8	8	0	0	0	0	0	0	0	0	0	0	0	0	0	0	0	0	0
Horse				14	5	5	5	0	0	0	0	0	0	0	0	0	0	0	0	0	0	0	0	0	0	0
Forest					14	26	26	10	10	0	0	0	0	0	0	0	0	0	0	0	0	0	0	0	0	0
Trees						5	5	0	0	0	0	0	0	0	0	0	0	0	0	0	0	0	0	0	0	0
Unfamiliar							36	23	20	8	8	8	0	0	0	0	0	0	0	0	0	0	0	0	0	0
Country								23	20	8	8	8	0	0	0	0	0	0	0	0	0	0	0	0	0	0
Dragon									45	36	45	66	58	29	16	42	48	46	28	28	17	33	13	13	0	0
Appeared										20	19	21	8	0	0	0	0	0	0	0	0	0	0	0	0	0
Kidnapping											37	43	19	8	6	0	0	0	0	0	0	0	0	0	0	0
Beautiful												50	25	20	15	8	0	0	0	0	0	0	0	0	0	0
Princess													59	38	20	10	8	8	0	0	0	23	5	46	37	20
Want-Free														26	16	26	24	23	8	8	5	11	3	20	8	0
Want-Marry															26	20	8	8	0	0	0	0	0	5	9	15
Love																10	0	0	0	0	0	0	0	0	0	0
Hurried-After																	20	19	8	8	5	0	0	0	0	0
Fought																		44	23	23	14	20	8	8	0	0
Life-Death																			20	20	12	20	8	8	0	0
Armor																				31	19	13	5	0	0	0
Scorched																					19	13	5	0	0	0
Fire																						8	3	0	0	0
Killed																							13	20	8	0
Sword																								5	0	0
Freed																									20	8
Thankful																										15
Married																										

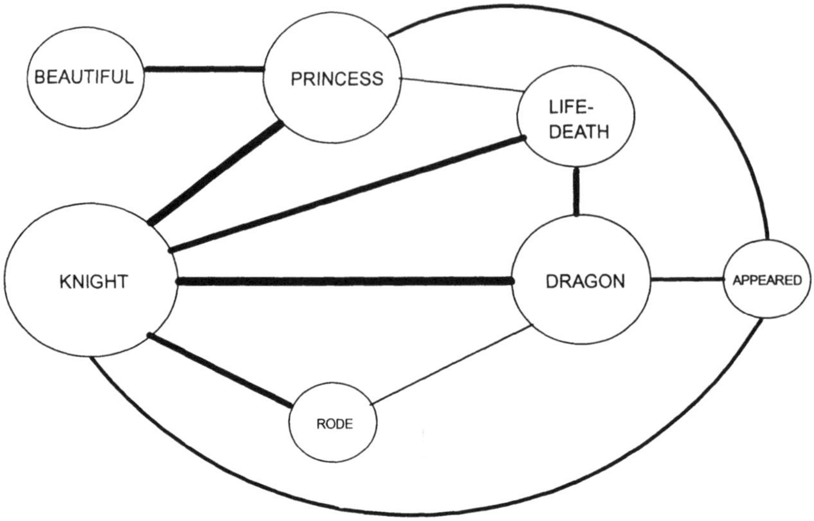

FIG. 6.2. Partial memory representation for the Knight story. (Size of circle indicates node strength; width of connection indicates strength of the relation between nodes.)

to the amount of activation that the concept received across the reading cycles, whereas the width of the connection between two concepts is proportional to the relational strength as calculated by Equation 1.

Testing the Model: Fluctuating Activation and Memory Representation

The model posits that the fluctuating activations during reading form the basis for the construction of a stable memory representation of the text. In a test of the model's hypotheses, each of the two stories used in the previously described experiment was read by 7 participants. After performing an intervening task, the participants engaged in a delayed free recall test. On the basis of the recall protocols, the probability of recall for each concept in the two texts was calculated.

If the model's hypotheses are correct, the total activation that a concept receives during reading and the extent to which it is activated concurrently with other concepts should be strongly related to the probability that it will be recalled. Furthermore, any observed relation between properties of the model and frequency of recall should be plausible in light of current models of memory retrieval (e.g., Ratcliff & McKoon, 1988; Raaijmakers & Shiffrin, 1981).

In our test of the model, two properties of recall were considered: frequency of recall and order of recall. A stepwise regression analysis was performed to test whether the model predicted frequency of recall. Three variables were

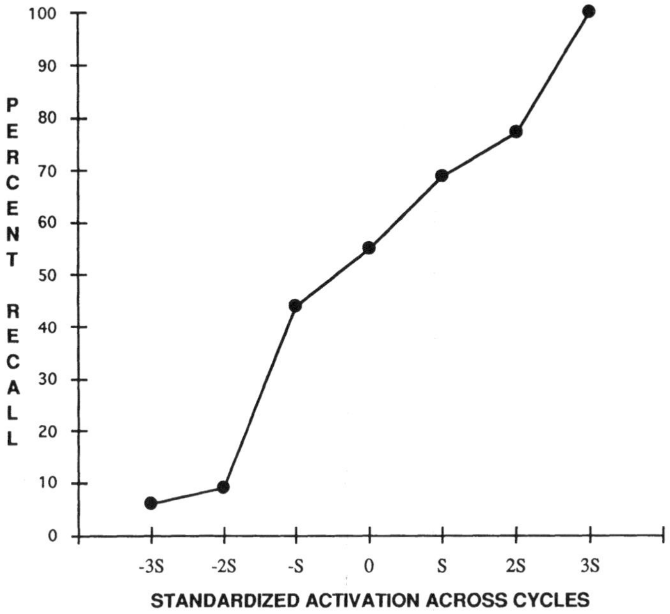

FIG. 6.3. Probability of recall as a function of node strength.

derived from the theoretical activation matrices used in the preceding experiment[6]: the number of cycles in which a concept had been activated, the overall strength of each node (i.e., activation across cycles), and the strength of relations (i.e., the cross-products of activation). The first variable to enter the regression model was node strength, or activation across cycles. As can be seen in Fig. 6.3, node strength strongly predicted the frequency of recall, $R^2 = .49$ ($p < .01$). The strength of the relations that a node had to other nodes in the network also contributed significantly to the frequency of recall, increasing R^2 to .64 (increase $p < .01$). Once these two factors were entered into the regression, the number of cycles in which a concept was processed during reading was not related to the frequency of recall.

With respect to the order of recall, two variables were considered: the likelihood of *first mention* and the conditional probability for *subsequent mention*. The probability that a particular concept was mentioned first during retrieval (i.e., first mention) was related directly to node strength: For both stories, 94% of the first-mentioned concepts consisted of the concept that overall had received the most activation during reading.

[6]The regression analyses reported in this section were repeated using the participant-generated activations, standardized for each participant, that had been obtained in the preceding experiment. The resulting correlations were very similar in pattern and magnitude to those reported here.

The conditional probability of subsequent mention was computed in the following fashion. For each pair of concepts in the text, we calculated the likelihood that the participants produced the second concept given that they had just recalled the first. This likelihood constituted the dependent variable. Only pairs of concepts that were actually produced by participants were considered in the analyses to avoid inflating correlations by including large numbers of pairs that were never produced. The independent variables were the node strength for the second member of the pair and the strength of the relation between the first and second members. Both independent variables were derived from the theoretical matrices.

As can be seen in Fig. 6.4, order of recall for subsequent concepts was strongly predicted by the strength of relations, $R^2 = .34$. In other words, the probability that a concept was retrieved was a function of the strength of its relation to the last recalled concept. This finding is in agreement with those of recent models of retrieval from memory for textual information (Fletcher, van den Broek, & Arthur, this volume; Golden & Rumelhart, 1993). Node strength had a small but significant effect as well, increasing the R^2 to .44 (increase $p < .01$). If two or more nodes had equal strength of relations to the previously recalled concept, the relative strengths of the individual nodes appear to determine which will be recalled next.

In summary, the probability of recall for a concept was determined primarily by the activation that the statement received during the reading process. This

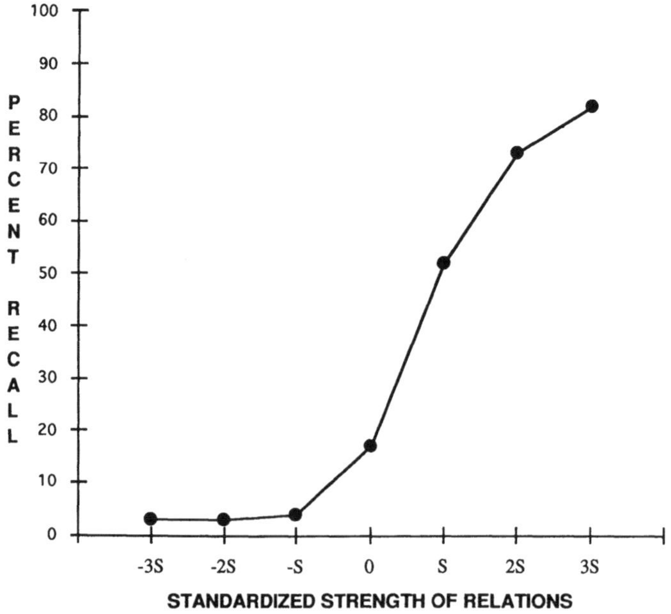

FIG. 6.4. Order effects in recall: Effect of relational strength on the conditional probability of recall.

probability also increased when the concept was strongly connected to other concepts. With respect to the order of recall, the concept that received the strongest activation over time was almost always recalled first. Once a concept was recalled, the next concept to be recalled was likely to be the one that had the strongest relation to the already recalled concept. When several concepts were related equally strongly to the last recalled concept, the total amount of activation that these candidate nodes had received across reading cycles determined which was selected and retrieved next.

CONCLUSION

The landscape model captures the dynamic processes of online comprehension as well as the way in which these processes lead to the construction of a stable memory representation of a text. In doing so, it provides a theoretical and methodological bridge between the empirical work on online comprehension processes and that on offline representation. The model posits that, during reading, concepts continually fluctuate in the amount of attention that they receive and, hence, in their activation. These fluctuations in activation, captured by the landscape model, form the basis for the representation of the text in memory. For example, the total amount of activation that a concept receives during the course of reading determines its strength in memory. Similarly, the patterns of co-occurrences, or simultaneous activations, of concepts (expressed as the sum of the cross-products of activations over reading cycles) determine the presence and strengths of connections between concepts in the memory representation.

In its general form, the landscape model provides an architecture for describing the relation between reading processes and memory that is independent of any particular theory of reading. In other words, any set of theoretical principles for determining fluctuations in activation can be implemented within this general architecture. Thus, the model constitutes a framework for investigating and testing specific theories of reading comprehension.

One potentially powerful source for fluctuating activations is the reader's efforts to understand each sentence that he or she encounters in the text. According to this notion, which is shared by many researchers (e.g., Casteel, 1993; Graesser & Kreuz, 1993; Kintsch, 1988; McKoon & Ratcliff, 1992; O'Brien & Albrecht, 1991; Singer, in press; Trabasso & Suh, 1993; van den Broek, 1990; van den Broek et al., in press), readers set for themselves a goal or standard for coherence and engage in inferential activity to attain the standard. These inferential processes, in turn, dictate the patterns of activation that occur during reading. In this fashion, different reading goals or standards for coherence will leave their unique "fingerprints" of activation patterns.

Reading goals and standards for coherence vary both within and between individual readers. Depending on his or her reading ability, reading purpose, motivation, and so forth a reader may adopt a wide range of standards of coherence (see Graesser & Kreuz, 1993; Lorch, Klusewitz, & Lorch, 1993; Lorch, Lorch, & Klusewitz, 1995; van den Broek et al., 1993). For example, as a reader strives for greater comprehension of the text, his or her standards for coherence become stricter. This adjustment of standards will result in a different landscape of activations and in the identification of different semantic relations. Any standard can be implemented in the landscape architecture, but in the current version of the model we focus on two standards of coherence that have received extensive attention in the literature and that are likely to form the building blocks for further coherence: anaphoric (or referential) clarity and causally sufficient explanation.

The standards of anaphoric clarity and causal coherence were found to have considerable psychological validity. The patterns of activation produced by the implementation closely resembled those produced by research participants. This pattern suggests that many readers indeed attempt to maintain anaphoric clarity and provide causal explanation for the events that are described. Furthermore, the fluctuating patterns of activation form the basis for the final memory representation of the text: Both activations of individual nodes and the extent to which concepts were activated concurrently strongly predicted frequency, as well as order of recall, for statements in the text.

Although these studies had relatively small sample sizes and hence must be interpreted with caution until further experimentation has been completed, the results suggest interesting patterns of recall. The first node to be recalled almost inevitably was the one that had received the largest sum total of activation during reading and had the strongest connections to other nodes in the network. The second node to be recalled usually was the node that had the strongest connection to the first recalled node, the third recalled node was strongly related to the second one, and so forth. Thus, it appears that after having selected the node that is most prominent in strength and relations in their network representation, readers follow the path of strongest relations in the network representation to recall subsequent nodes (with a small tendency to use individual node strengths as a tie-breaker). This pattern of recall is remarkably consistent with that described by Fletcher et al. (this volume) based on their implementation of Raaijmakers and Shiffrin's (1981) model of memory retrieval.

This implementation of the landscape model shares features with existing models of text comprehension (e.g., Fletcher & Bloom, 1988; Graesser & Kreuz, 1993; Just & Carpenter, 1992; Kintsch, 1988; Kintsch & van Dijk, 1978; McKoon & Ratcliff, 1992; Trabasso & Suh, 1993; van den Broek, 1990; van den Broek et al., in press). It is unique, however, in several respects. For example, it combines two criteria for coherence that frequently are treated in isolation: anaphoric clarity and causal explanation. Furthermore, the current model allows for activation to vary along a continuum rather than conceiving of activation as a dichotomous variable. As a result, concepts are activated to various degrees and hence the relations between co-occurring concepts vary in strength. In addition, it allows one to consider the possibility that the activations of concepts decay in a gradual rather than all-or-none fashion. As a final example, the model allows for standards to vary across individuals and even within an individual across occasions. Variations in standards lead to different patterns of activations and memory representations, but the computational principles for the construction of a memory representation remain the same. As a result, the model provides a general framework for testing a wide range of theories of comprehension.

The model and its implementation suggest several issues for further investigation. One issue concerns the extent to which the standards of anaphoric clarity and causal explanation are adequate to capture the richness of the reading process. Although the application of these standards did a remarkable job of explaining the activations and recall protocols that participants actually produced, the correspondence was not perfect. One interesting discrepancy between the model and the data concerns the generation of predictive inferences. At several points, readers activated concepts that had not been mentioned yet in the text. In other words, readers made forward inferences, anticipating aspects of what would happen next. For example, in the Knight story, several readers activated the concept *dragon* when the concept *knight* was introduced. Forward inferences can be implemented easily in the landscape model by including the factors that determine the generation of such inferences. There is considerable debate, however, about the extent to which forward inferences are generated during most reading (McKoon & Ratcliff, 1989; Singer, 1994). It seems likely that the average reader generates forward inferences in some circumstances but not in others. One possibility is that the constraints that the text provides affect the probability that a particular forward inference will be generated. For example, the Causal Inference Maker model (van den Broek, 1990) predicts that forward inferences will be drawn when the combination of a focal event and prior text is causally sufficient for a particular consequence. Empirical tests indeed have demonstrated this to be the case (Murray, Klin, & Myers, 1993; see also Keefe & McDaniel, 1993). By formalizing these *constraints for forward inferences* and including them in the model as a source of activation, one can test their psychological validity.

Many other factors are likely to influence the patterns of activation that occur during reading. For example, it is possible that events that evoke strong emotional reactions on the part of the reader receive additional activation. These and other factors can be implemented easily in the model and tested for their impact on comprehension and memory.

Further issues concern the details of the model. For example: Is co-occurrence sufficient for the establishment of a relation or is it merely necessary? If it is sufficient, then one would expect simple repetition effects to occur in memory: Concepts that occur frequently in the text, but are not necessarily semantically related to many other concepts, would be recalled frequently. Alternatively, it is possible that co-occurrence does not result in a association between concepts unless a semantic relation is identified.[7] In this case, simple repetition or primary effects are unlikely to occur. As a second example, the parameters of the decay function have potentially important consequences. If decay is relatively slow, then *adjacency* effects will occur: Concepts that are activated by sentences that are not semantically related would be connected more strongly in memory if the sentences are close to each other in the surface structure of the text than if they are further apart in the text. These and other aspects of reading can be investigated by comparing and contrasting different implementations of the landscape model.

The resolution of these and other issues will help us better understand the mechanisms and processes by which readers make sense (or fail to make sense) of a text. As readers understand each new part of a text, they construct the building blocks for comprehension of the text as a whole. How this is done is one of the central questions of cognitive psychology, but also of disciplines such as education and artificial intelligence. In addressing these issues, the landscape model makes a powerful contribution to our understanding of reading comprehension and memory for text.

ACKNOWLEDGMENTS

We would like to thank Tammy Bourg, Bruce Britton, Art Graesser, Bob Lorch, and Mike Young for their comments on an earlier draft of this chapter. The research presented here was supported by the Center for Research in Learning, Perception, and Cognition at the University of Minnesota through a grant from the National Institute of Child Health and Human Development (HD-07151).

REFERENCES

Britton, B., & Eisenhart, F. J. (1993). Expertise, text coherence, and constraint satisfaction: Effects on harmony and settling rate. *Proceedings of the 15th annual conference of the Cognitive Science Society*. Hillsdale, NJ: Lawrence Erlbaum Associates.

Casteel, M. A. (1993). Effects of inference necessity and reading goal on children's inferential generation. *Developmental Psychology, 29*(2), 346–357.

Dopkins, S., Klin, C., & Myers, J. L. (1993). The accessibility of information about goals during the processing of narrative texts. *Journal of Experimental Psychology: Learning, Memory and Cognition, 19*, 70–80.

Fletcher, C. R., & Bloom, C. P. (1988). Causal reasoning in the comprehension of simple narrative texts. *Journal of Memory and Language, 27*, 235–244.

---

[7]We thank Art Graesser for suggesting these two possibilities. Note that frequently co-occurrence is the result of the identification of a semantic relation between two events. For example, the reinstatement of a referential or causal antecedent leads to co-occurrence. A similar situation arises when background information is retrieved to provide coherence.

Fletcher, C. R., Chrysler, S. T., van den Broek, P., Deaton, J. A., & Bloom, C. (1995). The role of co-occurrence, co-reference, and causality in the coherence of conjoined sentences. In R. F. Lorch, Jr. & E. J. O'Brien (Eds.), *Sources of coherence in text comprehension* (pp. 203–218). Hillsdale, NJ: Lawrence Erlbaum Associates.

Gernsbacher, M. A. (1989). Mechanisms that improve referential access. *Cognition, 32*, 99–156.

Gernsbacher, M. A. (1990). *Language comprehension as structure building*. Hillsdale, NJ: Lawrence Erlbaum Associates.

Golden, R. M., & Rumelhart, D. E. (1993). A parallel distributed processing model of story comprehension and recall. *Discourse Processes, 16*(3), 203–238.

Graesser, A. C., & Bower, G. H. (1990). *Inferences and text comprehension*. San Diego, CA: Academic Press.

Graesser, A. C., & Clark, L. F. (1985). *The structures and procedures of implicit knowledge*. Norwood, NJ: Ablex.

Graesser, A. C., & Kreuz, R. J. (1993). A theory of inference generation during text comprehension. *Discourse Processes, 16*, 145–160.

Graesser, A. C., Singer, M., & Trabasso, T. (1994). Constructing inferences during narrative text comprehension. *Psychological Review, 101*, 371–395.

Huitema, J. S., Dopkins, S., Klin, C. M., & Myers, J. L. (1993). Connecting goals and actions during reading. *Journal of Experimental Psychology: Learning, Memory, and Cognition, 19*, 1053–1060.

Just, M. A., & Carpenter, P. A. (1992). A capacity theory of comprehension: Individual differences in working memory. *Psychological Review, 99*(1), 122–149.

Keefe, D. E., & McDaniel, M. A. (1993). The time course and durability of predictive inferences. *Journal of Memory and Language, 32*(4), 446–463.

Kintsch, W. (1988). The role of knowledge in discourse comprehension: A construction-integration model. *Psychological Review, 95*, 163–182.

Kintsch, W. A., & van Dijk, T. A. (1978). Toward a model of text comprehension and production. *Psychological Review, 85*, 363–394.

Lorch, R. F., Jr., Klusewitz, M. A., & Lorch, E. P. (1995). Distinctions among reading situations. In R. F. Lorch, Jr. & E. J. O'Brien (Eds.), *Sources of coherence in reading* (pp. 375–398). Hillsdale, NJ: Lawrence Erlbaum Associates.

Lorch, R. F., Jr., Lorch, E. P., & Klusewitz, M. A. (1995). College students' conditional knowledge about reading. *Journal of Educational Psychology, 85*, 239–252.

McKoon, G., & Ratcliff, R. (1980). Priming in item recognition: The organization of propositions in memory for text. *Journal of Verbal Learning and Verbal Behavior, 19*, 369–386.

McKoon, G., & Ratcliff, R. (1989). Semantic associations and elaborative inferences. *Journal of Experimental Psychology: Learning, Memory, and Cognition, 15*, 326–338.

McKoon, G., & Ratcliff, R. (1992). Inferences during reading. *Psychological Review, 99*, 440–466.

Miller, J. R., & Kintsch, W. (1980). Readability and recall of short prose passages: A theoretical analysis. *Journal of Experimental Psychology: Human Learning and Memory, 6*, 335–355.

Murray, J. D., Klin, C. M., & Myers, J. L. (1993). Forward inferences in narrative texts. *Journal of Memory and Language, 32*, 464–473.

Myers, J. L., & Duffy, S. A. (1990). Causal inferences and text memory. In A. C. Graesser & G. H. Bower (Eds.), *Psychology of learning and motivation: Inferences and text comprehension* (Vol. 25, pp. 35–51). San Diego, CA: Academic Press.

Myers, J. L., O'Brien, E. J., Albrecht, J. E., & Mason, R. A. (1994). Maintaining global coherence during reading. *Journal of Experimental Psychology: Learning, Memory, and Cognition, 20*, 876–886.

Myers, J. L., Shinjo, M., & Duffy, S. A. (1987). Degree of causal relatedness and memory. *Journal of Memory and Language, 26*, 453–465.

O'Brien, E. J. (1987). Antecedent search processes and the structure of text. *Journal of Experimental Psychology: Learning, Memory, and Cognition, 13*(2), 278–290.

O'Brien, E. J., & Albrecht, J. E. (1991). The role of context in accessing antecedents in text. *Journal of Experimental Psychology: Learning, Memory, and Cognition, 12*(3), 346–352.

O'Brien, E. J., & Myers, J. L. (1987). The role of causal connections in the retrieval of text. *Memory & Cognition, 15*, 419–427.

Potts, G. R., Keenan, J. M., & Golding, J. M. (1988). Assessing the occurrence of elaborative inferences: Lexical decision versus naming. *Journal of Verbal Behavior and Verbal Learning, 27*, 399–415.

Raaijmakers, J. G. W., & Shiffrin, R. M. (1981). Search of associative memory. *Psychological Review, 88*, 93–134.

Ratcliff, R., & McKoon, G. (1988). A retrieval theory of priming. *Psychological Review, 21*, 139–155.

Singer, M. (1994). Inference generation during reading. In M. A. Gernsbacher (Ed.), *Handbook of psycholinguistics* (pp. 479–515). New York: Academic Press.

Singer, M., Graesser, A. C., & Trabasso, T. (1994). Minimal or global inference during reading. *Journal of Memory and Language, 33*, 421–441.

Smith, E. E., Shoben, E. J., & Rips, L. J. (1974). Structure and process in semantic memory: A featural model for semantic decisions. *Psychological Review, 81*, 214–241.

Smolensky, P. (1986). Information processing in dynamical systems: Foundations of harmony theory. In D. E. Rumelhart & J. L. McClelland (Eds.), *Parallel distributed processing: Explorations in the microstructure of cognition* (pp. 194–281). London: MIT Press.

Stein, N. L., & Glenn, C. G. (1979). An analysis of story comprehension in elementary school children. In R. O. Freedle (Ed.), *New directions in discourse processing* (Vol. 2, pp. 53–120). Hillsdale, NJ: Lawrence Erlbaum Associates.

Thurlow, R. E. (1991). *The inference of causal antecedents during the reading of narratives*. Unpublished doctoral dissertation, University of Minnesota.

Trabasso, T., & Sperry, L. (1985). Causal relatedness and importance of story events. *Journal of Memory and Language, 24*, 595–611.

Trabasso, T., & Suh, S. Y. (1993). Understanding text: Achieving explanatory coherence through on-line inferences and mental operations in working memory. *Discourse Processes, 16*(1-2), 3–34.

Trabasso, T., Secco, T., & van den Broek, P. W. (1984). Causal cohesion and story coherence. In H. Mandl, N. L. Stein, & T. Trabasso (Eds.), *Learning and comprehension of text* (pp. 83–111). Hillsdale, NJ: Lawrence Erlbaum Associates.

Trabasso, T., van den Broek, P. W., & Suh, S. Y. (1989). Logical necessity and transitivity of causal relations in stories. *Discourse Processes, 12*, 1–25.

Turner, A., & Greene, E. (1978). *Construction and use of a propositional text base*. JSAS catalogue of selected documents in psychology, MS 1713.

van den Broek, P. W. (1988). The effects of causal relations and hierarchical position on the importance of story statements. *Journal of Memory and Language, 27*, 1–22.

van den Broek, P. W. (1990). The causal inference maker: Toward a process model of inference generation in text comprehension. In D. A. Balota, G. B. Flores d'Arcais, & K. Rayner (Eds.), *Comprehension processes in reading* (pp. 423–445). Hillsdale, NJ: Lawrence Erlbaum Associates.

van den Broek, P. W. (1994). Comprehension and memory of narrative texts: Inferences and coherence. In M. A. Gernsbacher (Ed.), *Handbook of psycholinguistics* (pp. 539–588). New York: Academic Press.

van den Broek, P. W., Fletcher, C. R., & Risden, K. (1993). Investigations of inferential processes in reading: A theoretical and methodological integration. *Discourse Processes, 16*, 169–180.

van den Broek, P. W., & Lorch, R. F., Jr. (1993). Causal relations in memory for narrative texts: Evidence from a priming task for network representations. *Discourse Processes, 16*, 75–98.

van den Broek, P. W., Risden, K., & Husebye-Hartmann, E. (1995). Comprehension of narrative events: Maintaining sufficient explanation. In R. F. Lorch, Jr. & E. O'Brien (Eds.), *Sources of coherence in text comprehension* (pp. 353–373). Hillsdale, NJ: Lawrence Erlbaum Associates.

van den Broek, P. W., Rohleder, L., & Narvaéz, D. (in press). Causal inferences in the comprehension of literary texts. In R. J. Kreuz & M. S. McNealy (Eds.), *The empirical study of literature*. Norwood, NJ: Ablex.

van den Broek, P. W., & Thurlow, R. (1990, November). *Reinstatements and elaborative inferences during the reading of narratives*. Paper presented at the annual meeting of the Psychonomic Society, New Orleans, LA.

van den Broek, P. W., & Trabasso, T. (1986). Causal networks versus goal hierarchies in summarizing text. *Discourse Processes, 9*, 1–15.

van Dijk, T. A., & Kintsch, W. (1983). *Strategies of discourse comprehension*. New York: Academic Press.

CHAPTER

7

THE ROLE OF INFERENTIAL PROCESSING IN READING ABILITY

Debra L. Long
Mark R. Seely
Brian J. Oppy
University of California, Davis

Jonathan M. Golding
University of Kentucky, Lexington

Skilled reading requires the coordination of numerous component comprehension processes. At the word level, processes are necessary to encode the printed word and access its meaning in memory. At the sentence level, processes are devoted to the formation of structures that specify the syntactic and conceptual relations among words in a phrase or a clause. These processes help to encode propositions, which are abstract units that represent the meaning of a sentence. At the text level, processes are required to construct connections among successive propositions in a text. One important mechanism for linking propositions in memory involves identifying instances of *argument overlap*. Argument overlap refers to the recurrence of a noun phrase concept in different propositions (Kintsch & van Dijk, 1978). Researchers generally agree that the normal execution of such processes results in a text representation comprised of a set of interrelated propositions (Kintsch & van Dijk, 1978; Perfetti, 1985).

The processes just described are primarily linguistic. They involve accessing knowledge about the language (e.g., word meanings, syntax) to construct a representation of a text. However, numerous studies have demonstrated that comprehension also involves access to knowledge about the world (Bransford & Johnson, 1973; Chiesi, Spilich, & Voss, 1979; Dooling & Lachman, 1971; Markman, 1977; Spilich, Vesonder, Chiesi, & Voss, 1979). If readers are unable to make inferences that connect explicit information in a text to relevant world knowledge, they feel as though they have not comprehended the text and have difficulty remembering it. In their classic experiment, Bransford and Johnson (1973) asked readers to comprehend and recall paragraphs that contained a number of vague referring expressions. These passages elicited low comprehension ratings and poor recall. Comprehension ratings and recall dramatically improved by providing readers with a title that evoked relevant world knowledge. Dooling and Lachman (1971) found similar comprehension difficulties when readers were unable to identify the referents of metaphorical phrases.

Although these studies demonstrate that access to world knowledge can be obligatory in the sense that a text cannot be completely understood without it, the extent to which skilled readers have access to world knowledge as they execute linguistic processes during reading is controversial. The purpose of this chapter is to (a) discuss the controversy surrounding the role of inferential processing in reading and (b) describe research in our laboratory that was conducted to discriminate between two very different views of text comprehension.

The controversy surrounding the role of inferential processing during reading can be explained best by distinguishing between two components of a text representation (Gerrig, 1986; Perfetti, 1989). The first component involves a representation of the meaning of a text (e.g., the microstructure or textbase). Meaning is extracted by the automatic execution of linguistic processes and consists of word meanings and propositional structure. Inferential processing plays a role in constructing meaning to the extent that inferences are necessary to link an incoming proposition with immediately preceding propositions. The second component involves the construction of an interpretation of information presented in the text (Gerrig, 1986; Perfetti, 1989). This process of interpretation operates on the propositional structure (i.e., the meaning) and constructs a referential representation. This representation includes information about the real world referents of words, properties attributed to objects, and knowledge about the situation. Interpretation relies on inferential processes that function to integrate explicit information in the text with general world knowledge.

Although researchers generally agree that both meaning and interpretation play important roles in comprehension, they disagree about whether interpretation occurs during reading or at some later time. According to one view of text comprehension, a text representation is comprised almost solely of the meaning of a text and is constructed by means of linguistic processes, such as word decoding and syntactic and semantic analyses (McKoon & Ratcliff, 1986, 1988, 1989a, 1989b, 1990, 1992; Perfetti, 1989). These processes are executed automatically as a function of receiving language inputs and are not influenced by the goals and strategies of a reader. Interpretation of the text occurs at a later point in processing. Interpretation involves strategic, problem-solving processes that operate on the propositional representation that is constructed automatically during reading (McKoon & Ratcliff, 1992). Thus, skilled reading consists first and foremost of the ability to execute linguistic processes to derive the meaning of a text. The ability to make knowledge-based inferences plays a secondary or peripheral role.

According to an alternative view of text comprehension, the representation constructed during reading consists of meaning plus interpretation (Graesser & Clark, 1985; Schank, 1986; Trabasso & Sperry, 1985; Trabasso & van den Broek, 1985; Trabasso, van den Broek, & Suh, 1989; van den Broek, 1988, 1990). World knowledge is accessed continually during reading to construct a representation of the situation described by the text. Moreover, the text representation contains more inferences than are required to forge connections among propositions. The text representation is likely to include inferences that specify (a) spatial relations among objects, (b) goals and motivations of characters in a story, and (c) causal relations among events, actions, and episodes. Thus, the ability to make knowledge-based inferences is viewed as an important component of skilled reading.

One way to assess the contribution of inferential processing to reading ability is to examine the extent to which skilled readers make knowledge-based inferences on-line; that is, as they comprehend a text. If inferential processing is an important component of reading ability, readers should reliably and spontaneously make inferences other than those required to construct a propositional representation. Another way to address this issue is to determine whether high ability readers are more likely to make knowledge-based inferences than are low ability readers. In the following sections, we discuss (a) two models of inferential processing that make different predictions about the on-line status of knowledge-based inferences, (b) studies conducted in our laboratory to discriminate between these models, and (c) the implications of our work for examining the relation between inferential processing and individual differences in reading ability.

MINIMAL INFERENCE PROCESSING VERSUS GLOBAL-COHERENCE PROCESSING

Predictions regarding the on-line status of knowledge-based inferences can be derived from two opposing models of inference processing. The first model, called Minimal Inference Processing, has been summarized by McKoon and Ratcliff (1986, 1988, 1989a, 1989b, 1990, 1992). The model is consistent with a view of comprehension that equates reading with the construction of meaning and regards integration at a global level as a secondary, strategic, or problem-solving, activity. The model distinguishes inferences that are encoded automatically to establish text coherence (i.e., bridging inferences) from those that are made strategically and function to elaborate or refine a text representation. Automatic inferences are not robustly influenced by the goals and strategies of the reader. In addition, they are encoded within a few hundred milliseconds of processing.

A major claim of the Minimal Inference Processing model is that inferences are encoded automatically during reading to the extent that these inferences are necessary to establish *local* text coherence. A reader's attention is focused on a small amount of information in short-term memory. This information includes an incoming proposition and a few immediately preceding propositions. Inferences are encoded automatically if they are required to establish referential connections among propositions residing in short-term memory. For example, inferences will be encoded automatically to establish *argument overlap* (Kintsch & van Dijk, 1978). These inferences include those that specify that the same word across two propositions refers to the same concept and those that specify that an anaphor and its antecedent refer to the same concept (Dell, McKoon, & Ratcliff, 1983; McKoon & Ratcliff, 1980). In addition, causal inferences will be encoded automatically during reading to the extent that they are (a) required to establish a referential connection between an incoming proposition and an immediately preceding proposition and (b) can be drawn from knowledge that is readily available (Bloom, Fletcher, van den Broek, Reitz, & Shapiro, 1990; Fletcher, Hummel, & Marsolek, 1990; McKoon & Ratcliff, 1992; Potts, Keenan, & Golding, 1988).

According to the Minimal Inference Processing model, inferences that are not required to establish local coherence (i.e., elaborative inferences) are encoded only to the extent that they are supported by readily available world knowledge. For example, McKoon and Ratcliff (1989b) found that some elaborative inferences, such as the contextually appropriate semantic features of noun concepts, are encoded automatically if they are supported by strong semantic associates in the text. Elaborative inferences that are not supported by such associations are typically not encoded automatically during comprehension. The latter type include inferences that specify the typical instruments of verbs (Corbett & Dosher, 1978; McKoon & Ratcliff, 1981), ongoing states (Graesser & Clark, 1985; Long, Golding, Graesser, & Clark, 1990; Seifert, Robertson, & Black, 1985), and the predictable consequences of events (McKoon & Ratcliff, 1986; Potts et al., 1988; Singer & Ferreira, 1983; but see Keefe & McDaniel, 1993, and Murray, Klin, & Myers, 1993, for contradictory evidence).

We have proposed an alternative to the Minimal Inference Processing model, called the Global-Coherence Processing model (Long & Golding, 1993; Long, Golding, & Graesser, 1992; Long et al., 1990). The Global-Coherence model is similar to the Minimal Inference Processing model in two respects. First, both predict that inferences will be automatically encoded to the extent that they are required to establish local coherence (i.e., bridging referential inferences, bridging causal inferences). Second, both models predict that inferences that are not necessary for coherence are not encoded during comprehension (e.g., inferences that specify ongoing states, instruments of verbs, predictable consequences of events). However, the two models define coherence very differently and, thus, make different predictions about the on-line status of certain classes of inferences.

According to the Global-Coherence model, coherence is established when readers generate (a) referential connections among the small set of propositions available in short-term memory (i.e., local coherence) and (b) causal connections that link each episode in a text from beginning to end (Graesser & Clark, 1985; Long & Golding, 1993; Long et al., 1990; Long et al., 1992; Schank, 1986; Trabasso, van den Broek, & Suh, 1989; van den Broek, 1988, 1990; Wilensky, 1983). Readers establish causal connections by determining why each action and event has occurred. Thus, the model assumes that coherence is *explanation-based*; that is, actions and events are understood only to the extent that readers can provide explanations for what has occurred (Schank, 1986). Explanations are found by searching relevant knowledge structures (e.g., scripts, frames, MOPs) to place an event or action in an appropriate causal context. Explanations provide causal information regarding reasons, motivations, antecedents, and enabling conditions. If no causal connection can be established between a proposition and the current contents of short-term memory, readers search long-term memory for an appropriate connection (Bloom, Fletcher, van den Broek, Reitz, & Shapiro, 1990; Fletcher & Bloom, 1988; Fletcher, Hummel, & Marsolek, 1990).

In this model, then, inferential processing is analogous to a question-answering task. That is, inference generation is viewed metaphorically as a process in which readers ask themselves "why" questions about each action and event in the story and answer these questions by making appropriate inferences. We make the analogy between inferential processing and question answering explicit by deriving our predictions about the on-line status of particular inferences from a model of question answering, called QUEST. QUEST was developed by Graesser and his colleagues to explain readers' responses to questions about narrative and expository texts (Golding, Graesser, & Millis, 1990; Graesser, 1981; Graesser & Clark, 1985; Graesser & Franklin, 1990; Graesser, Gordon, & Brainerd, 1992; Graesser & Hemphill, 1991; Graesser, Lang, & Roberts, 1991; Graesser & Murachver, 1985; Graesser, Robertson, & Anderson, 1981; Graesser, Robertson, Lovelace, & Swinehart, 1980). A particular inference is predicted to be encoded on-line during comprehension if it conforms to the question-answering principles incorporated in QUEST.

The Use of Question-Answering Principles to Generate Predictions about Inferential Processing

As an example of how principles of question answering are used to generate predictions about the on-line status of various types of inferences, consider the story presented in Table 7.1. Graesser and his colleagues have developed a system, called a conceptual graph structure, for representing both explicit information presented in a text and world knowledge activated by specific words in the text (e.g., *dragon, kidnap, daughters*). A small portion of the *conceptual graph structure* for "The Czar and His Daughters" appears in Fig. 7.1. A conceptual graph structure contains a set of categorized *statement nodes*. Statement nodes are elementary units of meaning that correspond informally to propositions. In the figure, the statement nodes in squares refer to explicit statements in the

TABLE 7.1
The Czar and His Daughters

1.	Once there was a Czar
2.	who had three lovely daughters.
3.	One day the three daughters went walking in the woods.
4.	They were enjoying themselves so much that
5.	they forgot the time and
6.	stayed too long.
7.	A dragon kidnapped the three daughters.
8.	As they were being dragged off,
9.	the daughters cried.
10.	Three heroes heard the cries and
11.	set off to rescue the daughters.
12.	The heroes came and
13.	fought the dragon and
14.	rescued the maidens.
15.	When the Czar heard of the rescue,
16.	he rewarded the heroes.

text; the statement nodes in ovals are knowledge-based inferences exposed by asking readers questions about the explicit story statements. Each statement node is assigned to a node category such as Event, Goal, State, Style Specification. A node is connected to other nodes in the structure by means of categorized and directed arcs that describe the conceptual relations among the nodes. The arcs in Fig. 7.1 correspond to the arc categories of Reason (R), Consequence (C), Outcome (O), and Initiate (I).

Conceptual graph structures also contain important causal substructures, such as goal hierarchies and event chains. Fig. 7.1 contains a goal hierarchy that consists of nodes 3, 5, 6, and 8. These goals are related by Reason arcs that specify hierarchical relations between the goals. For example, goal-node 5 is superordinate in the hierarchy to goal-node 3. Fig. 7.1 also contains an event chain that consists of nodes 1, 2, 4, 11, and 12. Most nodes in an event chain are connected by means of Consequence arcs that specify temporal and causal relations between the nodes.

In addition to the representational system described above, QUEST specifies mechanisms that operate on conceptual graph structures to supply answers to questions. First, the model assumes that questions are categorized according to their conceptual type. A finite number of question categories have been identified, such as "why" action, "why" event, "how" action, and "how" event. Second, the model specifies a unique arc-search procedure associated with each question category. The procedure involves identifying an entry node in a conceptual graph structure (e.g., node 4 <Event-dragon kidnapped daughters> in Fig. 7.1) and sampling paths of arcs and nodes that connect the entry node to other nodes in the structure. The arc-search procedure specifies the set of arc categories and arc directions that produce legal responses to a particular question

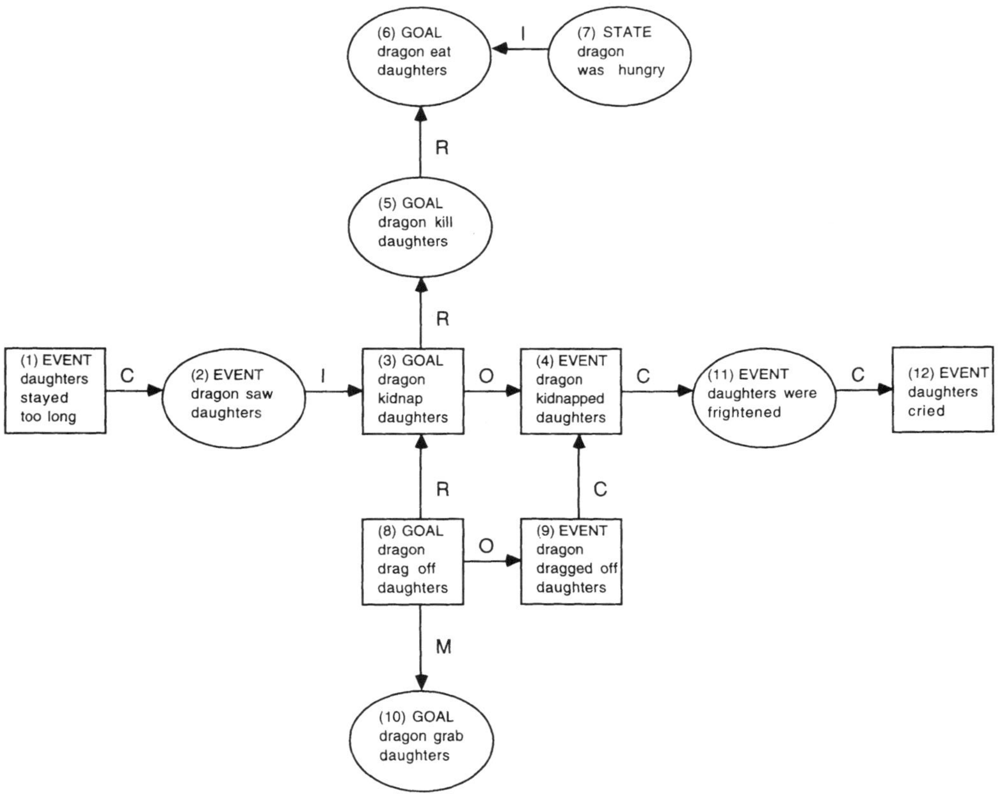

FIG. 7.1. Portion of the conceptual graph structure from *The Czar and His Daughters*. Statements in squares are explicit statements in the text. Statements in ovals are knowledge-based inferences produced as answers to questions about the text. (C = CONSEQUENCE, I = INITIATE, O = OUTCOME, R = REASON).

type. For example, the arc search-procedure that is associated with "how"-event questions allows sampling of nodes along backward Consequence arcs but not along forward Consequence arcs. Empirical evidence suggests that "good" answers to a question are those that conform to the arc-search procedure associated with that question type and are close to the entry node in the conceptual graph structure (Golding et al., 1990; Graesser et al., 1991).

According to the Global-Coherence model, readers establish causal connections by asking why each action and event has occurred. Thus, the on-line status of a particular inference can be determined by assessing its likelihood as a response to a "why" question. Consider the inferences that are likely to be produced as answers to the question:

(1) Why did the dragon kidnap the daughters?

The question corresponds to the category of "why"-action. An action is represented in a conceptual graph structure as an amalgamation of a goal and an event node linked by an Outcome arc (e.g., nodes 3 and 4 in Fig. 7.1). Once these entry nodes have been identified, the arc-search procedure associated with a "why" question is applied. This particular procedure allows sampling along backward Consequence arcs, forward Reason arcs, and backward Initiate arcs. By applying the search procedure to the structure in Fig. 7.1, we can identify those inferences that are likely to be made in response to the question: nodes 1, 2, 5, 6, and 7 in Fig. 7.1. Legal responses to "why"-action questions include superordinate goals, causal antecedent events, goal-initiating states, and enabling states. Legal responses to "why"-event questions include enabling states and causal antecedent events.

According to the Global-Coherence model, there should be a positive relation between the probability that an inference will be produced as a good answer to a "why" question about an action or event and the probability that the inference will be encoded on-line during comprehension. Thus, a good answer to a "why" question about an action or event will have a greater probability of being generated on-line during comprehension than will a "bad" answer (i.e., an illegal or distant node). Similarly, a good answer to a why question is more likely to be encoded automatically during comprehension than is a good answer to another question category, such as a "how" question or a "what-happened-next" question. According to the model, these explanation-based inferences are encoded on-line during comprehension because they help to establish overall coherence in a text by placing each action and event in a causal structure (e.g., goal hierarchy, causal event chain). These causal connections function to link each episode in a text from beginning to end. In contrast, the Minimal Inference Processing model predicts that causal inferences are typically not encoded automatically during comprehension because these inferences are seldom required to establish local coherence and unlikely to be supported by semantic associates in the text (McKoon & Ratcliff, 1992). In the following section, we describe studies conducted to test predictions derived from the two models regarding the on-line status of a particular class of causal inferences, referred to as *superordinate goal inferences.*

THE ON-LINE STATUS OF SUPERORDINATE GOAL INFERENCES

Many stories have a goal-subgoal hierarchical structure, such that higher level goals (i.e., superordinate goals) are accomplished by actions that achieve lower level goals (i.e., subordinate goals). Superordinate goals describe states of affairs that characters wish to achieve by performing intentional actions. In contrast, subordinate goals describe operations involved while performing actions, such as plans or instrumental actions. If a statement from a goal hierarchy appears in a story as an intentional action, the superordinate-subordinate status of other goals in the hierarchy is judged relative to the position of that action. Thus, any goal in the hierarchy (with the exception of the top node and the terminal nodes) can be superordinate in relation to one action but subordinate in relation to another.

Readers have considerable knowledge about the classes of goals that various characters in a story are likely to pursue. For example, fairy tale heroes want to slay dragons, rescue maidens, and marry princesses. Graesser and his colleagues have systematically examined the inferences that readers make when they answer questions about characters' intentional actions in stereotypical stories such as "The Czar and His Daughters" (Golding et al., 1990; Graesser, 1981; Graesser & Clark, 1985; Graesser et al., 1991; Graesser & Murachver, 1985; Graesser et al., 1981; Graesser et al., 1980). They found that readers reliably produce a small set of superordinate goal inferences in response to "why" questions about characters' actions (e.g., "the dragon wanted to eat the daughters"; "the dragon wanted to kill the daughters"). In addition, they have found that superordinate goal inferences are more likely to be produced in response to these questions than are other types of causal inferences, such as inferences about goal-initiating states (e.g., "the dragon was hungry"), causal antecedent events (e.g., "the dragon saw the daughters"), or enabling conditions (e.g., "the dragon was near the daughters").

Previous research has demonstrated that goal and planning knowledge influence performance on tasks other than question answering, such as reading time, recall, and summarization. If readers are aware of a character's goals and motivations, they are able to comprehend easily subsequent statements that describe the plans that have been implemented by characters to achieve their goals (Foss & Bower, 1986; Seifert et al., 1985; Wilensky, 1983). In addition, readers frequently include superordinate goal inferences in their recall and summarization protocols (Abbott & Black, 1986; Black & Bower, 1980; Graesser, 1981; Graesser & Clark, 1985; Graesser et al., 1981; Schank & Abelson, 1977; van den Broek & Trabasso, 1986; Wilensky, 1983). However, it is unclear whether goal-related inferences are encoded automatically as readers comprehend stories. Recall, summarization, and question-answering tasks do not discriminate between inferences drawn during comprehension and those drawn at some later time (e.g., at test).

Different predictions about the on-line status of goal-related inferences can be derived from the Global-Coherence and the Minimal Inference Processing models. According to the Global-Coherence model, readers should spontaneously encode superordinate goal inferences because overall text coherence cannot be established unless an action is placed in the context of a relevant causal structure (which includes a goal-subgoal hierarchy). However, readers should not spontaneously encode subordinate goal inferences during reading because these inferences do not provide causal information that is necessary to establish global coherence. According to the Minimal Inference Processing model, neither superordinate nor subordinate goal inferences are likely to be encoded automatically during reading because they are not usually required to establish local coherence, nor are they typically supported by semantic associates in the text.

Empirical Tests of the On-Line Status of Superordinate Goal Inferences

Support for the Minimal Inference Processing Model. Recently, McKoon and Ratcliff (1992) conducted a series of studies to test the on-line status of goal-related inferences. In one study, the participants were asked to read stories such as the one in the Appendix. This story has a common goal-subgoal hierarchical structure. Fulfillment of a superordinate goal (e.g., rescue of the daughter) requires fulfillment of lower level subordinate goals (e.g., finding the daughter; getting into fortress). A small portion of the goal structure for this story is presented in Fig. 7.2. According to McKoon and Ratcliff, the Minimal Inference Processing model predicts only local, referential connections among propositions and no inferential connections among goals and outcomes that are far from each other in the surface structure of the text. In contrast, the Global-Coherence model predicts that a goal should be connected to its eventual outcome by inferential links even if the goal and outcome are distant in the surface structure.

McKoon and Ratcliff (1992) tested their predictions by means of a priming procedure. Participants read two stories and then were asked to verify a list of test statements. The list included *outcome targets* (e.g., "Ali drove with Jon hidden in the trunk"), *goal primes* (e.g., "Jon had to find help to get into the fortress") and two types of control primes: *action-near-goal primes*, which described some action that was near to the goal in the surface structure of the story but not directly related to the goal (e.g., "Jon met an old friend who was a double agent"),

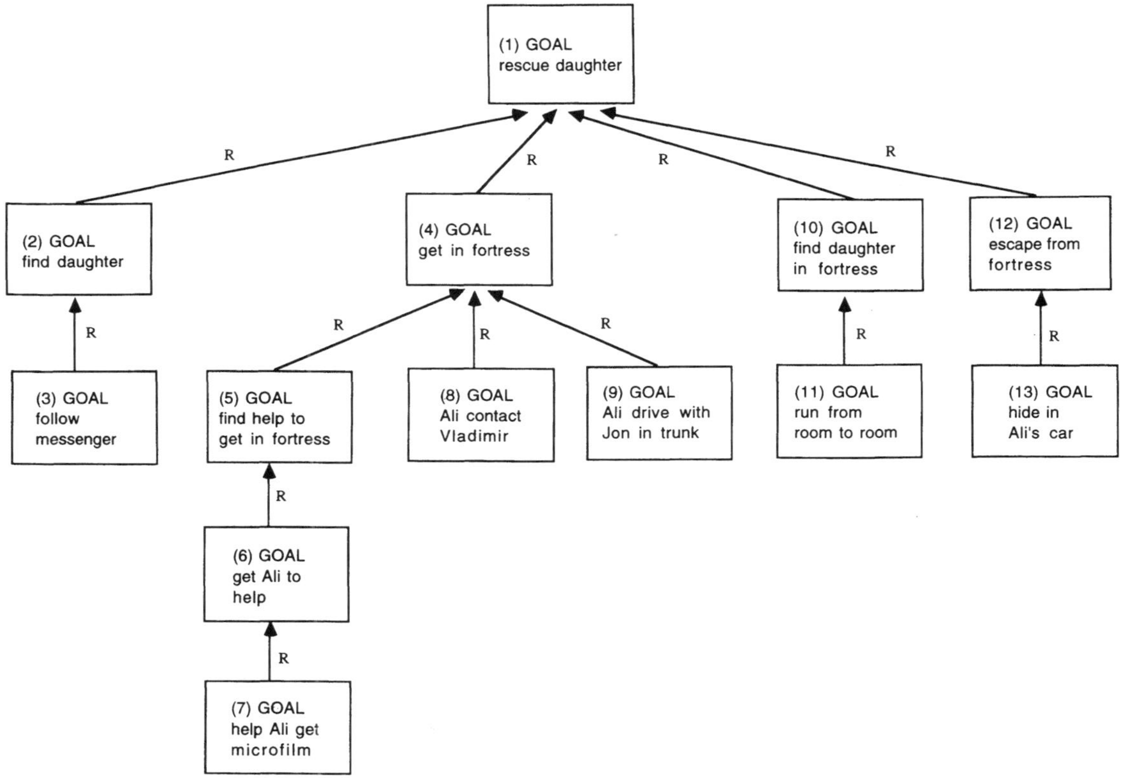

FIG. 7.2. Portion of the goal-subgoal hierarchy from *Kidnapped*. R = REASON.

and *near-primes*, which described an action that was near to the outcome target in the surface structure of the text but not causally related to it (e.g., "Jon kept the people at the embassy occupied"). If readers automatically encode goal relations during reading, responses to outcome targets should be facilitated by the prior presentation of a goal prime, but not by the prior presentation of an action-near-goal prime or a near prime. However, if only local relations are established during reading, responses to outcome targets should be facilitated by the prior presentation of near primes, but not the prior presentation of goal primes or action-near-goal primes.

The pattern of data yielded support for the Minimal Inference Processing model. The participants responded faster to outcome targets when they were preceded by an action that was near to the target outcome in the surface structure of the text (i.e., a near prime). Responses to outcome targets were not facilitated by the prior presentation of a goal prime. McKoon and Ratcliff (1992) concluded that these results disconfirm predictions from the Global-Coherence model. However, the Global-Coherence model proposed by Long et al. (1990) and Long et al. (1992), in fact, does not predict direct inferential links between lower level goals in a goal-subgoal hierarchy (e.g., terminal outcome nodes) and all superordinate goals.

Consider the goal hierarchy in Fig. 7.2. The Global-Coherence model does not predict an inferential connection between the outcome, "Ali drove with Jon hidden in the trunk," and the goal, "Jon had to find help to get into the fortress." QUEST's arc-search procedure for "why" questions allows sampling of goal nodes along forward REASON arcs. The model, therefore, would predict direct inferential connections between the outcome target (i.e., node 9 in Fig. 7.2) and goal-nodes 1 and 4 in Fig. 7.2. A direct inferential connection between the outcome target and goal-node 5, "Jon had to find help to get into the fortress," would require sampling along a backward Reason arc, a procedure that would produce an inappropriate response to a "why"-action question. That is, it would be inappropriate to say "Ali drove with Jon hidden in the trunk *because* Jon had to find help to get in the fortress." Thus, the global-coherence model described by Long et al. would not predict that goal-node 5 would prime responses to outcome node 9. Goal-node 5 does not lie along a path that constitutes a legal answer to a "why"-action question. By deriving our predictions about the on-line status of particular inferences from a question-answering model, we theoretically constrain the set of goal relations that are likely to be inferred during reading.

Support for the Global-Coherence Model. We recently conducted a series of studies to investigate the extent to which readers encode superordinate goal inferences during reading (Long et al., 1990; Long et al., 1992; Long & Golding, 1993). In these studies, we combined a question-answering procedure with on-line measures of inference generation. The question-answering procedure provided normative data on the likelihood that a particular inference would be produced as an answer to a why question about an action. Our procedure involved three steps. First, the question-answering task was used to identify potential on-line inferences. Consider "The Czar and His Daughters" story in Table 7.1. As the participants read each successive statement in the story, they answered a variety of questions, such as "why," "how," and "what-happened-next." Their answers constituted a corpus of inferences that were reliably produced in response to each statement. Second, theoretical predictions were generated about which of these inferences should be encoded on-line as the text is comprehended. For example, as readers comprehended an action statement (e.g., *The dragon kidnapped the daughters*), they were expected to make superordinate goal inferences (e.g., "the dragon wanted to eat the daughters"), but not subordinate goal inferences (e.g., "the dragon grabbed the daughters"). As discussed previously, superordinate goal inferences provide causal connections that contribute to overall coherence, whereas subordinate goal inferences do not. Third, on-line measures were used to test these predictions. For example, a lexical-decision task was used to test the prediction that concepts related to superordinate goal inferences (e.g., "eat") would be facilitated relative to concepts related to subordinate goal inferences (e.g., "grab").

We had two reasons for comparing the activation levels of concepts related to superordinate and subordinate goals rather than comparing the activation levels of superordinate goal and unrelated control concepts (Long et al., 1992). First, both superordinate and subordinate goal inferences tend to be drawn from the same knowledge structures (i.e., knowledge about the plans and actions of animate agents). To the extent that all concepts contained within a particular knowledge structure receive some activation when that structure is accessed, both inference concepts should be activated during comprehension. Second, each pair of superordinate and subordinate goal inferences was produced in response to questions about the same action statement. Any differences in their activation levels, therefore, could not be attributed to differences in their compatibility with the preceding context; both sets of words should be equally susceptible to the influence of context checking at the time of test. Thus, a comparison of the activation levels of concepts related to superordinate and subordinate goal inferences provides a stronger test of the on-line status of superordinate goal inferences than does a comparison of the activation levels of superordinate goal concepts and unrelated controls.

In our initial studies, we assessed the on-line status of superordinate goal inferences using a lexical-decision task (Long et al., 1990; Long et al., 1992). We selected the lexical-decision targets from the question-answering protocols of four short narrative stories reported by Graesser and Clark (1985). In their procedure, participants read short stories, such as "The Czar and His Daughters." As they read each successive statement in the text, participants answered a variety of questions, such as "why," "how," and "what-happened-next." We selected the lexical-decision targets by identifying a sample of explicit action statements in the stories (e.g., *The dragon kidnapped the daughters*). We then examined the participants' answers to "why" and "how" questions about the actions and selected one superordinate goal inference and one subordinate goal inference. Finally, we selected the most distinctive content word (typically the predicate) from each of the inferences. The superordinate and subordinate goal inference words were similar with respect to several lexical characteristics, such as number of letters, category, and frequency. In addition, the two sets of words appeared with approximately equal frequency in the question-answering protocols.

The activation levels of the superordinate and subordinate goal inference words were tested in two contexts. The words appeared in their inference context (i.e., the context in which they had been produced as answers to questions about action statements) or in a control context (i.e., an unrelated story). The control context was included to ensure that any facilitation elicited by superordinate goal inference words could not be attributed to characteristics of the test words that differentially affected lexical-decision latencies. The participants read each story as it was presented on a computer terminal one sentence at a time; each sentence was followed by a delay and then a lexical-decision target. After the participants had read all the stories and responded to the lexical decision items, they were administered a paper-and-pencil comprehension test. The test consisted of simple open-class questions to assess memory for the stories (e.g., *What did the dragon do to the daughters?*). Performance on the comprehension test was uniformly high ($M = .97$).

An analysis of the lexical-decision data showed strong support for the Global-Coherence Model. Decision latencies to words from superordinate goal inferences were facilitated relative to words from subordinate goal inferences in the inference context (M = 677 ms and M = 739 ms, respectively), but not in the control context (M= 803 ms and M= 789 ms, respectively). Our failure to observe any differences between the two sets of words in the control context suggests that the facilitation elicited by the superordinate goal inference words in the inference context was not due to variations in the intrinsic characteristics of the two sets of words (Long et al., 1992).

Alternative explanations for these results have been tested in subsequent experiments (Long & Golding, 1993; Long et al., 1992). First, we investigated the possibility that our pattern of results was due to the influence of context on post-access processes. Previous research has shown that lexical-decision latencies can be facilitated by context checking at the time of test (Balota & Chumbley, 1984; Chumbley & Balota, 1984; Forster, 1981; Potts, Keenan, & Golding, 1988). Thus, our participants might not have encoded superordinate goal inferences when they comprehended action statements. Rather, it might have been the case that presentation of a test word from a superordinate goal inference elicited a backward association between the test word and the preceding action sentence, with fewer such associations being elicited by words from subordinate goal inferences. We investigated this context-checking interpretation by replicating our experiment using a naming task in place of the lexical-decision task (Long et al., 1992). Again, we found faster responses to superordinate than to subordinate goal inference words in the inference context (M = 586 ms and M = 601 ms, respectively), but not in the control context (M = 652 ms and M = 608 ms, respectively). If word naming is less sensitive to context-checking effects than is lexical decision (Keenan, Golding, Potts, Jennings, & Aman, 1990; Lorch, Balota, & Stamm, 1986; Seidenberg, Waters, Sanders, & Langer, 1984), our results provide evidence against a context-checking explanation.

Second, we investigated the possibility that our results were due to differences in the extent to which our test words were semantically related to lexical items in the preceding text (Long et al., 1992). That is, test words from superordinate goal inferences might have been supported by a greater number of semantic associations with individual lexical items in the preceding action sentence than were test words from subordinate goal inferences. We examined this possibility using a procedure developed by Foss (1982). We used the same materials as in our previous experiments; however, we scrambled the content words in all of the stories to prevent participants from developing a coherent representation of the text. Latencies to superordinate goal inference words were not significantly shorter than were latencies to subordinate goal inference words in either the inference context (M = 740 ms and M = 765 ms, respectively) or the unrelated context (M = 800 ms and M = 787 ms, respectively); however, both superordinate and subordinate goal inference word showed facilitation in the inference context relative to the unrelated context. This pattern of findings suggests that both superordinate and subordinate goal inference words receive approximately equal facilitation from semantic associations with lexical items in the preceding action statements.

Finally, we investigated the possibility that aspects of our testing procedure encouraged more elaborative inferential activity than ordinarily occurs during reading (Long & Golding, 1993). In our previous studies, the participants read sentences at their own pace and pressed a key when they had comprehended each sentence. The test probe was presented 1,000 ms after a participant's key press. Thus, the *stimulus onset asynchrony* (SOA), the interval between the onset of the action statement and the onset of the test probe, was approximately 2,000 to 2,500 ms (i.e., the time it took to read the sentence plus the 1,000 ms delay). We chose a relatively long SOA to ensure that we were not assessing temporary activations of the inference concepts; temporary activations decay within 1,000 ms. However, the long SOA could have allowed readers the time needed to engage in more elaborative inferential processing than usually occurs. That is, superordinate goal inferences might have been reliably encoded only because readers were given an artificially long time to respond. This possibility is consistent with evidence about the time course of inferential processing obtained by Till, Mross, and Kintsch (1988), who found that readers spontaneously encoded topic-related inferences at long SOAs (i.e., 1,000–1,500 ms), whereas they did not encode these inferences at shorter SOAs (i.e., 200 to 500 ms).

Verification of the conclusion that superordinate goal inferences are automatically encoded during reading requires demonstrating that these inferences can be encoded within the time constraints of normal reading. Thus, we conducted a study to assess the activation of superordinate goal inferences under relatively demanding time constraints. The materials and design were similar to those we used previously; however, we used a *rapid serial visual presentation* (RSVP) procedure in which we presented the stories one word at a time. Each word appeared for 200 ms with a 50 ms interval between words. Lexical-decision targets followed the final word of each sentence by the same interval (i.e., a 250 ms SOA). As in our previous studies, we administered a comprehension test to assess the participants' memory for the stories. To our surprise, performance on the comprehension test was quite variable. Comprehension scores ranged from 8% to 100% correct. Because the participants exhibited such variability in their comprehension performance, we included comprehension as an explicit factor in our analysis. The median comprehension score was used to divide the participants into two groups: high scorers ($M = 84\%$) and low scorers ($M = 39\%$). The pattern of decision latencies exhibited by the two groups is depicted in Fig. 7.3. High scorers exhibited a pattern of decision latencies predicted by the Global Coherence model; latencies to test words from superordinate goal inferences

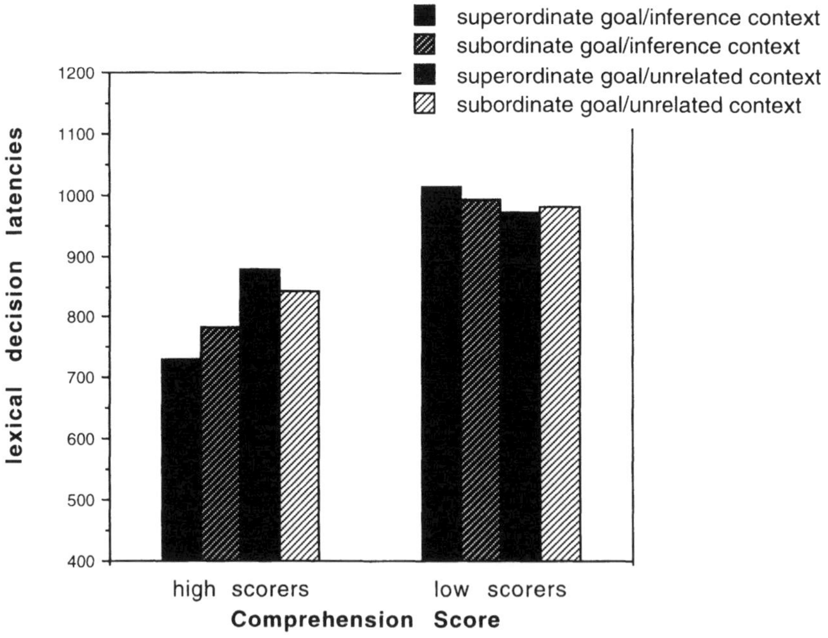

FIG. 7.3. Lexical-decision latencies (in milliseconds) to superordinate and subordinate goal inference words in inference and unrelated contexts as a function of comprehension score.

were faster than latencies to test words from subordinate goal inferences in the inference context, but not in the unrelated context. In contrast, low scorers exhibited no reliable differences in their responses to the two sets of test words in either the inference or the unrelated context. The failure of low scorers to encode superordinate goal inferences might have resulted from using the RSVP procedure in place of the self-paced reading task that we had used previously. The RSVP procedure might have limited reading time to the point at which a subset of readers failed to form an adequate discourse representation.

In summary, the pattern of results found in these experiments supports a Global-Coherence model of inferential processing. Concepts related to superordinate goal inferences are facilitated when readers comprehend action statements in stories. We have demonstrated that this facilitation is not due to (a) characteristics of the test words that differentially influence lexical-decision latencies, (b) the influence of context on post-access processes, or (c) semantic associations between the superordinate goal inference words and lexical items in the preceding sentences. In addition, we demonstrated that readers who score well on a comprehension test exhibit facilitation to concepts related to superordinate goal inferences within 250 ms. This latter finding is interesting for two reasons. First, it is problematic for the Minimal Inference Processing framework, which states that causal inferences are not automatically encoded during reading unless they are required for local coherence or supported by semantic associates in the text. Second, differences in the pattern of latencies exhibited by high and low scorers has interesting implications for assessing the role of inferential processing in reading ability. In the following section, we discuss some of these implications, as well as data from a recent study designed to investigate the relation between reading ability and inferential processing.

INDIVIDUAL DIFFERENCES IN READING ABILITY AND INFERENTIAL PROCESSING

It is tempting to speculate that the variability in comprehension scores observed by Long and Golding (1993) was due to individual differences in inferential ability. Readers who performed poorly on the comprehension test may have done so because they failed to encode superordinate goal inferences. These inferences may improve comprehension performance by providing causal connections that enhance the durability of a reader's text representation. Failure to encode such inferences could be attributed to a systematic failure to apply world knowledge during comprehension or a presentation rate (e.g., 200 ms per word) that did not allow sufficient time to execute inferential processes.

Although the failure of low scorers to encode superordinate goal inferences might have contributed to their poor comprehension performance, there is an alternative explanation. Low scorers might have performed poorly on the comprehension test because they failed to establish an accurate propositional representation of the stories. These readers could have deficits in lower level processes, such as word recognition or syntactic analysis. Such deficits would interfere with their ability to construct an accurate discourse representation, particularly under demanding time constraints. Certainly, our pattern of decision latencies suggests that word recognition is more effortful for low than for high scorers. Low scorers responded more slowly than did high scorers to both sets of test words. Thus, Long and Golding's (1993) data appear consistent with either explanation. Poor comprehension performance may have been due to failure to encode knowledge-based inferences or establish an accurate discourse representation.

Unfortunately, previous research on individual differences in comprehension performance suffers from similar difficulties in discriminating between these two explanations (Perfetti, 1989). Studies that have demonstrated inference problems among low-ability readers have not fully assessed the extent to which the failure to draw inferences is secondary to deficits in processes that are necessary to construct an accurate propositional representation (Oakhill, 1982, 1984; Oakhill, Yuill, & Parkin, 1986; Singer, Andrusiak, Reisdorf, & Black, 1992; Whitney, Ritchie, & Clark, 1991; Yuill, Oakhill, & Parkin, 1989). Similarly, studies that have shown comprehension performance to be related to individual differences in working memory capacity, word identification, and propositional encoding have not adequately assessed the role of inferential processing (Hunt, 1978; Hunt, Lunneborg, & Lewis, 1975; Perfetti, 1985; Perfetti, Finger, & Hogaboam, 1978; Perfetti & Hogaboam, 1975; Perfetti & Lesgold, 1977; Perfetti & Roth, 1981; Stanovich, 1980).

We recently conducted an experiment to examine the relation between reading ability and inferential processing more directly (Long, Oppy, & Seely, 1994). Our goal was to examine the extent to which low-ability readers execute processes necessary to represent the meaning of a text, but fail to encode knowledge-based inferences to elaborate this representation. Our experiment was designed to answer three questions. First, do high- and low-ability readers differ in the extent to which they execute processes that are required to understand the meaning of a sentence? If low-ability readers fail to construct accurate propositional representations, they should be less likely than high-ability readers to execute meaning-required processes. Second, do high- and low-ability readers differ in the extent to which they encode knowledge-based inferences? If the ability to generate knowledge-based inferences is an important component of skilled reading, low-ability readers should fail to encode such inferences even if they demonstrate the ability to execute meaning-required processes. Third, do high- and low-ability readers exhibit differences in the time they need to execute meaning-required processes? If low-ability readers require more time to execute such processes than do high ability readers, then failure to encode knowledge-based inferences should be attributed to inefficient processing at word and sentence levels.

In an attempt to answer these questions, we replicated and extended an earlier study reported by Till et al. (1988). Till et al. investigated the effects of discourse context on the time course of sense selection and meaning elaboration. As regards sense selection, Till et al. investigated the time required to select the context-appropriate sense of a homograph. Consider the following sentence:

(2) The townspeople were amazed to find that all the buildings had collapsed except the mint.

Representing the meaning of the sentence in Example 2 requires that the reader determine that the homograph *mint* refers to "a building where money is made" and not to "a piece of candy." As regards meaning elaboration, Till et al. investigated the time required to make knowledge-based inferences that involved the topic or theme of a sentence (e.g., "earthquake" as the topic of Example sentence 2).

In their experiments, sense selection and inferential processing were assessed by means of a lexical-decision task. The participants read brief passages that were constructed around an ambiguous noun. The passages were presented via RSVP at a rate of 300 ms per word, and a lexical-decision trial immediately followed the homograph in each passage. The lexical decision targets were either (a) context-appropriate associates of homograph primes, (b) context-inappropriate associates of the primes, (c) words related to the topic of the sentence, (d) unrelated control words, or (e) nonwords. Example passages and lexical decision targets appear in Table 7.2.

Till et al. (1988) assessed sense selection by comparing response latencies to appropriate and inappropriate associates of the homograph primes. If readers select the context-appropriate sense of the homograph, they should exhibit faster latencies to appropriate associates than to inappropriate associates. For example, responses to the target *money* should be facilitated relative to the target *candy* in the context of the passage presented in the upper section of Table 7.2, whereas the opposite should be true in the context of the other passage presented in Table

TABLE 7.2
Example Passages and Target Items from Till, Mross, and Kintsch (1988)

	Target Items	
Passage	*Associate*	*Topic*
The townspeople were amazed to find that all the buildings had collapsed except the *mint*. Obviously, it had been built to withstand natural disasters.	money	earthquake
Thinking of the amount of garlic in his dinner the guest asked for a *mint*. He soon felt more comfortable socializing with the others.	candy	breath

7.2. Similarly, topic-related inferences were assessed by comparing latencies to topic-related and control words. If readers encode topic-related inferences, they should exhibit faster latencies to topic-related words than to control words. For example, responses to the target *earthquake* should be facilitated relative to the target *breath* in the context of the passage in the upper half of Table 7.2, whereas the opposite should occur in the context of the second passage in the table. The time course of sense selection and inferential processing was assessed by examining decision latencies to targets presented at the SOAs of 200, 300, 400, 500, 1,000, and 1,500 ms.

Till et al. (1988) found no differences in readers' responses to appropriate and inappropriate associates at short SOAs (i.e., 200 and 300 ms). However, the participants were faster to respond to appropriate than to inappropriate associates at 400 ms and longer SOAs. Topic-related inferences were not drawn until later in processing. Faster response times to topic-related than to unrelated control words were observed only in the 1,000 and 1,500 ms SOA conditions.

In our replication, we extended Till et al.'s (1988) research by adding a measure of reading ability to assess differences in the extent to which high- and low-ability readers execute meaning-required and knowledge-based inferential processes. Performance on the verbal portion of the Scholastic Aptitude Test (SAT) was used as a general measure of reading ability. Groups of high- and low-ability readers were selected according to their verbal SAT scores (the upper third and bottom third of our participants, respectively). The stimulus materials and presentation procedure were the same as those used by Till et al. with one exception. We added a 750 ms SOA condition in place of the 1,500 ms condition to obtain more precise information about the time course of elaborative processing.

The participants were 168 undergraduate psychology students. High-ability readers had verbal SAT scores that ranged from 540 to 730, with a mean of 585. Low-ability readers had verbal SAT scores that ranged from 230 to 450, with a mean of 394. With respect to the time course of sense selection, high- and low-ability readers exhibited similar patterns of facilitation. Neither group exhibited differences in response time to appropriate and inappropriate associates at short SOAs (i.e., 200 and 300 ms). However, both groups responded significantly faster to appropriate than to inappropriate associates at longer SOAs (i.e., 400 to 1,000 ms). Thus, it appears that both high- and low-ability readers constructed a representation of the meaning of a sentence that was more consistent with contextually appropriate associates than with contextually inappropriate associates.

With respect to the construction of topic-related inferences, however, high- and low-ability readers exhibited substantially different patterns of facilitation. High-ability readers showed no facilitation for topic-related words compared to unrelated words at short SOAs (i.e., 200 to 500 ms), but responded significantly faster to topic-related words than unrelated words at longer SOAs (i.e., 750 and 1,000 ms). In contrast, low-ability readers exhibited no differences in decision latencies to topic-related and unrelated words in any of the SOA conditions.

Thus, it appears that high-ability readers encoded knowledge-based inferences that low-ability readers failed to encode.

These results suggest that inferential processing makes a unique and important contribution to reading skill. Both high- and low-ability readers execute a process that is required to represent the meaning of a sentence (i.e., sense selection). However, only high-ability readers construct a representation that is consistent with the topic or theme of the passage.

CONCLUSIONS

The studies described in this chapter illustrate two empirical approaches to assessing the relation between inferential processing and reading ability. In the first approach, we examined the extent to which skilled readers encoded knowledge-based inferences on-line as they comprehended a text. If inferential processing is an important component of reading ability, readers should reliably and spontaneously encode inferences other than those required to construct a propositional representation.

In our investigation of superordinate goal inferences, we combined question-answering and on-line methodologies. The question-answering task was used to probe readers' developing representations and determine whether they contained nonexplicit information, such as how and why the events and actions in the text occurred. We then generated theoretical predictions with regard to which of these inferences should be encoded on-line as a text is comprehended. According to the Global-Coherence model, the probability that a particular inference is encoded on-line depends on whether (a) the inference provides an explanation for an action or event described in the text and (b) the inference is a "good" answer to a "why" question. Finally, we assessed our theoretical predictions by means of different on-line measures of inferential processing (e.g., lexical decision, word naming).

In the second empirical approach, we examined differences in the extent to which high- and low-ability readers executed meaning-required and inferential processes. If low-ability readers fail to encode knowledge-based inferences, as well as fail to execute a process required to represent the meaning of a sentence (i.e., sense selection), inferential processing should be constrained and contingent on more basic meaning construction processes. However, if low-ability readers execute meaning-required processes, but do not encode knowledge-based inferences, this would suggest that inferential processing is a functionally separate component of skilled reading.

The data summarized in this chapter is consistent with the view that inferential processing is an important and functionally separate component of skilled reading. First, our data suggest that one class of knowledge-based inferences, superordinate goals, is spontaneously and reliably encoded during reading. Although superordinate goal inferences are not required for local coherence, they provide causal information that is necessary to establish overall text coherence. Second, our data suggest that high-ability readers encode knowledge-based inferences that low-ability readers fail to encode. Although both high- and low-ability readers execute sense selection processes early in the time course of processing, only high ability readers encode topic-related inferences.

APPENDIX

Example Story from McKoon and Ratcliff (1992): "Kidnapped"

Jon was a CIA agent who often worked behind the Iron Curtain. He had made many enemies, and one of them, a KGB agent, kidnapped his daughter, Karyn, while she was on a trip to the Bahamas. It was all part of a plan to get revenge because Jon had foiled one of the enemy agent's plots many years before.

Jon wanted to get Karyn back from the KGB agent who had kidnapped her as quickly as possible. He had worked against the KGB agent, Vladimir, many years ago and was very worried about his daughter's safety. Although the authorities told Jon that he should stay at home and let the professionals do their job, Jon decided that he had to get to the Bahamas. Anxious, as any father would be, he made a reservation on the first plane he could find. In a few hours Jon arrived in the Bahamas.

Jon believed the only way he would get Karyn back safely was to find her himself. He had to find out where the kidnapper had taken her. As soon as the messenger left, Jon quietly followed Him. He hoped that the young man would lead him to Vladimir. After some time, Jon arrived at a large, old fortress that was once used as a prison. As Jon Watched the messenger go into the fortress, he was sure this was where his daughter was being held by Vladimir. He hoped that she was alright.

The fortress appeared to be completely impenetrable. Jon knew that if he was to rescue Karyn he would have to find help getting into it. Jon returned back to town, hoping to find a mercenary to help him. After visiting several bars, Jon met an old friend, Ali Al-Dib, a double agent he had known for many years. They had worked both against and with each other, but they always remained friends. Jon and Ali had some beers and talked over old times. Jon discovered that Ali had done business with Vladimir on several occasions. Jon explained his situation to Ali and asked him to help rescue Karyn.

Ali was busy with his own mission, stealing some microfilm that contained the locations of missile silos of certain west European countries. He hoped to sell it to the highest bidder. Ali agreed to help Jon if Jon would help him first. Jon thought it was a fair exchange and agreed to the bargain. They stay up late that night trying to come up with a plan to get the microfilm, which was hidden in the British embassy. They came up with a deceptively simple plan. Since Jon knew some people at the embassy, he would go in first and keep them occupied while Ali stole the microfilm. It worked.

Ali contacted Vladimir and asked him if he would be interested in buying the microfilm. Vladimir wanted to see it first, so Ali drove to the fortress with Jon hidden in the trunk. The guards recognized Ali and let him into the fortress without searching his car, so they did not find Jon in the trunk. While Ali kept Vladimir busy examining the microfilm, Jon ran from room to room and finally found the room where his daughter was being held hostage.

They escaped, undetected, and hid in Ali's car. Soon, Ali finished his business with Vladimir and got into the car. He drove Jon and Karyn to the airport before Vladimir realized Karyn had been rescued. In just a few hours, Jon and Karyn were safely back home.

REFERENCES

Abbott, V., & Black, J. B. (1986). Goal-related inferences in comprehension. In J. A. Galambos, R. P. Abelson, & J. B. Black (Eds.), *Knowledge structures* (pp. 123–142). Hillsdale, NJ: Lawrence Erlbaum Associates.

Balota, D. A., & Chumbley, J. I. (1984). Are lexical decisions a good measure of lexical access? The role of word-frequency in the neglected decision stage. *Journal of Experimental Psychology: Human Perception and Performance, 10*, 340–357.

Black, J. B., & Bower, G. H. (1980). Story understanding as problem solving. *Poetics, 9*, 223–250.

Bloom, C. P., Fletcher, C. R., van den Broek, P., Reitz, L., & Shapiro, B. P. (1990). An on-line assessment of causal reasoning during comprehension. *Memory and Cognition, 18*, 65–71.

Bransford, J. D., & Johnson, M. K. (1973). Considerations of some problems of comprehension. In W. G. Chase (Ed.), *Visual information processing* (pp. 383–438). New York: Academic Press.

Chiesi, H. L., Spilich, G. J., & Voss, J. F. (1979). Acquisition of domain-related information in relation to high- and low-domain knowledge. *Journal of Verbal Learning and Verbal Behavior, 18*, 257–274.

Chumbley, J. I., & Balota, D. A. (1984). A word's meaning affects the decision in lexical decision. *Memory and Cognition, 12*, 590–606.

Corbett, A. T., & Dosher, B. A. (1978). Instrument inferences in sentence encoding. *Journal of Verbal Learning and Verbal Behavior, 17*, 479–491.

Dell, G., McKoon, G., & Ratcliff, R. (1983). The activation of antecedent information during the processing of anaphoric reference in reading. *Journal of Verbal Learning and Verbal Behavior, 22*, 121–132.

Dooling, D. J., & Lachman, R. (1971). Effects of comprehension on retention of prose. *Journal of Experimental Psychology, 88*, 216–222.

Fletcher, C. R., & Bloom, C. P. (1988). Causal reasoning in the comprehension of simple narrative texts. *Journal of Memory and Language, 27*, 235–244.

Fletcher, C. R., Hummel, J. E., & Marsolek, C. J. (1990). Causality and the allocation of attention during comprehension. *Journal of Experimental Psychology: Learning, Memory, and Cognition, 16*, 233–240.

Forster, K. I. (1981). Priming and the effects of sentence and lexical contexts on naming time: Evidence for autonomous lexical processing. *Quarterly Journal of Experimental Psychology: Human Experimental Psychology, 33*, 465–495.

Foss, C. C., & Bower, G. H. (1986). Understanding action in relation to goals. In N. E. Sharkey (Ed.), *Advances in cognitive science* (pp. 94–124). New York: Ellis Horwood.

Foss, D. J. (1982). A discourse on semantic priming. *Cognitive Psychology, 14*, 590–607.

Gerrig, R. J. (1986). Process models and pragmatics. In N. E. Sharkey (Ed.), *Advances in cognitive science* (Vol. 1, pp. 23–42). New York: Wiley.

Golding, J. M., Graesser, A. C., & Millis, K. K. (1990). What makes a good answer to a question?: Testing a psychological model of question answering in the context of narrative text. *Discourse Processes, 13*, 305–326.

Graesser, A. C. (1981). *Prose comprehension beyond the word*. New York: Springer-Verlag.

Graesser, A. C., & Clark, L. F. (1985). *Structures and procedures of implicit knowledge*. Norwood, NJ: Ablex.

Graesser, A. C., & Franklin, S. P. (1990). QUEST: A cognitive model of question answering. *Discourse Processes, 13*, 279–304.

Graesser, A. C., Gordon, S. E., & Brainerd, L. E. (1992). QUEST: A model of question answering. *Computers and Mathematics with Applications, 23*, 733–745.

Graesser, A. C., & Hemphill, D. (1991). Question answering in the context of scientific mechanisms. *Journal of Memory and Language 20*, 186–209.

Graesser, A. C., Lang, K. L., & Roberts, R. M. (1991). Question answering in the context of stories. *Journal of Experimental Psychology: General, 120*, 254–277.

Graesser, A. C., & Murachver, T. (1985). Symbolic procedures of question answering. In A. C. Graesser & J. B. Black (Eds.), *The psychology of questions* (pp. 15–88). Hillsdale, NJ: Lawrence Erlbaum Associates.

Graesser, A. C., Robertson, S. P., & Anderson, P. A. (1981). Incorporating inferences in narrative representations: A study of how and why. *Cognitive Psychology, 13*, 1–26.

Graesser, A. C., Robertson, S. P., Lovelace, E., & Swinehart, D. (1980). Answers to why-questions expose the organization of story plot and predict recall of actions. *Journal of Verbal Learning and Verbal Behavior, 19*, 110–119.

Hunt, E. B. (1978). Mechanics of verbal ability. *Psychological Review, 85*, 199–230.

Hunt, E. B., Lunneborg, C., & Lewis, J. (1975). What does it mean to be high verbal? *Cognitive Psychology, 2*, 194–227.

Keefe, D. E., & McDaniel, M. A. (1993). The time course and durability of predictive inferences. *Journal of Memory and Language, 32*, 446–463.

Keenan, J. M., Golding, J. M., Potts, G. R., Jennings, T. M., & Aman, C. J. (1990). Methodological issues in evaluating the occurrence of inferences. In A. C. Graesser & G. H. Bower (Eds.), *The psychology of learning and motivation: Inferences and text comprehension* (Vol. 25, pp. 295–312). New York: Academic Press.

Kintsch, W., & van Dijk, T. A. (1978). Toward a model of text comprehension and production. *Psychological Review, 85*, 363–394.

Long, D. L., & Golding, J. M. (1993). Superordinate goal inferences: Are they automatically generated during comprehension? *Discourse Processes, 16*, 55–74.

Long, D. L., Golding, J. M., & Graesser, A. C. (1992). A test of the on-line status of goal-related inferences. *Journal of Memory and Language, 31*, 634–647.

Long, D. L., Golding, J. M., Graesser, A. C., & Clark, L. F. (1990). Goal, event, and state inferences: An investigation of inference generation during story comprehension. In A. C. Graesser & G. H. Bower (Eds.), *The psychology of learning and motivation: Inferences and text comprehension* (Vol. 25, pp. 89–102). New York: Academic Press.

Long, D. L., Oppy, B. J., & Seely, M. R. (1994). Individual differences in the time course of inferential processing. *Journal of Experimental Psychology: Learning, Memory, and Cognition, 20*, 1456–1470.

Lorch, R. F., Balota, D. A., & Stamm, E. G. (1986). Locus of inhibition effects in the priming of lexical decisions: Pre- or postlexical access? *Memory and Cognition, 14*, 95–103.

Markman, E. M. (1977). Realizing that you don't understand. *Child Development, 48*, 986–992.

McKoon, G., & Ratcliff, R. (1980). The comprehension processes and memory structures involved in anaphoric reference. *Journal of Verbal Learning and Verbal Behavior, 19*, 668–682.

McKoon, G., & Ratcliff, R. (1981). The comprehension processes and memory structures involved in instrumental inferences. *Journal of Verbal Learning and Verbal Behavior, 20*, 671–682.

McKoon, G., & Ratcliff, R. (1986). Inferences about predictable events. *Journal of Experimental Psychology: Learning, Memory, and Cognition, 12*, 82–91.

McKoon, G., & Ratcliff, R. (1988). Contextually relevant aspects of meaning. *Journal of Experimental Psychology: Learning, Memory, and Cognition, 14*, 331–343.

McKoon, G., & Ratcliff, R. (1989a). Inferences about contextually defined categories. *Journal of Experimental Psychology, Learning, Memory, and Cognition, 15*, 1134–1146.

McKoon, G., & Ratcliff, R. (1989b). Semantic associations and elaborative inference. *Journal of Experimental Psychology: Learning, Memory, and Cognition, 15*, 326–338.

McKoon, G., & Ratcliff, R. (1990). Dimensions of inference. In A. C. Graesser & G. H. Bower (Eds.), *The psychology of learning and motivation: Inferences and text comprehension* (Vol. 25, pp. 312–328). New York: Academic Press.

McKoon, G., & Ratcliff, R. (1992). Inference during reading. *Psychological Review, 99*, 440–466.

Murray, J. D., Klin, C. M., & Myers, J. L. (1993). Forward inferences in narrative text. *Journal of Memory and Language, 32*, 464–473.

Oakhill, J. (1982). Constructive processes in skilled and less skilled comprehenders. *British Journal of Psychology, 73*, 13–20.

Oakhill, J. (1984). Inferential and memory skills in children's comprehension of stories. *British Journal of Educational Psychology, 54*, 31–39.

Oakhill, J., Yuill, N., & Parkin, A. (1986). On the nature of the difference between skilled and less skilled comprehenders. *Journal of Research in Reading, 9*, 80–91.

Perfetti, C. A. (1985). *Reading ability.* New York: Oxford University Press.

Perfetti, C. A. (1989). There are generalized abilities and one of them is reading. In L. B. Resnick (Ed.), *Knowing, learning, and instruction: Essays in honor of Robert Glaser* (pp. 307–335). Hillsdale, NJ: Lawrence Erlbaum Associates.

Perfetti, C. A., Finger, E., & Hogaboam, T. (1978). Sources of vocalization latency differences between skilled and less-skilled young readers. *Journal of Educational Psychology, 70*, 730–739.

Perfetti, C. A., & Hogaboam, T. (1975). The relationship between single word decoding and reading comprehension skill. *Journal of Educational Psychology, 67*, 461–469.

Perfetti, C. A., & Lesgold, A. M. (1977). Discourse comprehension and sources of individual differences. In M. A. Just & P. A. Carpenter (Eds.), *Cognitive processes in comprehension* (pp. 141–183). Hillsdale, NJ: Lawrence Erlbaum Associates.

Perfetti, C. A., & Roth, S. F. (1981). Some of the interactive processes in reading and their role in reading skill. In A. M. Lesgold & C. A. Perfetti (Eds.), *Interactive processes in reading* (pp. 269–297). Hillsdale, NJ: Lawrence Erlbaum Associates.

Potts, G. R., Keenan, J. M., & Golding, J. M. (1988). Assessing the occurrence of elaborative inferences: Lexical decision versus naming. *Journal of Memory and Language, 27*, 399–415.

Schank, R. C. (1986). *Explanation patterns: Understanding mechanically and creatively.* Hillsdale, NJ: Lawrence Erlbaum Associates.

Schank, R. C., & Abelson, R. (1977). *Scripts, plans, goals, and understanding.* Hillsdale, NJ: Lawrence Erlbaum Associates.

Seidenberg, M. S., Waters, G. S., Sanders, M., & Langer, P. (1984). Pre- and postlexical loci of contextual effects on word recognition. *Memory and Cognition, 12*, 315–328.

Seifert, C. M., Robertson, S. P., & Black, J. B. (1985). Types of inferences generated during reading. *Journal of Memory and Language, 24*, 405–422.

Singer, M., Andrusiak, P., Reisdorf, P., & Black, N. L. (1992). Individual differences in bridging inference processes. *Memory & Cognition, 20*, 539–548.

Singer, M., & Ferreira, F. (1983). Inferring consequences in story comprehension. *Journal of Verbal Learning and Verbal Behavior, 22*, 437–448.

Spilich, G. J., Vesonder, G. T., Chiesi, H. L., & Voss, J. F. (1979). Text-processing of domain-related information for individuals with high and low domain knowledge. *Journal of Verbal Learning and Verbal Behavior, 18*, 275–290.

Stanovich, D. E. (1980). Toward an interactive compensatory model of individual differences in the development of reading fluency. *Reading Research Quarterly, 16*, 32–71.

Till, R. E., Mross, E. F., & Kintsch, W. (1988). Time course of priming for associate and inference words in a discourse context. *Memory & Cognition, 16*, 283–298.

Trabasso, T., & Sperry, L. L. (1985). Causal relatedness and importance of story events. *Journal of Memory and Language, 24*, 595–611.

Trabasso, T., & van den Broek, P. (1985). Causal thinking and representation of narrative events. *Journal of Memory and Language, 24*, 612–630.

Trabasso, T., van den Broek, P. & Suh, S. Y. (1989). Logical necessity and transitivity of causal relations in stories. *Discourse Processes, 12*, 1–25.

van den Broek, P. (1988). The effects of causal relations and hierarchical position on the importance of story statements. *Journal of Memory and Language, 27*, 1–22.

van den Broek, P. (1990). Causal inferences and the comprehension of narrative texts. In A. C. Graesser & G. H. Bower (Eds.), *The psychology of learning and motivation: Inferences and text comprehension* (Vol. 25, pp. 175–196). New York: Academic Press.

van den Broek, P., & Trabasso, T. (1986). Causal networks versus goal hierarchies in summarizing text. *Discourse Processes, 9*, 1–15.

Wilensky, R. (1983). *Planning and understanding*. Reading, MA: Addison-Wesley.

Whitney, P., Ritchie, B. G., & Clark, M. B. (1991). Working-memory capacity and the use of elaborative inferences in text comprehension. *Discourse Processes, 14*, 133–145.

Yuill, N., Oakhill, J., & Parkin, A. (1989). Working memory, comprehension ability and the resolution of text anomaly. *British Journal of Psychology, 80*, 351–361.

CHAPTER

8

Metaphor as a Constraint on Text Understanding

Raymond W. Gibbs, Jr.
University of California, Santa Cruz

Our enjoyment of literature very much depends on our ability to recognize and appreciate different figures of thought. Metaphor, metonymy, irony, and other instances of figurative language fill the pages of great literature and provide us with instruments for establishing imaginative connections between diverse emotions, ideas, and events. Consider as examples of metaphor the following passages from Vladimir Nabokov's novel *The Defense* about a genius chess-master, Luzhin, who suffers a nervous breakdown in the middle of an important match. Luzhin has so saturated his mind with chess that he sees his whole life in its terms. These passages describe his awkward courtship of the woman who will become his wife:

> Luzhin began with a series of quiet moves, the meaning of which he himself only vaguely sensed, his own peculiar declaration of love. "Go on, tell me more," she repeated, despite having noticed how morosely and dully he had fallen silent. (p. 97)

> He sat leaning on his cane and thinking that with a Knight's move of this lime tree standing on a sunlit slope one could take that telegraph pole over there, and simultaneously he tried to remember what exactly he had just been talking about. (p. 97)

> With one shoulder pressed against his chest she tried with a cautious finger to raise his eyelids a little higher and the slight pressure on his eyeball caused a strange black light to leap there, to leap like his black Knight which simply took the Pawn if Turati moved it out on the seventh move, as he had done at their last meeting. (p. 114)

Later in the book, Nabokov gives us a glimpse of Luzhin's mind soon after his breakdown:

> He found himself in a smokey establishment where noisy phantoms were sitting. An attack was developing in every corner—and pushing aside tables, a bucket with a gold-necked glass Pawn sticking out of it and a drum that was being beaten by an arched, thick-manned chess Knight, he made his way to a gently revolving door. (p. 139)

The power of chess over Luzhin's mind is not limited to the visual or spatial properties of chess. Much more pervasive is the discipline provided by the rules and tactics of the game. The abstract structure of chess obsessively drives much of Luzhin's thinking:

> [He] presently would note with despair that he had been unwary again and that a delicate move had just been made in his life, mercilessly continuing the fatal combination. Then he would decide to redouble his watchfulness and keep track of every second of his life, for traps could be everywhere. And he was oppressed most of all by the impossibility of inventing a rational defense, for his opponent's aim was still hidden. (p. 227)

Nabokov's characterization of Luzhin is a wonderful example of how we live our lives via metaphor. We may not be as psychologically fixated on one particular metaphorical theme as is poor Luzhin, but we still conceptualize our everyday life in terms of a system of metaphorical schemas that help us make sense of our inchoate experiences. One of the pleasures that we derive from reading literary works, both poetry and prose, is the metaphors that we discover in these texts that somehow speak to us, or remind us of our own struggles to find meaning and purpose in the chaos of ordinary living.

Metaphor is not seen only in literary texts; it also plays an important role in serious intellectual arguments. Consider this paragraph from an essay by H. Kallan (1915) entitled "Democracy Versus the Melting Pot," in which Kallen used the striking metaphor of an orchestra to define his ideal for American civilization:

> As in an orchestra, every type of instrument has its specific timbre and tonality, founded in its substance and form; as every type has its appropriate theme and melody in the whole symphony, so in society each ethnic group is the natural instrument, its spirit and culture are its theme and melody, and the harmony and dissonances and discords of them all make the symphony of civilization, with this difference: a musical symphony is written before it is played; in the symphony of civilization the playing is the writing, so there is nothing so fixed and inevitable about its progressions as in music, so that within the limits set by nature they may vary at will, and the range and variety may become wider and richer and more beautiful. (p. 34)

Although we applaud writers such as Nabokov and Kallan for their inventive uses of metaphor as a literary and rhetorical device, a closer look at metaphor in both everyday and literary language reveals that metaphor is not, as Aristotle once noted, "the mark of genius"; instead, it is an essential part of how each of us thinks, reasons, and understands. Speakers and authors cannot help but use metaphor because their conceptualization of everyday experience is primarily accomplished via the metaphorical mapping from one knowledge domain (the source) onto another (the target). Readers find metaphorical texts easy to understand precisely because much of their thinking is constrained by common metaphorical processes. We often miss the presence of metaphoric schemes of thought in texts because we mistakenly assume that metaphor is a special intellectual ability. In this chapter, my aim is to illustrate the ubiquity of metaphorical thought in a variety of texts and show how metaphorical thought constrains the psychological processes by which readers make sense of, and comprehend, texts.

THE UBIQUITY OF METAPHOR IN WRITTEN LANGUAGE

We have seen some notable examples of metaphor in written texts, but how frequently is metaphor used by speakers and writers? Many scholars have commented on the ubiquity of metaphor in literature, poetry, and even scientific writing. Psychologists have arrived at some rough approximations of the frequency with which speakers and writers employ metaphorical language. One analysis examined the metaphorical language found in various essays, the 1960 Kennedy-Nixon presidential debates, and transcripts of psychotherapy interviews (Pollio, Barlow, Fine, & Pollio, 1977). This analysis indicated that people use 1.80 novel and 4.08 frozen metaphors per min of discourse. If one assumes that people engage in conversation as little as 2 hours per day, a person would utter 4.7 million novel and 21.4 frozen metaphors over a 60-year lifetime (Glucksberg, 1989). Although this analysis focused primarily on spoken language, it is apparent that metaphor is not only used in special circumstances or by individuals with special intellectual talents.

One historical analysis of the metaphors used in American English prose from 1675–1975 revealed significant metaphoric activity in each of the six 50-year periods considered (Smith, Pollio, & Pitts, 1981). The most general area dealt with metaphorically by American authors over the past 300 years concerned issues related to the psychological nature of being human. Many human topics, such as rationality, emotions, and the meanings of life and death, were discussed primarily in metaphorical terms. Although different source domains, or vehicles, were used to make these issues metaphorical in different time periods, it is clear that metaphor has been in widespread use during the past 300 years.

Another interesting analysis of the occurrence of metaphor in written texts focused the evolution of mental metaphors in a corpus of articles published in the scholarly journal *Psychological Review* between 1894 and 1975 (Gentner & Grudin, 1985). During this period, four main categories of mental metaphors were employed: *animate-being metaphors*, *neural metaphors*, *spatial metaphors*, and *system metaphors*.

In *animate-being metaphors*, ideas or certain aspects of the human mind are compared with animate beings. For example:

> Through lying, the mind grows wary or strong from swimming against stream. (Dewey, 1894, p. 110)
>
> Reaction arcs block each other, varying in tension, until one waxes strong enough. (Dashiell, 1925, p. 59)
>
> Super discriminating prepreceiver who selectively prevents recognition. (Minard, 1965, p. 76)

In *neural metaphors*, the physical system is taken as a domain. For example:

> Wider ideas shortcircuit smaller ideas. (James, 1885, p. 17)
>
> Thinking is neural impulses shifting along associative fibers from one area to another. (Dashiell, 1925, p. 20)
>
> Loudness perhaps proportionate to number of mental impulses. (Zwicker & Scharf, 1965, p. 24)

Spatial metaphors are derived from the position or the movements of an object in space. For example:

> Anything hidden in the background is not mental activity. (James, 1905, p. 7)
>
> Habitual connections between ideas. (Peterson, 1935, p. 8)
>
> Reservoir model for fixed action patterns. (Moltz, 1965, p. 43)

System metaphors involve comparison of certain mental phenomena with a system of lawfully constrained interactions between elements. For example:

> A body moves in empty space by its own momentum as when our thoughts at their own sweet will. (James, 1905, p. 6)
>
> The nervous system is like a switchboard mechanism. (Gray, 1935, p. 111)
>
> Serial, iterative operations. (Carpenter & Just, 1975, p. 47)

In addition to these four main categories, a large number (71 of 265 metaphors) were found to be *conventional metaphors*. These expressions have some kind of metaphorical basis but are thought to have lost their metaphorical associations as in *mental health*, *intellectual growth*, *mental state*, and so forth. In fact, even conventional phrases, such as *intellectual growth*, may reflect the strong tendency of psychologists to conceive of the mind in metaphorical terms.

Gentner and Grudin's (1985) review discovered two main tendencies in the evolution of mental metaphors: a shift in the number of metaphors and a change in the kinds of metaphors. Their analysis of the metaphors used in three bidecades–an early period (1894–1915), a middle period (1925–1945), and a recent period (1955–1975)–showed a U-shaped distribution, with many metaphors used in the early and recent period and far fewer metaphors seen in the middle period. In the early period, spatial metaphors and animate-being metaphors dominated. The latter category showed a strong drop in use over the years. Use of spatial metaphors also dropped, although less severely. In contrast, system metaphors were an unimportant category in the early period. The decline of metaphors in the middle period likely was due to the influence of behaviorism as articles in this period (1925–1945) were most often straightforward reports of data without any discussion of the internal functionings of the mind. Mental metaphors and all other forms of mentalistic language were rarely employed during the middle period; metaphors that did occur in this period were either mathematical metaphors or neural ones. System metaphors were responsible for the overall increase in metaphors during the recent period. The primary reason for this increase in system metaphors was the cognitive revolution in psychology, which included a view of the mind as a type computing system.

Other analyses of the use of metaphors in the recent history of experimental psychology texts suggest that inferential statistics provide many new concepts for describing mental processes (Gigerenzer, 1991). Theories of cognition were cleansed of terms such as *restructuring* and *insight*, and the new mind has come to be portrayed as "drawing random samples from nervous fibers," "computing probabilities," "calculating analyses of variance," "setting decision criteria," and "performing utility analyses." As inferential statistics has become institutionalized, a wide range of cognitive processes, conscious and unconscious, elementary and complex, have been reinterpreted as involving "intuitive statistics" (Gigerenzer & Murray, 1987).

These empirical analyses of the metaphors used by experimental psychologists demonstrate the pervasiveness of metaphor in psychological theories of the mind. For the most part, we mostly are blind to these metaphors in our thinking as experimental psychologists, even though an analysis of our language reveals their ubiquity in theories of mind and behavior.

WHY DO WE USE METAPHOR?

Why do people use metaphor? For example, why is metaphor found so frequently in psychological texts? Scholars traditionally have focused on three reasons for using metaphor (Ortony, 1975). First, metaphors provide speakers with a way to express ideas that would be difficult to convey using literal language. This notion has been referred to as the *inexpressibility hypothesis*. Just as the poet Lord Byron used metaphor to express his idea about the abstract concept of love in his famous metaphorical expression *My love is like a red, red rose*, psychologists might use the *Mind is a computer* or *Memory is a push-down stack* to express their conceptions of the mind and memory in ways that seem impossible to do using literal language (Roediger, 1980).

A second reason to use metaphor is to provide a particularly compact means of communication (i.e., the *compactness hypothesis*). For instance, the assertion *Memory is a push-down stack* expresses a large amount of information about memory (i.e., that information is ordered as to storage and retrieval processes) using relatively few words. Literal language simply does not enable speakers and writers to convey information as succinctly as does metaphor.

Finally, metaphors might be used because they help capture the vividness of our phenomenological experience, a notion that has been labeled the *vividness hypothesis*. Metaphors can convey richer, more detailed, and vivid images of our subjective experiences than can be expressed by literal language. Thus, *My love is like a red, red, rose* is likely to evoke mental images that better reflect the writer's vivid communicative intentions about the concept and experience of love.

Educators and psychologists long have been interested in understanding the role of metaphor in learning and remembering textual material. One of the greatest challenges to educators lies in selecting metaphors that provide succinct and informative descriptions of a topic (Petrie, 1979). Does the introduction of metaphor make it easier to learn and recall text information? The inexpressibility, compactness, and vividness hypotheses suggest that metaphors should enhance understanding and learning of textual materials.

One analysis of fourth- and fifth-grade social science texts indicated that these texts contained an average of 4 metaphors per 1,000 words of text (Ortony, 1976), suggesting that textbook authors use metaphor to achieve a variety of pedagogical goals (e.g., summary, processing of new information, emphasis, advanced organization, and so forth). Analogies used as advance organizers could enhance the quality and quantity of what is learned and recalled from subsequent material (Glynn, 1991; Mayer, 1980). For example, introducing a text on electrical current by having students read a passage about water flowing through pipes might provide a conceptual framework for students to learn basic information about electricity (Gentner & Gentner, 1983; Glynn, 1991; Glynn, Britton, Semrud-Clikeman, & Muth, 1989).

Empirical evidence suggests that metaphors also facilitate prose comprehension. In one study, participants read short didactic prose passages that were written using either context-dependent metaphor sentences or literally equivalent paraphrases as concluding statements (Reynolds & Schwartz, 1984). For example:

The people of Nazi Germany were swayed by Hitler's rhetoric. Although he had committed his people to a course of war, he found it easy to persuade them of the virtue of his actions. Everyone in Europe at the time was aware of the consequences of war, but the Germans had a blind belief in Hitler.

The sheep followed the leader over the cliff. (Metaphorical target)
The German people blindly accepted Hitler's dangerous ideas. (Literal target)

The participants read stories ending in either metaphorical or literal targets. Their task was to rate the quality and effectiveness of the writing. Subsequently, they were asked to write down all the stories they read. An analysis of the recall protocols indicated that people were superior at remembering passages if the concluding statement was expressed metaphorically rather than literally. Not only were the concluding metaphors themselves better remembered than were the literal paraphrases, there also was an increase in recall of the preceding context. Thus, metaphor can enhance learning from prose materials, although one could no doubt increase the number of metaphors present in a passage so as to make the text incomprehensible.

A variety of other studies have involved an examination of the utility of metaphor in learning computers and computer programming from text materials. This research has demonstrated that novice BASIC programmers learned concepts such as "input," "output," and "program" more quickly and effectively if these concepts first were introduced through concrete metaphors, such as a ticket window, a pad of paper, and a shopping list (Mayer, 1975, 1978). Other anecdotal evidence suggests that novices find it easier to overcome problems learning to use a text editor by using a variety of metaphors. In one study, for instance, the "editor is a secretary" metaphor helped familiarize novices with the basic idea of mixing commands and text, but it also led them to errors, such as failing to signal the end of a text insertion before issuing a command (Rumelhart & Norman, 1981). However, the metaphor "the editor is a tape recorder" overcame this difficulty because it forced people to realize that once you have started recording you must first stop before doing anything else. Finally, in another investigation, students found it easier to learn abbreviated commands for a computer-command language when given metaphorical instructions than when presented with rule-based instructions (Payne, 1988).

These findings suggest three possibilities as to why metaphor has a positive influence on understanding and learning from written texts. First, metaphor may serve a mnemonic function, enriching the encoding and thereby facilitating subsequent recall of information. Second, metaphor may activate appropriate semantic frameworks from long-term memory, allowing the new knowledge to be assimulated into existing mental schemas. Third, metaphor may act as a prompt to active, hypothesis-driven learning because the intrinsic incongruity and incompleteness of metaphorical expressions stimulates experimentation on the part of the learner (Petrie, 1979).

HOW METAPHOR IS UNDERSTOOD

What psychological processes underlie readers' comprehension of metaphor in texts? The traditional view of figurative language assumes that metaphoric language is deviant and a violation of normal communicative maxims. One widely accepted proposal states that people comprehend metaphorical statements in a series of steps starting with a literal analysis of a sentence and ending with a figurative interpretation once the literal meaning has been rejected as contextually inappropriate (Grice, 1975; Searle, 1979). In this theory, it is assumed that metaphor requires special mental processes to be understood. Nevertheless, there are good reasons, as well as experimental evidence, for concluding that metaphor does not require additional cognitive effort to be understood (in comparison to understanding literal language), contrary to the widely held assumption in linguistics and philosophy that metaphor violates, or "flouts," norms of cooperative conversation (Gibbs,1993a, 1994). Instead, similar cognitive processes drive our understanding of both literal and metaphorical language (Gibbs & Gerrig, 1989).

In one study that supported this conclusion, the participants read sentences such as *Regardless of the danger, the troops marched on*, in either a literal context (e.g., a story about the infantry) or a metaphoric context (e.g., a story about some children annoying their babysitter) (Ortony, Reynolds, Schallert, & Antos, 1978). It was hypothesized that with sufficient context, people need not analyze the literal interpretation of a metaphorical utterance before deriving their intended metaphorical meanings. This was found to be true. When participants read the target sentences in short contexts, metaphorical targets took significantly longer to read than did literal sentences. However, when participants read the target sentences at the end of long contexts, there were no differences in the time taken to read literal and metaphorical target sentences. Other studies that have examined understanding of metaphorical comparisons (e.g., *Billboards are warts on the landscape*) yielded similar findings, and suggest that contextual information might well prime a type of processing strategy rather than a particular figurative meaning (Inhoff, Lima, & Carroll, 1984; Shinjo & Myers, 1987).

Readers of metaphor appear to be unable to ignore the figurative meanings of these expressions even when instructed to focus exclusively on their literal meanings. A study that dramatically demonstrated this point was conducted by Keysar (1989). Participants were given brief stories to read, such as:

> Bob Jones is an expert at such stunts as sawing a woman in half and pulling rabbits out of hats. He earns his living travelling around the world with an expensive entourage of equipment and assistants. Although Bob tries to budget carefully, it seems to him that money just disappears into thin air. With such huge audiences, why doesn't he ever break even?

The participants then decided, as quickly as possible, whether a target sentence, such as:

Bob Jones is a magician.

was true or false. This target sentence is literally true, but metaphorically false; that is, with respect to Bob's financial affairs, he is not a magician at all. If people simply stop with the literal meaning if it makes sense, the false metaphorical meaning should not play a role in their responding. In this study, however, the metaphorical meaning did play a role and actually interfered with participants' correct "true" decision to the true literal meaning that Bob Jones is a magician by profession. However, when Bob Jones was described in this same context as making a profit despite huge expenses, the participants quickly agreed that he was a magician by profession. Thus, the metaphorical meaning can reinforce or interfere with the literal meaning, even when that literal meaning is not defective (also see Gildea & Glucksberg, 1983; Glucksberg, Gildea, & Bookin, 1982).

Metaphors are not always understood as quickly as are the corresponding literal statements. Psycholinguistic research has demonstrated that readers easily determine the appropriate referents for metaphoric expressions in discourse (Gibbs, 1990). Thus, readers easily recognize that the word *creampuff* in the statement *The creampuff didn't show up for the fight* metaphorically refers to a boxer, despite the literal incongruity of this sentence in a text that described a boxing match. But readers find such statements more difficult to process than the corresponding literal expressions, such as *The boxer didn't show up for the fight.* Understanding some metaphorical expressions, such as those used in referential descriptions, requires that a process of *sense creation* must operate to supplement ordinary *sense selection*. For instance, the contextually appropriate meaning of *creampuff* cannot be selected from a short list of potential meanings in the lexicon because these potential senses are unlimited (cf. Gerrig, 1989). Instead, listeners must create a new meaning for this word that already has a conventional interpretation. Creating new senses for novel metaphorical utterances in texts may sometimes necessitate additional mental effort on the part of readers, even if these expressions are not always recognized by readers as violations of communication norms.

In some cases, the interpretation of a novel metaphor, such as *Love is a red, red rose*, results in the explicit, conscious recognition that a new metaphor is being understood and that greater imaginative powers are required to fully understand and appreciate it. Many uses of metaphor actually reflect novel ways of articulating underlying conceptual mappings between concepts that already structure part of our experience in the world. For example, the idea that "*life is a game*" provides one of the many metaphors by which we conceptualize our ordinary life experiences. Nabokov's novel *The Defense* and its chessmaster character offer one particular instantiation of the "*life is a game*" conceptual metaphor. Readers find Nabokov's description of the chessmaster's life quite memorable and apt because of the special, nonautomatic use to which an ordinary, automatic mode of thought is put. Many linguists, literary theorists, and psychologists miss this important point and assume that linguistic metaphors actually create entirely novel mappings from dissimilar conceptual domains; they fail to acknowledge the systematic, conceptual underpinnings of the vast number of linguistic expressions that are motivated by common metaphorical patterns of thought.

THE STRUCTURE OF METAPHORICAL CONCEPTS

The research on how metaphors are understood suggests that context can facilitate readers' processing of metaphorical expressions. Context facilitates metaphor comprehension partly because the information depicted in texts often reflects our common metaphorical understanding of various ideas and events (e.g., the "life is a game" metaphor in Nabokov's *The Defense*). However, not all metaphorical expressions in language juxtapose disparate conceptual categories that are themselves fixed by their objectively defined properties. In fact, the vast majority of metaphorical expressions reflect metaphorical concepts that are very much a part of our ordinary conceptual system. "Our ordinary conceptual system, in terms of which we both think and act, is fundamentally metaphorical in nature" (Lakoff & Johnson, 1980, p. 3). The way we think, what we experience, and what we do everyday is very much a matter of metaphor. Many actions, events, and objects are understood in terms of *experiential gestalts* (i.e., structurally meaningful wholes within experience). Meaning emerges at the level of experiential gestalts via the partial structuring of one domain of knowledge (the target domain) in terms of a dissimilar domain of knowledge (the source domain). What is frequently seen as a creative, metaphorical expression of an idea is often only a spectacular instantiation of specific metaphorical entailments that arise from a small set of conceptual metaphors shared by many individuals within a culture. At the same time, many mundane cliches in the language are motivated by conceptual metaphors that form a fundamental part of our everyday thought.

Consider one instance of cliched language that reflects well-known metaphors of everyday thought. This example comes from Cyra McFadden's popular novel *The Serial*, which concerns the life of an affluent suburban couple living outside of San Francisco in the late 1970s:

> It sent Kate into the pits when she learned from her "friend" Martha, who seemed to get off on laying bad trips on people, that Harvey was getting it on with Carol. . . . She kept her cool, since Harvey and his hangups were no longer her problem. He'd made his waterbed and he could lie in it, although she couldn't help wishing that both he and his Innerspace would spring a leak. (p. 112)

Most American readers would probably not experience much difficulty understanding these sentences. We might roughly paraphrase the first sentence as:

> Kate became depressed when she learned from her supposed friend, Martha, who seemed to enjoy telling people bad news, that Harvey was having a sexual affair with Carol.

The last two sentences might roughly be paraphrased as:

> She remained calm because Harvey's personal problems were no longer his concerns. He created the situation he was in and would just have to take responsibility for them himself, although couldn't help hoping that Harvey would become emotionally distressed.

A variety of conceptual mappings of a metaphorical nature motivate the meanings of these cliched expressions. To take just a few examples, the expression *laying bad trips* is motivated by the "touching is controlling" and "life is a journey" metaphor. *She kept her cool* refers to the metaphorical concept that "anger is heated fluid in a container," suggesting in this case that Kate did not get angry. Harry's hang ups are obstacles preventing the easy passage in the "life is a journey" metaphor. This short passage from *The Serial* shows how even the most cliched, conventional language reflects metaphorical knowledge that is very much a part of our ordinary conceptual system.

The idea that metaphor is conceptually based and structures much of our worldly experience comes from the emerging discipline of cognitive linguistics. Researchers have explored a large number of representative domains of human experience (e.g., time, causation, spatial orientation, ideas, anger, understanding) and demonstrated the pervasiveness of various metaphorical systems in our everyday thought, at least as these ideas are manifested in the language that people use (Lakoff, 1987, 1990; Lakoff & Johnson, 1980; Lakoff & Turner, 1989; Johnson, 1987; Kovecses, 1986; Sweetser, 1990; Turner, 1991).

Let us look closely at one widespread metaphorical concept. Consider the opening lines from *The Divine Comedy* by Dante Alighieri:

> In the middle of the journey of our life I came to myself in a dark wood where the straight way was lost. Ah! how hard a thing it is to tell what a wild, and rough, and stubborn wood this was, which in my thought renews the fear! So bitter is it, that scarcely more is death: but to treat of the good that I found there, I will relate the other things that I discerned.
>
> I cannot rightly tell how I entered it, so full of sleep was I about the moment that I left the true way. But after I had reached the foot of a Hill there, where that valley ended, which had pierced my heart with dear, I looked up and saw its shoulders already clothed with the rays of the Planet that leads men straight on every road. (p. 2)

The Divine Comedy is in the form of an autobiographical narrative, but the whole story is an allegory, depicting man's life journey beginning with sin (the *dark wood*) and ending through great human effort and divine inspiration with salvation. Although we can read this tale as a literal story, we can find deeper meaning through recognition of its higher message based on our general metaphorical understanding of life as a journey. There are many variants of the metaphorical "life is a journey" in classical texts (e.g., The *Bible*, the *Koran*, the *Tibetan Book of the Dead*). Comparative studies have shown that similar mythic tales revolving around the "life is a journey" metaphor. These myths are not falsehoods, but reflect patterns of imaginative thinking rooted in metaphor.

Many wonderful works of literature are structured around the "life as journey" metaphor. This metaphor forms, among other things, one of the fundamental beliefs of the Judeo-Christian tradition in which we instantly understand that God is a guide, there are alternative paths of good and evil through life, and death hangs over us (Lakoff & Turner, 1989). Perhaps the most famous use of the "life as journey" metaphor occurs in the 23rd psalm. It begins *The Lord is my shepherd* and later continues:

> He leadeth me in the paths of righteousness for his name sake. Yea, though I walk through the valley of death, I will fear no evil: for thou art with me; thy rod and thy staff they comfort me... Surely goodness and mercy shall follow me all the days of my life: and I will dwell in the house of the Lord forever.

The meaning that we construct from reading literature such as the 23rd psalm derives from our own ordinary metaphorical understanding of life as a kind of physical journey. A cognitive-linguistic analysis of most any literary work reveals many significant metaphorical concepts that are active parts of everyday thought. Another way to see the pervasiveness of metaphors, such as "life is a journey," in our conceptual systems is to examine some of the conventional expressions that we use to talk about life. Consider the following fairly mundane utterances that often are used to talk about various life experiences, such as relationships and careers:

> Look how far we've come.
> It's been a long, bumpy road.
> My career is at a crossroads.
> We may have to go our separate ways.
> My career is on the rocks.
> We're spinning our wheels.

Why are each of these expressions acceptable ways of talking about, and understanding, life? All of these (and other) conventional expressions cluster together under one basic metaphorical system of understanding, a system in which one domain of experience, life, is structured partly in terms of a very different, and more concrete, domain of experience, namely, journeys. This metaphorical mapping is tightly constrained such that entities in the domain of life (e.g., people, their personal and career goals, their personal relationships) correspond systematically to entities in the domain of a journey (e.g., the traveler, a vehicle, destinations). These mappings reflect a fixed pattern of ontological correspondences across conceptual domains.

Most linguistic theories of metaphor offer no explanation as to why conventional expressions such as those presented above cluster in the ways that they do. Nor do these theories establish any connection between various conventional expressions used by ordinary speakers and the poetic uses of metaphor found in literary works such as *The Divine Comedy* or *The Defense*. Even theorists of metaphor generally view such conventional expressions as having little to do with metaphor per se, although they sometimes view these expressions as reflecting different "dead" metaphors. However, what is conventional need not be dead (Gibbs, 1993b, 1994; Lakoff & Turner, 1989). For example, it is not just arbitrary or accidental that we use *bumpy roads, crossroads, going separate ways,* and *spinning wheels* when speaking of different life experiences. We do so because much of our conceptual understanding of life is metaphorically structured.

METAPHOR AND TEXT UNDERSTANDING

Many of the hypotheses about the prominence of metaphorical thought in everyday thinking and language have been examined experimentally by researchers in psycholinguistics. This work has been designed to demonstrate that conceptual metaphors, such as "life is a journey" or "life is a game," are not simply classificatory devices but reflect ubiquitous patterns of knowledge used in everyday thought. Metaphor might well play the same role as does other schematic knowledge in text understanding and memory. Consider the following brief text written by a graduate student in experimental psychology:

> When I started off in graduate school things went fairly smoothly at first. I had no problems keeping up with the course work and I felt that I had made the right choice in pursuing a PhD in psychology. But in the my second year, the work got harder and I began to stumble somewhat. Soon I found myself spinning my wheels in trying to do research. Eventually, I realized that I was totally sidetracked by my inability to think independently of my advisor. No matter what I did, it just seemed that I was bogged down in this terrible rut, while other students sailed along with little difficulty. Toward the beginning of my third year, I had an important breakthrough and began to be much more productive in doing research. I soon felt back on track and with a lot of hard work, I began to see the light at the end of the tunnel.

This tale is repleat with systematic expressions that illustrate the underlying metaphorical conceptualization of life as a journey and, it specifically manifests the idea that purposes (e.g., obtaining a PhD) are destinations. This way of talking about experience shows how the "purposes are destinations" metaphor is constitutive of our understanding of intentional action. Familiarity with this metaphorical idea of how we lead our lives and achieve important goals provides the necessary schematic knowledge to make sense of the above tale; that is, to understand it as a coherent whole rather than as an unconnected series of statements. The chain of inferences needed to understand this passage appears to be more metaphorical than strictly causal. The underlying theme manifested in the story of "life is a journey" has its own internal structure based on the fixed ontological correspondences that result from the mapping of the source domain for journeys onto the target domain of life.

This hypothesis about how metaphor constrains both text production and understanding is consistent with previous work in experimental psychology on the role of schematic knowledge in text comprehension (e.g., Bartlett, 1932; Bower, Black, & Turner, 1979; Bransford & McCarrell, 1977; Brewer & Nakamura, 1984; Rumelhart, 1980; Rumelhart & Ortony, 1977; Spillich, Vesonder, Chiesi, & Voss, 1979). Metaphorical schemas and their resulting entailments from the mappings of source to target domain knowledge specifically constrain the inferences drawn by readers in constructing meaningful interpretations of texts. Cognitive psychologists have argued that text comprehension is guided by the search for causal relations, and that these relations provide much of the global coherence of memory structures (Trabasso & Sperry, 1985; Trabasso & van den Broek, 1985; van den Broek, 1988). As they proceed through a text, readers construct a causal chain through the story that preserves the sequence of causally important events that serves as the backbone for the story. Trabasso, van den Broek, and their associates have constructed causal network representations for several short texts and have shown that the comprehension and memorability of the clauses in these texts can be predicted via the causal connectedness of each chain as well as whether it lies along the main causal chain of the story.

Although no experimental work has specifically investigated the role of metaphorical knowledge in constructing causal inferences in prose understanding, it is likely that the ability to construct causal chains during text comprehension is, in many cases, facilitated by pre-existing metaphorical schemas. Readers need not derive each inference to connect the different propositions in the passage into a causal network because they can infer an entire system of relationships based on the pre-existing metaphorical concepts in long-term memory (e.g., "life is a journey," "purposes are destinations"). In the case of the story of the student's experience in graduate school, the fixed ontological correspondences between the domains of life and journeys specify that a person in life is a traveler, the goal of life is to reach certain destinations, the means for achieving life's goals are routes, the difficulties experienced in life are obstacles to travel, and progress in life is the distance traveled. These mappings provide the conceptual foundation for understanding that, for example, *to stumble*, *spinning my wheels*, *getting stuck*, and *getting sidetracked* reflect obstacles along the path toward the goal or destination of obtaining a PhD. Such knowledge enables readers to tie together the various conventional expressions about travel into a meaningful story about one aspect of the author's life.

In the past few years, a number of researchers have begun to examine the influence of metaphorical knowledge on different aspects of text understanding. This emerging research tradition has investigated how metaphor motivates, in the sense of providing a conceptual basis for, people's understanding of individual verbal metaphors, metaphorical texts, idiomatic expressions, and poetry (Gibbs, 1993a, 1994). For instance, common metaphorical knowledge has been shown to facilitate readers' understanding of verbal metaphors that are motivated by conceptual metaphors (Kemper, 1989). In one series of studies, people were found to be faster at reading a verbal metaphor, such as *The eager suitor assaulted her defense*, than a literal statement, such as *The eager suitor wanted her affection*, if they were first presented with the statement "love is war." Moreover, participants were faster at deciding that two metaphorical expressions (e.g., *He laid siege to her heart* and *The eager suitor assaulted her defenses*) were related if these were motivated by the same conceptual metaphor (e.g., "love is war"). Participants also took significantly longer to understand pairs of verbal metaphors derived from conflicting conceptual metaphors such as *He laid siege to her heart* ("love is war") and *He swept her off her feet* ("love is a physical force") (Kemper, 1989).

More recent studies have demonstrated that verbal metaphors are easier to comprehend when they are embedded in texts that instantiate relevant conceptual metaphors (Allbritton, 1992). Consider the following story illustrating the conceptual mapping of "love is a physical force":

> John and Martha met at a party about a month ago.
> Since then they have hardly ever been seen apart from one another.
> The attraction between John and Martha was overwhelming.
> Sparks flew the moment they first saw one another.
> It was a classic case of love at first sight.

Participants in one of a series of studies read such stories, with each story instantiating a particular conceptual metaphor. Afterwards, the participants were presented with either of two prime sentences, one of which was relevant to the primary conceptual metaphor in an earlier story (e.g., *The attraction between John and Martha was overwhelming*), and the other a neutral prime (e.g., *John and Martha met at a party about a month ago*). Immediately after seeing the prime sentence, the participants were shown a test sentence, such as *Sparks flew the moment they first saw one another.* The participants' task was to decide as quickly as possible whether they had read the test sentence previously. A series of studies showed that people were significantly faster at making these recognition judgments when primed by the sentences that were relevant to the underlying conceptual metaphor in the stories than when primed by the neutral sentences. This result supports the hypothesis that metaphor-based schemas function to relate instances of schema-related information to one another during text processing.

Other studies in this series showed that people automatically instantiate metaphorical schemes (i.e., conceptual metaphors) as they read texts (Allbritton, 1992). Consider the following passage instantiating the metaphor "anger is heat":

> Edward was boiling with anger.
> The sales clerk had completely screwed up his order.
> The manager saw there might be trouble and rushed over.

The passages could be completed by novel schema-instantiating priming sentences, such as:

> Hoping to prevent a scene, she tried to lower his thermostat.

or by conventional schema-instantiating priming sentences, such as:

> Hoping to prevent a scene, she tried to cool him off.

or by neutral priming sentences, such as:

> Hoping to prevent a scene, she tried to fix the problem.

Participants read a passage and immediately afterwards read a test word (e.g., *boiling*) that related to the metaphorical schema in the story. These test words were related to the dominant metaphorical schema in the story (e.g., *boiling* for "anger is heat"). Participants were faster at recognizing the test words if they had just read a conventional schema-instantiating priming sentences rather than a neutral sentences. This result suggests that people actually instantiate an underlying conceptual metaphor such as "anger is heat" when reading conventional expressions, such as *Hoping to prevent a scene, she tried to cool him off.* Interestingly, however, the participants were not faster at recognizing the test words if they had read a novel schema-instantiating priming sentences rather than a neutral sentence. It appears that novel metaphorical expressions (e.g., *Hoping to prevent a scene, she tried to lower his thermostat*) are not immediately seen as being related to the general metaphorical schema for the story (e.g., "anger is heat"), at least as measured by this type of word recognition task.

These experimental studies provide some initial evidence that readers use their metaphorical schemas of various concepts in their immediate processing of some types of verbal metaphors presented in prose texts. Another series of studies provided evidence on the constraining role of pre-existing conceptual metaphors in people's interpretations of literary metaphors in love poetry (Gibbs

& Nascimento, 1995). Consider these lines from the poem entitled "Ode and Burgeonings" by Pablo Neruda (1972):

> My wild girl, we have had
> to regain time
> and march backward, in the distance
> of our lives, kiss after kiss,
> gathering from one place what we gave
> without joy, discovering in another
> the secret road
> that gradually brought your feet
> close to mine. (p. 44)

These lines illustrate how we conceptualize of our love experiences partly in terms of journeys. As was discussed previously, various entailments arise when we think of life or love as a journey. These entailments are elaborated on in many poetic descriptions of love such as in Neruda's poem and people's individual love experiences.

In a series of studies, Gibbs and Nascimento (1995) examined the hypothesis that readers make sense of poetry, and find poetry especially apt and meaningful, because they infer various underlying conceptual metaphors that motivate the ideas to which poetry refers. Perhaps the most important evidence in support of this hypothesis comes from one experiment that involved a talking-out-loud task to determine whether the inferences readers drew about the meanings of poems reflected their metaphorical understanding of the poets' own conceptions about love.

An analysis of the participants' statements made while reading 10 poems in a line-by-line manner provided strong evidence that conceptual metaphor structured their understanding of the poems. Across all poems and participants, 78% of the statements in the talking-out-loud protocols referred to the entailments of the underlying conceptual metaphors that had partially motivated the meanings of the poems. For example, when participants read the fragment from Neruda's poem, they referred to entailments of the "love is a journey" metaphor, such as the path (e.g., *They learned a better path to happiness, They had to retrace their steps to find true love, They found a special road that they could travel together on in the same direction.*), the goals (e.g., *The future of their love lay ahead of them, They had to catch up.*), and the impediments to travel (e.g., *They managed to get over the rough places, rediscovering what was missed*). It seemed clear that readers were partially making sense of what the poems meant by accessing their everyday metaphorical understanding of love. Although there is some debate as to whether the talking-out-loud procedure accurately reflects normal online mental processes, the present data at least suggest that people's conscious, reflective interpretations of poetry are constrained by their ordinary metaphorical knowledge. Readers do not necessarily create novel metaphorical mappings to understand novel, poetic language. The vast majority of novel metaphors in poetry and literature reflect fixed patterns of metaphorical mappings between dissimilar source and target domains. Although poets may present novel instantiations for these pre-existing metaphorical mappings, people do not necessarily have to draw novel mappings in any algorithmic sense to understand poetic instantiations of conventional metaphors.

The final source of evidence on how metaphorical knowledge constrains text understanding comes from research on readers' comprehension of idioms in texts. The traditional view of idiomaticity assumes that expressions, such as *blow your stack, flip your lid, hit the ceiling,* are "giant lexical items" whose meanings result from "dead" metaphors. However, recent work in cognitive linguistics and psycholinguistics suggests that idioms are not simple, dead metaphors, but actually retain a good deal of their metaphoricity because they are motivated by metaphorical mappings between dissimilar source and target domains. For example, the figurative meanings of *blow your stack, flip your lid,* and *hit the ceiling* are specifically motivated by two independent elements in our conceptual system: "mind is a container" and "anger is heat in a pressurized container." These conceptual metaphors allow speakers to refer to "getting angry" through particular instantiations of the mapping from a source domain (e.g., heated gas or steam) onto a target domain (e.g., anger). Speakers make sense of many idioms, such as *blow your stack* or *flip your lid,* precisely because their meanings are motivated by the conceptual mappings that link the individual words in idioms to their figurative meanings (Gibbs & O'Brien, 1990).

Psycholinguistic research has shown that people's knowledge of the metaphorical links between different source and target domains provides the basis for the appropriate use and interpretation of idioms in particular discourse situations (Nayak & Gibbs, 1990; Gibbs & Nayak, 1991). Participants in one study, for example, gave higher appropriateness ratings to *blew her stack* in a story that described a woman's anger as being like heat in a pressurized container, whereas *bit his head off* was seen as more appropriate in a story that described a woman's anger in terms of a ferocious animal. *Bite your head off* makes sense because people can link the lexical items in this phrase to the conceptual metaphor "angry behavior is animal behavior." An animal jumping down a victim's throat is similar to someone shouting angrily. In contrast, people understand the figurative meaning of *blow your stack* through the conceptual metaphor "anger is heated fluid in a container" in which a person shouting angrily has the same explosive effect as does the top of a container blowing open under pressure. Thus, readers' judgments about the contextual appropriateness of an idiom were influenced by the coherence between the metaphorical information depicted in a text and the conceptual metaphor reflected in the lexical make-up of the idiom.

A second series of experiments extended these earlier studies to show that people's understanding of idioms reflects the particular entailments of the underlying conceptual metaphors motivating these phrases (Gibbs, 1992). For example, people's understanding of the causes, intentionality, and manner of physical events, such as heating fluid in containers (i.e., source domains), should be similar to their understandings of the causes, intentionality, and manner of the anger to which idioms such as *blow your stack*, *flip your lid*, and *hit the ceiling* refer. That is, people's knowledge of a particular source domain (e.g., their understanding about the behavior of heated fluids in containers) should predict their understanding of a dissimilar target domain (e.g., what they understand about anger) that is partially structured by that source domain.

Several studies demonstrated that people find idioms to be more appropriate and easier to understand if they are embedded in discourse contexts that are consistent with the various entailments of these phrases (Gibbs, 1992). For example, people found it easy to process the idiomatic phrase *blow your stack* when it was read in a context that accurately described the cause of the person's anger as due to internal pressure and the expression of anger was unintentional and violent (i.e., entailments that were consistent with the entailments of the source to target domain mappings of heated fluid in a container onto anger). However, readers took significantly longer to read *blow your stack* if any of these entailments were contradicted in the preceding story context. These findings provide additional evidence that people's metaphorical concepts underlie their understanding of what idioms mean in written texts.

METONYMY AND TEXT UNDERSTANDING

Metaphor is usually perceived as the "master" trope. But other figures of thought also play important roles in our use and understanding of language. A figure of thought related to metaphor is the well known trope of metonymy. Metonymy is a fundamental part of our conceptual system whereby people use one well understood or easily perceived aspect of something to represent or stand for the thing as a whole. Metonymic thinking is very easy to find in everyday speech and writing. Consider this passage in which the satirist Erma Bombeck relays in her newspaper column her daughter's complaints about finding a suitable roommate (Clark, 1983):

> We thought we were onto a steam iron yesterday, but we were too late. Steam irons never have any trouble finding roommates. She could pick her own pad and not even have to share a bathroom. Stereos are a dime a dozen. Everyone's got their own systems. We've just had a streak of bad luck. First, our Mr. Coffee flunked out of school and went back home. When we replaced her, our electric typewriter got married and split, and we got stuck with a girl who said she was getting a leather coat, but she just said that to get the room.

It seems odd, literally speaking, to talk about steam irons having trouble finding roommates or electric typewriters getting married. Traditional theories of parsing will fail to handle many of these phrases even though we can easily understand what Bombeck's daughter is saying (Clark, 1983). For example, consider the sentence *Steam irons never have any trouble finding roommates.* Most parsers will search their lexicons for the sense of *Steam irons* that is intended, namely "a person who owns a steam iron" and will fail to find anything like this meaning. As would be the case with each of the metonymic expressions in this passage, most parsers are unable to create novel, or nonce sense, interpretations for common words and phrases precisely because they do not have the capacity to make the appropriate inferences about what speakers and authors mean. The difficulty that parsers, readers, and listeners face is that the meanings of contextual expressions appear to be nondenumerable, depending crucially on the time, place, and circumstance in which these utterances are made. However, the fact that we talk about people in terms of *steam irons, stereos, Mr. Coffee,* and so forth reflects the common conceptual mapping whereby we use a salient aspect of an object or event to stand for the thing or event as a whole.

As is true for metaphor, the conceptual basis of metonymy is best demonstrated by the similarity between various metonymic expressions. Consider the following statements (Lakoff & Johnson, 1980):

Washington has started negotiating with Moscow.
The White House isn't saying anything.
Wall Street is in a panic.
The Kremlin agreed to support the boycott.
Hollywood is putting out terrible movies.
Paris has dropped hemlines this year.

These examples do not occur one by one, but reflect the general cognitive principle of metonymy in which people use one well understood aspect of something to stand for the thing as a whole or for some other aspect of it (Lakoff & Johnson, 1980). All of these examples relate to the general principle by which a place may stand for an institution located at that place. Thus, a place such as Wall Street stands for a particularly salient institution located at that place, namely, the stock exchanges and major banks.

Various metonymic models in our conceptual system underlie the use of many kinds of figurative and conventional expressions (e.g., "object used for user," "controller for controlled," and "the place for the event"). The metonymic expressions in Bombeck's narrative reflect the well known metonymy in which an objects stands for, or represents, the users or owners. Our ability to conceptualize of people, objects, and events in metonymic terms provides the basis for much of the way we reason and make inferences during text processing. Many studies show that people metonymically infer entire sequences of actions having read only some salient subpart in a story. Consider the following simple tale:

John was hungry and went into a restaurant.
He ordered lobster from the waiter.
It took a long time to prepare.
Because of this he only put down a small tip when he left.

When people hear this brief episode, they presumably activate their knowledge of the activities normally associated with eating in a restaurant and use this information to fill in the gaps to make the story coherent. This type of knowledge, called a *script* (Schank & Abelson, 1977), consists of highly learned scenarios describing structured situations in everyday life. Comprehending the example passage requires that listeners first decide what script is relevant and then how it is to be modified to fit the situation at hand. A number of experiments have shown that people automatically infer appropriate script-related actions when these are not explicitly stated (Abbott, Black, & Smith, 1985; Bower, Black, & Turner, 1979; Gibbs & Tenney, 1980; Graesser, Woll, Kowalski, & Smith, 1980). Other studies suggest that prior activation of script-based knowledge provides readers with a highly available set of causal connections that can facilitate sentence-by-sentence integration (Bower et al., 1979; Garrod & Sanford, 1985; Sanford & Garrod, 1981; Seifert, Robertson, & Black, 1985; Sharkey & Sharkey, 1987). Writers can assume that readers will supply the necessary script-like inferences needed to understand what is being said and, thus, typically will leave implicit any information that listeners can supply themselves.

This work on script-based text processing illustrates the importance of metonymic models in everyday thought. People's knowledge in long-term memory for coherent, mundane series of events can be metonymically referred to by the mere mention of one salient subpart of these events. We see that mention of the subpart metonymically stands for the whole event. This inference increases our ability to assume unstated propositions about what writers mean and to make sense of seemingly anomalous and disconnected statements in texts.

CONCLUSION

Metaphor has been viewed mostly as a special linguistic device whose understanding requires the novel mapping of dissimilar knowledge domains. We often conceptualize of metaphor understanding as something that evolves as a product of our comprehension processes rather than as a type of pre-existing knowledge that we apply to the activity of reading and interpreting texts. My aim in this chapter has been to illustrate the ubiquity of metaphor in written language and to show some of the ways in which pervasive metaphorical schemas of thought constrain readers' understanding of texts. Not only do we apply metaphorical concepts in understanding literary and scientific texts, we also apply pre-existing metaphorical knowledge when we understand even cliched, conventional language. In fact, a close reading of written language provides some of the best evidence for the presence of metaphorical thought in our ordinary conceptual systems. Similar kinds of metaphorical knowledge appear to motivate our use and understanding of literary texts, scientific writing, conventional expressions, idiomatic phrases, and poetry. Metaphorical knowledge plays an important role in readers' making sense of why certain expressions in texts mean what they do and also constrains the inferences needed to link different elements in texts to form meaningful, coherent memory structures for these text materials.

One question for future research concerns the extent to which common metaphorical knowledge is applied automatically during text processing as opposed to being used only strategically by readers. Most studies on metaphorical knowledge in language understanding have focused on the role of metaphor in people's interpretation of discourse rather than on their immediate, online use of metaphorical concepts in their comprehension of texts. A recent proposal on the range of inferences that readers ordinarily compute posits that only those inferences that are essential to establish local coherence, or those that are easily available are actually generated during online reading (McKoon & Ratcliff, 1992). This *minimalist hypothesis* suggests that the application of metaphorical knowledge during text processing belongs to the category of inferences that readers compute selectively and strategically. However, the application of metaphorical knowledge (e.g., the specific correspondences that arise from metaphorical mappings) appears to facilitate local coherence in certain texts, such as in Bombeck's narrative or the passage written by the graduate student about his career. Of course, the ultimate answer to this issue of whether readers generate metaphorical inferences automatically will depend on further online studies. At the moment, though, psychologists should remain open to the possibility that common metaphorical knowledge is applied automatically during text understanding.

One other aspect of metaphoric thought and text understanding that deserves further attention is the distinction between metaphor processing and processing metaphoric language. The empirical studies on metaphorical discourse primarily have examined how different, specific instances of metaphoric language are understood. However, there are many situations, especially in reading literature, when a specific metaphoric type of processing is given to a particular text. Metaphor processing, as opposed to processing metaphoric language, may be distinguished as an intentionally selected strategy of reading (Steen, 1994). When readers adopt such strategies, the processing that occurs is metaphoric even though there is no specific linguistic or textual material that is metaphoric (e.g., Joseph Conrad's novel *Heart of Darkness*). Various literary theorists have noted how it is possible to produce a high poetic reading of a poem or text because of a reader's explicit literary way of interpreting it (Gerrig, 1993; Lodge, 1977; Steen, 1993; Welleck & Warren, 1947). In this way, metaphor legitimately can be viewed as a type of literary strategy that colors people's imaginative understanding of texts in addition to constraining how readers draw inference about the meanings of figurative expressions in written texts.

REFERENCES

Abbott, V., Black, J., Smith, E. (1985). The representation of scripts in memory. *Journal of Memory and Language, 24*, 179–199.

Alighieri, D. (1959). *The divine comedy.* New York: Vintage.

Allbritton, D. (1992). *The use of metaphor to structure text representations: Evidence for metaphor-based schemas.* Unpublished doctoral dissertation, Yale University.

Bartlett, F. (1932). *Remembering.* Cambridge: Cambridge University Press.

Bower, G., Black, J., & Turner, T. (1979). Scripts in memory for texts. *Cognitive Psychology, 11*, 177–220.

Bransford, J., & McCarrell, N. (1977). A sketch of a cognitive approach to comprehension: Some thoughts about understanding what it means to comprehend. In P. Johnson-Laird & P. Wason (Eds.), *Thinking: Readings in cognitive science* (pp. 191–212). Cambridge: Cambridge University Press.

Brewer, W., & Nakamura, G. (1984). The nature and function of schemas. In R. Wyer & T. Srull (Eds.), *Handbook of social cognition* (pp. 119–160). Hillsdale, NJ: Lawrence Erlbaum Associates.

Carpenter, P., & Just, M. (1975). Sentence comprehension: A psycholinguistic processing model of verification. *Psychological Review, 82*, 45–73.

Clark, H. (1983). Making sense of nonce sense. In F. Flores d'Arcais & R. Jarvella (Eds.), *The process of understanding language* (pp. 297–332). New York: Wiley.

Dashiell, J. (1925). A physiological-behavioristic description of thinking. *Psychological Review, 32*, 54–73.

Dewey, J. (1894). Psychological literature: Ethical. *Psychological Review, 1*, 109–113.

Garrod, S., & Sanford, A. (1985). On the real-time character of interpretation during reading. *Language and Cognitive Processes, 1*, 43–61.

Gentner, D., & Gentner, D. R. (1983). Flowing waters or teaming crowds: Mental models of electricity. In D. Gentner & A. Stevens (Eds.), *Mental models* (pp. 99–129). Hillsdale, NJ: Lawrence Erlbaum Associates.

Gentner, D., & Grudin, J. (1985). The evolution of mental metaphors in psychology: A 90-year retrospective. *American Psychologist, 40*, 181–192.

Gerrig, R. (1989). The time-course of sense creation. *Memory & Cognition, 17*, 194–207.

Gerrig, R. (1993). *Experiencing narrative worlds.* New Haven, CT: Yale University Press.

Gibbs, R. (1990). Comprehending figurative referential descriptions. *Journal of Experimental Psychology: Learning, Memory, & Cognition, 16*, 56–66.

Gibbs, R. (1992). What do idioms really mean? *Journal of Memory and Language, 31*, 485–506.

Gibbs, R. (1993a). Process and products in making sense of tropes. In A. Ortony (Ed.), *Metaphor and thought* (Vol. 2, pp. 252–276). New York: Cambridge University Press.

Gibbs, R. (1993b). Why idioms are not dead metaphors. In C. Cacciari & P. Tabossi (Eds.), *On idioms* (pp. 57–78). Hillsdale, NJ: Lawrence Erlbaum Associates.

Gibbs, R. (1994). *The poetics of mind: Figurative thought, language, and understanding.* New York: Cambridge University Press.

Gibbs, R., & Gerrig, R. (1989). How context makes metaphor comprehension seem "special." *Metaphor and Symbolic Activity, 4*, 154–158.

Gibbs, R., & Nascimento, S. (1995). How we talk when we talk about love: Metaphorical concepts and understanding love poetry. In R. Kreuz & M. MacNealy (Eds.), *Empirical and aesthetic approaches to literature.* Norwood, NJ: Ablex.

Gibbs, R., & Nayak, N. (1991). Why idioms mean what they do. *Journal of Experimental Psychology: General, 120*, 93–95.

Gibbs, R., & O'Brien, J. (1990). Idioms and mental imagery: The metaphorical motivation for idiomatic meaning. *Cognition, 36*, 35–68.

Gibbs, R., Tenney, Y. (1980). The concept of scripts in understanding stories. *Journal of Psycholinguistic Research, 9,* 275–284.

Gigerenzer, G. (1991). From tools to theories: A heuristic of discovery in cognitive psychology. *Psychological Review, 98,* 254–267.

Gigerenzer, G., & Murray, D. (1987). *Cognition as intuitive statistics.* Chicago: University of Chicago Press.

Gildea, P., & Glucksberg, S. (1983). On understanding metaphor: The role of context. *Journal of Verbal Learning and Verbal Behavior, 22,* 577–590.

Glucksberg, S. (1989). Metaphors in conversation: How are they understood? Why are they used? *Metaphor and Symbolic Activity, 4,* 125–144.

Glucksberg, S., Gildea, P., & Bookin, H. (1982). On understanding nonliteral speech: Can people ignore metaphor? *Journal of Verbal Learning and Verbal Behavior, 21,* 85–98.

Glynn, S. (1991). Explaining science concepts: A teaching with analogies model. In S. Glynn, R. Yeany, & B. Britton (Eds.), *The psychology of learning science* (pp. 219–240). Hillsdale, NJ: Lawrence Erlbaum Associates.

Glynn, S., Britton, B., Semrud-Clikeman, M., & Muth, K. (1989). Analogical reasoning and problem solving in science textbooks. In J. Glover, R. Ronning, & C. Reynolds (Eds.), *Handbook of creativity: Assessment, research, and theory* (pp. 383–398). New York: Plenum Press.

Graesser, A., Woll, S., Kowalski, D., & Smith, D. (1980). Memory for typical and atypical actions in scripted activities. *Journal of Experimental Psychology: Human Learning and Memory, 6,* 503–515.

Gray, J. (1935). An objective theory of emotion. *Psychological Review, 42,* 108–116.

Grice, H. (1975). Logic and conversation. In P. Cole & J. Morgan (Eds.), *Syntax and semantics 3: Speech acts* (pp. 41–58). New York: Academic Press.

Inhoff, A., Lima, S., & Carroll, P. (1984). Contextual effects on metaphor comprehension in reading. *Memory & Cognition, 12,* 558–567.

James, W. (1885). *The principles of psychology.* New York: Holt.

James, W. (1905). President's address: The experience of activity. *Psychological Review, 1,* 1–17.

Johnson, M. (1987). *The body in the mind: The bodily basis of reason and imagination.* Chicago: University of Chicago Press.

Kallen, H. (1915, February). Democracy versus the melting pot. *Nation,* p. 25.

Kemper, S. (1989). Priming the comprehension of metaphors. *Metaphor and Symbolic Activity, 4,* 1–18.

Keysar, B. (1989). On the functional equivalence of literal and metaphorical interpretations in discourse. *Journal of Memory and Language, 28,* 375–385.

Kovecses, Z. (1986). *Metaphors of pride, anger, and love.* Philadelphia: Johns Benjamins.

Lakoff, G. (1987). *Women, fire, and dangerous things.* Chicago: University of Chicago Press.

Lakoff, G. (1990). The invariance hypothesis: Is abstract reason based on image schemas? *Cognitive Linguistics, 1,* 39–74.

Lakoff, G., & Johnson, M. (1980). *Metaphors we live by.* Chicago: University of Chicago Press.

Lakoff, G., & Turner, M. (1989). *More than cool reason: A field guide to poetic metaphor.* Chicago: University of Chicago Press.

Lodge, D. (1977). *The modes of modern writing.* London: Arnold.

Mayer, R. (1975). Different problem solving competencies established in learning computer programming with and without meaningful models. *Journal of Educational Psychology, 67,* 143–150.

Mayer, R. (1978). Advance organizers that compensate for the organization of text. *Journal of Educational Psychology, 70,* 880–886.

Mayer, R. (1980). Elaboration techniques that increase the meaningfulness of technical text: An experimental test of the learning strategy hypothesis. *Journal of Educational Psychology, 72,* 770–784.

McFadden, C. (1977). *The serial.* New York: New American Library.

McKoon, G., & Ratcliff, R. (1992). Inferences during reading. *Psychological Review, 99*, 440–466.

Minard, J. (1965). Response-bias interpretation of "perceptual defense:" A review and evaluation of recent research. *Psychological Review, 72*, 74–88.

Moltz, H. (1965). Contemporary instinct theory and the fixed action pattern. *Psychological Review, 72*, 27–47.

Nabokov, V. (1933). *The defense*. New York: Vintage Books.

Nayak, N., & Gibbs, R. (1990). Conceptual knowledge in the interpretation of idioms. *Journal of Experimental Psychology: General, 119*, 315–330.

Neruda, P. (1972). *The captain's verses*. New York: New Directions Publishers.

Ortony, A. (1975). Why metaphors are necessary and not just nice. *Educational Theory, 25*, 45–53.

Ortony, A. (1976). On the nature and value of metaphor: A reply to my critics. *Educational Theory, 26*, 395–398.

Ortony, A., Reynolds, R., Schallert, D., & Antos, S. (1978). Interpreting metaphors and idioms: Some effects of context on comprehension. *Journal of Verbal Learning and Verbal Behavior, 17*, 465–477.

Payne, S. (1988). Metaphorical instructions and the early learning of an abbreviated-command computer system. *Acta Psychologica, 69*, 207–230.

Peterson, J. (1935). Aspects of learning. *Psychological Review, 42*, 1–27.

Petrie, H. (1979). Metaphor and learning. In A. Ortony (Ed.), *Metaphor and thought* (pp. 438–461). Cambridge: Cambridge University Press.

Pollio, H., Barlow, J., Fine, H., & Pollio, M. (1977). *Psychology and the poetics of growth: Figurative language in psychology, psychotherapy, and education*. Hillsdale, NJ: Lawrence Erlbaum Associates.

Reynolds, R., & Schwartz, R. (1984). Relation of metaphor processing to comprehension and memory. *Journal of Educational Psychology, 75*, 450–459.

Roediger, H. (1980). Memory metaphors in cognitive psychology. *Memory & Cognition, 8*, 231–246.

Rumelhart, D. (1980). Schemata: The building blocks of cognition. In R. Spiro, B. Bruce, & W. Brewer (Eds.), *Theoretical issues in reading comprehension: Perspectives from cognitive psychology, linguistics, artificial intelligence, and education* (pp. 33–58). Hillsdale, NJ: Lawrence Erlbaum Associates.

Rumelhart, D., & Norman, D. (1981). Analogical processes in learning. In J. Anderson (Ed.), *Cognitive skills and their acquisition* (pp. 335–360). Hillsdale, NJ: Lawrence Erlbaum Associates.

Rumelhart, D., & Ortony, A. (1977). The representation of knowledge in memory. In R. Anderson, R. Spiro, & W. Montague (Eds.), *Schooling and the acquisition of knowledge* (pp. 99–135). Hillsdale, NJ: Lawrence Erlbaum Associates.

Sanford, A., & Garrod, S. (1981). *Understanding written language*. Chitchester: Wiley.

Schank, R., & Abelson, R. (1977). *Scripts, plans, goals, and understanding: An inquiry into human knowledge structures*. Hillsdale, NJ: Lawrence Erlbaum Associates.

Searle, J. (1979). Metaphor. In A. Ortony (Ed.), *Metaphor and thought* (pp. 92–123). New York: Cambridge University Press.

Seifert, C., Robertson, S., & Black, J. (1985). Types of inferences generated during reading. *Journal of Memory and Language, 24*, 405–422.

Sharkey, N., & Sharkey, A. (1987). What is the point of integration? The loci of knowledge-based facilitation in sentence processing. *Journal of Memory and Language, 26*, 255–276.

Shinjo, M., & Myers, J. (1987). The role of context in metaphor comprehension. *Journal of Memory and Language, 26*, 226–241.

Smith, M., Pollio, M., Pitts, M. (1981). Metaphor as intellectual history: Concepts and categories underlying figurative usage in American English from 1675–1975. *Linguistics, 19*, 911–935.

Spillich, G., Vesonder, G., Chiesi, H., & Voss, J. (1979). Text processing of domain-related information for individuals with high and low domain knowledge. *Journal of Verbal Learning and Verbal Behavior, 18*, 275–290.

Steen, G. (1994). *Understanding metaphor in literature*. London: Longmans.

Sweetser, E. (1990). *From etymology to pragmatics: The mind-as-body metaphor in semantic structure and semantic change*. Cambridge, England: Cambridge University Press.
Trabasso, T., & Sperry, L. (1985). Causal relatedness and importance of story events. *Journal of Memory and Language, 24*, 595–611.
Trabasso, T., & van den Broek, P. (1985). Causal thinking and the representation of narratives events. *Journal of Memory and Language, 24*, 612–630.
Turner, M. (1991). *Reading minds: The study of English in the age of cognitive science*. Princeton: Princeton University Press.
van den Broek, P. (1988). The effects of causal relations and hierarchial position on the importance of story statements. *Journal of Memory and Language, 27*, 1–22.
Welleck, R., & Warren, A. (1949). *Theory of literature*. Harmondsworth: Penguin.
Zwicker, E., & Scharf, B. (1965). A model of loudness summation. *Psychological Review, 72*, 3–26.

CHAPTER

9

TOWARD A MODEL OF LITERARY COMPREHENSION

Rolf A. Zwaan
Florida State University

Contemporary models of text comprehension are not well equipped to account for the comprehension of literary texts. This is partly due to the persistent tendency of text comprehension researchers to focus on experimenter-generated text rather than on naturalistic text (Graesser, Haberlandt, & Magliano, 1994; van Oostendorp & Zwaan, 1994; Zwaan & van Oostendorp, 1993). However, literary texts prose specific problems for the comprehender that are not captured in experimenter-generated prose. For example, many literary texts are unique in the sense that they are deliberately constructed to be *inconsiderate*. In this chapter, I propose a model of literary comprehension that takes the "inconsiderateness" of literary discourse into account. The proposed model is essentially an extension of existing models of text comprehension that were developed by Kintsch and van Dijk (Kintsch & van Dijk, 1978; Kintsch, 1988; van Dijk & Kintsch, 1983).

My main assumption in this chapter is that readers develop cognitive control systems for specific types of discourse. These control systems are developed through repeated exposures to different types of text and through explicit instruction. Experienced readers develop a literary control system by reading literature and by their training in high school and college. The literary control system monitors the comprehension of inconsiderate literary texts. This control system may be triggered by the novelty of a book, the reader's goal, or an instruction to read a literary text.

LITERARINESS

In the early part of this century, the Russian formalists and Prague structuralists suggested a way to distinguish literary texts from nonliterary texts: Literary texts, but not nonliterary texts, typically contain devices that are meant to side-track routine comprehension processes (Jakobson, 1960; Mukarovsky, 1964; Shklovsky, 1916; Striedter, 1989). Examples of literary devices that occur primarily in poetry are rhyme, alliteration, and enjambment. Examples of literary devices that occur in prose are flashbacks, flash-forwards, unusual points of view (e.g., a story told from the perspective of a horse), and open endings. According to Shklovsky (1916), these procedures bring about the aesthetic effect of *defamiliarization*. They focus the reader's attention on the linguistic surface structure itself, which creates the aesthetic effect rather than on the situation to which the text refers. Mukarovsky (1964) introduced the concept of *foregrounding* to refer to the same process.

Jakobson (1960) identified several functions of language, two of which are relevant for the present purposes. The first is the *referential function*, which is dominant in discourse types such as scientific prose, manuals, and newspaper articles. If the referential function is dominant, the focus of the text is on the state of affairs it denotes. The second relevant function of language is the *poetic function*. The poetic function is dominant in literature, especially poetry. If the poetic function is dominant, attention is focused on the linguistic structure itself rather than on the situation that is described by the text.

The referential and the poetic functions of language can be regarded as antagonistic (Waugh, 1980). Metaphorically speaking, the more that a linguistic structure focuses attention upon itself, the more the language will get in the way of constructing a representation of the referential situation denoted by the text. Conversely, the more a text is tuned to conveying information about a particular state of affairs, the more transparent the text will be, and, consequently, the reader's attention will not be focused upon the linguistic structure itself. It should be pointed out that Jakobson's (1960) use of the term *dominant* suggests that the poetic function may to some extent be active in referential discourse and that the referential function may to some extent be active in literary discourse. The presence of literary devices sets literary texts apart from content-oriented types of prose, such as scientific prose. However, nonliterary types of discourse, such as advertisements or sermons, also may contain literary devices. Jakobson's famous example is the slogan *I like Ike*, which contains the literary device of rhyme, even though its primary function was a persuasive one: "vote for Eisenhower."

Most models of text comprehension presuppose that texts are considerate. Considerate prose minimizes the processing load on the reader, for example, by using simple words, simple sentences, and stating the main point at the outset. It is essential that content-oriented types of discourse, such as scientific discourse or manuals, be considerate. Therefore, guidelines for writing scientific prose stress considerateness. In doing so, they typically contrast considerate writing with literary writing. The *APA Publication Manual* (1992) is a good example:

> Scientific prose serves a different purpose than creative writing does. Devices that are often found in creative writing, for example, setting up ambiguity, inserting the unexpected, omitting the expected, and suddenly shifting the topic, tense, or person, can confuse or disturb readers of scientific prose. Therefore, these devices should be avoided in writing that aims at clear and logical communication. (p. 32)

> Devices that attract attention to words, sounds, or other embellishments instead of to ideas are inappropriate in scientific writing. Avoid heavy alliteration, accidental rhyming, poetic expressions, and clichés. (p. 43)

It is interesting to note that the formalists' notion of literary device and their focus on the language itself rather than its content is echoed in a publication manual for scientific prose. It should be noted, however, that the use of literary devices does not necessarily produce good literature. A successful literary author presumably uses literary devices in a manner that creates aesthetic effects (e.g., suspense), thereby making it appealing for the reader to try to overcome any processing difficulties created by the devices. In other words, good literary texts are inconsiderate in an interesting way.

LEVELS OF REPRESENTATION

Contemporary theories of language comprehension commonly assume that texts may be represented at three levels during and after comprehension (Kintsch, 1988; Singer, 1990; van Dijk & Kintsch, 1983; van Dijk, 1987). First, the *surface structure* is a verbatim representation of the surface form of the text. Second, the propositional *textbase* is a representation of the semantic meaning of the text. Third, the *situation model* is a representation of the situation (i.e., the characters, goals, events, actions, and space) that the text is about. The situation model is an integration of information from the text with the reader's knowledge base. It has been demonstrated empirically that it is possible to discriminate among these levels (Fletcher & Chrysler, 1990; Kintsch, Schmalhofer, Welsch, & Zimny, 1990; Schmalhofer & Glavanov, 1986).

The surface structure is typically regarded as a transient phenomenon in text comprehension. Several studies have shown that surface information may be lost after as little time as a few seconds (Kintsch et al., 1990; Sachs, 1967). However, these studies were carried out in contextually impoverished domains using experimenter-generated texts. More ecologically valid studies have demonstrated that surface information may be available long after the text has been processed. For example, Keenan, MacWhinney, and Mayhew (1977), in a study of natural conversation, found that statements that were high in interactional content yielded excellent memory for surface information, whereas statements low in interactional content led to no memory for surface form. Bates, Masling, and Kintsch (1978) reported similar results. Long (1994) found excellent long-term memory for the surface form of dialogues in literary prose. Surface form was encoded most strongly when it provided information about the speaker's attitudes, and especially when such information was conveyed by means of formulaic expressions. Therefore, the probability that a given surface form will be retained is a function, at least in part, of the pragmatic role that surface form plays in a given context (Bates et al., 1978).

The textbase captures the semantic meaning of a text. After readers have accessed the surface form of a word, they access the lexical meanings of that word and combine lexical nodes into propositions. These propositions are organized in the form of a network (Kintsch & van Dijk, 1978; Kintsch, 1988). The greater the local coherence of a text, the more coherent is the network and the fewer inferences the reader needs to make to arrive at a coherent representation of the meaning of the text. It is assumed that textbase construction proceeds in cycles (Kintsch & van Dijk, 1978; Kintsch, 1988). In each cycle, approximately five propositions are formed in working memory. The extent to which a proposition is integrated in the network depends on, among other things, whether it shares an argument with the network constructed thus far. The textbase usually is more durable in memory than is the surface structure (Kintsch et al., 1990). The more argument overlap there is in a text, the easier it is to comprehend; that is, the more considerate it is. Maximizing argument overlap between consecutive sentences is a successful strategy for making an expository text more considerate (Britton & Gülgöz, 1991). Britton and Gülgöz found that increasing argument overlap in an instructional text leads to better recall and interpretations of the text that are closer to the interpretation that the author had intended.

The situation model captures the referential dimension of a text. A situation model is an amalgamation of information obtained from the text and inferences constructed by the reader. The prevalent view is that situation models capture only certain aspects of the situation that is described. For example, characters and objects may be represented by tokens rather than by elaborate images (Johnson-Laird, 1983). Theoretically, situation models can capture various types of information, such as causal, temporal, visual, or spatial information, as well as information about the characters' goals, motives, traits, emotions, and opinions (van Dijk, 1987). However, most empirical research on situation models has focused on spatial information. Under constrained laboratory conditions, readers construct detailed spatial models. Objects that are spatially close to the main protagonist of a story are more available in the model than distal objects (Glenberg, Meyer, & Lindem, 1987; Haenggi, Gernsbacher, & Bolliger, 1994; Morrow, Greenspan, & Bower, 1987; Morrow, Bower, & Greenspan, 1989). However, in the case of more naturalistic texts, readers do not appear to construct detailed spatial models, unless they are specifically instructed to do so (Zwaan, 1993; Zwaan & van Oostendorp, 1993). Even when they are allowed to reread the text, subjects do not end up with a strong spatial representation (Zwaan & van Oostendorp, 1993). The results suggest that despite the attention it has received in empirical studies, spatial information may not be a very crucial component of situation models in story comprehension. Zwaan and van Oostendorp (1993) speculated that the extent to which spatial information will be incorporated into the situation model is dependent upon its thematic relevance. However, there is no empirical evidence to support this claim.

Several studies have suggested that causal and motivational information may form the backbone of the situation models that are constructed during narrative comprehension (Bloom, Fletcher, van den Broek, Reitz, & Shapiro, 1990; Trabasso & Sperry, 1985; Trabasso & van den Broek, 1985; van den Broek, 1990). The more causally important a statement, the better it is recalled (Trabasso & Sperry, 1985). Researchers have recently reported that character traits may be represented in situation models (Albrecht, Hakala, & O'Brien, 1992). In these studies, the participants read short texts about a protagonist performing some sort of action. Reading-time measurements showed that the participants slowed down at sentences that were inconsistent with a trait of the protagonist. Specifically, these sentences described the protagonist performing an action that was inconsistent with one of his or her traits that was mentioned earlier in the text. For example, if the main protagonist was described as an old man at the beginning of the text, readers slowed down when reading how he ran across the street to rescue a child. This suggests that characters may be represented in the situation model along with information about their traits. Information about characters' emotions may also be incorporated in the situation model. Readers appear to make inferences about the emotional states of characters (Gernsbacher, Goldsmith, & Robertson, 1992). There may be other dimensions of situation models, such as moral judgments (Kintsch, 1992; van Dijk, 1987), that are prominent during comprehension as well. However, no empirical evidence about the role of these types of information in the construction of a situation model is available.

In summary, it is possible to distinguish three levels of representation in text comprehension: the surface structure, textbase, and situation model. In the previous section, two functions of language were distinguished, namely, the referential function and the poetic function. When the referential function is dominant, as in scientific and news discourse, the reader's focus will be on the construction of a situation model. Conversely, when the poetic function is dominant, as in literature, the focus is on the surface structure and textbase levels. In the next section, I argue that literary texts are often inconsiderate at all three levels of representation.

LITERARY TEXTS

The fact that literary texts are inconsiderate at the surface level is shown most easily in the case of poetry. Devices such as rhyme and alliteration attract attention to the surface form of the text itself rather than to the content of the text. In terms of resource allocation in online comprehension, this implies that the shift of attention towards the linguistic surface occurs at the expense of other, presumably higher level, processes, such as the construction of a situation model. Kintsch (1992) has simulated this process in the context of counting-out rhymes, using his Construction-Integration model. This simulation shows demonstrated the manner in which a surface representation can completely override both textbase and situational representations.

In addition to directing attentional processes to the surface structure, literary devices also may directly sidetrack routine comprehension procedures. For example, an enjambment sidetracks normal syntactic parsing. Consider the following example from Shakespeare's sonnet 15:

When I consider everything that grows
Holds in perfection but a little moment.

This is an example of a garden-path sentence. The reader at first analyzes the first line in the example as a complete clause. However, this analysis breaks down as soon as the first word of the second line is encountered. When the reader realizes that this is the main verb of the sentence, the entire sequence is reanalyzed. The garden-path effect capitalizes on the reader's propensity to attempt immediately to assign a syntactic structure to a sentence. This strategy has become known as the *minimal attachment strategy* (Frazier & Rayner, 1990) or the *immediacy strategy* (Just & Carpenter, 1987). This is a successful strategy in the majority of cases. However, it breaks down when the reader encounters an enjambment, which slows down the reading process and focuses attention on the linguistic structure that caused the disruption of the comprehension process. It is important to note that the enjambment in the Shakespeare sonnet converges with the meaning of the sentence. The initial syntactic representation holds in perfection for just a moment in the reader's mind, until the word "holds" is encountered. This specific aesthetic effect is known as the *semantization of the form*. In psychological terms, it leads to a convergence of different levels of representation.

It often is argued that poetry is the most typical case of literature because of the abundance of literary devices in poems (Waugh, 1980). Literary prose is commonly considered to be a less extreme case. Nonetheless, literary prose can contain various devices that direct attention to the surface structure. For example, Donald Barthelme's (1988) story "Concerning the Bodyguard" consists almost exclusively of questions. Table 9.1 presents the opening sentences of this story.

Consistent with these claims, there is empirical evidence that the surface structure in literary prose may interfere with normal comprehension processes (Carpenter & Just, 1992). For example, Henry James's prose is characterized by sentences that are interspersed with asides and interjections. Theoretically, such a structure should tax working memory. In an eye-tracking study, Carpenter and Just (1992), found that James's surface structure caused the participants to make

TABLE 9.1
Excerpt from Donald Barthelme's "Concerning the Bodyguard"

Does the bodyguard scream at the woman who irons his shirts? Who has inflicted a brown burn on his yellow shirt purchased expensively from Yves St. Laurent? A great brown burn just over the heart?
Does the bodyguard's principal make conversation with the bodyguard as they wait for the light to change, in the dull grey Citroen? With the second bodyguard,, who is driving? What is the tone? Does the bodyguard's principal comment on the brown young women who flock along the boulevard? On the young men? On the traffic? Has the bodyguard ever enjoyed a serious political discussion with his principal?
Is the bodyguard frightened by the initials D.I.T.?

elaborate regressions. These regressions were far more elaborate and the reading times were much slower than the ones that occurred in nonliterary prose, indicating that routine comprehension was disrupted.

In addition to the surface structure of individual sentences, there also is the surface structure of longer sketches of text. It is common in literary analysis to make a distinction between the surface order of events, as they are reported in the story, and their chronological order (Genette, 1980; Rimmon-Kenan, 1982; Tomashevsky, 1965). In considerate prose, one would expect the reported and the chronological order of events to be isomorphic. However, literary authors usually deviate from this norm; they may report events later (flashback) or earlier (flash-forward) than they actually occurred in the story. These literary devices, especially flash-forwards, have been found to have a disruptive effect on comprehension (Ohtsuka & Brewer, 1992). However, the reason why flashbacks and flash-forwards are used is that they may create suspense (Ohtsuka & Brewer).

Literary texts also are inconsiderate at the textbase level. As mentioned previously, considerate prose should start with a topical sentence. The main point of the text should be clear from the outset. This would enable the reader to process the text in a top-down manner, guided by the topical sentence. In terms of Kintsch's (1988) construction-integration model, the propositions of the topical sentence receive high activation in the textbase network; consequently, they dominate incoming information. However, in literary prose, the main point of the text is typically preserved for the very end or is never stated at all. Consequently, the reader may be uncertain about the point of the text and will have to read in a bottom-up manner, scanning the text for information about the point of the text. For example, even after having read the 10 sentences of the Barthelme story in Table 9.1, the reader still may be unclear about the point of the story.

Two important properties of considerate prose are that it is coherent and unambiguous. In contrast, literary prose often is deliberately incoherent and ambiguous. A detail may be mentioned in a detective novel that does not seem to bear immediate relevance to information previously stated in the text. For example, the narrator may mention out of the blue that a particular character is left-handed. In nonliterary prose comprehension, this information probably would be quickly deactivated because it would not receive activation from other nodes in the propositional network. In literature, however, seemingly irrelevant information can be relevant at a later stage, for example, when it turns out that the murderer is left-handed. In the case of literary prose therefore, seemingly irrelevant information has to be kept active in memory for a relatively long period. This will place extra processing loads on the reader.

There are at least two aspects at the referential level of literary texts that make it difficult to construct situation models: The extent to which the fictional deviates from the real world, and the perspective from which the events are described. Literary texts often are (but not necessarily) about fictional events set in fictional worlds. It has been demonstrated that it is easier to construct a situation model if the reader has prior knowledge about the setting of a story (Zwaan & van Oostendorp, 1993). Therefore, the more that fictional settings and events deviate from real world setting and events, the harder it will be for the reader to construct a situation model. This difficulty is increased if fictional settings and events partly contradict world knowledge, as they do in, for example, various literary genres, such as fables, fairy tales, fantasy, and science fiction and various literary modes, such as surrealism, absurdism, and postmodernism.

Literary theorists commonly make a distinction between the author and the narrator. The narrator's point of view may make it difficult for the reader to construct a situation model. The narrator may perceive reality in a totally different way than the reader. For example, the first part of Faulkner's *The Sound and the Fury* is written from the perspective of an idiot, and Calvino's *Cosmicomics* are written from the perspective of a subatomic particle. Unusual perspectives make it difficult for the reader to construct a situation model because his or her knowledge base is of little use in generating the appropriate inferences.

Finally, many literary stories have open endings. In Gabriel Garcia Márquez's (1972) story "A Very Old Man With Enormous Wings," a creature is found in a small village. It is an old man with wings. Some of the townspeople believe he is an angel. However, the local priest doubts this. The text does not provide information indicating whether the old man really is an angel or not. At the end of the story, the old man simply flies away. In principle, readers could construct two situation models for the story. In the first one, the old man really is an angel and the townspeople are right. Many inferences would follow from this interpretation. The reader also would have to find a way of dealing with the old man's nonangelic appearance in the situation model. In the alternative situation model, readers agree with the priest that the old man is not really an angel, but a Norwegian with wings. These readers probably would assign more weight to the priest's reservations than in the "angel" situation model. Many literary analysts would argue that the most plausible interpretation of an open-ended story is precisely that it is open-ended, and one cannot decide between the two alternative interpretations. In such stories, the author probably wants the reader to oscillate between the two interpretations.

Theoretically, it is possible that readers keep the two interpretations simultaneously in mind. However, empirically, this seems implausible. Mani and Johnson-Laird (1982) have demonstrated that, in the domain of spatial descriptions, if a text gives rise to more than one situation model, readers refrain from constructing any situation model whatsoever. Instead, they merely construct a strong textbase representation because such a representation is flexible enough to be consistent with both situation models. Mani and Johnson-Laird used very short and simple texts that gave rise to simple situation models. Consequently, it is unlikely that people can keep two complex situation models active at the same time. Because many literary stories are indeterminate, at least at the beginning, experienced readers of literature can be expected to have tuned their control systems in such a way that they are able to deal with the indeterminacies of the literary comprehension process. Therefore, they might delay the construction of a situation model as long as possible.

EMPIRICAL DATA REGARDING LITERARY COMPREHENSION

If it is true that repeated exposures to literature induce a particular literary processing mode in the reader, the effects of activating the literary control system should occur even in the absence of particular literary devices. This hypothesis was tested in a series of experiments (Zwaan, 1991, 1993, 1994). These experiments were the same in format. Participants were assigned to either of two conditions. In one condition, the participants were told that they would read a series of news stories. In the other condition, the participants were told that they would read a series of literary stories. The critical aspect of the manipulation was that both groups read the same series of texts. This made it possible to attribute any differences in the readers' performance between the conditions to the readers' control systems rather than to specific text features.

In all experiments, the texts were presented line-by-line on a computer screen, in a participant-paced reading paradigm. The presentation of the texts typically was followed by a memory test. The texts that were used in the experiments were excerpts from literary novels and news stories. A pilot study had demonstrated that these texts could be read either as literary or as news stories. The participants were unable to determine reliably whether these texts belonged to the literary or the news genre (Zwaan, 1991).

Participants consistently constructed stronger surface structure representations in the literary condition than in the news condition. This is consistent with the claim that there is a relatively strong focus on the surface form of texts in literary comprehension, even when this focus is not triggered by the text.

No significant difference was found between the literary and news conditions with respect to general textbase information. Zwaan (1994, Experiment 2) reported that, whereas causally important textbase information was remembered equally as well in both the literary and the news conditions, causally unimportant information was remembered better in the literary condition. This suggests that the textbase representation that was constructed in the literary condition was more elaborate than the textbase constructed in the news condition. In the news condition, the participants appeared to emphasize causally important information at the expense of seeming unimportant information. In the literary condition, the participants expected the seemingly unimportant information to become important later on and decided to keep it available for further processing.

The experiments also consistently showed that the participants in the literary condition constructed weaker situational representations than did the participants in the news condition. The literary control system apparently causes the reader to focus less on situation model construction than does the news control system. Because the referential function is dominant in news discourse, the participants in the news condition focused on the construction of a situation model.

The reading times for the texts were consistently longer when the texts were presented as literary stories than when they were presented as news stories. Therefore, information about the genre of a text influenced online processing. This result suggests that there may be a literary mode of text comprehension, as well as a news mode. Zwaan (1994) recently performed a more detailed analysis of the reading times, the results of which were consistent with the memory data. Readers in the literary condition allocated more of their processing resources to the construction of a surface structure and a textbase than did the participants in the news condition, whereas the participants in the news condition allocated more resources to the construction of situation models.

Finally, Zwaan (1993, Experiment 4) reported that information that violated world knowledge, such as a statement about a horse that spread its wings and flew away, caused the participants in the news condition to read more slowly than did the participants in the literary condition. The participants in the literary condition had fewer problems in processing the anomalous sentence.

TOWARDS A COMPUTATIONAL MODEL

These findings can be modeled computationally by extending Kintsch's (1988) Construction-Integration model of text comprehension. The Construction-Integration model is to a large extent a connectionist model. It distinguishes two phases in text comprehension: the construction phase and the integration phase. In the construction phase, a textbase is formed that contains (a) the concepts and propositions directly corresponding to the linguistic input, (b) a small number of the most closely associated neighbors of these elements in the general knowledge network, and (c) some additional inferred propositions. During the construction phase, which runs automatically, connection strengths are assigned to all pairs of elements that have been generated. This results in an initial, enriched, but incoherent and possibly contradictory, textbase. During the integration phase, which is more strategic, this textbase network settles on a coherent representation in a connectionist manner. Irrelevant information is deactivated, whereas nodes encoding important information are assigned high activation. Kintsch (1988) points out that a highly integrated network is tantamount to a situation model.

In terms of the Construction-Integration model, news comprehension involves a radical integration process in which irrelevant or unimportant information is rapidly deactivated. In contrast, literary comprehension would involve a far less drastic integration process in which (seemingly) irrelevant or unimportant information is kept longer in an active state. The more radical integration process in news comprehension would result in a strong situation model. This model would dominate incoming information in that information that is consistent with the model and highly related to the model would receive high activation, whereas information inconsistent with the model would be deactivated. The less dramatic integration process in literary comprehension would result in a partly incoherent, loosely organized textbase. However, literary readers would have less trouble than news readers processing incoming information that either contradicts the representation constructed thus far or is unrelated to it. Therefore, if a story suddenly takes a supernatural turn, news readers would be slowed down more by this information than literary readers.

These processes could be simulated by extending the Construction-Integration model in such a way that it would incorporate a control system. Because the construction phase is assumed to run automatically, the control system would not affect the construction of the initial propositional network. However, the control system could affect the integration process because this process is strategic. The Construction-Integration model could be extended by a node, or layer of nodes, that affect the integration process. There are two ways in which a control system could be implemented. In the first implementation, the control system would be nothing more than a threshold at which to start the integration process. With this extension, the Construction-Integration model could simulate both a literary and a news control system. In a model of a literary control system, the threshold would have to be relatively lax, so that the model would be relatively tolerant to seeming irrelevancies and contradictions. This would slow down the integration process. By contrast, in a model of a news comprehension control system, the threshold at which to start integration would need to be more stringent. This simple extension of the Construction-Integration model would give rise to all of the findings reported in the previous section. However, it is not clear whether the threshold mechanism would be sufficient for modeling other aspects of literary comprehension that have not been empirically investigated to date.

In the second implementation of the literary control system, the control system would consist of a layer of nodes that are activated and clamped when the reader obtains information about the genre of the text that he or she is reading. These nodes would activate various other nodes that are relevant to literary understanding, such as nodes coding surface features and seemingly unimportant propositions. At the same time, the control system would inhibit nodes that coded aspects of the situation model. The control system also would activate background knowledge in long-term memory that was relevant to literary comprehension, such as knowledge about literary history, intertextuality, and stylistics. This implementation of the literary control system could also account for all the findings reported in the previous section. Although it is less parsimonious than the threshold implementation, it is more realistic.

It should be noted that the texts used in the experiments just reported were all rather short (around 220 words). It seems unlikely that literary readers can keep large amounts of unrelated but potentially relevant information in an active state for a long time. Therefore, one could assume that literary readers delay the construction of situation models rather than failing to construct any situation model at all when reading longer stretches of text, such as a short story or a novel. It may be that there are "wrap-up moments" in literary comprehension, at which the reader will have sufficient information to construct part of the situation model. Therefore, we do not have to assume that literary readers will never settle on a situation model; rather, it is assumed that they delay the construction of a situation model until sufficient information has been assembled. In other words, they will allow the elaborate textbase network to settle at the wrap-up moments.

The proposed extensions of the Construction-Integration model could readily simulate this process. The threshold implementation offers the following solution. At any given point (which may be at least 200 words from the beginning of a text), the threshold for literary comprehension would be reached. At that point, integration would begin, or become more intensive, and the network would settle on an interpretation. In the alternative implementation, the control system would stop inhibiting and start activating the situation model nodes.

DIFFERENCES AMONG READERS

The model described thus far assumes that readers develop a specific cognitive control system in response to the literary devices to which they are exposed. In its present state, the model does not accommodate individual differences among readers. However, future versions of the model should be able to account for individual differences, an important source of which is working memory span.

Daneman and Carpenter (1980) have demonstrated that readers differ in the extent to which they can keep information active in working memory. Participants with a low working memory span can keep only a small number of items in working memory, whereas subjects with large working memory span can keep relatively many items in working memory. Whitney and Clark (1989) have collected data that suggest that readers with a low working memory span use a top-down strategy when reading an ambiguous passage. They typically form an interpretation of the text relatively early on and force the rest of the text into that pattern. This is a successful strategy if the incoming text is consistent with the interpretation because the already constructed interpretation will facilitate further comprehension. However, this strategy fails when the incoming text is not consistent with the interpretation. At this point, comprehension will break down, and readers will have to reread portions of the text.

Readers with a high working memory span, in contrast, use a bottom-up strategy. They hold off deciding on an interpretation of the text for as long as possible and allow the text to guide their interpretation. A drawback of this mode of comprehension is that it is relatively slow because the reader dos not have a high level interpretation to direct further processing. However, the advantage of this strategy is that it is more flexible. Because the reader is not committed to one interpretation, he or she can deal easily with anomalous information.

Readers with a high working memory span should be better equipped to read literary texts than readers with a low working memory span. One could predict that low span readers will have difficulty in comprehending literary stories. They probably will prefer simple unambiguous stories. These individual differences could be captured by the model by setting the integration threshold at different levels for different readers.

CONCLUSION

At the beginning of this chapter, I argued that literary comprehension is a specific mode of text comprehension. The literary comprehension process is monitored by a control system that is tuned to dealing with the deliberate inconsiderateness of literary discourse. I have discussed empirical findings that support this view. In addition, I have proposed extensions of Kintsch's Construction-Integration model that capture these empirical findings. This extended model generates a large number of predictions that could and should be tested empirically. At present, the model is a drastic simplification of the actual literary comprehension process. However, there is no a priori reason why future versions of the model should not be capable of capturing more aspects of literary comprehension.

REFERENCES

Albrecht, J. E., Hakala, C. E., & O'Brien, E. J. (1992, November). *Updating a mental model: Maintaining both local and global coherence.* Poster session presented at the annual meeting of the Psychonomic Society, St. Louis, MO.

Barthelme, D. (1988). Concerning the bodyguard. In P. S. Prescott (Ed.), *The Norton book of American short stories* (pp. 587–595). New York: W. W. Norton.

Bates, E., Masling, M., & Kintsch, W. (1978). Recognition memory for aspects of dialogue. *Journal of Experimental Psychology: Human Learning and Memory, 4*, 187–197.

Bloom, C. P., Fletcher, C. R., van den Broek, P., Reitz, L., & Shapiro, B. P. (1990). An on-line assessment of causal reasoning during comprehension. *Memory and Cognition, 18*, 65–71.

Britton, B. K., & Gulgoz, S. (1991). Using Kintsch's computational model to improve instructional text: Effects of repairing inference calls on recall and cognitive structures. *Journal of Educational Psychology, 83*, 329–345.

Carpenter, P. A., & Just, M. (1992, May). *How mental capacity constrains literary comprehension.* Paper presented at the third congress of the International Association for the Empirical Study of Literature, Memphis, TN.

Daneman, M., & Carpenter, P. (1980). Individual differences in working memory and reading. *Journal of Verbal Learning and Verbal Behavior, 10*, 450–466.

Fletcher, C. R., & Chrysler, S. T. (1990). Surface forms, textbases, and situation models: Recognition memory for three types of textual information. *Discourse Processes, 13*, 175–190.

Frazier, L., & Rayner, K. (1990). Taking on semantic commitments: Processing multiple meanings vs. multiple senses. *Journal of Memory and Language, 12*, 181–200.

Genette, G. (1980). *Narrative discourse.* Ithaca, NY: Cornell University Press.

Gernsbacher, M. A., Goldsmith, H. H., & Robertson, R. (1992). Do readers represent characters' emotional states? *Cognition and Emotion, 6*, 89–111.

Glenberg, A. M., Meyer, M., & Lindem, K. (1987). Mental models contribute to foregrounding during text comprehension. *Journal of Memory and Language, 26*, 69–83.

Graesser, A. C. (1981). *Prose comprehension beyond the word.* New York: Springer.

Graesser, A. C., Haberlandt, K., & Magliano, J. P. (1994). Psychological studies of naturalistic text. In H. van Oostendorp & R. A. Zwaan (Eds.), *Naturalistic text comprehension* (pp. 9–33). Norwood, NJ: Ablex.

Haenggi, D., Gernsbacher, M. A., & Bolliger, C. M. (1994). Individual differences in situation-based inferencing during narrative comprehension. In H. van Oostendorp & R. A. Zwaan (Eds.), *Naturalistic text comprehension* (pp. 79–96). Norwood, NJ: Ablex.

Jakobson, R. (1960). Closing statement: Linguistics and poetics. In T. A. Sebeok (Ed.), *Style in language* (pp. 350–377). Cambridge, MA: MIT Press.

Johnson-Laird, P. N. (1983). *Mental models: Towards a cognitive science of language, consciousness, and inference.* Cambridge, MA: Cambridge University Press.

Just, M. A., & Carpenter, P. A. (1987). *The psychology of reading and language comprehension.* Newton, MA: Allyn and Bacon.

Keenan, J. M., MacWhinney, B., & Mayhew, D. (1977). Pragmatics in memory: A study of natural conversation. *Journal of Verbal Learning and Verbal Behavior, 16*, 549–560.

Kintsch, W. (1992). Kognitionspsychologische Modelle des Textverstehens: Literarische Text [Cognitive models of text comprehension: Literary texts]. In K. Reusser & M. Reusser (Eds.), *Verstehen lernen-Verstehen lehren: Verstehen als psychologischer prozess und aufgabe* (pp. 39–59). Bern: Hans Huber.

Kintsch, W. (1988). The role of knowledge in discourse comprehension: A construction-integration model. *Psychological Review, 95*, 163–182.

Kintsch, W., Schmalhofer, F., Welsch, D., & Zimny, S. (1990). Sentence memory: A theoretical analysis. *Journal of Memory and Language, 29*, 133–159.

Kintsch, W., & van Dijk, T. A. (1978). Toward a model of text comprehension and production. *Psychological Review, 85*, 363–394.

Long, D. L. (1994). Pragmatics and discourse style, and recognition memory for sentences. *Discourse Processes, 17*, 213–239.

Mani, K., & Johnson-Laird, P. N. (1982). The mental representation of spatial descriptions. *Memory and Cognition, 10*, 181–187.

Márquez, Gabriel G. (1972). A very old man with enormous wings. In G. García Márquez, *Leaf storm and other stories* (pp. 105–112). New York: Harper & Row.

Morrow, D. G., Bower, G. H., & Greenspan, S. L. (1989). Updating situation models during comprehension. *Journal of Memory and Language, 13*, 441–469.

Morrow, D. G., Greenspan, S. L., & Bower, G. H. (1987). Accessibility and situation models in narrative comprehension. *Journal of Memory and Language, 26*, 165–187.

Mukarovsky, J. (1964). Standard language and poetic language. In P. Garver (Ed.), *The Prague school reader on esthetics, literary structure and style* (pp. 17–30). Washington, DC: Georgetown Press.

Ohtsuka, K., & Brewer, W. F. (1992). Discourse organization in the comprehension of narrative order in texts. *Discourse Processes, 15*, 317–336.

Rimmon-Kenan, S. (1982). *Narrative fiction*. London: Methuen.

Sachs, J. (1967). Recognition memory for syntactic and semantic aspects of connected discourse. *Perception and Psychophysics, 2*, 95–100.

Schmalhofer, F., & Glavanov, D. (1986). Three concepts of understanding a programmer's manual: Verbatim, propositional, and situational representations. *Journal of Memory and Language, 25*, 279–294.

Shklovsky, V. (1965/1916). Art as technique. In L. T. Lemon & M. J. Reis (Eds.), *Russian formalist criticism: Four essays* (pp. 3–24). Lincoln: University of Nebraska Press.

Singer, M. (1990). *The psychology of language*. Hillsdale, NJ: Lawrence Erlbaum Associates.

Striedter, J. (1989). *Literary structure, evolution, and value: Russian formalism and Czech structuralism reconsidered*. Cambridge, MA: Harvard University Press.

Tomashevsky, B. (1965/1925). Thematics. In L. T. Lemon & M. T. Reis (Eds.), *Russian formalist criticism: Four essays* (pp. 65–95). Lincoln: University of Nebraska Press.

Trabasso, T., & Sperry, L. L. (1985). Causal relatedness and importance of story events. *Journal of Memory and Language, 24*, 595–611.

Trabasso, T., & van den Broek, P. (1985). Causal thinking and importance of story events. *Journal of Memory and Language, 24*, 612–630.

van den Broek, P. (1990). The causal inference maker: Towards a process model of inference making in text comprehension. In D. A. Balota, G. B. Flores d'Arcais, & K. Rayner (Eds.), *Comprehension processes in reading* (pp. 175–196). Hillsdale, NJ: Lawrence Erlbaum Associates.

van Dijk, T. A. (1987). Episodic models in discourse processing. In R. Horowitz & S. J. Samuels (Eds.), *Comprehending oral and written language* (pp. 177–195). San Diego: Academic Press.

van Dijk, T. A., & Kintsch, W. (1983). *Strategies of discourse understanding*. New York: Academic Press.

van Oostendorp, H., & Zwaan, R. A. (1994). *Naturalistic text comprehension*. Norwood, NJ: Ablex.

Waugh, L. R. (1980). The poetic function and the nature of language. *Poetics Today, 2*, 57–82.

Whitney, P., & Clark, M. B. (1989). Disambiguation and cognitive control. In D. S. Gorfein (Ed.), *Resolving semantic ambiguity* (pp. 239–251). New York: Springer.

Zwaan, R. A. (1991). Some parameters of literary and news comprehension: Effects of discourse-type perspective on reading rate and surface-structure representation. *Poetics, 20*, 139–156.

Zwaan, R. A. (1993). *Aspects of literary comprehension*. Amsterdam/Philadelphia: John Benjamins.

Zwaan, R. A. (1994). Effect of genre expectations on text comprehension. *Journal of Experimental Psychology: Learning, Memory, and Cognition, 20*, 920–933.

Zwaan, R. A., & van Oostendorp, H. (1993). Do readers construct spatial representations in naturalistic story comprehension? *Discourse Processes, 16*, 125–143.

CHAPTER

10

UNDERSTANDING AND RESOLVING ARGUMENTS: THE DYNAMICS OF NEGOTIATION

Nancy L. Stein
Ronan S. Bernas
David J. Calicchia
Anne Wright
University of Chicago

The goal of this chapter is to present theory and data that describe a model of argument understanding and conflict resolution. Settling disagreements, disputes, and differences of opinion are among the most frequent activities that take place during conversational interaction in daily life. Not only do conflicts occur among individuals, but they occur among groups at both the national and international levels. Given the frequency and importance of conflictual interaction, and the negative consequences that result when negotiations fail, it is critically important that we develop a theory of how arguments and conflicts are understood.

Despite the many different approaches to argument and conflict resolution, a theory of argument understanding has not been well formulated. When argumentative understanding has been investigated, it has been considered primarily within a framework in which arguers are thought to be biased, irrational, or lacking in the logical or formal abilities needed to pursue and understand disagreements between people (Bazerman, 1986; Kuhn, 1991).

Our theory of argumentation is different from most approaches because it assumes that arguers experience a clarity of attention during a dispute, undertake goal-directed action to resolve a disagreement, and possess an ability to understand and respond to the dialogic content that is generated during negotiation. Two dimensions particularly characterize our theory and set it apart from traditional approaches to argument and conflict resolution (e.g., Toulmin, 1958).

First, we believe that arguers always understand a dispute within the context of their personal and interpersonal goals. If the argumentative evidence and explanations fulfill an individual's personal and social goals, the reasoning, the dialogic interaction, and the outcomes of the negotiation will appear reasoned and rational to the arguer. If the arguers' personal goals conflict with each other, the intellectual evaluation of the issue will suffer with respect to the credibility of the opposition, errors in understanding the opposing stance and criticizing the favored position are more likely to occur, and negotiation strategies are more likely to fail. Moreover, the interaction is more likely to become emotional and prone to aggressive action.

Second, we believe that stances in arguments and the reasons given for supporting a position always are constrained by the social and personal operating conditions of a specific situation (Stein & Miller, 1993a). Although some arguers may consistently support a given position, most are sensitive to the specific conditions surrounding a conflict and will use this information to decide whether they support their favored position in the present circumstances (Stein & Miller, 1993a). We cannot conclude that arguers are inconsistent or illogical in their judgments if they vary their stances in supporting an issue in different contexts. Their chosen position and understanding of the argument may shift depending on which of their goals is to be accomplished and which is blocked. Thus, the study of argument must be embedded in a theory of social understanding.

This chapter is devoted to such a study of argument. We present a model of argument understanding within the framework of the resolution of interpersonal disagreements and disputes in everyday negotiation. We focus on the goals of arguers, which involve wanting to effect a compromise or to win an argument. We examine whether arguers' prior knowledge and support of a position are predictive of how they reason during a negotiation, and we attempt to demonstrate how interpersonal goals are interleaved with the intellectual goal of evaluating the strength of the favored and opposing positions. In our theory, the outcomes of negotiation are a product of interpersonal and intellectual goals, and both types of goals constrain the course of the interactive dialogue.

THE DYNAMICS OF ARGUING AND NEGOTIATION

We argue and resolve conflicts frequently in everyday interaction throughout the life span. As early as 2½ years of age, children show substantial, and growing, involvement in conversational interaction, especially when the achievement of their own goals is at stake (Dunn, 1989; Eisenberg & Garvey, 1981; Fivush & Kuebli, in press; Garvey & Shantz, 1988; Goodwin, 1990; Hay & Ross, 1982; Liwag & Stein, 1994; Ross & Conant, 1993; Ross, Filyer, Lollis, Pearlman, & Martin, 1993; Stein, Trabasso & Liwag, 1991, in press). Young children (a) recognize when they are in conflict with another person (Stein & Levine, 1989; Stein & Liwag, 1994; Stein & Miller, 1993a, 1993b; Stein & Trabasso, 1982), (b) report clear preferences for certain goals and outcomes, (c) provide reasons for why they want to attain these goals (Liwag & Stein, 1994; Stein & Levine, 1989; Trabasso, Stein, & Johnson, 1981), and (d) verbally defend their choice of goal when pitted against an opponent (Eisenberg & Garvey, 1981; Goodwin, 1990; Stein & Miller, 1993a, 1993b; Stein & Trabasso, 1982; Stein, Wade, & Liwag, in press). By late childhood, they have acquired a considerable wealth of knowledge about conflict.

Although knowledge about conflict is always evolving, the period of adolescence uniquely frames the nature and resolution of conflict (Cooper, Carlson, Keller, Koch, & Spradling, 1991; Hofer, 1990; Rafaelli, 1990; Rubenstein & Feldman, 1993). Adolescents undergo changes in physical appearance (e.g., in voice, height, weight, facial structure, hormonal regulatory systems), their beliefs about the importance and necessity of autonomy, and the way in which they conduct interpersonal relationships (Youniss & Smollar, 1985). The demands from environments outside the family often place extraordinary stress on the ability of adolescents to adapt effectively. Because of increased peer influence, most adolescents are forced to explore more fully their core beliefs and the sociomoral principles governing their behavior and that of peers and family members.

The reconsideration of core social beliefs and values often brings adolescents into direct conflict with one another and with members of their families (Hofer & Pikowsky, 1993; Vuchinich, 1987, 1990). Understanding how adolescents reason about these disagreements and resolve conflicts may provide insights into the impact that many of these changes create. During negotiations, adolescents discover what they and their opponents know about the problem at hand; they become aware of the beliefs they hold compared to those that their opponents hold; they explain their reasoning and bring forth critical experiences that have influenced their decision making; and they continually evaluate how much they like one another, and whether they want to maintain a relationship after a conflict is over. Thus, the negotiation process provides direct access into many of the appraisals, reasons, and values that adolescent arguers hold to be important for interpersonal and sociomoral conduct (Stein & Miller, 1990, 1993a).

Describing the process and outcomes of negotiation also allows us to demonstrate two different functions of arguing. First, arguing can serve as a mechanism for inducing learning and changes in position, as well as for encouraging compromise. Second, it can function to further entrench and polarize differences, thereby ensuring that a conflict between two people is maintained or exacerbated (Stein & Miller, 1993a). Because of the duality inherent in argumentation, it becomes imperative to understand the conditions and mechanisms that lead to these different (and mutually exclusive) conflict outcomes. By examining the dynamic flow of negotiation, we can determine just how compromises rather than wins and losses are effected. In the present study, therefore, we sought to examine the unfolding negotiation process, as well as the role of prior knowledge and beliefs in determining the outcomes of negotiation. The issues described in the following sections served as a conceptual frame for the study.

The Nature of Interactive Arguments

Arguing has different meanings and can take many forms. In this study, we focus on *interactive arguments* (Stein & Miller, 1990, 1993a, 1993b). This type of argument is social in nature and occurs when two or more individuals support positions that are initially incompatible with each other. Interactive arguments can occur in any setting in which dialogic interchanges are carried out. Arguments can involve personal, sociomoral, political, or scientific issues. Two key dimensions define an interactive argument: recognition of conflicting and incompatible goals, and a willingness to defend initially one side of an issue over the other. If either party to an argument is unaware of the conflict, an argument cannot be initiated. Even when mutual recognition occurs, both parties must seek to resolve the conflict by defending and advancing their position. If either of these dimensions is not present, an argument cannot be initiated. If both dimensions are operative, an argument can proceed.

Arguers normally begin their interchange with the goal of supporting their own position (Fisher & Brown, 1988; Gottman, 1979; Stein & Miller, 1990; Ury, 1991). They attempt to justify their position by bringing forth reasons that give validity to their claims, often including reasons for not supporting their opponent's position as well (Stein & Miller, 1990, 1993a, 1993b). In most arguments, but especially those in the sociomoral domain, reasons given in support of a position are intimately linked to personal preferences, values, and beliefs about the benefits and costs of upholding the favored position (Shantz, 1987; Stein & Miller, 1990, 1993b; Voss, Fincher-Keifer, Wiley, & Silfies, 1993). When arguers support one side of an issue rather than the other, the implications are that (a) the values and sociomoral principles that underlie their favored position are more important than those of their opponents' position (Stein & Miller, 1993a, 1993b), (b) upholding their position will have more positive benefits for themselves or others than will their opponents' position, and (c) their favored position should be allowed to prevail over their opponents' position.

Because arguers begin with support for their position and criticisms of their opponents' position, the characterization of the content and organization of argument knowledge becomes critical. Why is it that arguers choose to begin their interaction in this fashion? Do arguers have equal amounts of knowledge about their own and their opponents' position? Stein and Miller (1993b; Miller, 1991) attempted to answer these questions by asking elementary school children and adults to talk about four different types of argument knowledge: reasons for supporting a favored position, reasons for opposing a favored position, reasons for supporting an opponent's position, and reasons for opposing an opponent's position. These investigators discovered that participants in all age groups could generate supporting reasons for their own position and at least one reason in favor of their opponent's position. Although the participants easily generated problems associated with their opponent's position, they had great difficulty generating arguments that would weaken or negate their own position. They also did not generate the more fundamental principles that motivated their opponent's stance.

Stein and Miller (1993a) concluded that qualitative distinctions between supporting and problem-oriented knowledge were valid and might be seminal in determining support for one side over another. The greater the number of supporting reasons for one side, the more likely an arguer would be to support that side. Furthermore, the very fact that arguers could generate reasons in support of one side meant that they could generate reasons for not supporting the other side.[1] Stein and Miller (1993b) surmised that arguers might believe that they had generated a good argument if they supported their own position and criticized the opposition.

Stein and Miller's (1993a) description of argument knowledge, in terms of how arguers connect and organize their knowledge, stands in direct contrast to Toulmin's (1958) description of the *normative* form that argument knowledge should take. According to Toulmin, the concept of a good argument includes: a claim or assertion; evidence (i.e., facts or observable events) in support of a claim; a warrant (i.e., a belief or principle) that links the evidence to the claim; backing that further supports and justifies the warrant; qualifications that limit the conditions under which the claim is valid; and counterarguments that directly oppose the claim. Thus, for Toulmin, a good argument includes qualifications and counterarguments against a favored position, as well as reasons in support of the favored position.

Stein and Miller (1990, 1993a) note that Toulmin's concept of an argument may be prescriptive rather than psychologically valid. Lay arguers rarely generate evidence against their own position, and Stratman (1990) has shown the same to be true in legal circles. Judges who depend on unbiased summaries from lawyers are more often than not disappointed, because lawyers rarely introduce negative evidence against their own case. Criticisms come from an opponent rather than from the supporter of a position. Arguers also have a tendency to omit warrants that support their own position, often assuming that their listeners or readers have inferred the appropriate warrant.

The asymmetrical nature of knowledge for and against a position has important implications for the process and outcomes of negotiation. If arguers lack specific types of knowledge about both their own and their opponents' position, negotiation can serve the purpose of creating a context in which the missing information can be provided. If arguers come to a negotiation task with little knowledge about the problems characterizing their own position and the principles that underlie support for the opposition, each opponent can provide the missing information so that the pros and cons of each position can be represented in more detail. In theory, therefore, negotiation should be ideal for learning new information about each side of an issue.

---

[1]Stein and Miller (1993b) illustrated that, by definition, certain types of supporting reasons for one side are criticisms against the other side.

The problem with this hypothesis is that negotiating involves much more than the evaluation of evidence for and against an issue. When arguers engage in face-to-face interaction, personal and social goals become operative, as does the intellectual goal of evaluating evidence. As Stein and Miller (1990, 1993a) point out, personal goals are often more important than intellectual goals.[2] The type of personal goal that an arguer has constructed determines exactly what the arguer's focus will be, what the arguer thinks is important, and whether the arguer will consider evidence to be valid. If arguers value the relationship that they have with their opponent and are determined to maintain that relationship, they may take a less rigid stance on an issue. In this case, they may negotiate for an intermediate position, even though they are still opposed to such a position in principle. Depending on the importance of the relationship, arguers may choose to exercise flexibility in their commitment to a stance. The reasons are contingent on a long range analysis of the benefits and risks to the relationship, as well as the arguers' feelings toward each other. For example, arguers who are good friends may have a high degree of trust in each other's ability to evaluate evidence. When opposing information is introduced, a close friend may be far more willing to listen to an opposing viewpoint. If a high level of trust is not present, arguers may choose to focus on the limitations rather than the strengths of a position.

For some arguers, however, the moral importance of the issue and the need to be right or to win can stand in direct contrast to the importance of maintaining or furthering a relationship. In these situations, arguers contend that past violations of moral codes are too important to warrant continuation of a relationship. Furthermore, compromising is often perceived to result in the loss of dominance and power (Rahim, 1983; Rands, Levinger, & Gallinger, 1981). Therefore, adherence to their original position becomes imperative. In this context, arguers will continue a relationship with their opponent only if they are able to persuade their opponent to switch sides (Stein & Miller, 1993a).

An important point to note when evaluating the different styles and needs of arguers is that the outcomes of negotiations cannot be predicted solely on the basis of how much knowledge each arguer brings to the negotiation task. According to Stein and Miller (1993a), most arguers have asymmetrical knowledge about each other's positions simply by virtue of the fact that they have chosen to support one side of an argument versus the other. The question of interest here is: How can we predict whether arguers choose to compromise, win, lose, or end in a standoff position?

The present study was designed to answer this question by examining how adolescent males and females resolve disagreements in online negotiation tasks. The selection of tasks and participants was constrained by our theoretical in-

[2]Fisher and Brown (1988) as well as Ury (1991) also point out the importance of personal goals that involve the desire to continue or discontinue a relationship.

terests. We chose adolescents from the ages of 14 to 17, not only because conflicts are quite frequent during this time period (Cooper et al., 1991; Hofer, 1990), but also because of the counterintuitive findings on conflict resolution reported by Vuchinich (1987, 1990). Vuchinich demonstrated that naturalistic conflicts between adolescents and family members rarely get resolved, with approximately 61% of all family conflicts ending in standoffs. Only about 15% of these conflicts end in a form of compromise in which family members work out a solution that satisfies some of the goals of each disputant.

The fact that compromise is not common in family disputes also has been observed in younger children. Tesla and Dunn (1992) have shown that young children learn more about getting their own way as they get older, and they become more skilled at effecting outcomes that favor their own point of view. Rather than increasing the probability of compromise behavior, negotiation skill is directed toward learning how to become a more effective supporter for one's own position. Thus, children become more skilled at criticizing their opponents' position (Stein & Miller, 1993a), learn to refute their opponents' criticisms, and become skilled at demonstrating that their position has more benefits than their opponents' (especially when the opponent is a sibling). As one of the older children in our argument study remarked, "When I'm fighting with my brother, any time I can win and beat him is great. It really doesn't matter what we fight about. The important thing is that I'm right and I can win."[3]

A major goal of the present study was to determine whether negotiations would end in standoffs when two adolescents were the arguers and each had prior familiarity with the other, but was not intimately involved with or did not dislike the other. By focusing on peer interactions, we were able to assess the breadth of the phenomenon discovered by Smetana, Yau, Restrepo, and Braeges (1991) and Vuchinich (1987, 1990). The frequency of standoffs might be different in peer negotiations when compared to naturalistic negotiations within the family (see Smetana, 1989, for a similar argument). In family contexts, adolescents need not be as fearful about losing or upsetting a relationship as in peer interactions. Adolescents may have greater latitude in family situations than in peer interactions. Because the status of a relationship can be disrupted more quickly in peer settings, engaging in compromise negotiations may occur more frequently in such settings.

Another factor that might influence the frequency of conciliatory negotiations is to ask arguers explicitly to try to compromise. This instruction may predispose arguers to seek common ground, although it may not be effective if great disparities exist between two points of view. Because so little systematic information is available about the exact process and language of compromise, we chose to examine negotiations that were constrained by a request for a compromise. We do not focus here on the contrast between compromise and noncompromise

---

[3]This quote came from a 10-year-old boy who had recently engaged in a negotiation with his 6-year-old brother (Stein & Miller, 1993a).

instructions, even though we have access to such data (Stein, Calicchia, & Bernas, in prep.). Rather, our first goal was to more fully understand the effects of this instruction on argument outcomes, and whether or not similarities would exist between family and peer negotiations.

Strategies and Conversations about Compromises versus Wins and Losses

The fact that negotiations end in different outcomes (e.g., compromise, win–lose, and standoffs) suggests that these outcomes are determined, in part, by arguers' goals, strategies, and interactions. As we argued previously, the goal of maintaining a relationship is a powerful factor in effecting a compromise (Fisher & Brown, 1988; Stein & Miller, 1993a; Ury, 1991). Compromising, however, entails additional factors. Arguers must be willing to revise their initial goal and substitute a new goal; they need to construct reasons for supporting this new goal; and they need to modify or delete reasons for supporting their old goal. Thus, a major type of knowledge restructuring has to be accomplished.

Arriving at a compromise requires that certain strategies are used. First, the act of compromising usually requires choosing one side of the argument and modifying it by the addition of constraints. For example, suppose that two arguers are attempting to resolve a conflict between two of their friends regarding the borrowing of money. The arguers discover that their friends have gotten into a dispute because one of them, Diane, loaned Michael money to get his car tuned up. Diane needed Michael to be prompt about paying back the money because she could not buy concert tickets without the loan repayment. Michael did pay back the money, but he did so in a negligent fashion (see Appendix). He kept forgetting to give Diane the money, even after his parents gave him a loan to cover his debt. Finally, he remembered the money and paid it back to Diane in time for her to buy concert tickets. Diane, however, never wanted to lend money to Michael again. Michael got upset at this decision and claimed that he should be allowed to borrow money in the future.

In talking to the two arguers, we discover that one supports Diane and the other supports Michael. We suggest that they attempt to compromise in resolving the dispute. They agree that Michael can borrow money in the future, but only under constrained circumstances. The two arguers tell us that not allowing Michael to borrow money would probably destroy his relationship with Diane. Given that a compromise is to be effected, the two arguers have decided to preserve the relationship rather than end it. However, they also have decided that the conditions that led to the dispute must be avoided at all costs. Thus, they set about generating an informal contract that specifies the conditions under which money can be borrowed in the future.

In effecting a compromise, the arguers have changed their basic beliefs about how money is to be borrowed (e.g., under what conditions and what the appropriate procedures are for loan repayment). Additionally, the time orientation of their negotiation is very important. The entire negotiation, except for the initial listing of reasons for supporting a stance, was oriented toward the future; that is, the entire negotiating session was directed towards constructing a plan that would specify how, and under what conditions, lending could take place in the future. The past was referred to only for purposes of retrieving and reviewing the conditions that led to the initiation of the dispute between Michael and Diane. With that exception, the focus was forward-going.

In win–lose arguments, however, the focus is primarily on the past and the dissolution of a relationship (Stein & Miller, 1993a). If two arguers decide not to compromise, the general nature of their negotiation focuses on a discussion of the conditions that led up to a dispute, the ways in which behaviors of the disputants violated a moral code or social contract, the assignment of blame and responsibility, and the reasons for not being able to support a compromise. Explanations for not supporting a compromise are the only part of the negotiation that is directed toward the future. In win–lose arguments, the negative outcomes that will result if a compromise occurs are highlighted.

The content of the dialogue also varies when different outcomes result. Compromisers focus on plans of action and the setting of new constraints. Win–lose arguers focus on moral violations, the assignment of blame and responsibility, and negative outcomes that will result as a function of compromising. Thus, very different perspectives are taken as a function of the arguers' decision to compromise or win. A critical part of this decision revolves around the judgment of whether the personal relationship with the arguer is important.

In asking adolescents to compromise, we should be able to observe the dialogic differences that occur as a function of deciding to compromise, win, or forfeit a stance. If arguers decide to compromise, they are essentially looking for some way to preserve the personal aspect of the relationship. Thus, the side of the issue that guarantees the most flexibility in maintaining a personal relationship should be the one upon which arguers choose to conditionalize.

Gender and the Outcomes of Negotiations

The nature, process, and outcomes of negotiations also can be influenced by the gender of the two arguers. Much of the current work on adolescent and adult negotiation has focused on the role of gender in determining the quality, emotionality, and outcomes of conversational arguments (Noller, 1981, 1984; Ross & Holmberg, 1990, 1992; Shulman, 1987; Tannen, 1990; Weiss, 1990). The types of evidence used to support gender differences are quite varied, ranging from anecdotal presentations (Tannen, 1990) to recordings of online adolescent negotiations in high school settings (Shulman, 1987), conversations of married couples in therapeutic interaction (Noller, 1981, 1984) or autobiographical recall of conflict (Ross & Holmberg, 1990, 1992; Weiss, 1990).

Reports of gender differences vary, depending on the types of dimensions being discussed and the identity of the arguers. Ross and Holmberg (1990, 1992) report that wives are more likely to initiate arguments with their husbands, than the reverse, although wives are less likely to win. In contrast, Weiss (1990) reports that wives are more likely to both initiate and win arguments, except when arguments threaten the maintenance of the relationship. Gottman, Levenson, and Carstensen (1993) report findings similar to Weiss' in that they observed that women are more likely to win an argument when a resolution is requested.

Few investigators have studied gender differences in adolescent conflict resolution patterns. In addition, little attention has been given to the importance of describing male–female negotiation patterns in comparison to negotiations between two females or between two males. Comparisons across studies are difficult because studies have defined and measured winning and losing in different ways. Some studies have used subjective reports at the end of a negotiation session (Ross & Holmberg, 1990, 1992; Weiss, 1990), whereas others have used experimenter-determined outcomes. Few studies have used outcomes determined by the negotiators themselves.

In an attempt to remedy some of the difficulties that limit generalization across studies, we designed the present study such that comparisons could be made among three types of dyads (i.e., male–female, male–male, and female–female). In this way, we were able to determine the stability of outcome differences across different types of gender-based dyads.

METHOD

Subjects

A total of 88 high school students participated in the study, with 51% (n = 45) being female and 49% (n = 43) were male. All students attended the same high school located in a southwest suburb of Chicago. All four grade levels were represented in the student sample: 37% of the students were in ninth grade; 42% in 10th grade; 8% in 11th grade; and 13% in 12th grade. The sample was 77% African American, 18% Caucasian, and 5% "other" ethnic background. Participation in the study was voluntary, and students were paid for their participation.

Materials

Two conflict scenarios were constructed by surveying an additional 128 adolescents about recent conflicts they had experienced. These adolescents lived in the same suburban school district and had the same demographic characteristics as did the students who participated in the present study. Adolescents in the survey were requested to report two conflicts that occurred recently in their daily interactions with friends. Two frequent themes emerged: One theme dealt with the appropriate principles and behaviors involved in keeping contracts and promises between friends, and the other theme involved loyalty and the amount of time friends should spend with one another. From the survey data, two conflict scenarios were constructed.

The first conflict scenario focused on an adolescent who had been tardy in repaying money borrowed from a friend (the "Borrowing Money" scenario). An argument arose between the lender and the borrower when the lender announced that he or she would never again lend money to the borrower. The borrower disagreed with the lender and stated that he or she should be allowed to borrow money again from the lender. The scenario contained details of the sets of conditions that made the borrower late in repaying the loan and the conditions that the lender was forced to tolerate when the borrower was late in repaying the loan.

The second conflict concerned an adolescent who had moved to a new high school and was spending time with new friends to get better situated in school. The result, however, was that the adolescent ignored a long-standing friendship with a person who still attended the adolescent's former high school (the "Friendship" scenario). A conflict arose when the old friend asked the adolescent to join him or her at a dance at the old school. The adolescent turned down the old friend because a dance was being held at the new school, and the adolescent was obligated to be at the new school. The old friend disagreed and stated that the adolescent should be allocating time to the old friendship rather than to new friendships (see Appendix for narrative accounts of the two conflict scenarios).

Design

All students completed the following four tasks: a screening interview, a prenegotiation interview, a 10-min negotiation session in which an attempt to resolve the conflict was made, and a postnegotiation interview. After completing the screening interview, each participating student was paired with another participating student, which resulted in 44 dyads, 14 of which were all male, 15 male–female, and 15 all female. Within each dyad, partners were paired such that they held opposing positions and were equally committed to their favored position.

Each dyad read one of the two conflict scenarios: the Friendship scenario or the Borrowing Money scenario. Within each type of dyadic arrangement, half of the couples discussed the Friendship scenario, whereas the other half discussed the Borrowing Money scenario. In both the Friendship and Borrowing Money scenarios, a male and female were portrayed as disagreeing on an issue, and each took an opposing stance. The gender of the accuser was counterbalanced such that half of all scenario presentations portrayed a male as the accuser and half portrayed the female as the accuser.

Procedure

Screening Interview. Students were asked to read both conflict scenarios and indicate: (a) which position they favored in each of the conflict scenarios; (b) their degree of commitment to their favored position, ranked on a 5-point scale; and (c) the reasons for supporting and for opposing each side of the conflict portrayed in the two scenarios. The screening interview data were collected from an initial 389 students who completed the written questionnaire during school hours. Because the design of the study required that the students be paired according to gender, position preference, and degree of commitment, only 88 students were asked to participate in the study.

Prenegotiation Interview. Students were asked to indicate how they wanted to resolve the disagreement between themselves and their opponents. Using a forced-choice procedure, students chose among the following alternatives: (a) they wanted to win and have their opponent agree to support their position; (b) they wanted to compromise so that they and their opponent could build a position that both could support; or (c) they wanted their opponent to win, and they would agree to support their opponent's position (i.e., to lose).

Negotiation Session. The two students in each dyad were taken into a conference room, reminded that they disagreed with each other on a conflict, and were asked to resolve their differences of opinion by effecting a compromise. The two were given the following instructions:

> A compromise is defined as a process where the two of you find a position you both can support. Compromising can include some of each of your concerns, or it can be an entirely new position, as long as you both feel you can support the position.

Students were given about 7 min to reach a compromise. An extra 3 min was granted to couples who expressed the need for more time. At the end of the session, each member of the dyad was asked to describe how the negotiation ended. Only the dyad was in the room during the negotiation session. However, with the students' knowledge and permission, the negotiation sessions were both video- and audiotaped.

Postnegotiation Interview. After the negotiation session, both students were interviewed separately and asked which side of the conflict they would support if they were to engage in another negotiation involving the same conflict. Would they choose to support their original position, their opponent's position, or a new position (i.e., a middle ground or a third position)? All interviews were audiotaped.

RESULTS

Amount of Initial Knowledge

Stein and Miller (1993a) made several predictions concerning the kinds of knowledge that arguers bring to bear in an argument. These researchers stated that arguers have asymmetrical knowledge for the two conflicting positions. Arguers are more likely to generate supporting reasons for the favored position than for the opposed position, and they are more likely to generate problem-oriented reasons for the opposed position than for the favored position. Therefore, our first analysis examined the frequencies associated with the generation of each of the four types of argument knowledge (i.e., supporting and problem-oriented knowledge for the favored and opposed positions). The data were scored in terms of the number of reasons that arguers generated for each type of argument knowledge. The interrater reliability was .95 for classifying the reasons generated for both positions as either supporting or problem-oriented.

An ANOVA was conducted on the amount of argument knowledge that the participants expressed, with position (favored vs. opposed) and knowledge type (supporting vs. problem oriented) as within-subject factors. Both main effects were significant: position, $F(1, 87) = 15.18$, $p < .0002$; knowledge type, $F(1, 87) = 35.58)$, $p < .0001$. These effects, however, were qualified by a significant interaction that emerged between the two factors, $F(1, 87) = 83.79$, $p < .0001$.

Figure 10.1 shows the amount of supporting and problem-oriented knowledge arguers had for the favored and opposed positions. Pairwise contrasts revealed

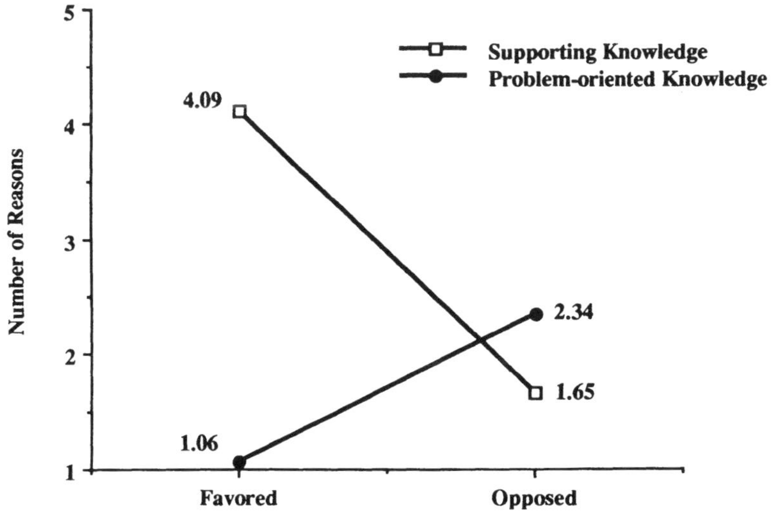

FIG. 10.1. Number of supporting and problem-oriented reasons for favored and opposed positions.

that the participants generated more supporting knowledge for the favored position than for the opposed position, $F(1, 87) = 72.27$, $p < .0001$. Further, the amount of problem-oriented knowledge that participants generated was less for the favored position than for the opposed position, $F(1, 87) = 19.75$, $p < .0001$. Therefore, Stein and Miller's (1993a) hypotheses about the asymmetry of argument knowledge were supported.

Specific Types of Supporting and Problem-Oriented Knowledge

A second coding of the participants' initial knowledge was carried out to examine the specific types of supporting and problem-oriented knowledge that they generated. Each reason was classified according to Toulmin's (1958) argument categories, as modified by Stein and Miller (1990). These argument categories are distinguished from one another according to the functions that they serve in an argument. Raters achieved a .91 coding reliability in classifying these reasons.

The two types of supporting reasons were *evidences* and *warrants*. Evidences can take the form of references to characters' actions in the conflict scenario, citations of events stated in the scenario, inferences about the motives, goals, or internal states of characters in the scenario, and evaluations or judgments of the characters' personality or behavior. Warrants are beliefs, values, and assumptions that explain why pieces of evidence support the favored position. They take the form of global statements about beliefs and values or prescribed courses of action.

Two types of problem-oriented reasons were identified: *qualifiers* and *counterarguments*. Qualifiers limit the conditions under which the supported position is deemed valid, whereas qualifiers weaken or limit a position, although they do not completely negate the position. Counterarguments are reasons that directly oppose or negate the position. In contrast to qualifiers, counterarguments focus on negating the values and basic assumptions of a position.

To illustrate the specific types of supporting and problem-oriented reasons, we provide an example of an arguer who takes the side of Michael, the borrower, in the Borrowing Money conflict scenario. The arguer generated the following supporting reasons for the favored position:

> *Evidence.* "Michael did return the money to Diane (the lender) in time for her to purchase the concert tickets she needed. No harm was done."
>
> *Warrant.* "It doesn't matter how long it takes to repay a debt so long as it is repaid in time to avoid any problems. Michael's tardiness in repaying the loan should not be cause enough to break his friendship with Diane."

The arguer also generated the following problem-oriented reasons against the favored position:

Qualifier. "(I support Michael), even though he was a bit irresponsible in forgetting to pay the money on time."

Counterargument. "Michael was insensitive to Diane's needs. This is cause enough for Diane to reconsider their friendship. Friends ought to be sensitive to each other's needs."

An ANOVA was conducted on the amount of supporting knowledge generated, with position (favored vs. opposed) and supporting knowledge type (evidences vs. warrants) as within-subject factors. A significant effect was found for the specific type of supporting reason used, $F(1, 87) = 34.62$, $p < .0001$. In line with the Stein and Miller (1993b) hypothesis, participants generated more evidences ($M = 1.96$) than warrants ($M = 0.91$) as supporting reasons. This finding generalized across both positions indicating that evidence is the most frequent type of supporting knowledge generated whether arguers focus on their own or the opponents' position. With respect to problem-oriented knowledge, no significant effects were found: qualifiers were generated as frequently ($M = 0.79$) as were counterarguments ($M = 0.91$) for both positions.

Relationship Between Initial Knowledge and Level of Commitment

The mean level of commitment for the favored position was 3.67, on a scale from 1 to 5. This score indicated a moderate to high level of commitment. However, 44.3% of the 88 participants expressed low commitment, and 55.7% expressed high commitment to their own position.

In all analyses, level of commitment was not significantly related to any other variable. Thus, commitment to the favored position was not a significant factor.

Amount of Initial Knowledge and Desired Conflict Resolution Strategy

Of the 88 participants, 81% wanted to effect a compromise, whereas 16% wanted to win. This difference in desired resolution strategies was found significant, $\chi^2(1, n = 86) = 39.1$, $p < .0001$.

No relationship was found, however, between the participants' desired resolution strategy and the amount of initial argument knowledge. Furthermore, no relationship was found between their desired strategy and level of commitment to their favored position. These data support our contention that knowledge about a position is independent of the personal goals that operate in a conflict.

Negotiation Outcomes

Arguers were instructed to state explicitly to each other how their negotiations ended. Given that we relied on the arguers' statements about the outcome of their negotiation, we analyzed the conversational interactions to determine how arguers, in fact, ended their negotiations. Outcome scores were determined using the individual arguer as the unit of analysis because of the possibility that dyads could disagree about how the negotiations were actually resolved.

The negotiation outcomes were scored as either a win, loss, compromise, or standoff. A *win* was scored when arguers maintained their original positions and made explicit statements that their original positions had been upheld. A *loss* occurred when arguers capitulated and explicitly stated that they had switched positions. Three examples of win–lose endings are:

(1) A: Yeah, that's true. I see what you're trying to say.
B: So, now could you please state that?
A: That I agree with you?
B: Yeah.
A: Yeah, I do.

(2) A: Yeah, I go with Steve too, because she not giving him any time. She can make new friends and stay friends with him, and spend time with him . . .
B: So we both voted for Steve?
A: Yeah, we did.

(3) B: Well, I still think Dwayne is right.
A: He was.
B: Don't you think both of them should just understand each other.
A: No. I think she shoulda paid up.
B: OK, she shoulda paid up on time.
A: Yeah, Marsha shoulda paid up on time. I lost.
B: You lost. Marsha shoulda paid up on time.
A: Yeah.

A *compromise* resulted when arguers explicitly stated that they had changed or modified their positions such that a compromise had been effected. In our theoretical framework, a compromise is defined as an outcome in which some element of each arguer's original position is changed such that common ground can be created between the two arguers. A frequent strategy used by arguers who compromised was to choose the position in the conflict scenario that would maintain the story characters' friendship, but then impose constraints on the characters' future actions. Three examples of compromise outcomes are:

(4) A: OK, we'll put it like this. The next time that somebody borrows money from either one of them, they just tell the date, "Could you get it to me by this time?"
B: Yeah, so that would resolve our conflict.
A: Yeah, that would resolve everything. And you won't forget the date.

(5) A: Well, we can change it. We can compromise.
B: Compromise. That's it. Yeah, OK.
A: So, they can talk a little, see how things go. They both have to understand their positions. They can't see each other all the time like they used to. Steve has to realize this, and Roberta can't be a jerk about it. So, they can still talk and fix up some dates.
B: Right, and maybe Roberta can get her new friends together with Steve.
A: So then she could see more of Steve.

(6) A: I think if they talk to each other and he told her how he felt, that he wanted to still be friends with her.
B: Yeah, they could still remain a little bit friends, call each other on the phone. But I don't think they could be as much friends as they ever were.
A: Probably not.
B: Hey, that sounds like a compromise.
A: Yap! It sure does.

A *standoff* resulted when the two arguers each maintained their original positions and refused to consider changing their positions. In one standoff negotiation, arguers were able to agree on individual points of contention, but were not able to create a basis for resolving the conflict. The following is an example of a standoff:

(7) A: And I'll be like, no man, forget it. We may as well cut it short. We ain't even got no friendship no more.
B: I'd be like well forget it. We just friends cause, you know, you go your way and I'll go my way.
A: Right. So, don't you support both of the sides?
B: Yeah, don't you?
A: Right.
B: Finished.

At the very end of the negotiation, the two arguers agreed that they now supported both positions simultaneously. However, immediately before they had "agreed to disagree," they also stated that they wanted to cut short the negotiation because they had no common ground. By agreeing to disagree, the arguers acknowledged the merits of both positions, but did not reach a resolution that would force them to change their original positions or any future negotiations. In effecting a standoff, they were able to preserve some basis of friendship for the characters, but only by going their separate ways.

As regards reaching an agreement on the outcomes of negotiation, a majority (89%) of the dyads actually agreed on how their negotiations ended. Of the 44 dyads, only 2 dyads could not agree on how the negotiation ended. In 3 dyads,

TABLE 10.1
Distribution of Outcome Types for the Two Argument Scenarios

Argument Scenario	*Number of Dyads*	*Outcome Types*				
		Compromise	*Win–Lose*	*Standoff*	*Mixed*	*Unclassifiable*
Friendship	23	16	4	2	0	1
Money	21	9	6	2	2	2
TOTAL	44	25	10	4	2	3

the resolution was ambiguous enough to be deemed unclassifiable. The distribution of the four outcome types remained constant across the conflict scenarios. The frequency distribution for each scenario is presented in Table 10.1, where the dyad is the unit of analysis.

When the individual arguer was considered as the unit of analysis, 59% compromised, 12% won, 12% lost, 9% reported a standoff, and 6% of the individual reports could not be classified. The results of a chi-square analysis indicated significant differences among the frequencies of outcomes, $\chi^2(4, N = 88) = 85.06$, $p < .0001$. Compromises were more frequent than any other type of outcome.

We also examined differences in negotiation outcomes achieved by the three types of dyads (i.e., male–male, female–female, and male–female). The results indicated that two females arguing were no more likely to compromise than two males arguing, and neither of these dyads was more or less likely to compromise than were male–female dyads. However, with mixed-gender dyads, an interesting pattern of wins and losses reported by the individual members of the dyads was found. Table 10.2 contains the proportion of males and females in mixed gender dyads reporting the four different types of outcomes. Even though the number of mixed-gender dyads ending in a win–lose outcome was small (4 dyads, 8 arguers), the results indicate that all females won in their interactions with males. A Fisher exact probability test indicated that the probability of obtaining a win was significantly greater for females than males ($p < .0001$). This finding requires replication because of the small number of male–female dyads ending in a win–lose outcome. However, these findings contradict the notion that fe-

TABLE 10.2
Proportions of Males and Females in Mixed-Gender Dyads Who Compromised, Won, Lost, or Stoodoff

Types of Outcomes	*Males*	*Females*
Compromise	.60	.60
Win	0	.27
Lose	.27	0
Standoffs	.07	.07
Unclassifiable	.06	.06

males tend to compromise more when in conflicts with males (Cooper et al., 1991; Tannen, 1990).

The Focus and Content of the Negotiation Process

Two analyses were carried out to examine the exact nature of the negotiation process between the two adolescent arguers. First, we examined the side of the argument that was upheld at the end of the compromise negotiations. As indicated previously, compromising usually consists of choosing the side that has more potential for the story characters to maintain their relationship, and at the same time allows constraints to be placed on the characters' future actions. The upper half of Table 10.3 contains the position choices that were upheld in compromise resolutions. For the Friendship scenario, all but one of the dyads (94%) preferred that the two story characters maintain their long-term friendship. The adolescents agreed to discuss and renegotiate the nature and the conduct of the story characters' friendship. For the Borrowing Money scenario, all dyads chose to allow future borrowing of money, but under modified conditions.

The lower half of Table 10.3 provides the proportion of times each side prevailed in win–lose arguments. The data are collapsed across the two scenarios because no significant differences were found. The probability of supporting the continuation of friendship was somewhat higher than the probability of supporting the discontinuation of the friendship. These data show that win–lose negotiations can lead the participants to adopt either side of the argument as the

TABLE 10.3
Favored Positions in the Compromise and Win–Lose Negotiations

	Proportion of Dyads
Negotiations Ending in Compromise Outcomes	
Friendship scenario	
End friendship due to lack of time spent with each other	.06
Re-evaluate how friendship should be conducted, given new constraints	.94
Borrowing money scenario	
Do not lend money	.00
Lend under specific conditions	1.00
Negotiations Ending in Win–Lose Outcomes	
Collapsed across both scenarios	
End friendship	.60
Do not lend money again	
Do not accept new conditions for friendship	
Maintain friendship	.40

prevailing one depending on the two arguers and the context of the negotiations. These results, however, are different from the results for the compromise outcomes.

To explore the actual content of the negotiations, a taxonomy was inductively developed for each scenario by categorizing and coding the content of the dialogic interchanges. The taxonomies captured the content of the reasons given in support of, and against, each position; they described the plans and methods suggested for compromising; and they described the future consequences that were predicted if particular outcomes were, or were not, actualized. Thus, the taxonomies also captured the temporal-causal nature of reason-giving during the negotiation process. In effect, we were able to describe whether negotiators focused on the past or the future in their discussions.

After identifying the explicitly agreed upon outcomes in a negotiated interchange, all statements that had direct bearing on the outcome were coded and classified in the following way. First, a decision was made as to whether a statement referred to a past event, action, or condition (i.e., a *focus on the past*), or whether it referred to a future event, action, or condition (i.e., a *focus on the future*). Within each time category, the content of all statements referring to the outcomes then were subclassified. For the Friendship scenario, three types of statements focused specifically on the past: (a) the two scenario characters had been long standing friends (an existing condition), (b) one character had a right to have new friends (a belief about sociomoral conduct), and (c) one character responded inappropriately when presented with the conflict between goals.

For discussions that focused on the future, two classes of plans and actions captured most statements in the interchange: (a) reference to positive plans and actions that could be carried out by the characters to enact a compromise (i.e., *positive actions*); and (b) reference to negative consequences that would ensue if the characters were unable to resolve the conflict (i.e., *negative actions*). In the Friendship scenario, most of the positive plans and actions included suggestions for renegotiating both the basis and the conduct of the friendship. The category of negative actions focused on predicted negative outcomes and constraints on future actions. The Friendship taxonomy is described in Table 10.4 and the Borrowing Money taxonomy in Table 10.5. Interrater reliability was .94 across all taxonomic categories.

Tables 10.4 and 10.5 illustrate the striking differences in focus when compromise negotiations are compared to win–lose negotiations. The primary difference was that compromise negotiations were future oriented for the most part. They focused on the plans of actions that would result when two friends decide to maintain their relationship. Over two thirds of all statements in the Friendship-compromise negotiations were focused on positive future actions. Approximately half of the statements in the Borrowing Money-compromise negotiations were forward looking in this way. These proportions differ from those in the win–lose negotiations, where only 25% of the statements were future oriented.

TABLE 10.4
Friendship Scenario: Content of Interchanges in Compromise and Win–Lose Negotiations

	Compromise	*Win–Lose*
Focus on the Past		
R & S have been long-standing friends	.00	.14
R has a right to have new friends	.04	.07
R or S handled the situation poorly	.06	.21
Subtotal	.10	.43
Focus on the Future		
Positive Actions		
Plan to meet at another time	.30	.07
Spend more quality time w/each other	.13	.14
Two groups of friends should merge	.11	.00
Should talk on the phone	.09	.00
R should invite S to party	.08	.07
Develop a better plan to maintain friendship	.06	.00
Subtotal	.77	.29
Negative Actions		
Cannot be as close as before	.09	.21
S should make new friends	.04	.07
Subtotal	.13	.29

In contrast, winners and losers spent significantly more time talking about past actions, especially those that either supported their position or violated their sense of moral conduct. When winners and losers focused on the future, they did so by talking about the fact that their opposition would not be able to achieve the outcomes believed to be possible. For example, when one arguer tried to convince the opponent that the two characters in the Friendship scenario should part, the arguer stated that the two friends could never be as close as they were before, and, therefore, they should just forget the relationship and try to make new friends. The only positive aspect of this suggestion is that each of the friends in the scenario should try to make new friends, given the difficulty that they were experiencing in their relationship. Thus, arguers in win–lose negotiations focus on the negative consequences that could result if they took the other position. They do suggest some alternatives, but the alternatives are not in line with maintaining the story characters' current relationship.

The taxonomic data do indicate some overlap between the compromise and the win–lose outcomes, especially in mentioning future negative actions. This overlap occurred for at least two reasons. First, some arguers who eventually compromised started out by trying to convince their opponents of their own position. Their persuasive efforts continued until one arguer offered the other sufficient evidence that the second arguer's position would be problematic, and

TABLE 10.5
Borrowing Money Scenario: Content of Interchanges in Compromise and Win–Lose Negotiations

	Compromise	*Win–Lose*
Focus on the Past		
M was irresponsible	.11	.07
D was too harsh on M	.07	.07
M was the victim of circumstances	.00	.00
No harm was done to D	.00	.14
You would do the same	.00	.07
Subtotal	.18	.36
Focus on the Future		
Positive Actions		
Develop a better plan for lending money	.39	.14
M deserves a second chance	.11	.07
Lend in emergency situations only	.04	.00
Subtotal	.54	.21
Negative Actions		
Do not lie in the future	.11	.21
Do not trust as much	.04	.00
Do not forget to pay back	.11	.21
Do not make promises you can't keep	.04	.00
Subtotal	.29	.42

a compromise negotiation would be better. Thus, some of the compromise dialogues did not start out in a future-oriented direction. Second, arguers who agreed to compromise often needed reassurance that the other arguer would really incorporate their concerns into a compromise resolution, especially in the Borrowing Money scenario. Often an arguer would decide to compromise, but say to the opponent, *And he can't lie anymore about paying back the money*, or *He should have told her the truth right away*. Thus, not all future negative actions are dropped from compromise negotiations. The real difference between the two types of conversations is an orientation toward the future for the compromisers and a focus on the past and on blame and responsibility for the winners and losers.

Future-Oriented Support

Our final analysis focused on the position arguers would support, if they had to argue with the same person the next day. The future-position choices were classified into four categories: *maintain* the original position; *switch* to the opponent's position; *compromise* and support the position upheld and qualified at the end of the negotiation; or *none*, which meant supporting neither the original position nor a compromise position. Overall, 54% of the arguers voted to maintain their favored position, 21% voted to switch positions, 14% voted to compromise,

TABLE 10.6
Proportion of Arguers Reporting Different Future-Oriented Positions as a Function of Each Negotiation Outcome

Future-Oriented Support Category	Outcome Types			
	Compromise	*Win*	*Lose*	*Standoff*
Maintain	.58	.83	.18	.62
Switch	.15	.08	.73	.37
Compromise	.17	.08	.09	0
Neither	.10	0	0	0

and 6% voted not to support either of the positions. The responses of 4% were unclassifiable. The results of a chi-square test indicated that there were significant differences in the frequency of choosing a future position, $\chi^2(4, n = 88) = 73.93$, $p < .001$. However, the type of future-oriented support must be considered in the light of the specific negotiated outcomes. A chi-square analysis was carried out on these data as presented in Table 10.6. The results showed that the future-oriented positions were dependent on the negotiated outcomes, $\chi^2(9, n = 79) = 23.40$, $p < .005$.

As expected, participants who won were most likely to maintain their original positions (83%), and participants who lost were most likely to switch their positions (73%). Similarly, arguers who effected standoffs were most likely to maintain their positions (62%). Clearly, a difference exists in the proportion of winners versus losers willing to maintain their original positions. In deciding to switch positions, the losers were likely to undergo some type of conceptual reorganization in their thinking during the interactions.

The arguers who compromised were the most problematic because they were the least stable and, therefore, the least predictable. A clear majority of compromisers (58%) switched back to their original position when asked what position they would support in the future; only 17% adhered to a compromise solution offered at the end of the negotiation session. Part of their instability may have been due to the fact that although compromise negotiations involved suggestions for future constraints, they lacked specificity. These types of negotiations may give compromisers latitude to reinterpret the negotiation in a negative light, thereby forcing them to revert to their original position.

DISCUSSION AND CONCLUSION

Initial Argument Knowledge

Our analysis of actual argumentative negotiations provides strong support for Stein and Miller's (1993a, 1993b) hypothesis about the initial knowledge states of arguers. Arguers always had more supporting reasons for their own position than for the opposition, and they always had more problem-oriented knowledge about the opposition than their own position. Thus, as Stein and Miller (1993a) suggested, argument knowledge is asymmetrical with respect to the two positions.

The relation between initial knowledge states and the outcomes of negotiation, however, was less clear. We found no relation between level of commitment and initial knowledge, and no relation between the amount and kind of initial argument knowledge and outcomes of negotiation. These findings suggest that the content, process, and specific interactions that comprise the negotiation are critical in determining the outcomes. In future studies, more emphasis should be placed on the way in which specific evidence is introduced during negotiation, and the ways in which evidence influences the resolution process.

If we were to generate an initial hypothesis about the types of evidence that would be effective in changing the stance of an arguer, we would conclude that providing supporting evidence for the opposing position, without criticizing the arguer's favored position, might be the most successful way to begin the change process. Being given the opportunity to consider evidence supporting the opposition without considering criticisms of one's own position might allow deeper processing of the beliefs and values that underlie the opposing position. Furthermore, as we pointed out previously, accepting certain types of evidence in support of the opposition means that problems will be created for one's own position. Therefore, arguers who receive only supporting knowledge for the opposition should not only understand the opposition better, they also may spontaneously begin to critique their favored stance.

The role that problem-oriented knowledge plays in changing a stance, however, is not clear. Would we be more likely to change an arguer's stance if we presented only problem-oriented knowledge against a favored position, or if we presented only supporting evidence in favor of the opposition? What would happen to the support of a position if some combination of supporting and opposing knowledge were to be presented to an arguer? That is, what conditions are most effective in inducing a shift to the opposite position, and what conditions are most effective in continuing support for a position?

A small number of studies on conceptual change have attempted to address this issue (see Chinn & Brewer, 1993, for a review). Presenting problem-oriented knowledge to arguers who support a position often leads to further entrenchment and continued support of the original position. Instead of accepting negative evidence as valid, arguers counter-attack with rebuttals and resist the conceptual change that is being suggested. Resistance to change is often robust, even when qualifications and counterarguments are accepted as valid (Thagard, 1992). Arguers often retain a commitment to their original position because they have not yet collected enough convincing evidence to justify the abandonment of their position.

Multiple presentations of negative data often are necessary for conceptual change because support of a position is based upon a network of reasons and evidences. Providing only one counterargument against a position is seldom sufficient to induce change. The entire knowledge network that underlies a position must be disqualified or invalidated. Furthermore, an alternative system of reasons and supports must replace the old support network. Although arguers did change their positions in the present study, our methodology did not afford a precise determination of how different types of argument knowledge should be introduced or combined to result in a change of positions or acceptance of a compromise stance.

The Importance of Personal Goals in Determining Negotiation Outcomes

The results of the present study supported Stein and Miller's (1993a) hypothesis that goals other than the desire to evaluate evidence become operative during face-to-face interaction. The emotional style used to introduce evidence (e.g., using a derogatory or an accepting tone, the use of hedges, accepting evidence while qualifying it), the ability to listen to each other, and the rate of interrupting during negotiation (Bly & Stein, 1993) were all important in determining the outcomes. Because we did not vary the degree of liking that arguers had for each other, we cannot say whether this factor operated in determining outcomes. However, in analyzing our videotapes, especially those of male–female negotiators, we found high levels of social banter and social agenda setting. In some cases, these social processes dominated the negotiation. The fact that no male winners emerged when males and females agreed to a win–lose outcome suggests that personal goals were as important as intellectual goals.

Initial Desires and Subsequent Negotiation Outcomes

The fact that 81% of the adolescents wanted to compromise is not surprising, given that they lacked an intimate involvement and were not negatively predisposed to each other. The adolescent arguers were quite interested in getting to know each other better and "fooling around." In other words, most of them considered the negotiation session an opportunity to learn more about each other and develop a further relationship. In fact, some adolescents were initially distressed that discussions might further exacerbate their disagreement with their opponent.

Initial desires for compromising or winning, however, were not predictive of the outcome. Only half of the arguers who wanted to compromise did so, with the other half of the arguers winning, losing, or ending in standoffs. The same held true for the 16% of arguers who initially wanted to win. Although the participants initially wanted to win the argument, half compromised, and the rest won, lost, or ended in a standoff. These data again illustrate that the contextual constraints of a negotiation easily can change desires. Adolescents do not always get what they want. Evaluating the specific issue and the goals of an opponent are sometimes more critical in determining how a negotiation should end, no matter how much an arguer desires one type of resolution. Arguers, even those skilled in negotiation, simply do not have enough prior knowledge to predict the operating conditions surrounding each disagreement that they might have over a particular issue.

The important finding with respect to outcomes, however, is that the majority of adolescents were capable of compromise when given explicit instructions to do so. These data are different from those of Smetana et al. (1991) and Vuchinich (1987). However, we do not view our results as contradicting theirs because our negotiation situations were strikingly different; our adolescents were not arguing in family contexts, where patterns of interaction among family members are well established and routinized (Cooper et al., 1991; Ross et al., 1993), nor were they arguing at the family dinner table (Vuchinich, 1987).

The lack of an intimate relationship might be critical in regulating the frequency of compromises or standoffs. If two people have little common history, their expectations about what will happen during the negotiation process may be less specific and less structured. Clearly, our adolescent negotiators could not report what their opponent did in past conflicts or whether their opponent would be resistant to change or compromise. This lack of information might allow many arguers to proceed in a more positive fashion and showing a willingness to consider an opponent's point of view because the opponent is perceived not to be biased against the arguer. Although we did request a compromise, we do not view this suggestion as accounting for the sharp increase in compromise outcomes that we observed as compared to Vuchinich's (1987) and Smetana's (1991) results. Our current research focuses on conflict resolution under a control condition in which instructions to compromise are not given and the rate of compromise is equivalent to that found in the compromise condition of the present study (Stein, Calicchia, & Bernas, in prep.).

Gender Differences in Negotiation Outcomes

If females compromise more than males, different distributions of outcomes should have occurred when female dyads were compared with male dyads. The only significant gender differences in outcomes, however, were within the mixed-gender dyads, with all of the females winning in the win–lose outcomes. How can these findings be explained? Miller, Danaher, and Forbes (1986) found that females in mixed-sex contexts behave more like males than do females in same-sex contexts. This could explain why females are especially combative when they attempt to compromise with males. However, Miller et al.'s hypothesis does not explain the even rate of compromise across the three different dyads in the present study.

Although Ross and Holmberg (1992) found that husbands were judged to have won more reported arguments than were their wives, Weiss (1990) found that men generally avoided conflicts with their wives unless the issue was one of extreme personal importance. Although Weiss's study involved long-term intimate relationships, it is possible that adolescent males also avoid conflicts with adolescent females. It is difficult to resolve the discrepancy between our findings and those of others, however, for several reasons. Not only did we focus on adolescents rather than married couples, but our study also was designed differently than either Ross and Holmberg's or Weiss' studies. We examined online negotiation, whereas both Ross and Weiss examined memories for arguments. Our criteria for determining the outcomes were different: we actually asked arguers to tell us how their negotiation ended at the end of their negotiation session, while in full view of one another. These factors alone could alter the rate of winning and losing among males and females, whatever their age and the nature of their relationship. Further studies need to be conducted to explore these issues. However, one thing is certain. In online negotiation tasks, females hold their own just as well or better than males.

Implications for Theories of Argumentation and Conflict Resolution

The results of our study have clear implications for theories of argumentation and conflict resolution. We were able to demonstrate that the nature of the knowledge that people possess about an issue is closely related to their position choice. However, it is the interaction process itself during negotiation, and not the initial knowledge, that determines whether compromise can be achieved. Although arguers typically start out with insufficient knowledge of the specific values and beliefs that the opposing side holds, this does not mean that they are unable to change positions or to effect a compromise. One way of reaching an agreement might be to get arguers to recognize the warrants for each side of the conflict. Future work should examine the process in which such learning and shifts in knowledge and beliefs are undertaken during argumentation.

ACKNOWLEDGMENTS

This research was funded in part by grants from the Smart Foundation and from the University of Chicago Biomedical Grant to Nancy L. Stein, the National Institute of Child Health and Human Development (Grant No. HD 25742) to Tom Trabasso and Nancy L. Stein, and the Spencer Foundation to Tom Trabasso. Ronan S. Bernas and Anne Wright were supported by Irving B. Harris Fellowships from the Harris Center for Developmental Studies and the Harris Foundation. David J. Calicchia was funded by a Century Fellowship from the University of Chicago. This study was inspired, in part, by Judy Dunn, Bob Glaser, and the late Nate Maccoby, each of whom made critical suggestions and commentaries advancing the conceptual framework of this study. Our thanks are due to all three. We are grateful to the students at Rich Central High School and to Dr. Anthony Moriarty, Associate Principal, for their help, participation and insight into the process of compromise. We are indebted to Maria D. Liwag, for her generosity in craftsmanship and intellectual collaboration, without which this chapter would not have been completed. Our appreciation is due to Tom Cook, Mike Ross, and Tom Trabasso for their advice and comments on an earlier version of this chapter, and to John Holmes for the superb suggestions and scholarship on conflict resolution and sex differences. We would also like to thank Joshua Stein, Emily Doolittle, and Rebecca Hutton for their help in data collection and administration of the study.

APPENDIX

Borrowing Money Scenario

Diane and Michael became friends when they entered junior high school and started playing in the band. They have been friends for about 5 years now. When they don't have a band rehearsal on a Friday afternoon, they usually go to the mall. There, they visit their friend who works at The Gap or play videogames. When the stores close, they often go to a movie in the mall.

A couple of months ago, Diane wanted to buy a shirt at Merry-Go-Round, but she didn't have enough money to pay for it. Michael offered to lend her the extra money, so Diane could buy the shirt. Diane borrowed the money from Michael and paid him back the next Monday at school.

A few weeks ago, Michael was getting his car tuned-up but he didn't have enough money to pay the whole bill. Because Diane was with him, she offered to loan Michael the extra $40 he needed. Michael thanked Diane and told her that he would try to pay her back early in the next week. But when the next week came, Michael did not have the money.

Michael told Diane that he would try to borrow money from his parents so he could pay Diane back the following week. Diane told Michael that she would really appreciate it if Michael paid her back soon because she wanted to buy tickets to a concert that she thought would sell out. But Michael did not pay Diane back in this second week either.

Finally, Michael did pay Diane back in the third week. Michael told Diane that his parents had given him the money several days beforehand so that he could pay her back. But Michael kept forgetting to bring the money to school. However, Diane was still able to get tickets to the concert that she wanted to attend.

Diane was upset that it took Michael so long to pay her back. Diane stated that she would not lend Michael money again. Diane felt that Michael was irresponsible in taking so long to repay her. Michael disagreed with Diane. He thought that Diane should loan him money in the future. Michael believed that he made an honest attempt to repay Diane.

Friendship Scenario

Roberta and Steve have lived a block away from each other as long as they can remember, and they have always gone to the same public schools. They often eat dinner over at each other's houses, do homework together, and talk about the people that they are interested in. They also really enjoy practicing new dance steps together. They usually practice in Roberta's basement, because there is a lot of room and Roberta's mom does not mind the music.

This fall they both started ninth grade, but for the first time, they are going to different schools. Roberta is going to a Catholic school and Steve is going to the local public school. Ever since school started, Roberta and Steve have been spending a lot less time together. While Steve is still getting together with his old friends, Roberta is making a lot of new friends. Steve often asks Roberta to join him and Roberta's old friends, but Roberta usually declines. Roberta has explained to Steve that since she is going to be at this Catholic school for the next 4 years, she needs to spend time getting to know new people.

Wednesday after school, Steve walked over to Roberta's house. Steve asked Roberta if she wanted to practice some new dance steps soon, because there was a dance scheduled for the next Saturday night at Steve's high school. Steve also invited Roberta to come to the dance with him. Roberta thanked Steve for the invitation, but told Steve that someone from her new school had already invited her to a party on Saturday.

Steve was upset that Roberta was spending so much time with her new friends. Steve told Roberta that they would not be able to maintain their friendship. Steve felt that Roberta did not think it was important enough to get together with him. Roberta disagreed with Steve. Roberta believed that she and Steve will always be friends. Roberta felt that Steve did not try to understand her need to make friends in a new school.

REFERENCES

Bazerman, M. H. (1986, June). Why negotiations go wrong. *Psychology Today*, 54–58.

Bly, B., & Stein, N. L. (1993, January). *Differences in interruptions when arguers compromise versus win or lose*. Paper presented at the Winter Text Conference, Jackson Hole, WY.

Chinn, C. A., & Brewer, W. F. (1993). The role of anomalous data in knowledge acquisition: A theoretical framework and implications for science instruction. *Review of Educational Research, 63*, 1–49.

Cooper, C. R., Carlson, C., Keller, J., Koch, P., & Spradling, V. (1991, April). *Conflict resolution in early adolescence*. Paper presented at the biennial conference of the Society for Research in Child Development, Seattle, WA.

Dunn, J. (1989). *The beginnings of social understanding*. Cambridge, MA: Harvard University Press.

Eisenberg, A. R., & Garvey, C. (1981). Children's use of verbal strategies in resolving conflicts. *Discourse Processes, 4*, 149–170.

Fisher, R., & Brown, S. (1988). *Getting together: Building relationships as we negotiate*. New York: Penguin.

Fivush, R., & Kuebli, J. (in press). Making everyday events emotional: The construal of emotion in parent-child conversations about the past. In N. L. Stein, P. A. Ornstein, C. J. Brainerd, & B. Tversky (Eds.), *Memory for everyday and emotional events*. Hillsdale, NJ: Lawrence Erlbaum Associates.

Garvey, C., & Shantz, C. (1988, April). *Varieties of conflict and development: A sociolinguistic perspective*. Paper presented at the Conference on Human Development, Charleston, S.C.

Goodwin, M. H. (1990). *He-said-she-said: Talk as social organization among Black children*. Bloomington, IN: Indiana University Press.

Gottman, J. M. (1979). *Marital interaction: Experimental investigations*. New York: Academic Press.

Gottman, J. M., Levenson, R. W., & Carstensen, L. L. (1993). *Emotional interaction in middle-aged and elderly long-term marriages*. Unpublished manuscript.

Hay, D. F., & Ross, H. S. (1982). The social nature of early conflict. *Child Development, 53*, 105–113.

Hofer, M. (1990, July). *The differential use of arguments in mother-daughter conflicts*. Paper presented at the International Conference on Dialogue Analysis, Bologna, Italy.

Hofer, M., & Pikowsky, B. (1993). Validation of a category system for arguments in conflict discourse. *Argumentation, 7*, 135–148.

Kuhn, D. (1991). *The skills of argument*. New York: Cambridge University Press.

Liwag, M. D., & Stein, N. L. (1994). *Children's memory for emotional events: The importance of emotion retrieval cues*. Manuscript submitted for publication.

Miller, C. A. (1991). *Learning to disagree: Argumentative reasoning in development*. Unpublished doctoral dissertation, University of Chicago.

Miller, P. M., Danaher, D. L., & Forbes, D. (1986). Sex-related strategies for coping with interpersonal conflict in children aged five to seven. *Developmental Psychology, 22*, 543–548.

Noller, P. (1981). Gender and marital adjustment level differences in decoding messages from spouses and strangers. *Journal of Personality and Social Psychology, 41*, 272–278.

Noller, P. (1984). *Nonverbal communication and marital interaction*. New York: Pergamon.

Rafaelli, M. (1990). *Sibling conflict in early adolescence*. Unpublished doctoral dissertation, University of Chicago.

Rahim, M. (1983). A measure of styles of handling interpersonal conflict. *Academy of Management Journal, 26*, 368–376.

Rands, M., Levinger, G., & Gallinger, G. (1981). Patterns of conflict in marital resolutions. *Journal of Family, 2*, 297–322.

Ross, H. S., & Conant, C. L. (1993). The social structure of early conflict: Interaction, relationships, and alliances. In C. U. Shantz & W. W. Hartup (Eds.), *Conflict in childhood and adolescence* (pp. 153–185). New York: Cambridge University Press.

Ross, H., Filyer, R., Lollis, S. P., Pearlman, M., & Martin, J. (1994). Administering justice in the family. *Family Psychology, 8*(3), 254–273.

Ross, M., & Holmberg, D. (1990). Recounting the past: Gender differences in the recall of events in the history of a close relationship. In M. Olson & M. P. Zanna (Eds.), *Self-inference processes: The Ontario Symposium* (Vol. 6, pp. 135–152). Hillsdale, NJ: Lawrence Erlbaum Associates.

Ross, M., & Holmberg, D. (1992). Are wives' memories for events in relationships more vivid that their husbands memories? *Journal of Social and Personal Relationships, 9*, 585–604.

Rubenstein, J. L., & Feldman, S. S. (1993). Conflict resolution in adolescent boys: A longitudinal study of predictors and correlates. *Journal of Research on Adolescence, 3*, 41–66.

Shantz, C. U. (1987). Conflicts between children. *Child Development, 58*, 283–305.

Shulman, A. (1987). *Storytelling rights*. New York: Cambridge University Press.

Smetana, J. (1989). Adolescents' and parents' reasoning about actual family conflict. *Child Development, 60*, 1052–1067.

Smetana, J., Yau, J., Restrepo, A., & Braeges, J. L. (1991). Adolescent-parent conflict in married and divorced families. *Developmental Psychology, 27*(6), 1000–1010.

Stein, N. L., Calicchia, D. J., & Bernas, R. S. (in prep.). *The dynamics of negotiation: The effects of compromise instructions*.

Stein, N. L., & Levine, L. (1989). The causal organization of emotion knowledge: A developmental study. *Cognition and Emotion, 3,* 343–378.

Stein, N. L., & Liwag, M. D. (1994). *Parents' and children's memories for emotional events.* Manuscript submitted for publication.

Stein, N. L., & Miller, C. A. (1990). I win-you lose: The development of argumentative thinking. In J. Voss, D. Perkins, & J. Segal (Eds.), *Informal reasoning and instruction* (pp. 265–290). Hillsdale, NJ: Lawrence Erlbaum Associates.

Stein, N. L., & Miller, C. A. (1993a). The development of memory and reasoning skill in argumentative contexts: Evaluating, explaining, and generating evidence. In R. Glaser (Ed.), *Advances in instructional psychology* (Vol. 4, pp. 285–335). Hillsdale, NJ: Lawrence Erlbaum Associates.

Stein, N. L., & Miller, C. A. (1993b). A theory or argumentative understanding: Relationships among position preference, judgments of goodness, memory and reasoning. *Argumentation, 7,* 183–204.

Stein, N. L., & Trabasso, T. (1982). Children's understanding of stories: A basis for moral judgment and dilemma resolution. In C. J. Brainerd & M. Pressley (Eds.), *Verbal processes in children: Progress in cognitive development research* (pp. 162–188). New York: Springer-Verlag.

Stein, N. L., Trabasso, T., & Liwag, M. D. (1991, April). *Children's and parents' memory for real life emotional events: Conditions for convergence or polarization.* Paper presented at the biennial conference of the Society for Research in Child Development, Seattle, WA.

Stein, N. L., Trabasso, T., & Liwag, M. (in press). The Rashomon phenomenon: Personal frames and future oriented appraisals in memory for emotional events. In M. Haith (Ed.), *Future oriented processes.* Chicago: University of Chicago Press.

Stein, N. L., Wade, E., & Liwag, M. (in press). A theoretical approach to understanding and remembering harmful events. In N. L. Stein, P. A. Ornstein, B. Tversky, & C. Brainerd (Eds.), *Memory for everyday and emotional events.* Hillsdale, NJ: Lawrence Erlbaum Associates.

Stratman, J. (1990). The emergence of legal composition as a field of inquiry: Evaluating the prospects. *Review of Educational Research, 60,* 153–235.

Tannen, D. (1990). *You just don't understand.* New York: Morrow.

Tesla, C., & Dunn, J. (1992). Getting along or getting your own way: The development of young children's use of argument in conflicts with mother and sibling. *Social Development, 1*(2), 107–121.

Thagard, P. (1992). *Conceptual revolutions.* Princeton, NJ: Princeton University Press.

Toulmin, S. E. (1958). *The uses of argument.* Cambridge, UK: Cambridge University Press.

Trabasso, T., Stein, N. L., & Johnson, L. R. (1981). Children's knowledge of events: A causal analysis of story structure. In G. Bower (Ed.), *Learning and motivation* (Vol. 15, pp. 237–281). New York: Academic Press.

Ury, W. (1991). *Getting past no: Negotiating with difficult people.* New York: Bantam.

Voss, J. F., Fincher-Kiefer, R., Wiley, J., & Silfies, L. N. (1993). On the processing of arguments. *Argumentation, 7,* 165–181.

Vuchinich, S. (1987). Starting and stopping spontaneous family conflicts. *Journal of Marriage and Family, 49,* 591–601.

Vuchinich, S. (1990). The sequential organization of closing in verbal conflict. In A. Grimshaw (Ed.), *Conflict talk* (pp. 118–138). New York: Cambridge University Press.

Weiss, R. (1990). *Staying the course: The emotional and social lives of men who do well at work.* New York: The Free Press.

Youniss, J., & Smollar, J. (1985). *Adolescent relationships with mothers, fathers, and friends.* Chicago: University of Chicago Press.

CHAPTER

11

THE STRUCTURE-BUILDING FRAMEWORK: WHAT IT IS, WHAT IT MIGHT ALSO BE, AND WHY[1]

Morton Ann Gernsbacher
University of Wisconsin-Madison

I have proposed previously that language comprehension can be described as structure building, and I have sketched a simple framework to use as a guide. I call this framework the Structure Building Framework. According to the Structure Building Framework, the goal of comprehension is to build cohesive mental representations, or structures. The first process involved in building a structure is laying a foundation. The next process involves developing the structure by mapping on incoming information when that information coheres with the previous information. However, if the incoming information is less coherent, comprehenders employ a different process: They shift to initiate a new substructure. Thus, most representations comprise several branching substructures.

The building blocks of mental structures are *memory nodes*. Memory nodes are activated by incoming stimuli. Their initial activation forms the foundation of mental structures. Incoming information often is mapped onto a developing structure because the more coherent the incoming information is with the previous information, the more likely it is to activate similar memory nodes. However, the less coherent the incoming information, the less likely it is to activate similar memory nodes. If the incoming information is less coherent, it activates different nodes, and the activation of these different nodes forms the foundation for a new substructure.

---

[1]This chapter is reprinted from chapter 6 of *Language Comprehension as Structure Building* (Lawrence Erlbaum Associates, 1990).

Once memory nodes are activated, they transmit processing signals. These processing signals either *enhance* (i.e., boost) or *suppress* (i.e., dampen) other nodes' activation. Memory nodes are enhanced if the information they represent is necessary for future structure building; they are suppressed if their information is no longer as necessary.

These three structure building processes (i.e., laying foundations for mental structures, mapping coherent information onto developing structures, and shifting to initiate new structures) and these two mechanisms (i.e., enhancement of some memory nodes but suppression of others) underlie numerous comprehension phenomena.

In Gernsbacher (1990), I described many of the phenomena that these general cognitive processes and mechanisms explain, including why adults differ in their comprehension skill. In the first section of this chapter, I briefly review these phenomena.

THE PROCESS OF LAYING A FOUNDATION

Because comprehenders first lay a foundation, they spend more time reading the first word of a clause or sentence (Aaronson & Ferres, 1983; Aaronson & Scarborough, 1976); they spend more time reading the first sentence of a paragraph or story episode (Haberlandt, 1984); they spend more time listening to the first word of a spoken clause or spoken sentence (Foss, 1969, 1982); and they spend more time viewing the first picture of a picture story or picture-story episode (Gernsbacher, 1983).

Comprehenders use these first segments (i.e., initial words, sentences, and pictures) to lay foundations for their mental representations of larger units, such as sentences, paragraphs, and story episodes. Because laying a foundation consumes cognitive effort, comprehenders slow down when comprehending initial segments. Indeed, none of these comprehension time effects emerges if the information does not lend itself to building cohesive mental representations, for example, if the sentences, paragraphs, or stories are self-embedded or scrambled (Foss & Lynch, 1969; Kieras, 1978, 1981).

The process of laying a foundation provides an explanation for why comprehenders are more likely to recall a sentence when cued by its first content word or a picture of that first content word (Bock & Irwin, 1980; Turner & Rommetveit, 1968); why comprehenders are more likely to recall a story episode when cued by its first sentence (Mandler & Goodman, 1982); and why comprehenders are more likely to consider the first sentence of a paragraph the main idea of that paragraph, even when the actual theme occurs later (Kieras, 1978, 1981). Initial words, sentences, and pictures are optimal cues because they form the foundations of their clause-level, sentence-level, and episode-level structures; only through initial words, sentences, and pictures can later words, sentences, and pictures be mapped onto the developing representation.

The process of laying a foundation explains why comprehenders access the participant mentioned first in a clause faster than they access a participant mentioned later (Gernsbacher & Hargreaves, 1988, 1992). This *advantage of first mention* occurs regardless of the first-mentioned participant's syntactic position or semantic role (see also Carreiras, Gernsbacher, & Villa, in press). First-mentioned participants are more accessible because they form the foundation of their clause-level substructures.

The process of laying a foundation also explains why the first clause of a multiclause sentence is most accessible shortly after comprehenders hear or read that multiclause sentence (even though while they are hearing or reading the sentence, the most recent clause is most accessible). According to the Structure Building Framework, comprehenders represent each clause of a multiclause sentence in its own substructure. Although they have greatest access to the information that is represented in the substructure that they are currently developing, at some point, the first clause becomes most accessible because the substructure representing the first clause forms the foundation for the whole sentence-level structure (Gernsbacher, Hargreaves, & Beeman, 1989).

THE PROCESSES OF MAPPING AND SHIFTING

The process of mapping explains why sentences that refer to previously mentioned concepts (and are, therefore, referentially coherent) are read faster than less referentially coherent sentences (Haviland & Clark, 1974); why sentences that maintain a previously established time frame (and are, therefore, temporally coherent) are read faster than sentences that are less temporally coherent (Anderson, Garrod, & Sanford, 1983); why sentences that maintain a previously established location or point of view (and are, therefore, locationally coherent) are read faster than sentences that are less locationally coherent (Black, Turner, & Bower, 1979); and why sentences that are logical consequences of previously mentioned actions (and are, therefore, causally coherent) are read faster than sentences that are less causally coherent (Duffy, Shinjo, & Myers, 1990; Keenan, Baillet, & Brown, 1984; Myers, Shinjo, & Duffy, 1987).

The process of mapping also explains why sentences that contain the definite article *the* are read faster than sentences that contain indefinite articles (Gernsbacher & Robertson, 1994); why clauses that convey events that are at least moderately causally related are read faster if the clauses are conjoined by the causal conjunction *because* (Deaton & Gernsbacher, in press); and why sentences that match the conceptual or syntactic structure of previous sentences are read faster than sentences that are not matched in this way (Frazier, Taft, Roeper, Clifton, & Ehrlich, 1984; Gernsbacher & Robertson, 1994).

The process of shifting from actively building one substructure to initiating another explains why words and sentences that change the topic, point of view, location, or temporal setting take substantially longer to comprehend than sentences that do not involve such changes (Anderson et al., 1983; Olson, Duffy, & Mack, 1984). The process of shifting also explains why information presented before a change in topic, point of view, location, or temporal setting is harder to retrieve than information presented afterward (Anderson et al., 1983; Clements, 1979). Such changes lead comprehenders to shift and initiate a new substructure; information presented before comprehenders shift is represented in a different substructure than information presented afterward.

The process of shifting also explains a well known language comprehension phenomenon: Comprehenders quickly forget the exact form of recently comprehended information. This phenomenon is not unique to language; it also occurs while comprehenders are viewing picture stories, and it also is exacerbated after comprehenders cross episode boundaries, even the episode boundaries of picture stories (Gernsbacher, 1985).

Finally, the process of shifting explains why comprehenders' memories for stories are organized by the episodes in which the stories were originally heard or read. Comprehenders shift in response to cues that signal a new episode; therefore, each episode is represented in a separate substructure (Beeman & Gernsbacher, 1994).

THE MECHANISMS OF SUPPRESSION AND ENHANCEMENT

The mechanism of suppression explains why only the contextually appropriate meaning of an ambiguous word, such as *bug*, is available to consciousness, even though multiple meanings, even contextually inappropriate ones, often are immediately activated (Swinney, 1979). The inappropriate meanings do not simply decay; neither do they decrease in activation because their activation is consumed by the appropriate meanings. Instead, the mechanism of suppression dampens the activation of inappropriate meanings. The mechanism of suppression also dampens the activation of less relevant associations of unambiguous words (Gernsbacher & Faust, 1991a).

The mechanisms of suppression and enhancement also explain how anaphoric devices (i.e., pronouns, repeated noun phrases, and so forth) improve the mental accessibility of their referents (i.e., the concepts to which they refer) (Gernsbacher, 1989). Anaphoric devices improve their referents' accessibility through the mechanism of enhancement: Referents are more highly activated after an anaphoric device is read or heard than they are before. Anaphoric devices also improve their referents' accessibility through the mechanism of suppression: Other concepts, which are not the referents, are activated less after an anaphoric device is read or heard than they are before. The net effect of the mechanisms of suppression and enhancement is that after an anaphoric device is heard or read, the referents to which the anaphoric devices refer are more highly activated than other concepts. Therefore, they are more accessible to listeners and readers and play a more prominent role in the developing mental structure.

The mechanisms of suppression and enhancement are triggered by information that specifies the anaphor's identity. More explicit anaphoric devices (such as explicitly repeated proper names) trigger more suppression and enhancement than do less explicit anaphoric devices (such as pronouns or zero anaphora). Information from other sources (such as the semantic, syntactic, and pragmatic context) also triggers suppression, but it does so less quickly and less powerfully.

Therefore, the mechanisms of suppression and enhancement explain why speakers and writers use more explicit anaphoric devices at longer referential distances, at the beginnings of episodes, and for less topical concepts (Fletcher, 1984; Givon, 1983). The mechanisms of suppression and enhancement also explain why comprehenders have more difficulty accessing referents at longer referential distances, at the beginnings of episodes, and for less topical concepts (Clark & Sengul, 1979; Clifton & Ferreira, 1987).

The mechanisms of suppression and enhancement explain how concepts marked with cataphoric devices, such as spoken stress and the indefinite article *this*, gain a privileged status in comprehenders' mental representations (Gernsbacher & Shroyer, 1989). Cataphoric devices improve their concepts' representational status through the mechanism of enhancement: If concepts are marked with cataphoric devices, they are more activated than if they are not marked by cataphoric devices. Cataphoric devices also improve their concepts' representational status through the mechanism of suppression: Concepts marked with cataphoric devices are better at suppressing the activation of other concepts, and they are better at resisting being suppressed themselves (Gernsbacher & Jescheniak, in press).

Finally, the mechanisms of suppression and enhancement explain why comprehenders typically forget surface information faster than they forget thematic information (Sachs, 1967, 1974); why comprehenders forget more surface information after they hear or read thematically-organized passages than after they hear or read seemingly unrelated sentences (Anderson & Bower, 1973; Peterson & McIntyre, 1973); and why comprehenders better remember the surface forms of abstract sentences but the thematic content of concrete sentences (Begg & Paivio, 1969; Pezdek & Royer, 1974). Typically, thematic information is repeatedly introduced; therefore, it gets enhanced. Further, typically, surface information is constantly changing; therefore, it gets suppressed. However, if the surface information is more constant than the thematic information (as in the case of abstract sentences or unrelated sentences that share their syntactic structure), surface information changes less rapidly than thematic information; therefore, surface information gets enhanced and thematic information gets suppressed.

INDIVIDUAL DIFFERENCES IN STRUCTURE BUILDING

The Structure Building Framework explains why skill at comprehending linguistic media (e.g., written and spoken stories) is highly related to skill at comprehending nonlinguistic media (e.g., picture stories). Comprehensible information, regardless of its media, is structured, and comprehenders differ in how skillfully they employ the cognitive processes and mechanisms that capture this structure (Gernsbacher, Varner, & Faust, 1990).

The process of shifting explains why less-skilled comprehenders have problems remembering recently comprehended information: They shift too often (Gernsbacher et al., 1990). The mechanism of suppression explains why, compared to highly skilled comprehenders, less-skilled comprehenders are less able to reject the contextually inappropriate meanings of ambiguous words (Gernsbacher et al., 1990); why they are less able to reject the incorrect forms of homophones (Gernsbacher & Faust, 1991b); why they are less able to reject typical-but-absent members of nonverbal scenes; why they are less able to ignore words written on pictures (Gernsbacher & Faust, 1991b); and why they are less able to ignore pictures surrounding words (Gernsbacher & Faust, 1991b). Less-skilled comprehenders have inefficient suppression mechanisms.

The distinction between the mechanism of suppression and the mechanism of enhancement explains why, compared to highly skilled comprehenders, less-skilled comprehenders are not less able to appreciate the contextually appropriate meanings of ambiguous words, and why they are not less able to appreciate typical members of nonverbal scenes (Gernsbacher & Faust, 1991b; Perfetti & Roth, 1981). It is less-skilled comprehenders' suppression mechanisms, not their enhancement mechanisms, that are faulty.

UNANSWERED QUESTIONS

Although the Structure Building Framework parsimoniously accounts for many comprehension phenomena, several questions remain unanswered. In this section, I briefly identify two of those questions.

Are These Cognitive Processes and Mechanisms Automatic or Are They Under Comprehenders' Conscious Control?

Some theories of cognition differentiate between automatic mental activity and mental activity that is more conscious, and, perhaps, controllable (Keele & Neill, 1978; Posner & Snyder, 1975a, 1975b). Do the three structure-building processes (i.e., foundation laying, mapping, and shifting) occur automatically or are they under comprehenders' conscious control?

I have described these processes implying both positions. For instance, I have described the process of mapping as something that comprehenders do. I have suggested previously that comprehenders develop mental structures by mapping on incoming information. This description implies that mapping is something that comprehenders actively and strategically accomplish. However, I have also described the process of mapping as something that gets done. I have suggested that "incoming information is mapped onto a developing structure when it activates similar memory nodes. The more the incoming information overlaps with the previous information, the more likely it is to activate similar memory nodes" (Gernsbacher, 1990, p. 52). This description implies that mapping is something that is accomplished automatically, perhaps mediated by some objective similarity detector.

I have also been equivocal about the other two structure-building processes (i.e., foundation laying and shifting). Do they occur automatically, or are they under comprehenders' conscious control? What about the two structure building mechanisms, suppression and enhancement? Do they occur automatically, or are they under comprehenders' control? Perhaps the three structure-building processes (i.e., foundation laying, mapping, and shifting) are under comprehenders' control, but the mechanisms that enable these processes (i.e., suppression and enhancement) occur automatically.

It also is possible that none of the structure-building processes or mechanisms is purely automatic or purely under comprehenders' control. Perhaps each is a combination of the two. For example, the process of mapping often feels conscious; indeed, in some situations, it feels effortful. In other situations, however, the process of mapping must surely occur without conscious attention (e.g., when the comprehenders are very skilled, and the information is very comprehensible).

Whether these cognitive processes and mechanisms are automatic or under comprehenders' control is an empirical question, with a theoretically and practically important answer. If any of these structure building processes or mechanisms are under comprehenders' control, they are amenable to training. For example, if highly skilled comprehenders' greater skill at suppressing irrelevant information is under their control, then this skill might be taught to less-skilled comprehenders.

In What Medium Are Mental Structures and Substructures Represented?

I also have been vague about the medium in which structures and substructures are mentally represented. Although I have empirically answered several questions about the representational *form* of mental structures and substructures (e.g., What units are packaged into substructures? How are dependencies between substructures represented? Are substructures built hierarchically?), I have avoided asking about their representational *medium*.

Given the Structure Building Framework's amodal approach, the medium of mental structures must handle nonlinguistic as well as linguistic input. This requirement demands either a theory that proposes a variety of (compatible) representational media or a theory that proposes that input modality is irrelevant (because all information is represented in a common medium). Theories that propose a variety of representational media have recently become popular.

In 1983, three new theories each proposed a three-media representation scheme. According to Anderson (1983), information is represented as linear strings, propositions, or spatial images. Language can be represented as linear strings or propositions, but not as spatial images. According to Johnson-Laird (1983, p. 165), information is represented as propositions ("strings of symbols that correspond to natural language"), mental models ("structural analogs of the world" [p. 165]), or images ("the perceptual correlates of mental models from a particular point of view" [p. 165]). According to van Dijk and Kintsch (1983), information is represented as verbatim forms, propositions, or situational models.

Johnson-Laird's (1983) and van Dijk and Kintsch's (1983) theories exemplify another direction in which theorists are moving, particularly when describing how language is represented. Several theorists have suggested that comprehenders' mental representations capture the real world situations conveyed by language. For example, according to Johnson-Laird (1983), language is often represented by *mental models*: "A mental model goes beyond the literal meaning of the discourse because it embodies inferences, instantiations, and references" (p. 245). Similarly, according to van Dijk and Kintsch (1983), language is often represented by *situational models*: "A situational model is the cognitive representation of the events, actions, persons, and in general the situation that a text is about" (pp. 11–12).

The proposal that comprehenders mentally represent the physical situations expressed by language is supported by the following phenomena. Consider Example 1:

(1) Three turtles rested on a floating log and a fish swam beneath them.

A short time after reading the sentence in Example 1, many comprehenders incorrectly accept the following sentence as the sentence they read:

(2) Three turtles rested on a floating log and a fish swam beneath it.

Sentences 1 and 2 convey similar physical situations. In the situation conveyed by 1, the fish swam beneath the turtles; in the situation conveyed by 2, the fish swam beneath the log. However, because the turtles were on the log, and the log was floating on water, the situations are similar: Swimming beneath the turtles is similar to swimming beneath the log.

In contrast, if comprehenders first read sentence 3:

(3) Three turtles rested beside a floating log and a fish swam beneath them.

they are unlikely to accept the sentence in Example 4 as the sentence they read:

(4) Three turtles rested beside a floating log and a fish swam beneath it.

The sentences 3 and 4 convey different situations: When the turtles are beside the log, swimming beneath *them* is not the same as swimming beneath *it* (Bransford & Franks, 1972).

Consider another example. Comprehenders can easily remember whether they read that:

(5) The hostess received a telegram at the furrier's.

as opposed to:

(6) The hostess received a telegram from the furrier.

In contrast, comprehenders have difficulty remembering whether they read that:

(7) The hostess bought a mink coat at the furrier's.

as opposed to:

(8) The hostess bought a mink coat from the furrier.

(Garnham, 1981). Buying a mink coat *at* the furriers is similar to buying a mink coat *from* the furrier, but receiving a telegram *at* the furriers differs from receiving a telegram *from* the furrier.

Finally, consider a story about John, who went out for a jog. Consider what happens if one group of comprehenders read:

(9) After doing a few warm-up exercises, John put on his sweatshirt and began jogging.

whereas another group of comprehenders read:

(10) After doing a few warm-up exercises, John took off his sweatshirt and began jogging.

Now, both groups read:

(11) John jogged halfway around the lake without too much difficulty.

For one group of comprehenders, John is now halfway around the lake with his sweatshirt on; for the other group, John is also halfway around the lake, but his sweatshirt is back on the other side. If both groups of comprehenders are asked whether the word *sweatshirt* occurred in the story, both groups correctly say "yes." However, those who read that John took off his sweatshirt are slower to say "yes" than are those who read that John put on his sweatshirt (Glenberg, Meyer, & Lindem, 1987). For those who read that John took off his sweatshirt (and left it on the other side of the lake), John's sweatshirt is no longer part of the current situation.

These demonstrations suggest that comprehenders develop relatively iconic representations of the physical situations conveyed by the texts. Indeed, for some theorists, envisioning the situation is tantamount to successful comprehension. For instance, according to van Dijk and Kintsch (1983), "if comprehenders are unable to imagine a situation in which certain individuals have the properties or relations indicated by the text, [they] fail to understand the text itself" (p. 337). Further, according to Bower and Morrow (1990), constructing "mental models of the situation that a writer or speaker is describing . . . is the basis of language comprehension" (p. 44).

Are the mental structures and substructures proposed by the Structure Building Framework the same as the mental models or situational models proposed by Johnson-Laird (1983) and van Dijk and Kintsch (1983)? Although I cannot answer that question here, I do know that the cognitive processes and mechanisms involved in structure building also depend on comprehenders' ability to envision real world situations. For instance, suppose that I am describing my participation in a marathon. During my description, I might say the sentence in Example 12:

(12) Half an hour later, it began to rain.

Alternatively, I might say the following:

(13) Three days later, it began to rain.

Comprehenders would map sentence 12 onto their developing structures, but they would shift in response to sentence 13 because it changes the temporal setting of my story. To appreciate this change, comprehenders must envision the real world situation; thus, the processes of mapping and shifting must depend on comprehenders' ability to envision the real world situation.

The mechanisms of suppression and enhancement must also depend on comprehenders' ability to envision real world situations. For instance, in Gernsbacher (1989), I found that after comprehenders read a pronoun, any person not referred to by that pronoun is suppressed. For instance, consider this pair of sentences:

(14) Bill lost the tennis match to John.

(15) Enjoying the victory, he walked slowly toward the showers.

After comprehenders read the pronoun *he* in sentence 15, *Bill* is suppressed. Now, consider the following sentences:

(16) Bill lost the tennis match to John.

(17) Accepting the defeat, he walked slowly toward the showers.

After comprehenders read the pronoun *he* in the sentence in Example 17, *John* is suppressed. Suppression of *Bill* following the sentence in 15 requires envisioning what happens when someone loses a tennis match; that is, who enjoys the victory? Similarly, suppressing *John* following the sentence in Example 17 requires envisioning what happens when someone loses a tennis match; who accepts the defeat?

These data suggest that comprehenders' success at building mental structures depends on their ability to envision real world situations. Whether these mental structures are represented by situation models, or whether mental structures are the same as situational models is unclear.

SIMILARITY TO OTHER APPROACHES

The processes and mechanisms identified by the Structure Building Framework are in some ways similar to processes and mechanisms proposed by other approaches. In this section of the chapter, I identify a few of the commonalities and differences between the Structure Building Framework and other models of cognitive processes and mechanisms in language comprehension.[2]

The Structure Building Framework's "process of laying a foundation" resembles MacWhinney's (1977) proposal that speakers and listeners use starting points. MacWhinney (1977) wrote:

---

[2]In this section, I purposely quote extensively from the original sources. My motivation is not laziness, but the belief that paraphrase is best reserved for investigating subjects' memory in laboratory experiments.

> The speaker uses the first element in the English sentence as a starting point for the organization of the sentence as a whole. Similarly, the listener uses the first element in a sentence as a starting point in comprehension. Both the speaker and the listener seem to use special techniques for attaching the body of the sentence to the starting point. Given the sentence *Mary ate the apple*, it seems that listeners take *Mary* as an initial node in processing, and then attach *ate the apple* to this node. Similarly, the speaker takes *Mary* as what he wants to talk about and then says something about *Mary*. (p. 152)

MacWhinney's starting points are like the Structure Building Framework's foundations. MacWhinney's process of "attaching the body of the sentence to the starting point" is like the structure building process of mapping information onto a foundation.

Would MacWhinney agree that starting points organize units larger than sentences, for instance, paragraphs in which the first sentence is the starting point for the other sentences? Would he agree that starting points are used outside the linguistic domain? Neither suggestion contradicts his proposal; his proposal is simply more constrained. In contrast, the Structure Building Framework explicitly proposes that the cognitive process of laying a foundation occurs whenever comprehenders are building mental structures, regardless of whether the units are clauses, sentences, story episodes, and regardless of modality.

The Structure Building Framework's *process of mapping* resembles a process that Hayes-Roth and Thorndyke (1979) call *integration*:

> We assume that the basic units for representing facts in memory are lexical. The meanings of lexical units derive from their associative connections to other lexical units. Semantically related lexical units are presumably more closely associated than unrelated lexical units. These assumptions imply that memory representations of facts that include identical wordings can include identical subrepresentations. Memory representations of facts that include paraphrased wordings cannot contain identical subrepresentations but may contain associatively connected subrepresentations. Of course, memory representations of facts that express unrelated information will have neither identical subrepresentations nor close associative connections.
>
> Memory representations can be "activated" in two ways. They can be activated directly, by apprehension of the information they represent in an external stimulus. They can also be activated associatively via excitation received from other activated memory representations. A memory representation can be activated more easily if (a) it has been activated recently; (b) it contains a subrepresentation of information in an external stimulus; or (c) it contains a subrepresentation that is identical to one in an activated memory representation. A memory representation is more difficult to activate if (a) it has not been activated recently; (b) it contains a subrepresentation of information that is synonymous with an external stimulus; or (c) it contains a subrepresentation that is associatively connected to one in an activated memory representation. Of course, a memory representation is least

> likely to be activated if the information it represents is unrelated to any information in an external stimulus or an activated memory representation.
>
> We assume that when two memory representations are simultaneously active and contain identical or associatively connected subrepresentations, the two representations are integrated into a single higher-order representation. In the case of identical subrepresentations, integration effectively "superimposes" the two representations upon one another so that they share a single subrepresentation. Thus, integration eliminates redundancy in memory for related facts. However, the integrated representation also preserves the identities of the original constituent representations. In the case of associatively connected subrepresentations, integration establishes a direct connection between the subrepresentations, reflecting the semantic relationship between them but preserving their individual identities. (pp. 92–93)

As in the Structure Building Framework's process of mapping, Hayes-Roth and Thorndyke's (1979) process of integration is affected by activation. Also, as is the case for Structure Building Framework's process of mapping, Hayes-Roth and Thorndyke's (1979) process of integration is affected by coherence.

In Hayes-Roth and Thorndyke's (1979) terminology, the greater the similarity between two representations (in terms of their content and their level of activation), the more likely they are to be integrated into a single, higher order representation. In the Structure Building Framework's terminology, the greater the similarity between incoming and previous information, the more likely they are to be mapped onto the same substructure.

The Structure Building Framework's process of mapping also resembles Hayes-Roth and Thorndyke's (1979) process of integration because in neither process is information recoded. Mapping (during structure building) simply connects information; it does not change it. Similarly, Hayes-Roth and Thorndyke's (1979) integration only "establishes a direct connection between the subrepresentation, reflecting [their] semantic relationship . . . but preserving their individual identities" (p. 93).

But Hayes-Roth and Thorndyke's (1979) process of integration differs from the Structure Building Framework's process of mapping in at least two ways. First, according to the Structure Building Framework, the building blocks of mental structures are memory nodes. Memory nodes can represent the meanings of words, the meanings of pictures, the "meanings" of tones, or any other meaningful unit. In contrast, the building blocks in Hayes-Roth and Thorndyke's model represent only the meanings of words.

The second way in which Hayes-Roth and Thorndyke's (1979) process of integration differs from the Structure Building Framework's process of mapping is that Hayes-Roth and Thorndyke's process of integration is driven primarily by lexical overlap and secondarily by semantic association. But coherence is not just a function of lexical overlap and semantic associations. Consider sentence pair 18 and 19:

(18) A waitress was counting her tips.

(19) A waitress was daydreaming about getting off early.

and the pair of sentences in 20 and 21:

(20) The waitress was counting her tips.

(21) The waitress was daydreaming about getting off early.

The sentences in 18 and 19 imply two waitresses, whereas the sentences in 20 and 21 imply only one. Thus, the sentences in Examples 20 and 21 are more referentially coherent than are the sentences in Examples 18 and 19. But the two sets of sentence pairs are equal in their lexical overlap and semantic association.[3]

The Structure Building Framework's *mechanism of suppression* resembles Neill and Westberry's (1987) conception of *selective inhibition*. They wrote:

> . . . the activation of information in memory must be followed by a process of narrowing down the range of activations to those specifically appropriate to current task demands. It has been suggested that this focusing process is accomplished through the direct, selective inhibition of distracting information. (p. 331)

As does the Structure Building Framework's mechanism of suppression, Neill and Westberry's (1987) selective inhibition actively dampens previously activated information. This active characteristic is critical; it differentiates selective inhibition from other conceptions of inhibition. Neill and Westberry (1987) wrote:

> Selective inhibition differs operationally and theoretically from other forms of inhibition . . . For example, Posner and Snyder (1975a, 1975b) refer to "inhibition" of processing unattended signals caused by the commitment of processing capacity to an attended signal (see also Neely, 1976, 1977). Inhibition here is *de facto* and nonselective, and it does not reflect an operation on specific unattended information (Posner, 1982). Other proposed forms of nonselective inhibition, such as attenuation of all unattended information (Treisman, 1964), or *dampening* of spreading activation (Anderson, 1976) also do not predict a specific bias against more recently activated information. Similarly, models based on an automatic *lateral inhibition* between cognitive or perceptual units (e.g., Brown, 1979; Estes, 1972; McClelland & Rumelhart, 1981; Walley & Weiden, 1973) do not make this prediction; because degree of inhibition would be directly determined by proximity (similarity) between activated units, more recently activated units should remain relatively more activated if such proximity is equated. (p. 327)

---

[3]The inadequacy of a criterion for coherence based only on lexical overlap also is demonstrated in the sentences in Examples 12 and 13. Those two sentences are equivalent in how much they overlap with the prior context, but one sentence leads to mapping, whereas the other leads to shifting.

As does Neill and Westberry's (1987) selective inhibition, the Structure Building Framework's mechanism of suppression also differs from the automatic loss of activation caused by attention to other information, global attenuation of unattended information, or lateral inhibition. However, the Structure Building Framework's mechanism of suppression differs from Neill and Westberry's (1987) selective inhibition in at least two ways. First, Neill and Westberry (1987) proposed that selective inhibition is always under conscious control. The Structure Building Framework does not make that assumption. Second, Neill and Westberry (1987) proposed that "suppression of irrelevant information requires conscious awareness of what is relevant" (p. 332). In this way, Neill and Westberry's (1987) selective inhibition mechanism is similar to the inhibition mechanisms proposed by Marcel (1980, 1983) and Allport, Tipper, and Chmiel (1985).

Is the Structure Building Framework's mechanism of suppression triggered only by comprehenders' conscious awareness of what is relevant? It does not seem to be. For instance, as I described in Gernsbacher and Faust (1991a), one of the vital roles that the mechanism of suppression plays in comprehension is that it dampens the activation of the contextually inappropriate meanings of ambiguous words (e.g., the playing card meaning of *spade* in the context *He dug in the garden with a spade*). If the mechanism of suppression is triggered by a conscious awareness of what is relevant, comprehenders' awareness of the contextually relevant meanings of ambiguous words would predict their ability to suppress the contextually irrelevant meanings. But that is not the case.

As described in Gernsbacher and Faust (1991b), less-skilled comprehenders are just as able as more-skilled comprehenders to consciously select the appropriate meaning of an ambiguous word (e.g., they are just as able to accept the *garden tool* meaning of *spade* as appropriate in the context *He dug in the garden with a spade*). However, less-skilled comprehenders are considerably less able to suppress the inappropriate meanings of an ambiguous word (e.g., they are less able to reject the *playing card* meaning of *spade* as inappropriate in the context *He dug in the garden with a spade*). These data demonstrate that although less-skilled comprehenders are aware of what is relevant, they are less able to suppress what is irrelevant. Therefore, the mechanism of suppression must be independent of comprehenders' conscious awareness of what is relevant.

The Structure Building Framework's *mechanism of enhancement* resembles the process of integration in Kintsch's (1988) Construction-Integration Model. In Kintsch's (1988) model, two processes build mental representations during language comprehension: The process of *construction* builds a propositional network (a textbase), and the process of *integration* edits that network. Kintsch (1988) described these two processes in the following way:

> The steps in constructing a textbase according to the construction-integration model involve: (a) forming the concepts and propositions directly corresponding to the linguistic input; (b) elaborating each of these elements by selecting a small number of its most closely associated neighbors from the general knowledge net;

> (c) inferring certain additional propositions; and (d) assigning connection strengths to all pairs of elements that have been created. (p. 166)
>
> The result of the construction process is, therefore, a network expressible as a connectivity matrix, consisting of all the lexical nodes accessed, all the propositions that have been formed, plus all the inferences that were made at both the local and global level and their interconnections. (p. 168)
>
> The network that has been constructed so far is not yet a suitable text representation. It was carelessly constructed and is therefore incoherent and inconsistent. At all levels of the representation, components associated with the text elements were included without regard to the discourse context, and many of them are inappropriate. An integration process in the connectionist manner can be used to exclude these unwanted elements from the text representation (e.g., see Rumelhart & McClelland, 1986, and Waltz & Pollack, 1985, for discourse).
>
> Text comprehension is assumed to be organized in cycles, roughly corresponding to short sentences or phrases (for further detail, see Kintsch & van Dijk, 1978; Miller & Kintsch, 1980). In each cycle a new net is constructed, including whatever is carried over in the short-term buffer from the previous cycle. Once the net is constructed, the integration process takes over: Activation is spread around until the system stabilizes. More specific, an activation vector representing the initial activation values of all nodes in the net is postmultiplied repeatedly with the connectivity matrix. After each multiplication the activation values are normalized: Negative values are set to zero, and each of the positive activation values is divided by the sum of all activation values, so that the total activation on each cycle remains at a value of one (e.g., Rumelhart & McClelland, 1986). Usually, the system finds a stable state fairly rapidly; if the integration process fails, however, new constructions are added to the net, and integration is attempted again. Thus, there is a basic, automatic construction-plus-integration process that normally is sufficient for comprehension.
>
> The result of the integration process is a new activation vector, indicating high activation values for some of the nodes in the net and low or zero values for many others. The highly activated nodes constitute the discourse representation formed on each processing cycle. In principle, it includes information at many levels: Lexical nodes, text propositions, knowledge-based elaborations (i.e., various types of inferences), as well as macropropositions. (p. 168)

As does the Structure Building Framework mechanism of enhancement, Kintsch's (1988) process of integration increases the activation of contextually relevant information. Moreover, the Structure Building Framework's mechanism of enhancement is similar to Kintsch's process of integration in that each operates after concepts have been initially activated.

In this way, both Kintsch's (1988) process of integration and the Structure Building Framework's mechanism of enhancement differ from "facilitation of activation" (Posner & Snyder, 1975b). Further, in this way, Kintsch's (1988) process of integration and the Structure Building Framework's mechanism of enhancement resemble the chemical transmission of neural information via neurotransmitters (which also occurs after initial activation) rather than the electrical transmission of neural information (which causes initial activation).

However, Kintsch's (1988) process of integration differs from the Structure Building Framework's mechanism of enhancement in at least two ways. First, Kintsch assumes that the process of integration is completed in cycles, but the Structure Building Framework does not assume that suppression signals are transmitted in cycles. Second, Kintsch's (1988) process of integration operates automatically, but (as mentioned previously) it is unclear whether the mechanism of enhancement operates automatically.

Finally, the Structure Building Framework's overall thesis that language depends on general cognitive processes and mechanisms resembles Bever's (1970) thesis. For instance, Bever began his classic (1970) paper, "The Cognitive Basis for Linguistic Structures" by writing:

> This article explores the ways in which specific properties of language structure and speech behavior reflect certain general cognitive laws. [It] begins an exploration of an alternative approach to the study of language: as a conceptual and communicative system which recruits various kinds of human behavior, but which is not exhaustively manifested in any particular form of language behavior. (p. 279)

The Structure Building Framework differs in several ways from Bever's (1970) thesis; one primary difference being breadth. Bever's thesis argues only for commonality among language behaviors (production, acquisition, comprehension). The Structure Building Framework suggests that there exist commonalities among behaviors that are not bound by language.

WHY DESCRIBE LANGUAGE COMPREHENSION AT A GENERAL LEVEL?

According to the Structure Building Framework, language comprehension is not a specialized skill driven by language-specific processes and language-specific mechanisms. Rather, the Structure Building Framework describes language comprehension as driven by general cognitive processes and general cognitive mechanisms, processes and mechanisms that are involved in nonlinguistic tasks.

Is this level of description too general? As B. Repp (personal communication, March 12, 1990) asked:

> Are the processes and mechanisms so general as to be applicable to any subject matter, be it cognition, social behavior, biological processes, evolution, or physics? A similar argument is often made in the area of speech perception research. By showing that certain general processes operate in speech perception, some believe they have shown that no speech-specific processes are required to explain speech

> perception. This does not follow, of course. To show that no speech-specific processes exist, all processes involved must be shown to be general. Quite apart from the fact that we shall never know all the processes, there is soon a point where knowledge specific to the subject matter begins to play a role in perception or cognition. On the other hand, has anyone ever claimed that speech perception is accomplished only via specific processes, and that there are no general processes at all?
>
> There are perhaps some exceptions, such as the "modular" systems for echolocation, stereopsis, and so forth. The division between modular and other systems may simply be that we are beginning to understand the neural architecture of the former, but not of the latter. Knowing the physiological mechanisms, we do not have to think about what those mechanisms might be. As soon as we psychologists need to engage our own cognitive faculties to make conjectures about processes, our limited inventory of general concepts (with a heavy dose of computer jargon) prescribes what those processes are going to be and insures their generality. We cannot think differently when we investigate language than when we investigate music or problem solving, and therefore the same general concepts will surface as hypothetical processes everywhere.

Why not focus on those aspects of language that distinguish it from everything else (B. Repp, personal communication, March 12, 1990)? By focusing on those aspects of comprehension that are specific to language, we might identify the limits of a general framework like structure building. In lieu of doing that, however, let me turn the tables and use the last section of this chapter to answer the question: What is gained by describing language comprehension at a general level?

Describing language comprehension at a general level saves me from committing five deadly sins, which according to Reber (1987, as cited in Gernsbacher, 1990) caused "the rapid rise and (surprisingly rapid) fall of psycholinguistics." In his essay bearing that title, Reber identifies these five transgressions:

> 1. *Believing in a Strong Version of Nativism.* Nativism is a position that is simply not conducive to the promotion of an empirical research program. Nativism, especially when blended with rationalism, looks for data in intuitions, introspections, and phenomenological experience; it does not encourage the kinds of research programs that experimental psychologists have typically felt comfortable with (p. 329). Moreover, nativism, almost by definition, down plays learning. In the Chomskyan form of psycholinguistics, . . . all the interesting questions that psychologists asked about acquisition were recast into questions about the "growth of organs." This is not the kind of notion that sits comfortably with psychologist. . . . And of course it becomes all the more difficult to accept when the psychologist is being told that the linguistic underpinning of psycholinguistics is actually a branch of cognitive psychology (p. 330).
>
> 2. *Isolating Psycholinguistics From Psychology.* The Chomsky-inspired psycholinguistics views language as the ultimate unique behavior for it is conceptualized as

doubly isolated from other psychological processes. Not only is language viewed as unique *to* man, but is also viewed as unique *within* man. The resulting psycholinguistic science becomes one in which it is presumed that nothing about language can be learned by the examination of any other cognitive or perceptual process—and vice versa. This is a very touchy point. Notice what it asks of a cognitive psychologist with an interest in language. It argues that linguistics and psycholinguistics, disciplines which have been put forward as properly within the umbrella of cognitive psychology, will, in the final analysis, only be admitted in a *sealed* box (p. 331).

3. *Preferring Theory Over Data.* The psychology of this century has been strongly in the data camp. Theory is not its long suit and whenever things start getting sticky psychologists will prefer empirical examination of phenomena to models of them (p. 332). [P]sycholinguistics was a good deal more linguistic than it was psychological and, given the tilt taken by the two contributing fields during the past two decades, it became a discipline whose prejudice was toward theory rather than data. [T]rying to fit such a field into the larger discipline of psychology—which not only did not share this prejudice but had a long history of battling against it—has not worked (p. 333).

4. *Relying on Linguistic Theories.* This problem was placed sharply in the attentional focus by the labored confusion in the study of sentence memory immediately following the publication of *Aspects of a Theory of Syntax* by Chomsky in 1965 (cited in Gernsbacher, 1990). In the preceding years, a number of studies had been published, primarily by George Miller and his co-workers, that seemed to show that people process sentential material in the fashion predicted by Chomsky's earlier model of language. Few of us around at the time can forget those marvelous graphs showing how the more transformations there were underlying a sentence the longer it took a subject to process it and the more errors the subject would typically make when trying to recall it. . . . *Aspects*, of course, pulled the rug out from under the new psycholinguists, as Miller was calling these frontier scientists. All of these transformations turned out not to be optional rules applied to terminal strings but parts of the deep structure tree. To this day many of us have wondered what to do with all that lovely data (pp. 333–334).

5. *Ignoring Functionalism.* Actually, within experimental psychology functionalism represents a loose confederation of attitudes more than anything else. It is not a theory of the organism nor is it a set of dictates or tenets. Rather, it is an approach to the examination of things psychological that is so much a part of the field that its existence is hardly noticed (p. 335). Adherence [to a functionalist perspective] simply means that one looks to the functional role that a given process or specific pattern of behavior has in the context within which it occurs (p. 336). The failure of [the Chomsky-inspired psycholinguistic] science to reckon with the deeply ingrained functionalist spirit is arguably the single most significant factor in its failure to establish itself as a robust science within psychology (p. 337).

What do I gain by describing language comprehension using the Structure Building Framework as a guide? I am not forced to accept nativism; isolate the psychology of language from the remainder of psychology; honor theory over data; depend on linguistic theory; or ignore functionalism. Instead, by describing language comprehension as structure building, I hope to map the study of language comprehension onto the firm foundation of cognitive psychology.

ACKNOWLEDGMENTS

The research reviewed in this chapter was supported by grants from the National Institutes of Health (RO1 NS 29926 and K04 NS 01376) and the Air Force Office of Sponsored Research (AFOSR 0258). Preparation of this chapter was supported by a grant from the Army Research Institute, DASW01-94-K-0004.

REFERENCES

Aaronson, D., & Ferres, S. (1983). Lexical categories and reading tasks. *Journal of Experimental Psychology: Human Perception and Performance, 9*, 675–699.

Aaronson, D., & Scarborough, H. S. (1976). Performance theories for sentence coding: Some quantitative evidence. *Journal of Experimental Psychology: Human Perception and Performance, 2*, 56–70.

Allport, D. A., Tipper, S. P., & Chmiel, N. R. J. (1985). Perceptual integration and postcategorical filtering. In M. I. Posner & O. S. M. Marin (Eds.), *Attention and performance XI* (pp. 107–132). Hillsdale, NJ: Lawrence Erlbaum Associates.

Anderson, A., Garrod, S. C., & Sanford, A. J. (1983). The accessibility of pronominal antecedents as a function of episode shifts in narrative text. *Quarterly Journal of Experimental Psychology, 35A*, 427–440.

Anderson, J. R. (1976). *Language, memory, and thought.* Hillsdale, NJ: Lawrence Erlbaum Associates.

Anderson, J. R. (1983). *The architecture of cognition.* Cambridge, MA: Harvard University Press.

Anderson, J. R., & Bower, G. H. (1973). *Human associative memory.* Washington, DC: Winston.

Beeman, M., & Gernsbacher, M. A. (1994). *Structure building and coherence inferencing during comprehension.* Unpublished manuscript, University of Wisconsin.

Begg, I., & Paivio, A. (1969). Concreteness and imagery in sentence meaning. *Journal of Verbal Learning and Verbal Behavior, 8*, 821–827.

Bever, T. G. (1970). The cognitive basis for linguistic structures. In J. R. Hayes (Ed.), *Cognition and the development of language* (pp. 279–362). New York: Wiley.

Black, J. B., Turner, T. J., & Bower, G. H. (1979). Point of view in narrative comprehension, memory, and production. *Journal of Verbal Learning and Verbal Behavior, 18*, 187–198.

Bock, J. K., & Irwin, D. E. (1980). Syntactic effects of information availability in sentence production. *Journal of Verbal Learning and Verbal Behavior, 19*, 467–484.

Bower, G. H., & Morrow, D. G. (1990, January). Mental models in narrative comprehension. *Science*, 44–48.

Bransford, J. D., & Franks, J. J. (1972). The abstraction of linguistic ideas: A review. *Cognition, 1*, 211–249.

Brown, A. S. (1979). Priming effects in semantic memory retrieval processes. *Journal of Experimental Psychology: Human Learning and Memory, 5*, 65–77.

Carreiras, M., Gernsbacher, M. A., & Villa, V. (in press). The advantage of first mention in Spanish. *Psychonomic Bulletin and Review.*

Clark, H. H., & Sengul, C. J. (1979). In search of referents for nouns and pronouns. *Memory & Cognition, 7*, 35–41.

Clements, P. (1979). The effects of staging on recall from prose. In R. O. Freedle (Ed.), *New directions in discourse processing* (pp. 287–330). Norwood, NJ: Ablex.

Clifton, C., Jr., & Ferreira, F. (1987). Discourse structure and anaphora: Some experimental results. In M. Coltheart (Ed.), *Attention and performance XII* (pp. 635–654). Hillsdale, NJ: Lawrence Erlbaum Associates.

Deaton, J. A., & Gernsbacher, M. A. (in press). Causal conjunctions and implicit causality cue mapping in sentence comprehension. *Journal of Memory and Language.*

Duffy, S. A., Shinjo, M., & Myers, J. L. (1990). The effects of encoding task on sentence pairs varying in causal relatedness. *Journal of Memory and Language, 29*, 27–42.

Estes, W. K. (1972). Interactions of signal and background variables in visual processing. *Perception and Psychophysics, 12*, 278–286.

Fletcher, C. R. (1984). Markedness and topic continuity in discourse processing. *Journal of Verbal Learning and Verbal Behavior, 23*, 487–493.

Foss, D. J. (1969). Decision processes during sentence comprehension: Effects of lexical item difficulty and position upon decision times. *Journal of Verbal Learning and Verbal Behavior, 8*, 457–462.

Foss, D. J. (1982). A discourse on semantic priming. *Cognitive Psychology, 14*, 590–607.

Foss, D. J., & Lynch, R. H., Jr. (1969). Decision processes during sentence comprehension: Effects of surface structure on decision times. *Perception & Psychophysics, 5*, 145–148.

Frazier, L., Taft, L., Roeper, T., Clifton, C., & Ehrlich, K. (1984). Parallel structure: A source of facilitation in sentence comprehension. *Memory & Cognition, 12*, 421–430.

Garnham, A. (1981). Mental models as representations of text. *Memory & Cognition, 9*, 560–565.

Gernsbacher, M. A. (1983). *Memory for the orientation of pictures in nonverbal stories: Parallels and insights into language processing.* Unpublished doctoral dissertation, University of Texas at Austin.

Gernsbacher, M. A. (1985). Surface information loss in comprehension. *Cognitive Psychology, 17*, 324–363.

Gernsbacher, M. A. (1989). Mechanisms that improve referential access. *Cognition, 32*, 99–156.

Gernsbacher, M. A. (1990). *Language comprehension as structure building.* Hillsdale, NJ: Lawrence Erlbaum Associates.

Gernsbacher, M. A., & Faust, M. (1991a). The role of suppression in sentence comprehension. In G. B. Simpson (Ed.), *Comprehending word and sentence* (pp. 97–128). Amsterdam: North Holland.

Gernsbacher, M. A., & Faust, M. E. (1991b). The mechanism of suppression: A component of general comprehension skill. *Journal of Experimental Psychology: Learning, Memory and Cognition, 17*, 245–262.

Gernsbacher, M. A., & Hargreaves, D. (1988). Accessing sentence participants: The advantage of first mention. *Journal of Memory and Language, 27*, 699–717.

Gernsbacher, M. A., & Hargreaves, D. (1992). The privilege of primacy: Experimental data and cognitive explanations. In D. L. Payne (Ed.), *Pragmatics of word order flexibility* (pp. 83–116). Philadelphia: John Benjamins Publishing Company.

Gernsbacher, M. A., Hargreaves, D., & Beeman, M. (1989). Building and accessing clausal representations: The advantage of first mention versus the advantage of clause recency. *Journal of Memory and Language, 28*, 735–755.

Gernsbacher, M. A., & Jescheniak, J. D. (in press). Cataphoric devices in spoken discourse. *Cognitive Psychology.*

Gernsbacher, M. A., & Robertson, R. R. W. (1994). *The definite article "the" facilitates mapping in story comprehension.* Manuscript submitted for publication.

Gernsbacher, M. A., & Shroyer, S. (1989). The cataphoric use of the indefinite *this* in spoken narratives. *Memory & Cognition, 17,* 536–540.

Gernsbacher, M. A., Varner, K. R., & Faust, M. (1990). Investigating differences in general comprehension skill. *Journal of Experimental Psychology: Learning, Memory, and Cognition, 16,* 430–445.

Givón, T. (1983). *Topic continuity in discourse: A quantitative cross-language study.* Amsterdam: Benjamins.

Glenberg, A., Meyer, M., & Lindem, K. (1987). Mental models contribute to foregrounding during text comprehension. *Journal of Memory and Language, 26,* 69–83.

Haberlandt, K. (1984). Components of sentence and word reading times. In D. E. Kieras & M. A. Just (Eds.), *New methods in reading comprehension research* (pp. 219–252). Hillsdale, NJ: Lawrence Erlbaum Associates.

Haviland, S. E., & Clark, H. H. (1974). What's new? Acquiring new information as a process in comprehension. *Journal of Verbal Learning and Verbal Behavior, 13,* 512–521.

Hayes-Roth, B., & Thorndyke, P. W. (1979). Integration of knowledge from text. *Journal of Verbal Learning and Verbal Behavior, 18,* 91–108.

Johnson-Laird, P. N. (1983). *Mental models.* Cambridge, MA: Harvard University Press.

Keele, S. W., & Neill, W. T. (1978). Mechanisms of attention. In E. C. Carterette & M. P. Friedman (Eds.), *Handbook of perception* (pp. 3–47). New York: Academic Press.

Keenan, J. M., Baillet, S. D., & Brown, P. (1984). The effects of causal cohesion on comprehension and memory. *Journal of Verbal Learning and Verbal Behavior, 23,* 115–126.

Kieras, D. E. (1978). Good and bad structure in simple paragraphs: Effects on apparent theme, reading time, and recall. *Journal of Verbal Learning and Verbal Behavior, 17,* 13–28.

Kieras, D. E. (1981). Component processes in the comprehension of simple prose. *Journal of Verbal Learning and Verbal Behavior, 20,* 1–23.

Kintsch, W. (1988). The role of knowledge in discourse comprehension: A construction-integration model. *Psychological Review, 95,* 163–182.

Kintsch, W., & van Dijk, T. A. (1978). Toward a model of discourse comprehension and production. *Psychological Review, 85,* 363–394.

MacWhinney, B. (1977). Starting points. *Language, 53,* 152–168.

Mandler, J. M., & Goodman, M. S. (1982). On the psychological validity of story structure. *Journal of Verbal Learning and Verbal Behavior, 21,* 507–523.

Marcel, A. J. (1980). Conscious and preconscious recognition of polysemous words: Locating the selective effects of prior verbal context. In R. S. Nickerson (Ed.), *Attention and performance VIII* (pp. 435–457). Hillsdale, NJ: Lawrence Erlbaum Associates.

Marcel, A. J. (1983). Conscious and unconscious perception: Experiments on visual masking and word recognition. *Cognitive Psychology, 15,* 197–237.

McClelland, J. L., & Rumelhart, D. E. (1981). An interactive activation model of context effects in letter perception: Part 1. An account of basic findings. *Psychological Review, 88,* 375–407.

Miller, J. R., & Kintsch, W. (1980). Readability and recall of short prose passages: A theoretical analysis. *Journal of Experimental Psychology: Human Learning and Memory, 6,* 335–354.

Myers, J. L., Shinjo, M., & Duffy, S. (1987). Degree of causal relatedness and memory. *Journal of Memory and Language, 26,* 453–465.

Neely, J. H. (1976). Semantic priming and retrieval from lexical memory: Evidence for facilitatory and inhibitory processes. *Memory and Cognition, 4,* 648–654.

Neely, J. H. (1977). Semantic priming and retrieval from lexical memory: Roles of inhibitionless spreading activation and limited capacity attention. *Journal of Experimental Psychology: General, 106,* 226–254.

Neill, W. T., & Westberry, R. L. (1987). Selective attention and the suppression of cognitive noise. *Journal of Experimental Psychology: Learning, Memory, and Cognition, 13,* 327–334.

Olson, G. M., Duffy, S. A., & Mack, R. L. (1984). Thinking-out-loud as a method for studying real-time comprehension processes. In D. E. Kieras & M. A. Just (Eds.), *New methods in reading comprehension research* (pp. 253–286). Hillsdale, NJ: Lawrence Erlbaum Associates.

Perfetti, C. A., & Roth, S. (1981). Some of the interactive processes in reading and their role in reading skill. In A. M. Lesgold & C. A. Perfetti (Eds.), *Interactive processes in reading* (pp. 269–297). Hillsdale, NJ: Lawrence Erlbaum Associates.

Peterson, R. G., & McIntyre, C. W. (1973). The influence of semantic "relatedness" on linguistic information and retention. *American Journal of Psychology, 86*, 697–706.

Pezdek, K., & Royer, J. M. (1974). The role of comprehension in learning concrete and abstract sentences. *Journal of Verbal Learning and Verbal Behavior, 13*, 551–558.

Posner, M. I. (1982). Cumulative development of attention theory. *American Psychologist, 37*, 168–179.

Posner, M. I., & Snyder, C. R. R. (1975a). Attention and cognitive control. In R. L. Solso (Ed.), *Information processing and cognition: The Loyola symposium* (pp. 55–85). Hillsdale, NJ: Lawrence Erlbaum Associates.

Posner, M. I., & Snyder, C. R. R. (1975b). Facilitation and inhibition in the processing of signals. In P. M. A. Rabbitt & S. Dornic (Eds.), *Attention and performance V* (pp. 669–682). New York: Academic Press.

Reber, A. S. (1987). The rise and (surprisingly rapid) fall of psycholinguistics. *Synthese, 72*, 325–339.

Rumelhart, D. E., & McClelland, J. L. (1986). *Parallel distributed processing. Explorations in the microstructure of cognition: Vol. 1. Foundations.* Cambridge, MA: MIT Press.

Sachs, J. S. (1967). Recognition memory for syntactic and semantic aspects of connected discourse. *Perception & Psychophysics, 2*, 437–442.

Sachs, J. S. (1974). Memory in reading and listening to discourse. *Memory & Cognition, 2*, 95–100.

Swinney, D. A. (1979). Lexical access during sentence comprehension: (Re)consideration of context effects. *Journal of Verbal Learning and Verbal Behavior, 18*, 645–659.

Treisman, A. M. (1964). The effect of irrelevant material on the efficiency of selective listening. *American Journal of Psychology, 77*, 533–546.

Turner, E. A., & Rommetveit, R. (1968). Focus of attention in recall of active and passive sentences. *Journal of Verbal Learning and Verbal Behavior, 7*, 543–548.

van Dijk, T., & Kintsch, W. (1983). *Strategies of discourse comprehension.* New York: Academic Press.

Walley, R. E., & Weiden, T. D. (1973). Lateral inhibition and cognitive masking: A neuropsychological theory of attention. *Psychological Review, 80*, 284–302.

Waltz, D. L., & Pollack, J. B. (1985). Massively parallel parsing: A strongly interactive model of natural language interpretation. *Cognitive Science, 9*, 51–74.

CHAPTER

12

THE MENTAL MODELS THEORY OF LANGUAGE COMPREHENSION

Alan Garnham
Jane Oakhill
University of Sussex

> *Sentences are not viewed as linguistic objects to be remembered. Instead they are viewed as information which [participants] can use to construct semantic descriptions of situations. These constructed descriptions may contain more information than is represented in the linguistic inputs.*
>
> —Bransford, Barclay, and Franks (1972, p. 194)

Imagine reading a newspaper report about the events that took place in Manhattan on February 26, 1993, when the World Trade Center was bombed. The point of reading the report would be to find out about those events. The report would be based, though perhaps at some distance, on the firsthand accounts of people who witnessed the events directly. From a psychological point of view, the reader of such a report, in extracting information from it, would be aiming to create in his or her own mind a mental representation of those events. That representation would not be as rich as those of the firsthand witnesses, but it probably would be less fragmented. Language is the medium by which the information about the events would be transmitted. Indeed, without language this information could not be transmitted in such detailed form. Nevertheless, such a newspaper report would convey information about a series of events, not information about language.

This much, one might say, is common sense. However, it is common sense that was lost on cognitive psychologists in the 1970s who spoke of propositional representations and semantic representations. In thinking about language processing, these cognitive psychologists singularly failed to engage in what David

Marr (1982) called *task analysis* and, hence, they failed to develop a *computational theory* of what happens when people understand texts, and why. What we referred to as common sense is an, admittedly sketchy, task analysis of text comprehension. More precisely, it is a task analysis of the comprehension of a factual text about events in the world by a reader who wants to find out about those events. Modifications are needed for other types of text, such as fictional texts, texts about abstract matters, and so on, and for readers with other goals (e.g., discourse analysts). Moreover, we have said nothing about the broader "why" question of the computational theory: Why do people want to find out about faraway events or read novels or chapters about theories of text comprehension? The answers are numerous and varied, and there is no need to answer them to present a theory of what people do when they understand texts. Marr was able to provide a (slightly) more satisfactory answer to the why question in vision: Why do animals (particularly humans) rapidly construct a three-dimensional representation of the world around them? His answer was that they are "building a description of the shapes and positions of things from images" (p. 36). However, the impact of this answer on the form of his theory was minimal.

In Marr's (1982) account of low-level vision, several representations intervened between the grey-level representation of the image and the final three-dimensional model representation of the scene. Thus, we do not exclude the possibility that something we might want to call a propositional representation, or something we might want to call a semantic representation, is constructed in the course of text comprehension. However, we do claim that it is not the reader's purpose to construct such representations; instead that purpose is to construct a mental representation of what the text is about: a sequence of events, a place, a psycholinguistic theory, and so on. We call these representations *mental models*. Their nature is, to some extent, an empirical matter, just as it is an empirical matter how three-dimensional objects in the world are represented.

BRANSFORD'S THREE IDEAS ABOUT TEXT COMPREHENSION

Around 1970, John Bransford (e.g., Bransford & Franks, 1971; Bransford, Barclay, & Franks, 1972) put forward a set of interrelated ideas about text comprehension. These ideas were, in large part, a reaction to the syntax-based theories that had been popular in the 1960s. We now know that some of Bransford's ideas were wrong. For example, on the basis of memory experiments, he overestimated the amount of (elaborative) inferencing that people engage in as they read texts, as opposed to afterwards, when they are asked questions. Nevertheless, three of Bransford's central ideas remain at the heart of our mental models theory.

The first of these ideas was that the mental representation of a text does not correspond to any of its linguistic representations. We use syntactic and compositional semantic rules to work out the meaning of the phrases and clauses of a text (though see the subsequent discussion for some caveats). However, we do not typically retain detailed syntactic or semantic representations of what we hear or read. In most cases, detailed information about the form of a text disappears rapidly although we can commit it to memory (with difficulty) if we have been asked to do so by an experimenter, or if we want to do so for some other reason, such as learning a part in a play. We also can remember the wording of a text if it contributes to the text's meaning, as it might in the case of a joke. However, even in this latter case memory may be partly or wholly reconstructive; changing the wording of a joke, even in some cases the substitution of one synonymous word for another, can destroy its point. Similarly, in remembering a poem it may be possible to reconstruct which of two synonyms has been used, using the rhyme, scansion, or alliteration.

Bransford's second idea was that comprehension is an *integrative process*. Syntactically based theories of comprehension inevitably focus on individual sentences. Indeed, such theories often seemed to suggest that a text representation is simply a concatenation of sentence representations. However, a moment's thought suggests that there is more to integrating the information from the different sentences of a text than juxtaposition. Referential links between expressions, such as *the table* and *it*, have to be established, as do links of other kinds, such as causal relations between the events, states, and processes described. It is in some ways unfortunate that Bransford's best known empirical work on the integrative nature of comprehension (Bransford & Franks, 1971) diverted attention from the important questions about integration. In that study, complex sentences, such as:

(1) The ants in the kitchen ate the sweet jelly that was on the table.

were divided into their component "ideas" (e.g., the ants were in the kitchen), and shorter sentences expressing one, two, or three of these ideas were mixed with sentences that also had been derived from other complex sentences. The results of the Bransford and Franks (1971) study suggested that the component ideas from individual complex sentences were integrated by the readers, and that these integrated representations were used, in a subsequent unexpected recognition test, to make judgments of which sentences had been in the original list. This study provoked numerous follow-up studies, some of which challenged the original interpretation of the findings. However, we are not concerned here with whether Bransford and Franks' results were artifactual. Our point is that, even if they were not, they probably reflected a process, or set of processes, that is relatively unimportant in the normal course of text comprehension.

Presumably, the main grouping principle used by Bransford and Franks' (1971) participants was one based on content. However, a coherent text does not consist of randomly ordered packages of information. For the most part, continuity of content can be assumed and used to guide other integrative processes. Thus, a reader or listener does not have to decide that two bits go together because they are both about ants; instead, they use a general assumption about the continuity of subject matter to conclude that the pronoun *they* in one sentence refers to the set of ants introduced by the definite noun phrase *the ants* in a previous sentence. Bransford and Franks' study also obscures another important aspect of integration: Text comprehension is an incremental process. The mental model of a text constructed to a particular point forms (part of) the context for the interpretation of the next clause of the text. This process of interpretation changes the context by incrementing the model (Isard, 1975), and the new model forms (part of) the context for the interpretation of the next clause.

Bransford's third contribution to theories of text comprehension was his realization that understanding is a *constructive process* (Bransford, Barclay, & Franks, 1972). By making this claim, Bransford was pointing out that, in creating a mental representation of the content of a text, information that is explicit in the text (almost always) has to be combined with relevant knowledge about the world. This knowledge comes from long-term memory and it may be specific knowledge about particular people, places, and things or general knowledge about types of people, places, and things. Construction and integration are closely connected because, in many cases, background knowledge contributes crucially to the integration of information from different clauses of a text.

The constructive aspect of text comprehension also is related to the notion that the representation of a text is not a representation of its linguistic form, but is, instead, "a wholistic description of the overall situation linguistically communicated" (Bransford et al., 1972, p. 202). According to constructive theories, the combination of information that is explicit in a text with information about people and things in the world is entirely straightforward because both types of information have the same form; both are representations of, or templates for representing, aspects of the world. By using the term *template*, we are claiming that general knowledge is knowledge about categories of things; for example, knowledge about dogs could be used as a template for the representation of a particular dog (although texts can also be about dogs in general). In addition, the information extracted from a clause in a text before it has been integrated into the model might be a schematic representation of an event. For example, the sentence:

(2) The dog chased the ball.

could describe any one of an indefinitely large set of events. Only when this sentence has been interpreted in its context will a representation of a particular event have been derived from it.

SYNTAX AND MENTAL MODELS

We have already mentioned that the construction of mental models is an incremental process. Information from the current clause is extracted and added to the model of the text constructed to that point. The incremented model is then used as part of the context for interpreting the next clause. In extracting information from the current clause, readers and listeners use stored knowledge about words, the way that words can be grouped into phrases and clauses (syntax), and the way in which the meaning of those phrases and clauses depends on their structure. Information is integrated into the model by establishing referential and other types of links that are derived from the temporal, spatial, logical, causal, intentional, and moral (Miller & Johnson-Laird, 1976) connections between the pieces of information in the text. The manner in which these two sets of processes (i.e., those that extract information from a clause and those that integrate that information with the model) interact remains to be determined. However, because some semantic integration occurs within clauses (e.g., Marslen-Wilson, 1975) and some is delayed until clause boundaries (e.g., Mitchell & Green, 1978), the nature of the interaction is undoubtedly complex.

We assume that, in the case of clearly articulated speech and clearly written or printed text, word identification proceeds primarily on the basis of perceptual information. Although some researchers (e.g., Smith, 1988) favor an account of reading as a "psycholinguistic guessing game," this idea has been largely discredited (e.g., Adams, 1990; Oakhill & Garnham, 1988, chapter 4). In the case of syntax, however, matters are more complex. Some sentences cannot be interpreted correctly without a full syntactic analysis (Marcus, 1984). Nevertheless, semantic and pragmatic information affects the interpretation of sentences, and if such information suggests an interpretation that is not the linguistically correct one, people sometimes produce it (e.g., Norris, 1985).

A study of our own makes a similar point. Garnham and Oakhill (1987) found that people sometimes interpreted:

(3) The patient had been examined by the doctor during the ward round. The nurse had too.

to mean that the nurse, as well as the doctor, had examined the patient during the ward round. Although that interpretation is a plausible interpretation, it is not correct. Furthermore, Caramazza and Zurif (1976) reported the first of several studies to show that agrammatic aphasics, as well as having severe language production difficulties, also have more specific comprehension difficulties. These difficulties result from a partial or total inability to use syntax to compute meaning. Interestingly, the ability to judge whether a sentence is grammatically ill-formed is largely preserved in these patients (Linebarger, Schwartz, & Saffran, 1983). They have not lost their knowledge of syntax, but rather the ability to use it in comprehension.

Further evidence that people do not always use detailed syntactic analyses to understand a sentence comes from studies of the manner in which certain sentences are systematically misinterpreted (see Sanford & Garrod, 1994). For example:

(4) This book fills a much needed gap.

is often assumed to be a positive comment about the book. As another example, people fail to see the anomaly in the question:

(5) Following an air crash on the border between two countries, where should the survivors be buried?

(Barton & Sanford, 1993; Sanford, Barton, Moxey, & Paterson, 1995). In each case, the individual words or their components suggest a plausible interpretation. For example, there is a gap that needs filling and the book fills it; air crashes often cause deaths, dead people have to be buried, and if the crash is on the border, there might be problems in deciding where.

A more complicated example was studied by Wason and Reich (1979). The sentence:

(6) No head injury is too trivial to be ignored.

is typically construed as an injunction not to ignore any head injury. However, a proper analysis of the sentence shows that it should be taken as an injunction to ignore head injuries. Because the "verbal illusion" created by this sentence is so powerful, it is profitable to analyze the sentence further.

A predicate of the form "too *X* to be *Y*-ed" means that an entity or event has so high a value on the *X* dimension that one cannot or should not perform action *Y* on it. For example, if something is *too hot to be touched* it is so hot that one should not touch it. Such a predicate can only be felicitously used if it is assumed that the more *X* something becomes the less likely one would be to perform action *Y* on it. The hotter something gets the less likely it is that one will be able to touch it. Thus, to say that something is *too hot to be touched* means that it has gone beyond a threshold on the dimension of hotness at which it is possible to touch it. Instead of predicating "too *X* to be *Y*-ed" of a particular object, we might say that "no *Z* is too *X* to be *Y*-ed." This would mean that although as something gets more *X* it becomes more and more likely that we should not perform action *Y* on it, as we consider *Z*s that are more and more *X*, we will never cross the threshold beyond which we cannot or should not *Y* them. *No mountain is too high to be climbed* means that, although as mountains get higher and higher, it becomes less and less likely that they can be climbed; in fact, none of them is so high that it cannot be climbed.

With this analysis established, we can return to Example 6. This sentence presupposes that as head injuries get more and more trivial it is less and less likely that we will ignore them. This presupposition conflicts with our everyday beliefs about head injuries or, indeed, about injuries in general, that is, it is the serious ones that should not be ignored, not the trivial ones. If a head injured patient arrived at a hospital, the claim that *this case is too trivial to be ignored* would not make sense. In contrast, the claim that it was *too trivial to be treated* would make linguistic sense, if not medical sense. The claim that it was *too serious to be ignored* would make both linguistic and medical sense. The universal negative claim that *no head injury is too trivial to be ignored* says that as one considers more and more trivial head injuries, one never reaches a point where it is not possible to ignore those injuries (i.e., they always can be ignored). Thus, as Wason and Reich (1979) point out Example 6 (a) carries an incorrect presupposition about the relation between the triviality of head injuries and the reasonableness of ignoring them, and (b) makes the false claim that all head injuries should be ignored. These two problems, together with the negatives (both explicit and implicit) in the sentence and its quantifier (also negative) conspire to cause its misinterpretation.

Wason and Reich (1979) also point out that the two problems associated with Example 6 do not necessarily go together. For example:

(7) No head injury is too serious to be ignored.

carries the sensible presupposition that the more serious a head injury, the less likely one should be to ignore it. However, Example 7 still makes the false claim that all head injuries should be ignored. In contrast:

(8) No head injury is too serious to be treated.

carries the implausible presupposition that the more serious a head injury, the less likely one should be to treat it. However, Example 8 conveys the reasonable claim that all head injuries should be treated. According to Wason and Reich, neither Example 7 nor Example 8 is as likely to be misinterpreted as correctly conveying a plausible claim as is Example 6. The fact that Example 6 is misinterpreted, together with the extreme resistance that many people display to the claim that there is something wrong with it, indicates that it is almost impossible to use syntax to derive the correct meaning of a sentence when other factors conspire in the right way. This observation raises the question of how syntax is used in understanding sentences that do not have anomalous interpretations. In contrast to Broca's aphasics, healthy individuals do not usually make the mistake of assuming that:

(9) The horse that the girl kicked is brown.

is about a horse kicking a girl. Therefore, they cannot be relying wholly on semantic factors to interpret what they hear and read. Nevertheless, the contribution of syntax to comprehension is not particularly robust, and, thus, people can be led by considerations of plausibility to construct incorrect mental models.

INFERENCE IN MENTAL MODELS THEORY

It is sometimes argued (e.g., McKoon & Ratcliff, 1992) that the theory of mental models is committed to the idea that numerous inferences inevitably will be made during comprehension so that a detailed representation of a specific situation can be built. In fact, the theory makes no particular claims about which inferences are made (Garnham, 1992, 1993). Indeed, it is recognized in the theory that the reader's goals determine this matter, as much as the text itself. The theory, however, does have much to say about what an inference is, and what processes would have to contribute to the making of particular inferences. In this section, we attempt to clarify the much misunderstood position of the mental models theory on inference making.

Local Links and Referential Continuity

As we have already mentioned, mental models are constructed incrementally by incorporating information that is explicit in the current clause into the model of the text constructed to that point. Perhaps the most important aspect of this incorporation process is the establishment of referential links. In the mental models framework, establishing a referential link means identifying something in the world that one of the tokens in the model-so-far stands for as the referent of a linguistic expression in the current clause. In a straightforward case, such as:

(10) The cup was in front of the saucer.
The fork was to the left of the cup.

this process of identification is relatively straightforward, although it depends, for example, on the use of definite articles (e.g., *the*) rather than indefinite articles (e.g., *a* or *some*). Thus, *the cup* in the second sentence of Example 10 refers to the object introduced by the same phrase in the first sentence.

More often, however, the referring expression in the current clause takes a different form from the one used in a previous clause.

(11) The cup was in front of the forks.
It was full of milk.

Nevertheless, given knowledge of how the English pronoun system works, there is little difficulty in explaining why *it* must refer to the cup. If the process of determining reference were to be described as inferential in such cases, the inferences would be based primarily on a knowledge of linguistic conventions. A minor change in Example 11 complicates matters considerably, for the theorist, if not for the reader:

(12) The cup was in front of the fork.
It was full of milk.

In this version, the referent of *it* is not determined by the fact that it is a neuter third-person singular pronoun because such a pronoun could legitimately refer to either *the cup* or *the fork*. Nevertheless, given the content of the second sentence in Example 12, there is no doubt that *it* is intended to refer to *the cup*. The reader knows this from a combination of the information that is explicit in the text and background knowledge. The text explicitly states that the referent of *it* was full of milk. Background knowledge about cups, forks, and milk shows that cups, not forks, can be full of milk. Thus, the integration of the information in the two sentences of Example 12 is brought about by a process that is clearly inferential. Furthermore, the process also satisfies Bransford et al.'s (1972) definition of a constructive process: one that "use[s] linguistic information in conjunction with previous knowledge to construct semantic descriptions" (p. 207). As Garnham (1992) has argued, even inferences that make local links between the parts of a text–those that establish what McKoon and Ratcliff (1992) refer to as *local coherence*–frequently involve constructive processing.

In the simple examples considered thus far, the referential links have been between adjacent sentences. A text containing such links throughout is *referentially continuous* (Garnham, Oakhill, & Johnson-Laird, 1982). According to the mental models theory, referential continuity is one of the major factors that determines whether a text is easy to understand (Ehrlich & Johnson-Laird, 1982; Garnham et al., 1982). Nevertheless, referential continuity is not essential. Consider the type of referentially discontinuous texts used by Ehrlich and Johnson-Laird, for example:

(13) The knife is in front of the pot.
The glass is behind the dish.
The pot is to the left of the glass.

Such texts are not particularly problematic for readers or listeners. As is the case in other theories of text comprehension (e.g., Kintsch & van Dijk, 1978), the mental models theory assumes that (local) integrative processes take place in a limited capacity short-term memory buffer. The mental models theory differs, however, in its account of the nature of those processes and of the representations they construct. Furthermore, it is not unreasonable to assume that short-term memory can hold information from more than two clauses simultaneously and, therefore, that links between close, but nonadjacent, clauses can be established without much difficulty. Nevertheless, Ehrlich and Johnson-Laird explain the additional difficulty of referentially discontinuous passages, and its primary locus at the third sentence of such passages, in terms of a hypothesized increase in temporary storage and processing in working memory at that point.

Kintsch and van Dijk (1978) provided a further mechanism by which referential links might readily be established between nonadjacent clauses. In each cycle of processing in their model, it is not necessarily the most recent propositions that are retained in the short-term memory store, but rather, those judged likely to be important in processing upcoming material. The precise mechanisms involved in deciding what is likely to be important remain to be determined but, at least for certain types of text, information from the first sentence of each paragraph is important for understanding the remainder of the paragraph. According to the mental models theory, it is not propositions, but, rather, (parts of) mental models that are held in working memory and used to process upcoming text. However, the mental models theory provides much the same account as does the Kintsch and van Dijk model of why coreference can sometimes be established in the absence of referential continuity. Given a relatively complex method for deciding what parts of the model to hold in working memory, and, thus, what parts are probable sources of referents for the next clause, a referent that was not mentioned in an immediately preceding clause may, nonetheless, be readily available.

The idea that the structure of working memory is the principal determinant of the ease of integrating material from different clauses is an attractive one. However, other considerations complicate the picture considerably. Stenning, Shepherd, and Levy (1988) suggested that referential continuity is just a special case of predictable referential change. Furthermore, they showed that discontinuous, but predictable, changes of reference, as in the following passage:

(14) There is a nurse. There is a chef. The nurse is French. The chef is Greek. The nurse is young. The chef is old. The nurse is strong. The chef is strong.

resulted in no measurable comprehension difficulty compared to a comparable referentially continuous passage. However, when switching between the referents was unpredictable, referential change did result in processing costs (Stenning, Nelson, Levy, Patel, & Gemmell, 1992).

These considerations suggest that the question of whether an inference is local or whether it establishes local coherence does not necessarily have a straightforward answer (see also Singer, 1993). Fortunately, if one wishes to ask which inferences are given priority in comprehension, the mental models theory provides a better answer than does any theory that suggests that inferences needed to establish local coherence are given priority. The mental models theory claims that the inferences given priority are those needed to establish the referents of the referring expressions in the current clause.

When Are Inferences Made?

We will return subsequently to the question of what is meant by *global* inferences or inferences that establish *global coherence*. However, before we leave the topic of local, or referent establishing, inferences, we consider the long-standing question of whether these are the only inferences made as a text is read. In the 1970s, Bransford and others argued that readers make many other inferences as they read texts. However, this argument was based on memory experiments, which provide no evidence as to what occurs during reading. Moreover, it became obvious that the results of these experiments primarily reflected reconstructive processes at retrieval. Numerous researchers, therefore, began to consider the idea that inferencing during reading is restricted to just those inferences that are necessary for a coherent interpretation of the text (e.g., Corbett & Dosher, 1978; Dosher & Corbett, 1982; Singer, 1980; Thorndyke, 1976). On this view, other inferences, labelled *merely elaborative*, are not made during reading, but can be made later on the basis of the mental representations of the text constructed at the time of reading. One circumstance under which they might be made would be if they were needed to answer a question posed by the experimenter.

Although plausible, this idea depends on a clear account of what is meant by "necessary for a coherent interpretation of a text." In particular, might some inferences that do not link adjacent clauses or make referential links be necessary in this sense? The answer to this question is "yes." For example, we have argued (Garnham & Oakhill, 1992) that the inferences about text characters' emotional states, such as those studied by Gernsbacher and Robertson (1992), probably have this status. In one of Gernsbacher and Robertson's passages, Joe gets fired from his job in a store. The money in his till did not balance one evening because his friend, Tom, had come into the store and stolen money while Joe went out into the storage room. At the end of the story, Tom learns that Joe has been fired. Although making the inference that Tom is likely to feel guilty would not help to make local referential links, someone who did not make this inference would not have understood the story properly. In our view, it would be surprising if such inferences were not made in ordinary reading, and Gernsbacher and Robertson's data suggest that they are made. However, such inferences are problematic for a new version of the idea that coherence-producing inferences are made automatically during reading, McKoon and Ratcliff's (1992) *minimalist hypothesis*.

Despite the problems involved in defining local and global coherence described above, McKoon and Ratcliff (1992) claim that inferences that establish global coherence are not made routinely during reading. The only way that minimalism can accommodate Gernsbacher and Robertson's (1992) findings, therefore, is to assume that the inferences are based on "readily available knowledge" and made automatically, even if they are not needed to produce local coherence. However, the notion of "ready availability" is a problematic one in the minimalist framework and certainly does not fit with our everyday intuitions.

For example, McKoon and Ratcliff can account for established findings on case-filling inferences only by assuming that information, such as scissors are usually used to cut paper, is not readily available. It seems unlikely, therefore, that information about characters' emotional states would be readily available in this sense, and thus, Gernsbacher and Robertson's findings are problematic for minimalism.

Might an Inference Be Made in Stages?

A further problem for the claim that the inferences necessary to establish coherence are made during reading is that it assumes an all-or-none account of inference making: either an inference is made or it is not. However, this overly simplistic view of inference making can be attacked in several ways. First, an inference could be made in several stages. Anderson and Ortony (1975) showed that *bottle* was a better cue than *basket* for recalling:

(15) The container held the cola.

whereas the reverse was true for:

(16) The container held the apples.

They argued that the meaning of *container* was instantiated differently in the two sentences. An obvious question is whether *can* and *glass* also would be good cues for the first sentence. Gumenik (1979) showed that they were. Anderson and Ortony's experiments looked at merely elaborative instantiation, so their only error was to overspecify the inferences made by the participants in their experiment. On reading Example 15, the participants did not really infer that the container was a bottle, but, rather, that it was either a bottle, a can, a glass, or something similar. However, instantiations sometimes are necessary for establishing local coherence. Therefore, in a passage such as:

(17) The container held the cola.
I always used that glass.

the referent of *that glass* in the second sentence is the container introduced by the first sentence. If the container in the first sentence is immediately represented as a bottle, or a can, or a glass, or something similar, and it must be stressed that Anderson and Ortony's data do not prove that it is, some of the work needed to resolve the reference of *the glass* is carried out as the first sentence is read and some as the second sentence is read. A different division of labor would occur for a similar passage in which the first sentence did not narrow down the set of possible containers as much; for example:

(18) The container was on the table.
I always used that glass.

Another way the work of inference making might be distributed is indicated in Garnham's (1982) *omission theory*. Garnham considered elaborative case-filling inferences and, in particular, the finding that highly probable explicit case fillers are confused in memory with implicit case fillers. The standard account of this finding is that an implicit case filler, such as "a knife" in:

(19) The teacher cut into the juicy steak.

is encoded when the sentence is read. Another possibility is that a highly probable explicit case filler, for example, in:

(20) The teacher cut into the juicy steak with a knife.

is omitted from the representation of the content, but encoded briefly in the representation of surface form. Once the representation of the surface form has decayed, the mental representations of the sentences with and without the case filler would be the same, and both would encode the content "the teacher cut into the juicy steak." In the omission theory, the case filler is constructed at recall, if required, just as it is constructed at encoding in the standard account: if it can be constructed from the original text (without the case filler), it can be constructed from an adequate representation of the content of that text.

According to the omission theory, making a case-filling inference is explained partly by what happens at encoding and partly by what happens at retrieval. At encoding, explicit case fillers have to be checked to see if they can be omitted, which is only possible if they can be reconstructed. Implicit case fillers are not encoded at all. At retrieval, case fillers are reconstructed if needed. Furthermore, reconstruction is necessary, even if the case filler was originally explicit. It is incorrect, therefore, to identify reconstruction with inference making in the everyday sense because no inference is required when the original sentence has an explicit case filler.

Does Only Partial Integration of Information Occur?

Oakhill, Garnham, and Vonk (1989) discuss a different type of inference that has potentially separable aspects. Oakhill et al. suggest that there are (at least) two aspects to the process of integrating the information from a clause containing a pronoun into the existing mental model: *role-to-name mapping* and *role-to-role mapping*. Consider the interpretation of the sentence:

(21) Sue blamed Carol because she spilled some coffee.

Each verb (e.g., *blame* and *spill* in Example 21) has associated with it a set of roles (e.g., the person who carries out the action, and the person or thing that is the object of the action). One view (Carlson & Tanenhaus, 1988) is that there is a small set of *thematic roles*, such as agent, goal, theme and instrument, each of which is associated with many verbs. In this context, we need not commit ourselves to this hypothesis. Instead, we can describe the roles associated with each verb in a theory-neutral way. Thus, the action of blaming includes a person who does the blaming (the blamer) and a person who gets blamed (the blamee), and the action of spilling has a person who does the spilling (the spiller) and something that gets spilled. In Example 21, Sue is the blamer and Carol the blamee, the coffee is the substance that gets spilled and the referent of *she* is the spiller. Role-to-name mapping associates the spiller (i.e., role) with the referent of Carol (i.e., name). Role-to-role mapping associates the spiller with the blamee.

In a full interpretation of the sentence in Example 21, both role-to-role mapping and role-to-name mapping would be effected: The person who was blamed would be identified with the person who spilled the coffee and that person's name would be determined to be Carol. However, it is possible to imagine either sort of mapping without the other. For example, in a psycholinguistic experiment in which many names are used out of context and with no real-world referents, the particular names may be ignored, especially if the task demands do not require participants to remember them. Participants nevertheless may decide that the sentence is about one person blaming another because the second has spilled some coffee. This would be an example of role-to-role mapping with no role-to-name mapping. Conversely, in a superficial reading of a related sentence:

(22) Sue blamed Carl because he spilled some coffee.

a reader might decide that *he* must be Carl because of its morphological form and the usual sexes of people called Sue and Carl, but they may fail to register the exact nature of the connection between the blaming and the spilling. A related possibility is that, at any point in a text, there is a favored entity for subsequent pronominal reference and that, when a pronoun is encountered, it is at least tentatively assumed to have that referent (e.g., Greene, McKoon, & Ratcliff, 1992; Grosz, Joshi, & Weinstein, 1983). Such an assignment would involve a pronoun-to-name mapping without any role-to-role or even any role-to-name mapping.

As we have just illustrated, the gender of a pronoun can, in certain circumstances, provide an unambiguous indication of what its referent must be. In such cases, the reader knows which entity takes the role assigned to the referent of the pronoun by the verb in its clause (e.g., the spiller), regardless of that entity's roles in previous clauses. A "gender cue," therefore, aids role-to-name mapping. A factor that can help role-to-role mapping, without necessarily effecting role-to-name mapping, is *implicit causality* (Garvey & Caramazza, 1974). Use of the verb *blame*, for example, suggests an act that is likely to have been caused by the person who gets blamed. Therefore, a pronominal subject of a subsequent *because* clause is likely, although not certain, to be the person playing the role of the blamee in the main clause. To the extent that implicit causality is associated specifically with verbs, it can guide role-to-role mapping in a way that is independent of how the entities filling the roles are "named."

Oakhill et al. (1989) argued that, because role-to-role and role-to-name mapping are at least partly independent, readers might sometimes perform one without the other. The result would be a representation of the content of the text that was incomplete with respect to the information that is either explicit in the text or introduced by inferences necessary for a coherent interpretation. Garnham, Oakhill, and Cruttenden (1992) and Cruttenden (1993) provide empirical evidence that gender cue and congruity between the information in a *because* clause and the implicit causality of the verb in the main clause affect different aspects of comprehension. Indeed, it appears that the effects of bias may be automatic, whereas gender cues only differentially affect comprehension when a participant's attention is drawn to them.

Signals for Inference versus Knowledge Underlying Inference

A different division of inferential processes also suggests that different parts of an inference might be computed at different times, or that some may not be computed at all. The need for an inference may be signaled by an explicit marker, such as a coordinating or subordinating conjunction, or a relational property of a text, such as the order of its sentences. However, such signals only indicate the kind of relation that holds between the different parts of the text (e.g., in "the window broke because the stone hit it," *because* signals a causal relation), they do not determine how the relation is grounded (e.g., in the knowledge that when stones are thrown at windows they often break). As this example shows, it is usually background knowledge related to the explicit content of the text that provides the grounding.

Texts contain many signals that inferences are required. The use of the word *because* to indicate a causal, inferential, or reason-based relation between the information in two clauses is just one example (see Examples 21 and 22). Furthermore, there are conventions about the kinds of relations that hold between clauses that are merely juxtaposed. For example, Sanders, Spooren, and Noordman (1992) point out that a "list" of events, such as:

(23) It's Jane's birthday and Robin has invited all her friends.

is often interpreted as implicitly expressing a relation of cause and consequent. Further, Kamp's (1979; Kamp & Rohrer, 1983) account of the use of tenses shows how the temporal relations between the events described in a text can be signaled.

Recognizing such signals of the types of relations that hold between parts of a text generally depends only on readers' or listeners' knowledge of their language: knowing what *because* and other connectives mean, how tenses are used, or how information can be conveyed implicitly or indirectly. For example, readers who see and understand the word *but* know that some kind of contrastive relation is being signaled. There is little doubt that this much is registered during all but the most cursory reading. However, it is another matter whether the general knowledge that underlies the contrastive relation is activated during reading and used to complete the inference. Indeed, readers who do not have the general knowledge may recognize that there is a contrastive relation, but be unable to activate the relevant knowledge. They can, in fact, derive at least some of that knowledge on the assumption that the text is both well-written and true (or true of the world it is about). Thus, someone who does not know much about detergents and reads that a detergent is *biological, but does not wash colors out*, could assume from this text that biological detergents are likely to wash colors out. However, Noordman and Vonk (1992) showed, in a laboratory study where the participants had no strong motivation to learn from the texts they were reading, that such inferences were not made as texts were read. However, they were made subsequently when the participants were forced to verify the inferable information as part of the experimental task.

ANAPHORA FROM A MENTAL MODELS PERSPECTIVE

One of the major linguistic devices for indicating local links between parts of a text is the use of anaphoric expressions, such as pronouns and verbal ellipses. We have discussed some of the inferences needed to interpret pronouns in the previous section. In this section, we treat anaphora, which has been a topic of special concern in mental models theory (see Garnham & Oakhill, in prep., for a fuller treatment).

In the simplest cases, an anaphoric expression has the same meaning—either the same referent or the same sense—as another expression in the preceding text. For example, a definite pronoun, such as *he*, *she*, *it*, or *they*, usually refers to the same thing (or things) as a previous noun phrase, as in:

(24) John came into the room. He sat down.

In contrast, an indefinite pronoun, such as *one*, may refer to another thing of the same kind as a previous noun phrase. Thus, it has the same sense, but not the same referent as a previous expression in the text, for example:

(25) John has a spaniel and my sister has one, too.

However, there are many uses of anaphoric expressions which do not have the same meaning as a previous expression in the text. These cases complicate matters to such an extent that a satisfactory definition of anaphora is difficult to formulate, and none has been suggested to date (see Bosch, 1983, chapter 1, for a historical summary). However, the lack of a comprehensive definition will not affect the ensuing discussion. Indeed, the lack of a clear distinction between anaphora and deixis, in which an expression takes its meaning from an indicated component of the nonlinguistic context (e.g., *that one* accompanied by a pointing gesture), and between anaphoric expressions and other referring expressions, is not surprising from a mental models perspective. It is a reflection of two facts: (a) one of the most important aspects of comprehension is determining what expressions refer to, and (b) both linguistic and nonlinguistic contexts are represented in models of the real or an imaginary world.

Garnham (1987) identified three, possibly overlapping, sets of processes in the interpretation of an anaphoric expression:

1. The expression must be identified as anaphoric.
2. The linguistic and nonlinguistic context relevant to its interpretation must be determined.
3. An interpretation must be assigned to the expression on the basis of its form and its context.

In fact, to say that an expression must be identified as anaphoric is misleading. Expressions must invoke appropriate procedures for computing their meanings. For example, once a definite pronoun has been identified—a relatively straightforward task in clear speech or print—an attempt can be made to find its referent in the model of the text constructed so far. However, various factors conspire to make the assignment of a referent to a definite pronoun more complicated than it first appears. For example, it might be thought that the referent for a pronoun could be found by searching the model constructed to that point for an entity that could be referred to by a pronoun of that number and gender. For a short text, such as:

(26) John came into the room. He sat down.

such a procedure might work. The first sentence introduces two entities into the model, a (presumably) male person called John and a room. Of these two, only John can be appropriately referred to using the singular male pronoun *he*.

One complication arises because pronouns do not always agree in number and gender with the antecedent noun phrases that introduce their referents. Inanimate objects can be referred to using masculine or feminine pronouns (e.g., *the ship . . . she*). Moreover, even if such references are sexist, they are readily understood. A more important complication is that many items introduced in a text can be referred to by, for example, a masculine singular pronoun. Thus, although the existence of a mental model imposes strong constraints on the referents of pronouns, those constraints are not always strong enough to make a pronoun's referent determinate.

Many attempts to solve this problem have invoked the notion of *focus* (e.g., Grosz, 1981; Grosz, Joshi, & Weinstein, 1983; Grosz & Sidner, 1986; Joshi & Weinstein, 1981; Reichman, 1978; Sanford & Garrod, 1981; Sidner, 1981). In terms of the three component processes of anaphor interpretation mentioned previously, focus is a device that restricts the relevant context for interpreting an anaphor. Unfortunately, there is no satisfactory definition of focus. However, the basic idea is that a subset of the entities in a mental model has a special status and might be, for example, the locus of the most probable referents for anaphoric pronouns. Most accounts agree that there is not a single focused subset of entities, but a structured set of *focus spaces*. One view is that focus, or the set of focus spaces, guides the search for the referent of an anaphoric pronoun after it has been encountered. Another view is that focusing involves preselecting an entity as the most likely referent for a subsequent pronoun, and that it is automatically associated with any pronoun unless subsequent information shows that such an assignment is impossible. This idea would be attractive if there were always, or nearly always, a single entity that was much more likely than any other to be the subject of pronominal reference. However, pairs of sentences such as:

(27) Max confessed to Bill because he wanted a reduced sentence.
Max confessed to Bill because he offered a reduced sentence.

suggest that this is unlikely to be the case, because neither member of the pair is particularly difficult to understand.

Another important idea for a theory of anaphoric processing is that there are two types of anaphoric expression, each of which receives its meaning in different ways (Hankamer & Sag, 1976; Sag & Hankamer, 1984). Hankamer and Sag distinguished between *deep* and *surface* anaphors, and suggested that they were interpreted from mental models and from representations of the surface form of texts, respectively. We subsequently present reasons for questioning this idea. However, it is clearly a proposal for how the context relevant to interpreting an anaphoric expression might be limited.

Deep anaphors do not need explicit linguistic antecedents. They can be used deictically. For example, it is acceptable to say *he's a friend of mine* when the referent of *he* has not been mentioned, but is a salient person in the nonlinguistic context. Furthermore, when deep anaphors do have explicit antecedents, those antecedents need not have the same form as the most natural expansion of the anaphor. For example, if someone says, *those shelves will have to be painted*, a linguistically correct response would be *I'll do it*. In this example, *do it* is most naturally expanded as the active verb phrase "paint those shelves," although the antecedent is passive. Surface anaphors are judged to be used incorrectly if they do not have explicit linguistic antecedents, and they typically have antecedents that parallel the natural expansion of the ellipsis. Hankamer and Sag (1976) claimed that the elliptical form *I will* is a linguistically inappropriate response to *those shelves will have to be painted*, and that it should not be used when the fact that the shelves need painting is obvious from their appearance rather than being explicitly stated.

Deep anaphors include many definite noun phrases, pronouns, *do it*, and null complements. If such anaphors are encountered in a text, according to Sag and Hankamer (1984), they take their meaning (sense or reference) directly from an element in (the focused part of) a mental model. Constraints provided by the anaphor itself, therefore, should be interpreted semantically. Thus, a feminine singular pronoun, such as *she*, should match something represented as a single entity and as female. Surface anaphors are elliptical verbal constructions other than *do it* and null complements. If an expression of this type is encountered, its antecedent must be located in a representation of the surface form of the recently processed text (or, occasionally, the subsequent text). Because representations of surface form are short-lived, surface anaphors have to occur close to their antecedents—almost always in the adjacent clause. Once the antecedent has been found, its form can be used to derive a meaning for the anaphor. Although it has long been established that the surface form of a text is briefly stored, there is some controversy about the aspects of the surface form that are represented. The representation used to interpret surface anaphors cannot be too superficial because indexical expressions can retain their referents, rather than their forms, across speakers. For example, in the following dialogue, the ellipsis following *will* is interpreted as "explain my theory of text comprehension to you." Thus, *your* changes to *my* but continues to mean JO's, and *me* changes to *you* but continues to mean AG:

(28) AG: Are you going to explain your theory of text comprehension to me.
JO: I will, but can we leave it till tomorrow?

Sag and Hankamer suggested that the relevant surface representation might be Chomsky's logical form (LF).

Sag and Hankamer's (1984) account of the interpretation of deep anaphors is plausible for most English pronouns. However, in languages with nonsemantic gender (e.g., most European languages other than English), pronouns can be associated with their antecedents on the basis of morphological features. For example, in a French sentence beginning:

(29) *La cape a protégé le manteau parce qu'elle. . . .*
The (FEM) cape protected the (MASC) coat because it (FEM). . . .

the feminine singular pronoun *elle* must refer to the cape and not the coat. However, if a mental model involved simply the representation of objects, information about the genders of nouns typically used to describe those objects might not be included in the model. In any case, an object can be referred to using different nouns, which, in a language such as French, can have different genders (e.g., *le paquet*, masculine; *la boîte*, feminine). Furthermore, pronouns that refer to objects that can be resolved on the basis of their nonsemantic gender are understood more rapidly, just as pronouns that can be resolved on the basis of their semantic gender (Carreiras, Garnham, & Oakhill, 1993).

In English, there also are cases, particularly in the domain of number, where the morphological marking of a noun conflicts with its conceptual status. Although the plurality of English nouns, such as *scissors*, *pliers*, *trousers*, and *pants*, is not entirely arbitrary, a pair of trousers is, nonetheless, a single object. However, the correct pronoun in a sentence such as:

(30) Pass me those trousers and I'll press ___.

is *them*. Thus, although a pair of trousers is represented as a single entity in a mental model, a text about trousers may contain plural pronouns that must be interpreted as referring to such single entities.

Tasmowski-De Ryck and Verluyten (1982) have pointed out that, in language production, the gender of the noun that would most naturally be used to refer to an object determines the form of a pronoun if there is no linguistic antecedent. For example, in talking about a table (in French, *la table*, feminine) it is appropriate to say:

(31) *Tu n'arriveras jamais à la faire entrer dans la voiture.*
You'll never manage to get it (FEM) into the car.

But for a desk (in French, *le bureau*, masculine), one would have to say:

(32) *Tu n'arriveras jamais à le faire entrer dans la voiture.*
You'll never manage to get it (MASC) into the car.

The importance of morphological markings that do not have a semantic reflex, however, is short lived. For example, a woman government minister would be referred to in French as *le ministre* (masculine); subsequent references may use either a masculine or a feminine pronoun. Choice of pronoun is governed by a variety of factors (Cornish, 1986, 1988), but as the distance between the pronoun and the overtly masculine noun phrase (*le ministre*) increases, the likelihood of using a masculine pronoun decreases.

In light of these observations, Sag and Hankamer's (1984) theory must be modified. Either a representation of the superficial features of a text is important for interpreting pronouns, or mental models contain information that one might not have expected in a representation of content (e.g., about nonsemantic gender). A subsidiary finding from an experiment in English reinforces the view that, whatever the nature of mental models, a superficial representation is used to interpret pronouns. Garnham and Oakhill (1988) investigated pronominal references into so-called *anaphoric islands*, in which the pronoun's antecedent is introduced indirectly; for example, by using a verb phrase whose main verb (e.g., *dreamed*) is morphologically related to the head noun (e.g., *dreams*) of the noun phrase that would be the standard antecedent.

(33) Tom dreamed a lot but he never remembered them.
Tom had a lot of dreams but he never remembered them.

References into anaphoric islands were less preferred and took longer to process than did anaphoric references with noun phrase antecedents. However, the effect was less marked if the verb and the corresponding plural noun were identical, as in:

(33) Tom dreams a lot but he never remembers them.
Tom has a lot of dreams but he never remembers them.

This effect can only be explained if aspects of the form of a text influence the way pronouns are interpreted.

MENTAL MODELS OF ABSTRACT SITUATIONS

Much of the discussion, both in this chapter and in the mental models literature generally, has focused on simple texts describing concrete situations. The mental model of such a text is a representation of the situation in the real or imaginary world that the text is about. Real texts, however, are rarely entirely descriptive, and their subject matter is rarely entirely concrete. The question arises, therefore, as to how the concept of a mental model can be extended to nondescriptive and abstract texts. We do not believe that there are major obstacles to generalizing the theory. However, the focus on spatial mental models, although understandable insofar as the difference between the representation of a situation and the representation of a description of it is particularly clear in the spatial domain, has obscured some of the issues.

Descriptive texts are usually about specific people, things, and places. As we said previously, the representation of, for example, a chair in the model of such a text is a representation of an exemplar of a thing of a particular type, although the amount of detail that is incorporated into the representation of a specific chair from our general knowledge of chairs varies from context to context. Some references to abstract objects are essentially similar. For example, a text describing the political system of the United States may be represented in a mental model with exemplars of general concepts such as a *president* and a *supreme court*. More mundanely, even in a simple narrative, we may classify an act of one of the characters as a kind act, and represent it using, in part, our general knowledge of kind acts.

There is, however, another kind of abstract text, one that includes discussion of, for example, the general concept of a *presidency*, a *chair*, or even of a *mental model*. In understanding such texts, the distinction between the concept and its exemplars (the so-called *type-token* distinction) is no longer directly relevant. Such texts tell us what a president is, what a mental model is, or what a chair is.

Because mental models are representations of particular situations, the following question arises: How does the notion of a mental model apply to texts of this kind, or even to texts of the first more abstract kind? In generalizing the theory, we need to broaden our ideas about what counts as a representation of "part of the world." The world must be taken to include not just the physical world, but also the world of ideas. The crucial similarity is that, although there is an unbreakable link between complex abstract ideas and our ability to use language, a set of ideas is independent of any particular account of it. Just as a concrete situation can be described in indefinitely many different texts, so, too, can an abstract concept or theory. The components of the theory and the relations between them can be referred to in different ways, and understanding an abstract text involves mapping between the particular linguistic account of the abstract theory, and the elements of the theory and the relations between them.

An important feature of abstract texts (e.g., the texts that psycholinguists read most of the time in their professional capacity) is that they do not simply describe or set out abstract ideas; instead, they provide arguments for and against different theoretical positions. Arguments are structured, and thus, texts that set out those arguments also have structure. One way of characterizing that structure is to recognize *coherence relations* as holding between the different parts of a text (e.g., Grimes, 1975; Hobbs, 1983; Longacre, 1976; Mann & Thompson, 1986). Garnham (1991) argued that there is no need to postulate a separate set of coherence relations to explain the relations between the information in the different parts of a text; rather, the relations between the parts of a text reflect relations between the parts of the "world" that they are about. In the case of narratives, for example, the relations are typically spatial, temporal, causal, intentional, and moral and are signaled in the text by a variety of devices, such as spatial relational terms, temporal relational terms, temporal anaphora, tense, explicit causal connectives, and so on. For these relations, the argument against the idea that they are specifically textual relations, originally couched in response to the notion of a story grammar (Garnham, 1983), generalizes immediately. If two clauses refer to an effect and its cause, the correct account of why they cohere is not that a causal coherence relation holds between them; instead, their coherence arises indirectly from the fact that they describe events, states, or processes that are causally related in the world that the text is about.

Furthermore, a full account of the lexical, structural, and discourse semantics and pragmatics of markers of spatial, temporal, causal, intentional, and moral relations would leave no task for coherence relations to perform. For example, nothing is gained by saying that, in addition to the relations between events, states, and processes signaled by temporal markers, two segments of a text are linked by a temporal coherence relation.

The set of relations between the parts of a text that reflect the structure of its arguments are not so easily dismissed. Indeed, coherence-relation theorists typically offer a more detailed and more sophisticated account of these relations than of temporal relations, for example. However, just as a situation can be described in different texts, the same argument can be expressed in different texts. Furthermore, a text that presents its arguments clearly will be coherent, much as a descriptive text that presents a sequence of events clearly will be coherent. It helps if the arguments are also good ones, but a text that presents a poor argument still can be coherent. If it is expounding an argument that is not the author's, there may sometimes be no choice but to present a poor argument.

Because arguments exist independently of the particular texts that expound them, we need a theory of what makes a good argument or how arguments are structured. Once we have such a theory, we will be able to say that a text is coherent if it presents arguments in a way that makes their structure clear. In constructing such a theory, it will be necessary to recognize that there is not just one way in which arguments can be good or bad. In particular, good arguments might be valid or convincing (or both). Thus, a theory of what makes a good argument will draw on both logic and rhetoric. It will not, however, draw on a theory of coherence. Rather, once we have a theory about arguments, we will be able to explain the coherence of texts, at least in part, with reference to that theory. Texts that present arguments are not coherent because their parts are related by argumentative coherence relations. Rather, the parts are indirectly related because they reflect some other structure—in this case the structure of arguments rather than the structure of the world.

CONCLUSIONS

The mental models theory provides a framework for thinking about text comprehension (and other aspects of cognition). It places a greater emphasis on task analysis and computational theory, in Marr's (1982) sense, than do other theories of text comprehension. It does so in the belief that unless we can give an account of what it is to make an inference or to interpret an anaphoric expression, it is unlikely that we will be able carry out sensible empirical investigations of comprehension processes.

The origins of mental models theory can be found in Bransford's three insights: (a) a mental representation of the content of a text is not a representation of its linguistic form, (b) comprehension is an integrative process, and (c) comprehension is a constructive process. The theory has elaborated and refined these ideas, and at least in the case of the first two insights, has built considerably on Bransford's original suggestions. In the case of the constructive aspect of comprehension, it is not clear that much in the way of a theoretical advance has been made, but much more is known about inference making than was known in the early 1970s when Bransford was suggesting, incorrectly, that many elaborative inferences are made online.

In developing an account of the integrative aspect of comprehension, particular attention has been paid to local coherence and anaphoric links. Indeed, the study of anaphoric processing has been one of the primary concerns of mental models theorists working on text comprehension. Another focus of attention has been spatial mental models because, in the spatial domain, it is easy to distinguish between the structure of a spatial layout and the structure of a linguistic description of it. The application of the theory, however, is intended to be more general, and we have outlined how its major insights can be applied to abstract and to argumentative texts.

ACKNOWLEDGMENTS

Our work on mental models theory and the interpretation of anaphoric expressions was supported by grant C00232439 "Mental Models and the Interpretation of Anaphora" from the ESRC and by NATO Collaborative Research Grant CRG 890527 "A Cross-Linguistic Study of Anaphor Interpretation."

REFERENCES

Adams, M. J. (1990). *Beginning to read*. Cambridge, MA: MIT Press.

Anderson, R. C., & Ortony, A. (1975). On putting apples into bottles: A problem of polysemy. *Cognitive Psychology, 7*, 167–180.

Barton, S. B., & Sanford, A. J. (1993). A case study of anomaly detection: Shallow semantic processing and cohesion establishment. *Memory and Cognition, 21*, 477–487.

Bosch, P. (1983). *Agreement and anaphora: A study of the role of pronouns in syntax and discourse*. London: Academic Press.

Bransford, J. D., Barclay, J. R., & Franks, J. J. (1972). Sentence memory: A constructive versus interpretive approach. *Cognitive Psychology, 3*, 193–209.

Bransford, J. D., & Franks, J. J. (1971). The abstraction of linguistic ideas. *Cognitive Psychology, 2*, 331–350.

Caramazza, A., & Zurif, E. B. (1976). Dissociation of algorithmic and heuristic processes in language comprehension: Evidence from aphasia. *Brain and Language, 3*, 572–582.

Carlson, G. N., & Tanenhaus, M. K. (1988). Thematic roles and language comprehension. In W. Wilkins (Ed.), *Syntax and semantics 21: Thematic relations* (pp. 263–288). New York: Academic Press.

Carreiras, M., Garnham, A., & Oakhill, J. V. (1993). The use of superficial and meaning-based representations in interpreting pronouns: Evidence from Spanish. *European Journal of Cognitive Psychology, 5*, 93–116.

Corbett, A. T., & Dosher, B. A. (1978). Instrument inferences in sentence encoding. *Journal of Verbal Learning and Verbal Behavior, 17*, 479–491.

Cornish, F. (1986). *Anaphoric pronouns in English and French: A discourse perspective*. London: Croom Helm.

Cornish, F. (1988). Anaphoric pronouns: Under linguistic control or signalling particular discourse representations? A contribution to the debate between Peter Bosch, and Liliane Tasmowski and Paul Verluyten. *Journal of Semantics, 5*, 233–260.

Cruttenden, H. L. (1993). *The role of implicit causality and gender cue in the interpretation of pronouns*. Unpublished doctoral dissertation, University of Sussex, Brighton, UK.

Dosher, B. A., & Corbett, A. T. (1982). Instrument inferences and verb schemata. *Memory and Cognition, 10*, 531–539.

Ehrlich, K., & Johnson-Laird, P. N. (1982). Spatial descriptions and referential continuity. *Journal of Verbal Learning and Verbal Behavior, 21*, 296–306.

Garnham, A. (1982). Testing psychological theories about inference making. *Memory and Cognition, 10*, 341–349.

Garnham, A. (1983). What's wrong with story grammars. *Cognition, 15*, 145–154.

Garnham, A. (1987). Understanding anaphora. In A. W. Ellis (Ed.), *Progress in the psychology of language* (Vol. 3, pp. 253–300). Hillsdale, NJ: Lawrence Erlbaum Associates.

Garnham, A. (1991). Where does coherence come from? A psycholinguistic perspective. *Occasional Papers in Systemic Linguistics, 5*, 131–141.

Garnham, A. (1992). Minimalism versus constructionism: A false dichotomy in theories of inference during reading. PSYCOLOQUY 3(63) reading-inference.1.1.

Garnham, A. (1993). Dichotomy or not dichotomy? That is the question: Reply to Keenan on Garnham on reading-inference. PSYCOLOQUY 4(16) reading-inference.10.

Garnham, A., & Oakhill, J. V. (1987). Interpreting elliptical verb phrases. *Quarterly Journal of Experimental Psychology, 39A*, 611–627.

Garnham, A., & Oakhill, J. V. (1988). "Anaphoric islands" revisited. *Quarterly Journal of Experimental Psychology, 40A*, 719–735.

Garnham, A., & Oakhill, J. V. (1992). Discourse representation and text processing from a "mental models" perspective. *Language and Cognitive Processes, 7*, 193–204.

Garnham, A., & Oakhill, J. V. (in prep.). *Mental models and the interpretation of anaphora*.

Garnham, A., Oakhill, J. V., & Cruttenden, H. (1992). The role of implicit causality and gender cue in the interpretation of pronouns. *Language and Cognitive Processes, 7*, 231–255.

Garnham, A., Oakhill, J. V., & Johnson-Laird, P. N. (1982). Referential continuity and the coherence of discourse. *Cognition, 11*, 29–46.

Garvey, C., & Caramazza, A. (1974). Implicit causality in verbs. *Linguistic Inquiry, 4*, 459–464.

Gernsbacher, M. A., & Robertson, R. R. W. (1992). Knowledge activation versus sentence mapping when representing fictional characters' emotional states. *Language and Cognitive Processes, 7*, 353–371.

Greene, S. B., McKoon, G., & Ratcliff, R. (1992). Pronoun resolution and discourse models. *Journal of Experimental Psychology: Learning, Memory and Cognition, 18*, 266–283.

Grimes, J. E. (1975). *The thread of discourse*. The Hague, Netherlands: Mouton.

Grosz, B. J. (1981). Focusing and description in natural language dialogues. In A. K. Joshi, B. L. Webber, & I. A. Sag (Eds.), *Elements of discourse understanding* (pp. 84–105). Cambridge, England: Cambridge University Press.

Grosz, B. J., Joshi, A. K., & Weinstein, S. (1983). Providing a unified theory of definite noun phrases in discourse. *Proceedings of the 21st annual meeting of the Association for Computational Linguistics*, 44–50.

Grosz, B. J., & Sidner, C. L. (1986). Attention, intentions, and the structure of discourse. *Computational Linguistics, 12*, 175–204.

Gumenik, W. E. (1979). The advantage of specific terms over general terms as cues for sentence recall: Instantiation or retrieval? *Memory and Cognition, 7*, 240–244.

Hankamer, J., & Sag, I. A. (1976). Deep and surface anaphora. *Linguistic Inquiry, 7*, 391–428.

Hobbs, J. R. (1983). Why is discourse coherent? In F. Neubauer (Ed.), *Coherence in natural language texts* (Vol. 38, pp. 29–70). Hamburg: Helmut Buske Verlag.

Isard, S. D. (1975). Changing the context. In E. L. Keenan (Ed.), *Formal semantics of natural language* (pp. 287–296). Cambridge, England: Cambridge University Press.

Joshi, A. K., & Weinstein, S. (1981). Control of inference: Role of some aspects of discourse structured-centering. *Proceedings of the 7th International Joint Conference of Artificial Intelligence*, 385–387.

Kamp, H. (1979). Events, instants and temporal reference. In R. Bauerle, U. Egli, & A. von Stechow (Eds.), *Semantics from different points of view* (pp. 376–417). Berlin: Springer-Verlag.

Kamp, H., & Rohrer, C. (1983). Tense in texts. In R. Bauerle, C. Schwarze, & A. von Stechow (Eds.), *Meaning, use, and interpretation of language* (pp. 250–269). Berlin: de Gruyter.

Kintsch, W., & van Dijk, T. A. (1978). Towards a model of text comprehension and reproduction. *Psychological Review, 85*, 363–394.

Linebarger, M., Schwartz, M., & Saffran, E. (1983). Sensitivity to grammatical structure in so-called agrammatic aphasics. *Cognition, 13*, 361–392.

Longacre, R. E. (1976). *An anatomy of speech notions*. Lisse, The Netherlands: Peter de Ridder Press.

Mann, W. C., & Thompson, S. A. (1986). Relational propositions in discourse. *Discourse Processes, 9*, 57–90.

Marcus, M. P. (1984). Some inadequate theories of human language processing. In T. G. Bever, J. M. Carroll, & L. A. Miller (Eds.), *Talking minds: The study of language in the cognitive sciences* (pp. 253–278). Cambridge, MA: MIT Press.

Marr, D. (1982). *Vision: A computational investigation into the human representation and processing of visual information*. San Francisco: Freeman.

Marslen-Wilson, W. D. (1975). Sentence perception as an interactive parallel process. *Science, 189*, 226–228.

McKoon, G., & Ratcliff, R. (1992). Inference during reading. *Psychological Review, 99*, 440–466.

Miller, G. A., & Johnson-Laird, P. N. (1976). *Language and perception*. Cambridge: Cambridge University Press.

Mitchell, D. C., & Green, D. W. (1978). The effects of context and content on immediate processing in reading. *Quarterly Journal of Experimental Psychology, 28*, 325–337.

Noordman, L. G. M., & Vonk, M. (1992). Reader's knowledge and the control of inference in reading. *Language and Cognitive Processes, 7*, 373–391.

Norris, D. (1985). Comprehension strategies and lexical priming. *Language and Speech, 27*, 355–366.

Oakhill, J. V., & Garnham, A. (1988). *Becoming a skilled reader*. Oxford, England: Basil Blackwell.

Oakhill, J. V., Garnham, A., & Vonk, W. (1989). The on-line construction of discourse models. *Language and Cognitive Processes, 4*, 263–286.

Reichman, R. (1978). Conversational coherency. *Cognitive Science, 2*, 283–327.

Sag, I. A., & Hankamer, J. (1984). Toward a theory of anaphoric processing. *Linguistics and Philosophy, 7*, 325–345.

Sanders, T. J. M., Spooren, W. P. M., & Noordman, L. G. M. (1992). Toward a taxonomy of coherence relations. *Discourse Processes, 15*, 1–35.

Sanford, A. J., Barton, S. B., Moxey, L. M., & Paterson, K. (1995). Cohesion processes, coherence, and anomaly detection. In G. Rickheit & C. Habel (Eds.), *Focus and processing in discourse coherence* (pp. 201–211). Berlin: de Gruyter.

Sanford, A. J., & Garrod, S. C. (1981). *Understanding written language: Explorations in comprehension beyond the sentence*. Chichester: Wiley.

Sanford, A. J., & Garrod, S. C. (1994). Selective mechanisms in text understanding. In M. Gernsbacher (Ed.), *Handbook of psycholinguistics* (pp. 699–719). San Diego: Academic Press.

Sidner, C. L. (1981). Focusing for interpretation of pronouns. *Computational Linguistics, 7*, 217–231.

Singer, M. (1980). The role of case-filling inferences in the comprehension of brief passages. *Discourse Processes, 3*, 185–201.

Singer, M. (1993). Minimalism: A hedged analysis of restricted inference processing: Commentary on Garnham and on Glenberg and Mathew on reading-inference. PSYCOLOQUY 4(1) reading-inference.2.

Smith, F. (1988). *Understanding reading: A psycholinguistic analysis of reading and learning to read* (4th ed.). Hillsdale, NJ: Lawrence Erlbaum Associates.

Stenning, K., Shepherd, M., & Levy, J. (1988). On the construction of representations for individuals from descriptions of texts. *Language and Cognitive Processes, 3*, 129–164.

Stenning, K., Nelson, A. W. R., Levy, J., Patel, M. J., & Gemmell, M. (1992). Representations of individuals and the processing of reference change. *Quarterly Journal of Experimental Psychology, 45A*, 373–398.

Tasmowski-De Ryck, L., & Verluyten, P. (1982). Linguistic control of pronouns. *Journal of Semantics, 1*, 323–346.

Thorndyke, P. W. (1976). The role of inferences in discourse comprehension. *Journal of Verbal Learning and Verbal Behavior, 15*, 437–446.

Wason, P. C., & Reich, S. S. (1979). A verbal illusion. *Quarterly Journal of Experimental Psychology, 31*, 591–597.

CHAPTER

13

FIVE METAPHORS FOR TEXT UNDERSTANDING

Arthur C. Graesser
University of Memphis

Bruce K. Britton
University of Georgia

What are the requirements for an ideal psychological model of text understanding? Such a model would capture the cognitive representations that are constructed during comprehension, and as a result of comprehension. It would specify the processing mechanisms that participate in the construction of these representations. The output of the model would match behavioral indices of online representations and processes, such as think-aloud protocols, reading times, and naming latencies for test words interspersed in the text. The output of the model would also match behavioral indices of the final representation that are achieved after comprehension is complete, such as recall, summarization, question answering, and ratings of the relatedness of text constituents. An ideal model would be applicable to different classes of texts, readers with different cognitive styles, and readers with different reading goals. It would be grounded in major theories of cognition. An ideal model would be specified in enough qualitative or mathematical detail to offer decisive predictions about human thought and behavior.

None of the contributors to this volume have developed an ideal model of text understanding. Each contributor is concentrating on a different piece of the puzzle. However, the enterprise in which they are engaged is moving closer toward an ideal model of text understanding. Indeed, most scientists would be impressed with the analytical and mathematical sophistication of the models presented in the chapters by Graesser, Turner, Goldman, Mannes, Fletcher, and van den Broek. (For ease of exposition, we refer to the chapters by first author only throughout this chapter.) Twenty years ago, quantitative models were entirely absent from the field of text and discourse processing; now the field is replete with numerous such models, or pieces of such models. As regards the match between data and theory, the results reported in some of the chapters in this volume show an impressive correspondence between human behavior and model output. As regards breadth, the collective contributions cover an impressive array of text and discourse genre: exposition (the chapters by Turner, Goldman, and Mannes), simple stories (the chapters by Fletcher, van den Broek, and Long), literary narrative (the chapters by Gibbs and Zwaan), argumentation (the chapter by Zwaan), everyday conversation (the chapters by Graesser and Gibbs), and short experimenter-generated texts (the chapters by Garnham and Gernsbacher). The field showed minimal sensitivity to the diversity of genre 20 years ago.

We are convinced that there has been visible progress in the science of text understanding. At the same time, it is important not to become overly infatuated with mathematical precision, analytical detail, and complexity. Sometimes a verbal articulation of a model is adequate for expressing a comprehension mechanism. The first author of this chapter recalls a conversation with a colleague who had suffered through an abstruse presentation at a conference. The presenter had reported on a complex mathematical model of text processing and memory that had six parameters. The colleague remarked that he was quite impressed with the model's mathematical precision, its scope, its complexity, and its close fit to the data. However, he then grumbled that he was not sure whether he had learned anything about understanding.

One way of organizing the contributions in this volume is to identify the pervasive metaphors that underlie the various models of text understanding. There no doubt are dozens of useful metaphors, but five were particularly salient to us:

1. Understanding is the assembly of a multileveled representation.
2. Understanding is the construction of a coherent representation.
3. Understanding is a complex dynamical system.
4. Understanding is the process of managing working memory.
5. Understanding is inference generation.

In this final chapter, we discuss the other 12 chapters from the perspective of these five metaphors.

UNDERSTANDING IS THE ASSEMBLY OF A MULTILEVELED REPRESENTATION

According to this metaphor, comprehenders build representations, codes, and structures at different levels of text and context. For example, most of the chapters adopted Kintsch's three-level contrast of the surface structure code, the propositional textbase, and the referential situation model (van Dijk & Kintsch, 1983;

Kintsch, 1988). Readers normally attend to and remember the referential situation model when they have extensive world knowledge about the text content, as in the case of a simple story or a newspaper article. In chapter 12, Garnham argued rather persuasively that a newspaper conveys information about events, not language. However, it is not always the case that readers focus on the situation model. In chapter 9, Zwaan presented theory and data that suggested that readers concentrate on the surface structure, and attenuate attention to the situation model, when reading narrative as literature. It is the textbase that apparently reigns supreme in the case of expository text, for which readers normally have little world knowledge about the topics being discussed. In chapters 2 and 3 by Turner and Goldman, respectively, the models were focused entirely at the level of the textbase, but they nevertheless provided an impressive account of memory for propositions in expository text (see also Britton & Gulgoz, 1991). Although Turner and Goldman advocated adding world knowledge to their future models, such an augmentation may yield minimal gains in the case of expository text. Expository text is normally written to inform the reader about new topics; by definition, readers have little world knowledge about these topics and, therefore, a minimal foundation for assembling a situation model.

There are other ways of cutting the pie in addition to Kintsch's three-level distinction. We can differentiate the text-message level from the pragmatic level of interaction (i.e., between writer and reader, speaker and listener, or narrator and reader). In chapter 10, Stein emphasizes the situated pragmatic interaction between speakers who are engaged in arguments. In contrast, in the case of decontextualized expository text, the pragmatic level plays a minimal, if not invisible, role. We can contrast the literal propositional meaning of the text from the intended meaning of the writer or speaker, as discussed by Gibbs in chapter 8. We can contrast the local level of text structure (i.e., contiguous or short sequences of clauses) from the global macrostructure of text, as discussed in the chapters by Graesser, Fletcher, van den Broek, Long, Gibbs, and Garnham. There probably are other ways of cutting the pie as well.

In chapter 12, Gernsbacher proposed a Structure Building Framework that specifies how structures are built within any particular level (see also Gernsbacher, 1990). In her model, initial information lays the foundation for the representation being assembled. This comparatively time-consuming process provides an explanation of why it takes longer to read initial words in sentences than later words, and initial sentences in paragraphs than later sentences. The initial foundation is subsequently elaborated as additional information in a text is comprehended. If an incoming proposition is relevant to the foundation, coherence within the level is maintained, and the time to comprehend the proposition is comparatively fast. Additional processing time is needed to handle coherence breaks or to shift focus from one structural foundation to another structural foundation. The Structure Building Framework can account for a large body of empirical data in psycholinguistics and text comprehension.

Most researchers have represented knowledge in the form of a structured set of nodes that are linked by relational arcs. Thus, the comprehender essentially assembles new nodes and relational arcs in a fashion analogous to a child building structures with tinker toys. This "node-and-arc" metaphor has proven useful because it allows researchers to keep track of analytical details and generate nontrivial predictions. It has been applied to most levels of representation, including the syntactic, the propositional textbase, belief systems, world knowledge, and the situation model. There have been arguments in cognitive science that challenge the aptness of the "node-and-arc" metaphor and similar symbolic notational systems. Alternative representational systems include distributed connectionist models (Rumelhart & McClelland, 1986; St. John, 1992) and the so-called "embodied" cognitive representations (Varela, Thompson, & Rosch, 1991). Future research in text and discourse should consider these alternative metaphors for representation more seriously.

One of the persistent mysteries in this area lies in the mappings and "communication" between levels of representation. It is widely acknowledged that the mapping between any two levels involves weak constraints rather than elegant, rigid algorithms. Thus, we may never find a simple parser that takes a syntactic structure as input and produces the appropriate textbase. Similarly, there may be no simple computational procedure that takes us from the textbase to the referential situation model. The construction of the situation model is a product of weak constraints from several sources of information: syntax, the lexicon, the textbase, world knowledge, the pragmatic level of interaction, and the immediate world being discussed. Although the mapping between any two levels is underdetermined, researchers must document and explain the many ways that the various levels constrain one another. We suspect that this will be one of the pressing challenges for many years to come.

UNDERSTANDING IS THE CONSTRUCTION OF COHERENT REPRESENTATIONS

Comprehenders believe that they understand text to the extent that they can conceptually relate the text elements and constituents. Suppose that a text has N explicit propositions. There would be $[N \times (N - 1)]/2$ potential pairwise connections. A text is fully connected if each proposition is conceptually connected to one or more other propositions. In this case, the text would satisfy a minimal formal criterion for coherence. A network of propositions achieves greater coherence to the extent that there are multiple connections with any given node. A network is incoherent to the extent that it includes propositions that are not connected to other propositions. A text with sparse connections is predicted to be difficult for a reader to understand.

The "understanding-as-coherence" metaphor was embraced, explicitly or implicitly, by the authors of most of the chapters in this volume. However, the types of connections that were thought to link propositions vary somewhat from chapter to chapter. The contributors to several chapters (Turner, Goldman, Mannes, Fletcher, van den Broek, and Gernsbacher) regarded the noun-phrase arguments of propositions as critical for connecting propositions and establishing text coherence; that is, two propositions are connected if they share at least one noun argument. The emphasis on argument overlap can be attributed, in part, to Kintsch's early claim that argument overlap is an important foundation for establishing text coherence (Kintsch, 1974). However, subsequent research has established that argument overlap is neither a necessary nor sufficient criterion for establishing coherence; instead, it is merely one type of connection among many. This has led researchers to consider other types of connections. In chapter 2, Turner examined connections between the predicates of propositions. The chapters by Fletcher, van den Broek, and Long examined the causal connections and goals of story characters that explain why actions and events occur. Gibbs identified the strands that tie deep metaphors to lexical items and explicit expressions. Clearly, there are many classes of connections that tie text constituents together, and text constituents to information units in world knowledge structures.

The "understanding-as-coherence" metaphor offers a number of predictions that have been confirmed in empirical research. As reported in chapter 6, by van den Broek, a proposition has a greater likelihood of being recalled to the extent that it has more connections to other propositions in the text. Reading time for a proposition increases if there is a break in coherence (see chapter by Gernsbacher) and if the incoming proposition needs to be connected to a proposition mentioned much earlier in the text (see the chapters by Fletcher and van den Broek). In chapter 4, Mannes reported that there are more connections (or stronger connections) between text and world knowledge if there is a discrepancy between an outline and text content; this results in improved problem solving, but not recall for the text per se. The "understanding-as-coherence" metaphor supplies a large number of predictions about comprehension performance. Some of the predictions are intuitively compelling, whereas others are counterintuitive.

UNDERSTANDING IS A COMPLEX DYNAMICAL SYSTEM

This metaphor is inspired by theoretical developments that have occurred in virtually all sciences. Many mechanisms in the natural and physical sciences unfold in a complex dynamic fashion. Simple finite-state automata assume that a system can be described adequately by a small finite set of states and a small set of transition matrices, one for each process, that specify the likelihood that a theoretical entity will change states. Complex dynamical systems are not that simple. There is a large, if not infinite, set of states. There also is a large set of invariant transition matrices. In addition, a complex dynamical system can evolve along an unpredictable chaotic trajectory, at least from the perspective of a human's interpretation of the system. Thus, it may be impossible to capture a complex dynamical system with a set of linear equations or with a set of simple rules.

Consider a complex dynamical system in the arena of text comprehension. Most of the contributors in this volume would assume there is a set of *P* explicit nodes (such as propositions), a limited-capacity working memory, and a set of *M* nodes stored in long-term memory. The activation level of each node in *P* and *M* is potentially modified as each explicit node is comprehended online. There is a final activation value for each node, once the text is finished being comprehended. The goal is to identify a mechanism that accurately specifies the correct activation values of the nodes as the text is incrementally comprehended, word by word or sentence by sentence. The adequacy of the mechanism is tested by observing the goodness-of-fit between the activation values of nodes and behavioral indices that should correspond to these activation values. For example, the behavioral indices were recall probabilities for the *P* explicit nodes in the chapters by Turner, Goldman, Mannes, Fletcher, and van den Broek.

There were two major computational architectures that the contributors to this volume found useful for simulating the complex dynamical systems involved in comprehension. The first was a classical computational architecture in cognitive science; namely, that of a production system (Anderson, 1983; Laird, Rosenbloom, & Newell, 1987). The chapters by Turner, Goldman, and Fletcher explicitly adopted the production system architecture.

A production system consists of a set of production rules that (a) govern the operation of working memory, (b) scan explicit input, (c) change activation values of information in long-term memory and working memory, and (d) produce output. Each production rule has an "*if* <state> *then* <action>" form; that is, if the contents of working memory includes state *S*, then action *A* is executed. All the production rules are evaluated in a parallel fashion. The state and action slots are complex entities in the recent models that have simulated comprehension processes, such as Just and Carpenter's (1992) CAPS/READER (collaborative activation-based production system) model. That is, a state slot may consist of a long list of substates, such that each substate is satisfied if it meets or exceeds some threshold of activation. An action slot can consist of the modification of activation values of nodes in *P* and *M*; the action involves spreading activation to other particular nodes in the system. Therefore, the production rules in the CAPS/READER model are hardly brittle, discrete, and simple. The activation values of the nodes in the text and long-term memory are modified along a quantitative continuum in a complex but systematic fashion. The behavior of the system is sometimes difficult to trace and capture by simple rules or formulae.

The second computational architecture includes connectionist models. These models have become quite popular in cognitive science during the last decade, and are regarded as a radical alternative to the classical symbolic architectures (Rumelhart & McClelland, 1986). Connectionist modeling was first applied to text comprehension by Kintsch (1988). Since then, researchers have used connectionist architectures to model memory for explicit text (Golden & Rumelhart, 1993), the activation of inferences (St. John, 1992), and other mechanisms involved in text comprehension. In this volume, the chapters by Graesser, Goldman, Mannes, van den Broek, and Zwaan incorporated connectionism in their modeling efforts.

Consider a simple connectionist model that includes only the *P* explicit nodes. The activation value of each node fluctuates systematically during the course of comprehension, proposition by proposition. A set of weights specifies the extent to which each node activates or inhibits the activation of each of the other nodes. There would be $[P \times P - P]$ weights in the weight space. If a particular node reaches some threshold of activation, it spreads activation to the other nodes according to the weights in the weight space. This spreading activation evolves over several cycles until the process settles on a stable set of activation values for the entire set of nodes. This process of spreading activation and settling occurs as each proposition is incrementally interpreted. Memory for any particular node reflects the final activation value of the node at the end of the text, or the number of cycles in which the proposition achieves some minimal threshold of activation. Two nodes are related to the extent that they share high activation as the propositions are incrementally comprehended.

It is important to acknowledge that some models are hybrids that incorporate connectionism, production systems, and other computational architectures. In chapter 3, for example, Goldman combined Just and Carpenter's (1992) CAPS model (a production system architecture) with Kintsch's Construction-Integration model, which has a connectionist architecture. In chapter 5, Fletcher combined production systems with Shiffrin's Search of Associative Memory (SAM) model (Raaijmakers & Shiffrin, 1981). Hybrid models such as these take advantage of the positive features of multiple models and circumvent the shortcomings of any particular model.

It is not easy to test the psychological plausibility of models that involve complex dynamical systems. These models have a large number of assumptions, parameters, and production rules. It would require too much time to explore the total space of parameter values to determine the combination of values that provides the best fit to the data. It also would require too much time to determine the set of production rules, properly tuned, that have the closest match to data. Once the best fitting model is found, there remains the labor-intensive task of performing a sensitivity analysis for each production rule or parameter value. That is, the researcher must determine how much the system deteriorates when a particular production rule is removed or a particular parameter value varied. Similarly, it would take too much time to provide a thorough comparison of the models. Because of these practical limitations, the enterprise has settled for a more modest goal, namely, building the model and determining the extent to which it produces output that significantly correlates with human data. Thus, the contributors to this volume frequently reported how much variance in the data was explained by their model or whether there was a reasonable qualitative fit to a pattern of means. This is indeed an important first step in evaluating a model. However, it is important to acknowledge that this is not a thorough test. In the future, researchers must give more thought to providing rigorous tests when evaluating models, comparing models, and assigning credit to particular model components.

UNDERSTANDING IS THE MANAGEMENT OF WORKING MEMORY

The contributors to this volume have assumed that comprehension is managed in a limited-capacity working memory. As argued by Baddeley (1986), working memory contains a passive storage component and an active component that manipulates the contents of both long-term memory and working memory. The exact upper bound of working memory is a less pressing issue than is the fact that working memory has an upper bound in storage capacity and processing resources. Several predictions can be derived from the notion that working memory has capacity limitations. First, reading time should slow as working memory approaches the upper bound of capacity limitations. Second, if the demands of text comprehension exceed the limitations of working memory, there should be a catastrophic deterioration in comprehension performance. Third, readers with high working memory spans should enjoy advantages in comprehension to the extent that comprehension components are demanding on working memory. These predictions have been confirmed in empirical studies of Just and Carpenter (1992).

The central question, from the standpoint of text understanding, is as follows: What information is inserted or maintained in working memory as comprehension proceeds, sentence by sentence? Stated differently, what nodes occupy working memory when a particular sentence is comprehended? Some of the contributors to this volume make very specific claims about the management of working memory. In chapter 2, Turner's Prediction Semantics Model reduces complex sentences (e.g., *Australia has more sheep than any other country*) to simple descriptions (e.g., *Australia has sheep*) by eliminating less important predicates. Propositions are held over in working memory to the extent that they are connected to other propositions in the network. In the chapters by Fletcher and van den Broek, working memory tends to maintain the following classes of propositions while reading stories: propositions that share arguments with other propositions; the goals of protagonists that motivate their actions; and events that have causal antecedents but no consequences. In chapter 3, Goldman developed a dynamic model of working memory management by including in the model production rules that are sensitive to the goals of the reader, working memory load, and text elements. In chapter 7, Long proposed that information is active in working memory to the extent that it explains why actions and events occur in stories (see also Graesser, Singer, & Trabasso, 1994; Trabasso & Suh, 1993). These models offer distinctive predictions that can be tested with online behavioral measures, such as reading times, naming latencies for test words, lexical-decision latencies for test strings, and think-aloud protocols. There are also indirect tests of these working memory assumptions. For example, later recall of the text propositions increases as a function of the number of cycles that the proposition is held in working memory (as reported in the chapters by Turner, Goldman, Fletcher, and van den Broek).

Once again, comprehension deteriorates when working memory is not adequately managed. Deterioration occurs if the processing demands of the text exceeds working memory resources, and if the reader has a low working memory span. In chapter 12, Gernsbacher argued that poor comprehenders have problems suppressing irrelevant information from working memory. Thus, good readers know what cards to keep and what cards to throw away.

UNDERSTANDING IS INFERENCE GENERATION

Understanding involves more than interpreting explicit text propositions. It involves accessing relevant world knowledge and generating inferences that are needed to provide local and global coherence. Some of these inferences are copied from the content of activated world knowledge structures, whereas other inferences are novel constructions that are needed to construct the referential situation model. A satisfactory model of text understanding should be able to accurately predict those inferences that are generated online versus those that are not generated online during comprehension. The chapters by Graesser, Mannes, Long, Gibbs, and Garnham directly confronted the problem of inference generation.

There is an important distinction between inferences that are quickly or automatically made during comprehension and those that are time consuming. Consider first those inferences that are quickly generated. At one end of the continuum, McKoon and Ratcliff's (1992) *minimalist hypothesis* predicts that very few inferences are quickly generated online. These include inferences that are readily accessible in working memory or long-term memory and inferences that are necessary for achieving local text cohesion. At the other end of the continuum, the *promiscuous inference generation* hypothesis predicts that virtually all classes of inferences are quickly generated. The truth probably lies somewhere between these two extremes. For example, the *constructionist theory* proposed in chapter 1 by Graesser (see also Graesser et al., 1994) predicts that readers quickly generate the following classes of inferences: inferences that address the reader's goals, inferences that assist in establishing coherence at local or global levels, inferences that explain why actions and events occur in stories, and inferences that are highly activated from multiple information sources. In chapter 7, Long reported data that show that readers of stories quickly activate the superordinate goals that motivate protagonists' actions (e.g., *the heroes fought the dragon* generates the superordinate goal "helping a victim"). These superordinate goals are very quickly generated by readers who have highly developed reading ability. The superordinate goals are not needed to establish local text cohesion, and, thus, Long's data are incompatible with the minimalist hypothesis. Instead, the data support Graesser's constructionist theory and other models that predict more than minimal inference generation.

Consider next the inferences that are more time-consuming to generate. Some of these are a struggle to generate because there is modest world knowledge about the topic discussed in the text. Others are a result of contradictions, anomalies, or irrelevant propositions in the text; the reader attempts to generate explanations and justifications that accommodate the contradictions, anomalies, and irrelevancies. In chapter 1, Graesser reported that comprehenders ask questions that address such incompatible information. In chapter 4, Mannes reported that more elaborative inferences are generated when there is an incompatibility between an outline and the text content. These processes assisted readers in a later problem-solving task, but lowered performance when they were asked to recall the explicit material. The process of generating these elaborative inferences is time consuming and may be circumvented by readers with low motivation.

The status of deep global inferences merits more attention in future research. For example, Graesser et al. (1994) lamented that there is virtually no research on the online status of global thematic inferences that capture the point of a story (e.g., "haste makes waste"), inferences about the author's intent or attitude in writing the text (e.g., "the author resents workaholics"), and inferences that capture the appropriate emotional reaction of the reader (e.g., "the reader should be shocked"). In chapter 8, Gibbs offered persuasive arguments that deep metaphors are very prevalent in literature and discourse. However, the empirical evidence is lacking when it comes to determining when and whether these metaphors are generated online. Global inferences need more attention in future research.

FINAL COMMENTS

Now that all is said and done, someone might ask the following question: What is text understanding? In light of the five metaphors discussed in this chapter, we would offer the following definition: Text understanding is the dynamic process of constructing coherent representations and inferences at multiple levels of text and context, within the bottleneck of a limited-capacity working memory. To some, this definition is comprehensive and general, but rather vague. Fortunately, we are rescued by the modeling efforts of the contributors to this volume.

The models help elevate our enterprise from a collection of vague ideas to a coordinated system that furnishes claims with teeth. As a consequence, we have had much to say that our grandparents never told us.

REFERENCES

Anderson, J. R. (1983). *The architecture of cognition*. Cambridge, MA: Harvard University Press.

Baddeley, A. D. (1986). *Working memory*. New York: Oxford University Press.

Britton, B. K., & Gulgoz, S. (1991). Using Kintsch's computational model to improve instructional text: Effects of repairing inference calls on recall and cognitive structures. *Journal of Educational Psychology, 83*, 329–345.

Gernsbacher, M. A. (1990). *Language comprehension as structure building*. Hillsdale, NJ: Lawrence Erlbaum Associates.

Golden, R. M., & Rumelhart, D. E. (1993). A parallel distributed processing model of story comprehension and recall. *Discourse Processes, 16*, 203–237.

Graesser, A. C., Singer, M., & Trabasso, T. (1994). Constructing inferences during narrative text comprehension. *Psychological Review, 101*, 371–395.

Just, M. A., & Carpenter, P. A. (1992). A capacity theory of comprehension: Individual differences in working memory. *Psychological Review, 99*, 122–149.

Kintsch, W. (1974). *The representation of meaning in memory*. Hillsdale, NJ: Lawrence Erlbaum Associates.

Kintsch, W. (1988). The role of knowledge in discourse comprehension: A constructive-integration model. *Psychological Review, 95*, 163–182.

Laird, J., Rosenbloom, P. S., & Newell, A. (1987). SOAR: An architecture for general intelligence. *Artificial Intelligence, 33*(1), 1–64.

McKoon, G., & Ratcliff, R. (1992). Inference during reading. *Psychological Review, 99*, 400–466.

Raaijmakers, J. G., & Shiffrin, R. M. (1981). Search of associative memory. *Psychological Review, 88*, 93–134.

Rumelhart, D. E., & McClelland, J. L. (1986). *Parallel distributed processing: Explorations in the microstructure of cognition* (Vol. 1). Cambridge: MIT Press.

St. John, M. F. (1992). The Story Gestalt: A model of knowledge-intensive processes in text comprehension. *Cognitive Science, 16*, 271–306.

Trabasso, T., & Suh, S. Y. (1993). Using talk-aloud protocols to reveal inferences during comprehension of text. *Discourse Processes, 16*, 3–34.

van Dijk, T. A., & Kintsch, W. (1983). *Strategies of discourse comprehension*. New York: Academic Press.

Varela, F. J., Thompson, E., & Rosch, E. (1991). *The embodied mind*. Cambridge, MA: MIT Press.

AUTHOR INDEX

A

Aaronson, D., 290, *308*
Abbott, V., 198, *211*, 235, *237*
Abelson, R., 17, *30*, 198, *213*, 235, *239*
Adams, M. J., 317, *336*
Albrecht, J. E., 166, 167, 181, *185*, *186*, 245, *253*
Alighieri, D., 225, *237*
Allbritton, D., 229, 230, *237*
Allen, J., 104, *110*
Allprot, D. A., 302, *308*
Alterman, R., 54, *69*
Aman, C. J., 203, *212*
Amster, H., 133, *138*
Anderson, A., 291, 292, *308*
Anderson, J. R., 153, *162*, 293, 296, 302, *308*, 346, *351*
Anderson, P. A., 13, 16, *29*, 193, 197, 198, *212*
Anderson, R. C., 115, *138*, 324, *336*
Andrusiak, P., 206, *213*
Antos, S., 222, *239*
Austin, J. L., 3, *27*

B

Bach, K., 3, *27*
Baddeley, A. D., 348, *351*
Baggett, W. B., 6, 19, 20, *29*, *31*
Baillet, S. D., 158, *162*, 291, *310*
Balota, D. A., 202, 203, *211*, *212*
Barclay, J. R., 313, 314, 316, 321, *336*
Barger, J., 22, *31*
Barlow, J., 217, *239*
Barsalou, L. W., 103, 105, *110*
Barthelme, D., 246, *254*
Bartlett, F. C., 16, *27*, 228, *237*
Barton, S. B., 318, *336*, *339*
Bates, E., 243, 244, *254*
Bazerman, M. H., 257, *285*
Beckwith, R., 57, 59, *71*
Beeman, M., 291, 292, *308*, *309*
Begg, I., 293, *308*
Berlyne, D. E., 16, 22, *27*
Bernas, R. S., 264, 282, *286*
Bever, T. G., 37, *70*, 305, *308*
Birnbaum, L., 22, *31*
Black, J. B., 17, *27*, 144, *162*, 192, 197,198, *211*, *213*, 228, 235, *237*, *239*, 291, *308*
Black, N. L., 206, *213*
Bloom, B. S., 23, *27*
Bloom, C. P., 15, *28*, 75, *111*, 141, 142, 146, 147, 150, 156, 157, *162*, 167, 176, 182, *184*, *185*, 192, 193, *211*, 245, *254*
Bly, B., 281, *285*

Bock, J. K., 290, *308*
Bolliger, C. M., 244, *254*
Bookin, H., 223, *238*
Bosch, P., 329, *336*
Bovair, S., 154, *162*
Bower, G. H., 11, 12, 17, 27, 28, 30, 123, 138, 144, 162, 166, 185, 197, 198, 211, 212, 228, 235, 237, 244, 255, 291, 293, 298, 308
Braeges, J. L., 263, 282, *286*
Brainerd, L. E., 193, *212*
Bransford, J. D., 115, *138*, 189, *211*, 228, *237*, 297, *308*, 313, 314, 315, 316, 321, *336*
Brewer, W. F., 228, *237*, 247, *255*, 280, *285*
Britt, M. A., 101, *112*
Britton, B. K., 11, 15, 27, 60, 69, 74, 75, 76, 109, 112, 168, 184, 220, 238, 244, 254, 343, 351
Brooks, C., 133, *138*
Brooks, R. A., 11, *27*
Brown, A. L., 22, *30*
Brown, A. S., 302, *309*
Brown, J. S., 22, *28*
Brown, P., 158, *162*, 291, *310*
Brown, S., 260, 264, *285*
Bruner, J., 11, *27*

C

Calicchia, D. J., 264, 282, *286*
Campbell, J. P., 22, *27*
Caramazza, A., 317, 326, *336*, *337*
Carlson, C., 259, 263, 275, 282, *285*
Carlson, G. N., 326, *336*
Carpenter, P. A., 12, 14, *29*, 73, 74, 76, 102, 103, *111*, *112*, 182, *185*, 218, *237*, 246, 252, *254*, 346, 347, 348, *351*
Carreiras, M., 291, *309*, 332, *337*
Carroll, P., 222, *238*
Carstensen, L. L., 266, *286*
Casteel, M. A., 181, *184*
Chen, A. H., 101, *112*
Chiesi, H. L., 59, *71*, 73, *112*, 146, *163*, 189, *211*, *214*, 228, *239*
Chinn, C. A., 280, *285*
Chmiel, N. R. J., 302, *308*
Chrysler, S. T., 176, *185*, 243, *254*
Chumbley, J. L., 202, *211*
Clark, H. H., 2, 8, *27*, 104, *111*, 233, 234, *237*, 291, 293, *309*, *310*
Clark, L. F., 14, 16, 18, 19, 20, 21, *28*, *29*, 54, 59, *70*, 167, 175, *184*, 191, 192, 193, 197, 198, *212*
Clark, M. B., 73, *113*, 206, *214*, 253, *255*
Clark, N. K., 146, *162*
Clark, S. E., 150, *163*
Cleeremans, A., 5, *27*
Clements, P., 292, *309*
Clifton, C., Jr., 291, 293, *309*
Cohen, R., 4, 6, *31*
Collins, A., 22, 23, *28*
Companario, J. M., 23, *30*
Conant, C. L., 258, *286*
Cooper, C. R., 259, 263, 275, 282, *285*
Corbett, A. T., 192, *211*, 323, *337*
Cornish, F., 332, *337*
Cote, N., 89, 103, *111*, *112*
Crain, M., 4, *31*
Cruttenden, H. L., 327, *337*
Cullingford, R. E., 2, *31*
Curtis, M. E., 58, *71*

D

D'Andrade, R. G., 2, 3, *28*
Daft, R. L., 22, *27*
Dahlgran, K., 59, *69*
Danaher, D. L., 282, *286*
Daneman, M., 252, *254*
Dashiell, J., 218, *237*
de Beaugrande, R., 37, *70*
Deaton, J. A., 176, *185*, 291, *309*
DeJong, G., 17, *28*
Dell, G., 192, *211*
Denhiere, G., 76, 105, *112*
Dewey, J., 218, *237*
Dillon, J. T., 22, 23, *28*
Doane, S. M., 123, 125, *139*
Donlan, D., 22, *31*
Dooling, D. J., 189, 190, *211*
Dopkins, S., 21, *28*, 167, 168, *184*, *185*
Dosher, B. A., 192, *211*, 323, *337*
Duffy, S. A., 13, 22, *30*, 158, *163*, 168, 175, *185*, 291, 292, *309*, *310*, *311*
Dunbar, K., 22, *29*
Duncan, M. K., 4, *31*
Dunn, J., 258, 263, *285*, *287*
Dyer, M. G., 16, 17, *28*

E

Eckart, T., 23, *28*
Ehrlich, K., 291, *309*, 321, *337*
Eisenberg, A. R., 258, 259, *285*
Ellis, H. C., 124, 134, *139*
Elman, J. L., 5, *28*
Elsenhart, F. J., 168, *184*
Epstein, W., 23, *28*

Estes, W. K., 302, *309*
Evans, E., 22, *30*
Eymard, L. A., 56, *71*

F

Faust, M., 292, 294, 303, *309*, *310*
Feldman, S. S., 259, *286*
Fellbaum, C., 57, 59, *71*
Ferguson, W., 22, *31*
Ferreira, F., 192, *213*, 293, *309*
Ferres, S., 290, *308*
Fillmore, C. J., 35, *70*
Filyer, R., 258, 282, *286*
Fincher-Kiefer, R., 260, *287*
Fine, H., 217, *239*
Finger, E., 206, *213*
Fishbein, H. D., 23, *28*
Fisher, R., 260, 264, *285*
Fivush, R., 258, *286*
Flammer, A., 23, *28*
Fleet, J., 22, *30*
Fletcher, C. R., 15, *28*, 57, *70*, 74, 75, 76, 109, *111*, *112*, 141, 142, 146, 147, 150, 156, 157, *162*, 166, 167, 176, 182, *184*, *185*, *186*, 192, 193, *211*, 243, 245, *254* , 293, *309*
Fodor, J. A., 37, *70*
Foley, J. M., 23, *30*
Forbes, D., 282, *286*
Forster, K. I., 202, *211*
Foss, C. C., 197, *212*
Foss, D. J., 203, *212*, 290, *309*
Franklin, S. P., 6, *31*, 193, *212*
Franks, J. J., 297, *308*, 313, 314, 315, 316, 321, *336*
Frazier, L., 246, *254*, 291, *309*

G

Gallinger, G., 262, *286*
Garner, R., 100, *111*
Garnham, A., 12, *28*, 297, *309*, 317, 320, 321, 323, 325, 327, 328, 329, 332, 333, 334, *337*, *338*
Garrett, M. F., 37, *70*
Garrod, S. C., 235, *237*, *239*, 291, 292, *308*, 318, 330, *339*
Garvey, C., 258, 259, *285*, *286*, 326, *337*
Gemmell, M., 322, *339*
Genette, G., 247, *254*
Gentner, D., 218, 219, 220, *237*
Gernsbacher, M. A., 21, *28*, 103, *111*, 166, 168, *185*, 244, 245, *254*, 290, 291, 292, 293, 294, 295, 299, 303, 306, 307, *308*, *309*, *310*, 323, *337*, 343, *351*
Gerrig, R. J., 190, *212*, 222, 223, 236, *237*
Gholson, B., 56, *71*
Gibbs, R., 222, 223, 227, 229, 230, 231, 232, 233, 235, *237*, *238*, *239*
Gigerenzer, G., 219, *238*
Gildea, P., 223, *238*
Gillingham, M. D., 100, *111*
Gillund, G., 142, 148, 150, 156, *162*
Givon, T., 293, *310*
Gjellstad, L., 89, *111*
Glavanov, D., 116, *139*, 243, *255*
Glenberg, A. M., 12, 23, *28*, 244, *254*, 298, *310*
Glenn, C. G., 158, *163*, 173, *186*
Glucksberg, S., 217, 223, *238*
Glynn, S. M., 11, 15, *27*, 60, *69*, 220, *238*
Goffman, E., 2, *28*
Golden, R. M., 14, *28*, 167, 180, *185*, 347, *351*
Golding, J. M., 19, 20, 21, *29*, 168, *186*, 192, 193, 196, 197, 200, 201, 202, 203, 205, 206, *212*, *213*
Goldman, S. R., 73, 74, 77, 78, 80, 81, 89, 100, 101, 103, 105, 107, *111*, *112*
Goldsmith, H. H., 21, *28*, 245, *254*
Goodchild, F., 22, *30*
Goodman, M. S., 290, *310*
Goodwin, M. H., 258, 259, *286*
Gordon, S. E., 17, *28*, 193, *212*
Gottman, J. M., 260, 266, *286*
Graesser, A. C., 2, 6, 11, 13, 14, 15, 16, 17, 18, 19, 20, 21, 22, 23, 24, 25, 26, *28*, *29*, *30*, *31*, 54, 56, 59, *70*, *71*, 106, *111*, 166, 167, 168, 169, 175, 181, 182, *184*, *185*, *186*, 191, 192, 193, 196, 197, 198, 200, 201, 202, 203, *212*, 235, *238*, 241, *254*, 349, 350, *351*
Gray, J., 218, *238*
Green, D. W., 317, *338*
Greene, E., 55, *71*, 154, *163*, 169, *186*
Greene, S. B., 326, *337*
Greeno, J. G., 141, 146, 147, *162*
Greenspan, S. L., 12, *30*, 244, *255*
Greising, M., 22, *31*
Grice, H., 222, *238*
Grimes, J. E., 334, *337*
Gross, D., 57, 59, *71*
Grosz, B. J., 326, 330, *337*, *338*
Gruber, J., 35, *70*
Grudin, J., 218, 219, 220, *237*
Gulgoz, S., 60, *69*, 244, *254*, 343, *351*
Gumenik, W. E., 324, 338

H

Haberlandt, K., 19, 21, 28, 56, *71*, 241, *254*, 290, *310*
Haenggi, D., 244, *254*
Hakala, C. E., 245, *253*
Hankamer, J., 330, 331, 332, *338*
Hargreaves, D., 291, *309*
Harnish, R. M., 3, *27*
Haviland, S. E., 104, *111*, 291, *310*
Hay, D. R., 258, *286*
Hayes-Roth, B., 300, 301, *310*
Hemphill, D., 11, 15, *27*, 60, *69*, 193, *212*
Hilton, D. J., 22, *29*
Hobbs, J. R., 334, *338*
Hofer, M., 259, 263, *286*
Hogaboam, T., 206, *213*
Holmberg, D., 265, 266, 282, *286*
Huber, J., 23, *29*
Huitema, J. S., 167, *185*
Hulin, C. L., 22, *27*
Hummel, J. E., 142, *162*, 192, 193, *211*
Hunt, E. B., 206, *212*
Husebye-Hartmann, E., 166, 168, *186*

I

Inhoff, A., 222, *238*
Irwin, D. E., 290, *308*
Isard, S. D., 316, *338*

J

Jackendoff, R., 35, *70*
Jacob, R. J. K., 7, *29*
Jakobson, R., 242, *254*
James, W., 218, *238*
Jennings, T. M., 203, *212*
Jescheniak, J. D., 293, *309*
Johnson, B. K., 19, 20, *29*
Johnson, L. R., 259, *287*
Johnson, M. K., 115, *138*, 189, *211*, 224, 225, 234, *238*
Johnson, N. S., 15, *30*, 49, *71*, 158, *162*
Johnson-Laird, P. N., 12, 17, *29*, 244, 249, *254*, 296, 298, *310*, 317, 321, *337*, *338*
Joshi, A. K., 326, 330, *338*
Just, M. A., 12, 14, *29*, 73, 74, 76, 102, 103, *111*, *112*, 182, *185*, 218, *237*, 246, *254*, 346, 347, 348, *351*

K

Kahneman, D., 12, *29*
Kajer, W. K., 23, *30*
Kallen, H., 216, *238*
Kamp, H., 327, *338*
Keefe, D. E., 183, *185*, 192, *212*
Keele, S. W., 294, *310*
Keenan, J. M., 37, 57, *71*, 158, *162*, 168, *186*, 192, 202, 203, *212*, *213*, 243, *254*, 291, *310*
Keeton, J., 89, *111*
Keller, J., 259, 263, 275, 282, *285*
Kemper, S., 229, *238*
Kerry, T., 23, *29*
Keysar, B., 222, *238*
Kieras, D. E., 49, 57, *70*, 81, 103, *111*, 154, *162*, 290, *310*
King, A., 22, *29*
Kintsch, E., 73, 74, 75, 76, 100, 101, 103, 105, 109, *111*, *112*, *113*
Kintsch, W., 11, 12, 14, 15, 17, 20, *29*, *32*, 33, 34, 36, 37, 49, 52, 54, 56, 57, *71*, 116, 117, 118, 119, 121, 122, 123, 125, 134, *139*, 141, 142, 144, 146, 148, 150, 158, *162*, *163*, 166, 167, 171, 175, 176, 181, 182, *184*, *185*, *187*, 189, 192, 203, 207, 208, *212*, *214*, 241, 243, 244, 245, 246, 247, 250, 251, *254*, *255*, 296, 298, 303, 304, 305, *310*, *311*, 321, 322, *338*, 342, 343, 345, 347, *351*
Klahr, D., 22, *29*
Kletzien, S. B., 73, *112*
Klin, C. M., 21, *28*, 167, 168, 183, *184*, *185*, 192, *213*
Klusewitz, M. A., 182, *185*
Koch, P., 259, 263, 275, 282, *285*
Koizumi, D., 19, 21, *28*
Kovecses, Z., 225, *238*
Kowalski, D.,235, *238*
Kozminsky, E., 57, *71*
Kreuz, R. J., 11, 16, *28*, 166, 181, 182, *185*
Kuebli, J., 258, *286*
Kuhn, D., 257, *286*

L

Lachman, R., 189, 190, *211*
Laird, J., 346, *351*
Lakoff, G., 224, 225, 226, 227, 234, *238*
Lang, K. L., 16, 18, 22, *28*, 193, 196, 197, *212*
Langer, P., 203, *213*
Langmeyer, D., 23, *28*
Langston, M. C., 22, *28*
Larkin, K. M., 22, *28*
Lauver, E., 23, *28*
Lee-Sammons, W. H., 73, *112*

Lehnert, W. G., 17, *29*
Lesgold, A. M., 58, *71*, 206, *213*
Levenson, R. W., 266, *286*
Levine, L. J., 17, *31*, 258, 259, *287*
Levinger, G., 262, *286*
Levy, J., 322, *339*
Lewis, J., 206, *212*
Lima, S., 222, *238*
Lindem, K., 12, *28*, 244, *254*, 298, *310*
Linebarger, M., 317, *338*
Little, L. D., 23, *29*
Liwag, M. D., 258, 259, *286*, *287*
Lodge, D., 236, *238*
Lollis, S. P., 258, 282, *286*
Long, D. L., 19, 20, 21, *29*, 192, 193, 200, 201, 202, 203, 205, 206, *212*, 243, *254*
Longacre, R. E., 334, *338*
Lorch, E. P., 101, 112, 166, 167, 175, 182, 185, 186
Lorch, R. F., Jr., 15, 21, *31*, 81, 101, 105, *112*, 182, *185*, 203, *212*
Lovelace, E., 193, 197, *212*
Lucas, S., 133, *138*
Lunneborg, C., 206, *212*
Lynch, R. H., Jr., 290, *309*

M

MacDonald, C. D., 4, *31*
MacDonald, M. C., 103, *112*
Mack, R. L., 13, 22, *30*, 292, *311*
Mackie, J. L., *162*
MacWhinney, B., 243, *254*, 299, *310*
Magliano, J. P., 11, 14, 19, 20, 23, *29*, *30*, 56, *71*, 241, *254*
Maki, R. H., 23, *30*
Mandler, J. M., 11, 15, 30, 49, 71, 158, 162, 290, 310
Manelis, L., 57, *71*
Mani, K., 249, *254*
Mann, W. C., 334, *338*
Mannes, S. M., 74, 75, 76, 101, 109, 112, 116, 117, 118, 119, 120, 121, 122, 123, 125, 139
Marcel, A. J., 303, *310*
Marcus, M. P., 317, *338*
Markman, E. M., 23, *30*, 189, *212*
Marquez, G. G., 248, *255*
Marr, D., 314, 335, *338*
Marslen-Wilson, W. D., 317, *338*
Marsolek, C. J., 142, *162*, 192, 193, *211*
Martin, J., 258, 282, *286*
Masling, M., 243, 244, *254*
Mason, R. A., 167, *185*
Mayer, R., 220, 221, *238*
Mayhew, D., 243, *254*
McCarrell, N., 228, *237*
McClelland, J. L., 5, *27*, *30*, *139*, 302, 304, *310*, *311*, 344, 347, *351*
McDaniel, M. A., 183, *185*, 192, *212*
McFadden, C., *238*
McIntyre, C. W., 293, *311*
McKoon, G., 11, 15, 17, *30*, 57, *71*, 144, 150, *162*, *163*, 166, 168, 178, 181, 182, 183, *185*, *186*, 190, 191, 192, 197, 198, 200, 210, *211*, *213*, 236, *239*, 320, 321, 323, 326, *337*, *338*, 349, *351*
McMahen, C. L., 24, 25, 26, *29*
McNamara, D. S., 76, *111*
Mehan, H., 2, *30*
Meichenbaum, D., 22, *30*
Meyer, B. J. F., 105, *112*
Meyer, M., 12, *28*, 244, *254*, 298, *310*
Miller, C. A., 258, 259, 260, 261, 262, 263, 264, 265, 269, 270, 271, 279, 280, 281, *286*, *287*
Miller, G. A., 33, 34, 36, 37, 52, 54, 56, 57, 59, *71*, 317, *338*
Miller, J. R., 146, *163*, 175, *184*, 304, *310*
Miller, K., 57, 59, *71*
Miller, P. M., 282, *286*
Millican, C., 89, *111*
Millis, K. K., 19, *30*, 193, 196, 197, *212*
Minard, J., 218, *239*
Minsky, M., 11, *30*
Mitchell, D. C., 317, *338*
Miyake, N., 22, *30*
Moltz, H., 218, *239*
Morrow, D. G., 12, *30*, 244, *255*, 298, *308*
Moxey, L. M., 318, *339*
Mross, E. F., 20, *31*, 203, 207, 208, *214*
Mukarovsky, J., 242, *255*
Murachver, T., 193, 197, *212*
Murray, D., 219, *238*
Murray, J. D., 183, *184*, 192, *213*
Muth, K., 220, *238*
Myers, J. L., 14, 21, *28*, *30*, 134, *139*, 158, *163*, 167, 168, 175, 183, *184*, *185*, *186*, 192, *213*, 222, *239*, 291, *309*, *310*

N

Nabokov, V., 215, 216, 217, 223, 224, *239*
Nakamura, G., 228, *237*
Narvaez, D., 166, 181, 182, *187*
Nascimento, S., 230, 231, *237*
Nathan, M. J., 74, 75, 76, 109, *112*

Nayak, N., 232, *237*, *239*
Neely, J. H., 302, *310*
Neill, W. T., 294, 302, 303, *310*
Neisser, U., 102, *112*
Nelson, A. W. R., 322, *339*
Nelson, K., 11, *30*
Neruda, P., 231, *239*
Newell, A., 141, 147, 153, *163*, 346, *351*
Noller, P., 265, *286*
Noordman, L. G. M., 327, 328, *338*
Norman, D. A., 22, *30*, 221, *239*
Norris, D., 317, *338*

O

Oakhill, J. V., 206, *213*, *214*, 317, 321, 323, 325, 327, 328, 332, 333, *337*, *338*
O'Brien, E. J., 14, *30*, 134, *139*, 166, 167, 168, 175, 181, *185*, *186*, 245, *253*
O'Brien, J., 232, *237*
Ohtsuka, K., 247, *255*
Olson, G. M., 13, 22, *30*, 292, *311*
Oppy, B. J., 206, *212*
Ortega, J., 107, *111*
Ortony, A., 219, 220, 222, 228, *239*, 324, *336*
Otero, J. C., 23, *30*, 105, *112*
Ozyoruk-gee, N., 133, *138*

P

Paivio, A., 293, *308*
Palincsar, A. S., 22, *30*
Parente, F. J., 124, 134, *139*
Parkin, A., 206, *213*, *214*
Patel, M. J., 322, *339*
Payne, S., 221, *239*
Pearlman, M., 258, 282, *286*
Perfetti, C.A., 101, *112*, 189, 190, 206, *213*, 294, *311*
Person, N. K., 23, *29*
Peterson, J., 218, *239*
Peterson, K., 318, *339*
Peterson, R. G., 293, *311*
Petrie, H., 220, 221, *239*
Pezdek, K., 293, *311*
Pichert, J. W., 115, *138*
Pikowsky, B., 259, *286*
Pitts, M., 217, *239*
Pollack, J. B., 304, *311*
Pollio, H., 217, *239*
Pollio, M., 217, *239*
Polsonk, P. G., 123, 125, *139*
Posner, M. I., 294, 302, 304, *311*
Potts, G. R., 168, *186*, 192, 202, 203, *212*, *213*
Pressley, M., 22, *30*

R

Raaijmakers, J. G. W., 142, 148, 150, 156, *163*, 178, 182, *186*, 347, *351*
Rafaelli, M., 259, *286*
Rahim, M., 262, *286*
Rands, M., 262, *286*
Ratcliff, R., 11, 15, 17, *30*, 57, *71*, 144, 150, *162*, *163*, 166, 168, 178, 181, 182, 183, *185*, *186*, 190, 191, 192, 197, 198, 200, 210, *211*, *213*, 236, *239*, 320, 321, 323, 326, *337*, *338*, 349, *351*
Ray, G. E., 4, *31*
Rayner, K., 14, *30*, 246, *254*
Reber, A. S., 306, *311*
Reich, S. S., 318, 319, *339*
Reichman, R., 330, *338*
Reiger, C., 60, *71*
Reisdorf, P., 206, *213*
Reitz, L., 142, 157, *162*, 192, 193, *211*, 245, *254*
Restrepo, A., 263, 282, *286*
Reynolds, R., 220, 222, *239*
Riesbeck, C. K., 22, *30*
Rimmon-Kenan, S., 247, *255*
Rips, L. J., 12, *30*, 167, *186*
Risden, K., 166, 167, 168, 182, *186*
Ritchie, B. G., 73, *113*, 206, *214*
Roberts, R. M., 16, 18, *28*, 193, 196, 197, *212*
Robertson, R. R., 21, *28*, 245, *254*, 291, *310*, 323, *337*
Robertson, S. P., 13, 16, *29*, 192, 193, 197, 198, *212*, *213*, 235, *239*
Roediger, H., 220, *239*
Roeper, T., 291, *309*
Rohleder, L., 166, 181, 182, *187*
Rohrer, C., 327, *338*
Rommetveit, R., 290, *311*
Rosch, E., 344, *351*
Rosenbloom, P. S., 346, *351*
Ross, H. S., 258, 282, *286*
Ross, M., 265, 266, 282, *286*
Roth, S. F., 58, *71*, 206, *213*, 294, *311*
Royer, J. M., 293, *311*
Rubenstein, J. L., 259, *286*
Rumelhart, D. E., 5, 7, 14, *28*, *30*, *31*, *139*, 158, *163*, 167, 180, *185*, 221, 228, *239*, 302, 304, *310*, *311*, 344, 347, *351*
Rutter, D. R., 146, *162*

S

Sachs, J. D., 116, *139*, 243, *255*, 293, *311*
Sacks, H., 2, 7, *31*
Saffran, E., 317, *338*
Sag, I. A., 330, 331, 332, *338*
Sanders, T. J. M., 327, *338*
Sandres, M., 203, *213*
Sanford, A. J., 235, *237*, *239*, 291, 292, *308*, 318, 330, *336*, *339*
Saul, E. U., 73, 81, 101, 103, 105, 107, *111*
Sawyer, J. D., 17, *28*
Scarborough, H. S., 290, *308*
Schaefer, E. R., 2, 8, *27*
Schallert, D., 222, *239*
Schank, R. C., 11, 17, 22, *30*, *31*, 144, *163*, 191, 193, 198, *213*, 235, *239*
Scharf, B., 218, *240*
Schegloff, E. A., 2, 7, *31*
Schmalhofer, F., 76, *112*, 116, *139*, 150, *162*, 243, 244, *254*, *255*
Schwartz, M., 317, *338*
Schwartz, R., 220, *239*
Searle, J. R., 3. *31*, 222, *239*
Sebrechts, M. M., 22, *31*
Secco, T., 166, 175, *186*
Seely, M. R., 206, *212*
Seidenberg, M. S., 203, *213*
Seifert, C. M., 192, 197, *213*, 235, *239*
Selfridge, O. G., 102, *112*
Sell, M. A., 4, 6, *31*
Semrud-Clikeman, M., 220, *238*
Sengul, C. J., 293, *309*
Shank, D. M., 14, *30*
Shantz, C. U., 260, *286*, 258, *286*
Shapiro, B. P., 142, 157, *162*, 192, 193, *211*, 245, *254*
Sharkey, A., 235, *239*
Sharkey, N., 235, *239*
Shepherd, M., 322, *339*
Shiffrin, R. M., 142, 148, 150, 156, *162*, *163*, 178, 182, *186*, 347, *351*
Shinjo, M., 158, *163*, 168, 175, *185*, 222, *239*, 291, *309*, *310*
Shklovsky, V., 242, *255*
Shoben, E. J., 167, *186*
Shroyer, S., 293, *310*
Shulman, A., 265, *286*
Sidner, C. L., 330, *338*, *339*
Silfies, L. N., 260, *287*
Simon, H. A., 141, 147, *162*, *163*
Singer, H., 22, *31*
Singer, M., 11, 15, 16, 21, *29*, *31*, 104, 106, *111*, *112*, 166, 168, 169, 181, 183, *185*, *186*, 192, *206*, *213*, 243, *255*, 322, 323, *339*, 349, 350, *351*
Slovic, P., 12, *29*
Smetana, J., 263, 282, *286*
Smith, D., 235, *238*
Smith, E. E., 167, *186*, 235, *237*
Smith, F., 317, 339
Smith, M., 217, *239*
Smolensky, P., 168, *186*
Smollar, J., 259, *287*
Snyder, C. R. R., 294, 302, 304, *311*
Songer, N., 76, *111*
Sperry, L. L., 75, *112*, 175, *186*, 228, *240*, 141, 142, 144, *163*, 191, *214*, 245, *255*
Spilich, G. J., 59, *71*, 73, *112*, 146, *163*, 189, *211*, *214*, 228, *239*
Spooren, W. P. M., 327, *338*
Spradling, V., 259, 263, 275, 282, *285*
St. John, M. F., 14, *30*, 344, 347, *351*
Stamm, E. G., 203, *212*
Stanovich, D. E., 206, *214*
Steen, G., 236, *239*
Stein, N. L., 17, 31, 158, 163, 173, 186, 258, 259, 260, 261, 262, 263, 264, 265, 269, 270, 271, 279, 280, 281, 282, 285, 286, 287
Stenning, K., 322, *339*
Stephenson, G. M., 146, *162*
Sternberg, R. J., 22, *31*
Stevens, A. L., 7, *31*
Stratman, J., 261, *287*
Streby, W. J., 57, *71*
Striedter, J., 242, *255*
Suh, S. Y., 13, 16, 21, 31, 143, 163, 166, 167, 171, 175, 181, 182, 186, 191, 193, 214, 349, 351
Swamer, S. S., 6, *31*
Swartz, M. L., 22, *31*
Sweetser, E., 225, *240*
Swinehart, D., 193, 197, *212*
Swinney, D. A., 292, *311*

T

Taft, L., 291, *309*
Tanenhaus, M. K., 326, *336*
Tannen, D., 265, 275, *287*
Tapiero, I., 76, 105, *112*
Tasmowski-De Rych, L., 332, *339*
Tenney, Y., 235, *238*
Tesla, C., 263, *287*

Tesser, A., 60, *69*
Thagard, P., 280, *287*
Thompson, E., 344, *351*
Thompson, R. C., 23, *30*
Thompson, S. A., 334, *338*
Thorndyke, P. W., 158, *163*, 300, 301, *310*, 323, *339*
Thurlow, R. E., 168, 169, *186*, *187*
Till, R. E., 20, *31*, 203, 207, 208, *214*
Tipper, S. P., 302, *308*
Tomashevsky, B., 247, *255*
Toulmin, S. E., 257, 261, 270, *287*
Trabasso, T., 13, 15, 16, 21, 29, 31, 75, 106, 111, 112, 141, 142, 143, 144, 163, 166, 167, 168, 169, 171, 175, 181, 182, 185, 186, 187, 191, 193, 198, 214, 228, 240, 245, 255, 258, 259, 287, 349, 350, 351
Treisman, A. M., 302, *311*
Turner, A., 55, *71*, 154, *163*, 169, *186*
Turner, E. A., 290, *311*
Turner, E. H., 2, *31*
Turner, M., 225, 226, 227, *238*, *240*
Turner, T. J., 17, *27*, 228, 235, *237*, 291, *308*
Tversky, A., 12, *29*

U, V

Ury, W., 260, 264, *287*
van den Broek, P. W., 15, 16, 21, 31, , 75, 112, 141, 142, 143, 144, 157, 158, 162, 163, 166, 167, 168, 169, 171, 175, 176, 181, 182, 183, 185, 186, 187, 191, 192, 193, 198, 211, 214, 228, 240, 245, 254, 255
van der Meij, H., 23, 24, *31*, *32*
van Dijk, T. A., 12, 14, 15, 29, 31, 37, 49, 57, 71, 73, 74, 75, 76, 100, 103, 105, 112, 113, 116, 117, 139, 141, 142, 144, 146, 148, 162, 163, 166, 167, 171, 176, 182, 185, 187, 189, 192, 212, 241, 243, 244, 245, 254, 255, 296, 298, 304, 310, 311, 321, 322, 338, 342, 351
van Dusen, L., 11, 15, *27*, 60, *69*
Van Leeuwen, R., 23, *28*
van Oostendorp, H., 241, 244, 245, 248, *255*
Varela, F. J., 344, *351*
Varner, K. R., 294, *310*
Verluyten, P., 332, *339*
Verma, S., 74, 77, 78, 80, 81, 100, 103, 105, 107, *111*
Vesonder, G. T., 59, *71*, 73, *112*, 146, *163*, 189, *214*, 228, *239*
Villa, V., 291, *309*
Vipond, D., 81, *113*, 146, *162*
Vonk, M., 325, 327, 328, *338*
Voss, J. F., 59, *71*, 73, *112*, 146, *163*, 189, *211*, *214*, 228, *239*, 260, *287*
Vuchinich, S., 259, 263, 282, *287*

W

Wade, E., 259, *287*
Walker, C. W., 124, 134, *139*
Walley, R. E., 302, *311*
Waltz, D. L., 304, *311*
Warren, A., 236, *240*
Wason, P. C., 318, 319, *339*
Waters, G. S., 203, *213*
Waugh, L. R., 242, 246, *255*
Weaver, C. A., 23, *32*
Weiden, T. D., 302, *311*
Weinstein, S., 326, 330, *338*
Weiss, R., 265, 266, 282, *287*
Welleck, R., 236, *240*
Welsch, D. M., 74, 76, *112*, 150, *162*, 243, 244, *254*
Westberry, R. L., 302, 303, *310*
White, C. S., 100, *111*
Whitney, P., 11, *32*, 73, *112*, *113*, 206, *214*, 253, *255*
Wilensky, R., 193, 197, 198, *214*
Wiley, J., 260, *287*
Wilkinson, A. C., 23, *28*
Willert, M. G., 23, *30*
Wish, M., 2, 3, *28*
Woll, S., 235, *238*

Y

Yau, J., 263, 282, *286*
Yekovich, F. R., 57, *71*, 158, *163*
Yochum, N., 73, *113*
Youniss, J., 259, *287*
Yuill, N., 206, *213*, *214*

Z

Zajachewski, R., 22, *30*
Zimny, S., 76, *112*, 150, *162*, 243, 244, *254*
Zurif, E. B., 317, *336*
Zwaan, R. A., 241, 244, 245, 248, 249, 250, *255*
Zwicker, E., 218, *240*

Subject Index

A

Activation, 166, 171, 174, 176
fluctuation in, 171, 173, 174, 178, 181
online, 171, 176
reading cycles and, 166, 167, 171, 173, 176, 181
spread of, 122, 125, 134
Adjacency pairs, 2
Agrammatic aphasics, 317, 319
Anaphora, 292–293, 328–333, 336
deep anaphors, 330–333
surface anaphors, 330–333
Anaphoric islands, 333
Argument overlap, 123–125, 134
Argumentation, 257–285
assymetry of knowledge, 259–262, 269–270, 279–280
in childhood and adolescence, 258–259
dynamics of, 258–266
functions of, 259
interactive, 260–262
theory of understanding, 257–258, 260–262, 283
and Toulmin, 261
Arguments, 33, 34, 36, 57, 65, 335, 336
best argument, 42
obligatory arguments, 35
optional arguments, 35
ARTN, *see* Augmented recursive transition network
Associates, 104
Attention, 166
limitations in, 166
Augmented recursive transition network (ARTN), 10–11

B, C

Background knowledge, 167, 168
Causal antecedent, 16–17, 21
Causal connections, 142–144
Causal consequences, 17, 21
Causality, 166
causal inference maker, 183
coherence and, 166, 167
enablements and causes, 171
explanation and, 166
sufficiency, 166, 168
Classes, *see* Predicate classes
Coherence, 77, 104, 105, 106, 165, 166, 167, 169, 175, 321, 322, 323, 336
anaphoric/referential, 166, 167, 168, 169, 175, 176, 182

breaks in, 167
causal, 166, 167, 183
causal explanation and, 166, 167, 168, 169, 175, 182
global, 323
local, 321, 322, 336
standards of coherence, 166, 169, 181, 182
Coherence relations, 334–335
Compactness hypotheses, 220
Comprehension, 341–342
Computational theory, 314, 335
Conceptual graph structure, 19
Conflict resolution, *see* Negotiation
Connected network, 45
Connectedness, 35, 36, 37, 38, 55, 56, 64, 67
Connectionism, 3–6, 10, 11, 344, 346–347
recurrent network, 5–7, 10
Constructing propositions, 57
Construction-integration, 74, 76, 78, 85, 100, 102, 347
Construction-integration model, 121–122, 134, 250, 251, 252, 253, 303–305
connectivity matrix, 304
Constructionist model, 15, 16, 19, 20, 21, 349
Constructive processing, 316, 336
Contiguity, 123–125, 127–132, 134–135, 137
Control systems, 241, 249, 251, 252, 253
literary control system, 241, 249, 250, 251
Current-state selection strategy (CSS), 15–16, 18, 20–21
Cyclical model of comprehension, 144–147
narrative comprehension, 150–153
model of comprehension component, 150–151, 158–160
model of computer simulation, 153, 158–162
model of empirical tests, 153–156
model of free recall component, 152–153, 160–162
problem solving in narrative comprehension, 142–144
problem solving, state-space search of models of, 147–148

D

Deixis, 329, 330
Dialogue patterns, 2
Discourse representation, *see* Text representation
Discourse structure, 101, 105
content structure, 99, 106
informational text, 80, 89, 105
signaling, 101
superordinate, 109
Domain knowledge, 11

E

Elaboration, 119, 133, 134
Expectation-violation, 133, 134
Experiential gestalts, 224
Expert–novice differences, 59

F

Figurative language, 215, 222, 236
Focus, 330, 331
focus spaces, 330
Functionalism, 307, 308
Functions of language, 242, 245
poetic function, 242, 245
referential function, 242, 245

G

Gist, 33, 40, 42
Global coherence processing model, 192, 200–205
Goal hierarchies, 197–200

I

Idioms, 232–233
Implicit causality, 326–327
(In)considerate prose, 241–245, 247, 253
Inexpressibility hypothesis, 220
Inference, 1, 11–22
nference generation, 349–350
Inferences, 60, 105, 165, 169, 181, 320–328, 336
associations and, 166
case-filling, 325
causal antecedent, 12, 16–17, 21
causal consequences, 12, 17, 21
causal inference maker, 183
character emotion, 13
connecting, 169
during reading/online, 165, 181
elaborations, 169
elaborative, 323
forward, 183
constraints on, 183
instantiation, 324–325
knowledge-based inferences, 11–14, 19, 21
landscape of, 171, 174, 175, 181, 182, 184
logic-based inferences, 12
necessary, 323

offline, 11
online, 11, 13, 15, 17–19, 21
quantitative inferences, 12
reinstatements, 167, 168, 169
role-to-name mapping, 325–327
role-to-role mapping, 325–327
state inference, 13, 19
subordinate goal, 12
superordinate goal, 12
Input, 33
Input phase, 36, 61
completeness, 37
connected chain, 36
cycles, 33
internal completeness, 55
Integration, 116, 120–121, 133–135, 137, 300–302
Integrative processing, 315–316, 336
Irony, 215

K

Knowledge,
knowledge structure, 109
prior knowledge, 50, 75, 77, 95, 99, 101, 104, 105, 108
procedural knowledge, 58, 102
procedural prior knowledge, 57, 60
representations, 101
schemata, 107
seductive detail, 100
semantic knowledge, 58
semantic prior knowledge, 57
world knowledge, 58, 59
Knowledge-based inferences, 189–193, 197–205, 207–209
goal-related, 197–205
subordinate goal, 197–198, 200–205
superordinate, 197–198, 200–205
online inferences, 191–193, 197–198, 200–205, 207–209
topic-related, 207–209

L

Language experience, 55
Leading edge strategy, 34, 39, 45
Learning, 100
Levels of representation, 116, 117
situation model, 116, 117
textbase, 116, 117, 137
macrostructure, 116
microstructure, 116
verbatim, 116
Lexical-decision task, 19–21
Literary devices, 242, 243, 245, 246
Literary texts, 215–216, 225–226, 231–232, 235
Literary texts (stories), 241–242, 245–250, 253
Logic, 335
Long-term memory, 35, 49, 58, 123, 133
long-term memory traces, 47
long-term memory value, 48
network, as a, 117, 121, 123, 134
network, as a construction of, 124
Long-term memory abilities, 60

M

Macropropositions, 54
Macrorules, 54
Meaning, 54
Memory, 14, 165, 184
decay in, 171, 184
dynamic memory, 99
for texts, 165, 178, 182
long-term memory, 14, 76, 79, 83, 89, 91
primacy, 100
recall data, 81, 85, 93, 97
network model of, 175, 178
representations and, 165, 175, 176, 178, 181
short-term, 14, 166
two-stage access of, 167
working memory, 14, 22, 77
activation, 76, 79, 85, 104
resource allocation, 101
Mental models, 296, 298, 313–336
of abstract situations, 333–335, 336
spatial, 333, 336
Metaphor
concepts, 221, 224–227, 230
conventional, 218–219, 225–227
language
understanding, 222–224, 227–230
use, 217–220
learning, 217–219, 221
Metastatement, 119
Metonymy
concepts, 234
models, 235
text understanding, 233–235
Minimal inference processing model, 191–192, 198–200
Minimalist hypothesis, 236, 323–324
Modeling
activation-based production system (3 CAPS), 74, 77, 102
capacity-constraints, 73, 101, 102, 109

reader, 102
reader model, 102
capacity-constrained construction-integration, 74, 76, 78, 85, 100, 102
competition, 109
lexical processing, 103, 107
monitoring, 105, 106, 107
productions, 106
semantic field, 103
settling, 103
syntax, syntactic, 103, 104
connectionist, 75, 78
construction-integration, 74, 78
argument overlap, 75, 78
carryover, 76
cycles, 77, 79
propositional embedding, 75, 78
propositions, 77, 107
situation model, 75, 105, 106
textbase, 75, 103, 106
simulation, 74, 79, 89
Modular systems, 306

N

Nativism, 306, 308
Negotiation, *see also* Argumentation
compromise, 264–265, 272
conceptual change, 280–281
gender, 265–266, 282–283
goals of resolution, 260, 262, 281
knowledge, role of, 259–262, 280–281
outcomes, 271, 281
Network, 33, 56, 77, 108
links, 77, 83, 97
node, 83, 89, 97
propositional network, 104
semantic network, 77, 93
News stories, 249, 250

O, P

Omission theory, 325
Overlap, 33, 34, 36
Poetry, 230, 232
Pragmatics, 1, 343
Predicate classes, 54, 58
cause, 46
contrast, 42, 46, 65
contrasts with, 65
extent of, 43, 46
hedge, 40, 41, 45, 65
intensifier, 46
location, 46
number, 46
possess, 41
purpose, 46
qualify, 46
quantify, 43, 46
range, 46
reference, 46
time, 46
time:when, 58
topic, 46
Predicates, 33, 34, 35, 45, 57, 58, 61
Predication reduction rules, *see* Reduction
Predication semantics, 33, 40, 47, 52
Predication semantics model, 52, 54, 348
Prior knowledge, 115, 116
instructions as, 116
organization of, 115, 117, 133
title as, 115
Processing
flexibility, 101, 107
local processing, 95
parsing, 101, 103
Production system, 346
Pronouns, 328, 329–330, 331–332, 333
Propositional representation, *see* Text representation
Propositions, 57
Psycholinguistics, isolation of, 306–307, 308

Q

Question answering, 193–197, 200–201
arc categories, 194–196
arc search procedures, 194–196
conceptual graph structure, 193–196, 200–201
Quest model, 193–196
question categories, 194–196
statements nodes, 194–196

R

Rapid serial visual presentation (RSVP), 20–21
Reading, 165–166
ability, 166, 181
activation during, 171, 174
cycles in, 166, 167, 171
motivation for, 166, 181
purpose, 181

standards of coherence, 166
Reading ability, 205–209
Reading strategies, 60
Recall, 178
Recency, 35, 37, 46, 56, 65
Recursive transition network (RTN), 7–11
Reduction, 33, 34, 37, 40, 59, 64, 65, 67
priority, 45, 48, 67
intermediate coordinators, 48, 65
local predicates, 46
remote coordinators, 46, 48
simplify rules, 40, 44
reduction abilities, 60
reduction phase, 40, 58
reduction process, 39, 54, 56, 60
active connections, 61
activity, 45
argument overlap, 56
connections, 40
core, 40, 44, 68
core:hedge, 65
core rule, 40, 41, 43
generalization rule, 68
generalize, 40
generalize rules, 42, 44
holdover, 45, 46
Referential connections, 144, 146
first mention in, 179, 182
frequency of, 178, 179, 182
order of, 178, 179, 180, 182
Referential continuity, 320–322
Relatedness, 120–126, 133–135, 137
Representational medium, 295–299
Rhetoric, 335
Rules, 37

S

Schema, 115
Search of Associative Memory (SAM), 148–150
free parameters in, 149
recovery process in, 148–149
sampling process in, 148–149
short-term memory role in comprehension, 144–147
Selective inhibition, 302–303
Semantic, 33, 34, 52
Semantic memory, 59, 60
Semantics, 35, 45, 47, 54
Sense-selection, 206–209
Short-term buffer, 122–124, 127, 134–135, 137
Simulations, 50, 51
alpha, 47, 61, 50
computer simulations, 47
free recall, 55
interest, 51
prior knowledge, 58
ratings of interest, 50
recall, 52
Situation model, 12, 243, 244, 245, 248, 249, 250, 252, 342–344
Situational models, 296, 298
Speech act categories, 3–4
assertion, 3
directive, 3
evaluation, 4
indirect directive, 3
juncture, 4
nonverbal response, 4
question, 3
reply to question 3
verbal response, 4
Speech acts, 2–4, 8–9, 19
Starting points, 299–300
Story grammars, 334
Strategies, 73, 101
repair strategies, 107
rereading, 103, 107
strategic reading, 77
strategy competition, 100, 101, 106, 107
Strength, 34, 35, 37, 38, 39, 40, 42, 45, 47, 56, 60, 65
strength values, 42, 59, 64
decay, 39
number of connections, 39
strength parameter, 50
Structure building framework, 289–308, 343
amodality, 296
automatic processes vs. conscious process, 294–295
coherence, 289–290, 291, 301–302
anaphoric devices, 292–293
because, as conjunction, 291
cataphoric devices, 293
enhancement, 290, 292–293, 303–305
foundation laying, 289–291
advantage of first mention, 291
general cognitive processes, 290, 305–308
individual differences, 294–299
mapping, 289, 291–292, 300–302
memory nodes, 289–290, 295
mental representation, 289

processing signals, 290
shifting, 289, 291–292
suppression, 290, 292–293, 302–303
ambiguous words, 292, 303
sentence context, 303, 304
surface forms, forgetting of, 292, 293
Subordinate goals, 17, 21
Superordinate goal, 16–17, 21
Surface structure, 243, 244, 245, 246, 247, 249, 250, 252
SWALE, 22
Syntax, 317–320

T

Task analysis, 314, 335
Text representation, 189–191, 205–206
Textbase, 12, 14–15, 17
Textbase (level), 243, 244, 245, 247, 249, 250, 251, 252
Three-pronged method, 14, 18, 21
Tree, 34

V

Verbal protocols, 13, 14, 18
question-answering protocols, 13, 18–19, 20
question-asking protocols, 13, 22–26
think-aloud protocols, 13, 341
Vividness hypothesis, 220

W

Working memory, 14, 22, 33, 34, 35, 37, 47, 48, 60, 64, 65, 67, 321–322, 348–349
working memory overload, 43
working memory parameters, 50

Printed in Dunstable, United Kingdom

b62ed225-f6f6-49b1-9cce-4700f2bfbaf6R01